FISCAL YEAR 2013

BUDGET

OF THE U.S. GOVERNMENT

OFFICE OF MANAGEMENT AND BUDGET

BUDGET.GOV

THE BUDGET DOCUMENTS

Budget of the United States Government, Fiscal Year 2013 contains the Budget Message of the President, information on the President's priorities, budget overviews organized by agency, and summary tables.

Analytical Perspectives, Budget of the United States Government, Fiscal Year 2013 contains analyses that are designed to highlight specified subject areas or provide other significant presentations of budget data that place the budget in perspective. This volume includes economic and accounting analyses; information on Federal receipts and collections; analyses of Federal spending; information on Federal borrowing and debt; baseline or current services estimates; and other technical presentations.

The *Analytical Perspectives* volume also contains supplemental material with several detailed tables, including tables showing the budget by agency and account and by function, subfunction, and program, that is available on the Internet and as a CD-ROM in the printed document.

Historical Tables, Budget of the United States Government, Fiscal Year 2013 provides data on budget receipts, outlays, surpluses or deficits, Federal debt, and Federal employment over an extended time period, generally from 1940 or earlier to 2013 or 2017.

To the extent feasible, the data have been adjusted to provide consistency with the 2013 Budget and to provide comparability over time.

Appendix, Budget of the United States Government, Fiscal Year 2013 contains detailed information on the various appropriations and funds that constitute the budget and is designed primarily for the use of the Appropriations Committees. The *Appendix* contains more detailed financial information on individual programs and appropriation accounts than any of the other budget documents. It includes for each agency: the proposed text of appropriations language; budget schedules for each account; legislative proposals; explanations of the work to be performed and the funds needed; and proposed general provisions applicable to the appropriations of entire agencies or group of agencies. Information is also provided on certain activities whose transactions are not part of the budget totals.

AUTOMATED SOURCES OF BUDGET INFORMATION

The information contained in these documents is available in electronic format from the following sources:

Internet. All budget documents, including documents that are released at a future date, spreadsheets of many of the budget tables, and a public use budget database are available for downloading in several formats from the Internet at *www.budget.gov/budget*. Links to documents and materials from budgets of prior years are also provided.

Budget CD-ROM. The CD-ROM contains all of the budget documents in fully indexed PDF format along with the software required for viewing the documents. The CD-ROM has many of the budget tables in spreadsheet format and also contains the materials that are included on the separate *Analytical Perspectives* CD-ROM.

For more information on access to electronic versions of the budget documents (except CD-ROMs), call (202) 512-1530 in the D.C. area or toll-free (888) 293-6498. To purchase the budget CD-ROM or printed documents call (202) 512-1800.

GENERAL NOTES

1. All years referenced for budget data are fiscal years unless otherwise noted. All years referenced for economic data are calendar years unless otherwise noted.

2. Detail in this document may not add to the totals due to rounding.

3. Under the President's Government consolidation proposal announced on January 13, 2012, a number of agencies and programs would be consolidated into a new department focused on supporting the growth of American business and the resulting job creation, with the goal of improving services and reducing costs. The specific proposal to create the new department will be submitted to the Congress once the consolidation authority requested by the President is enacted. The Administration's budget proposal, including the request in this Budget and agencies' supporting materials, is presented in terms of the existing agency structures, and appropriate adjustments will be submitted once consolidation authority is enacted.

Table of Contents

THE BUDGET MESSAGE OF THE PRESIDENT

To the Congress of the United States:

America was built on the idea that anyone who is willing to work hard and play by the rules, can make it if they try—no matter where they started out. By giving every American a fair shot, asking everyone to do their fair share, and ensuring that everyone played by the same rules, we built the great American middle class and made our country a model for the world.

Today, America is still home to the world's best universities, most productive workers, and most innovative companies. But for many Americans, the basic bargain at the heart of the American Dream has eroded.

Long before this recession hit, there was a widespread feeling that hard work had stopped paying off; that fewer and fewer of those who contributed to the success of our economy actually benefited from that success. Those at the very top grew wealthier while everyone else struggled with paychecks that did not keep up with the rising cost of everything from college tuition to groceries. And as a result, too many families found themselves taking on more and more debt just to keep up—often papered over by mounting credit card bills and home equity loans.

Then, in the middle of 2008, the house of cards collapsed. Too many mortgages had been sold to people who could not afford—or even understand—them. Banks had packaged too many risky loans into securities and then sold them to investors who were misled or misinformed about the risks involved. Huge bets had been made and huge bonuses had been paid out with other people's money. And the regulators who were supposed to prevent this crisis either looked the other way or did not have the authority to act.

In the end, this growing debt and irresponsibility helped trigger the worst economic crisis since the Great Depression. Combined with new tax cuts and new mandatory programs that had never been paid for, it threw our country into a deep fiscal hole. And millions of hardworking Americans lost their jobs, their homes, and their basic economic security.

Today, we are seeing signs that our economy is on the mend. But we are not out of the woods yet. Instead, we are facing a make-or-break moment for the middle class, and for all those who are fighting to get there. What is at stake is whether or not this will be a country where working people can earn enough to raise a family, build modest savings, own a home, and secure their retirement. This is the defining issue of our time.

This Budget reflects my deep belief that we must rise to meet this moment—both for our economy and for the millions of Americans who have worked so hard to get ahead.

We built this Budget around the idea that our country has always done best when everyone gets a fair shot, everyone does their fair share, and everyone plays by the same rules. It rejects the "you're on your own" economics that have led to a widening gap between the richest and poorest Americans that undermines both our belief in equal opportunity and the engine of our economic growth. When the middle class is shrinking, and families can no longer afford to buy the goods and services that businesses are selling, it drags down our entire economy. And countries with less inequality tend to have stronger and steadier economic growth over the long run.

The way to rebuild our economy and strengthen the middle class is to make sure that everyone in America gets a fair shot at success. Instead of lowering our standards and our sights, we need to win a race to the top for good jobs that pay well and offer security for the middle class. To succeed and thrive in the global, high-tech economy, we need America to be a place with the highest-skilled, highest-educated workers; the most advanced transportation and communication networks; and the strongest commitment to research and technology in the world. This Budget makes investments that can help America win this race, create good jobs, and lead in the world economy.

And it does so with the understanding that we need an economy that is no longer burdened by years of debt and in which everyone shoulders their fair share to put our fiscal house in order. When I took office 3 years ago, my Administration was left an annual deficit of $1.3 trillion, or 9.2 percent of GDP, and a projected 10-year deficit of more than $8 trillion. These deficits were the result of a previous 8 years of undertaking initiatives, but not paying for them—especially two large tax cuts and a new Medicare prescription drug benefit—as well as the financial crisis and recession that made the fiscal situation worse as revenue decreased and automatic Government outlays increased to counter the downturn.

We have taken many steps to re-establish fiscal responsibility, from instituting a statutory pay-as-you-go rule for spending to going through the budget line by line looking for outdated, ineffective, or duplicative programs to cut or reform. Importantly, we enacted the Affordable Care Act, which will not only provide Americans with more affordable choices and freedom from insurance company abuses, but will also reduce our budget deficits by more than $1 trillion over the next two decades.

As economic growth was beginning to take hold last year, I took further steps to put our Nation on a fiscally sustainable path that would strengthen the foundation of the economy for years to come. In April of 2011, I put forward my Framework for Shared Prosperity and Shared Fiscal Responsibility that built on the 2012 Budget to identify $4 trillion in deficit reduction. During negotiations over extending the debt ceiling in the summer, I presented to congressional Republicans another balanced plan to achieve $4 trillion in deficit reduction. Finally, in September, I sent my Plan for Economic Growth and Deficit Reduction to the Joint Select Committee on Deficit Reduction, which detailed a way to achieve $3 trillion in deficit reduction on top of the $1 trillion already achieved in the Budget Control Act of 2011 that I signed into law the previous month.

I also made sure that this plan covered the cost of the American Jobs Act—a set of bipartisan, commonsense proposals designed to put more people back to work, put more money in the pockets of the middle class, and do so without adding a dime to the deficit at a time when it was clear that global events were slowing the economic recovery and our ability to create more jobs. Unfortunately, Republicans in Congress blocked both our deficit reduction measures and almost every part of the American Jobs Act for the simple reason that they were unwilling to ask the wealthiest Americans to pay their fair share.

In the year ahead, I will continue to pursue policies that will shore up our economy and our fiscal situation. Together with the deficit reduction I signed into law this past year, this Budget will cut the deficit by $4 trillion over the next decade. This will put the country on a course to a level of deficits below 3 percent of GDP by the end of the decade, and will also allow us to stabilize the Federal debt relative to the size of the economy. To get there, this Budget contains a number of steps to put us on a fiscally sustainable path.

First, this Budget implements the tight discretionary spending caps that I signed into law in the Budget Control Act of 2011. These caps will generate approximately $1 trillion in deficit reduction over the next decade. Building on reductions we already have made, this will result in a cut in discretionary spending of $42 billion since 2010 when higher levels of Federal spending were essential to provide a jumpstart to the economy. Meeting the spending targets in this Budget meant some very difficult choices: reforming, consolidating, or freezing programs where we could; cutting programs that were not effective or essential and even some that were, but are now unaffordable; and precisely targeting our investments. Every department will feel the impact of these reductions as they cut programs or tighten their belts to free up more resources for areas critical to economic growth. And throughout the entire Government, we will continue our efforts to make programs and services work better and cost less: using competition and high standards to get the most from the grants we award; getting rid of excess Federal real estate; and saving billions of dollars by cutting overhead and administrative costs.

Second, this Budget begins the process of implementing my new defense strategy that reconfigures our force to meet the challenges of the coming decade. Over the past 3 years, we have made historic investments in our troops and their capabilities, military families, and veterans. After a decade of war, we are at an inflection point: American troops have left Iraq; we are undergoing a transition in Afghanistan so Afghans can assume more responsibility; and we have debilitated al Qaeda's leadership, putting that terrorist network on the path to defeat. At the same time, we have to renew our economic strength here at home, which is the foundation of our strength in the world, and that includes putting our fiscal house in order. To ensure that our defense budget is driven by a clear strategy that reflects our national interests, I directed the Secretary of Defense and military leadership to undertake a comprehensive strategic review.

I presented the results of the review, reflecting my guidance and the full support of our Nation's military leadership, at the Pentagon on January 5. There are several key elements to this new strategy. To sustain a global reach, we will strengthen our presence in the Asia Pacific region and continue vigilance in the Middle East. We will invest in critical partnerships and alliances, including NATO, which has demonstrated time and again—most recently in Libya—that it is a force multiplier. Looking past Iraq and Afghanistan to future threats, the military no longer will be sized for large-scale, prolonged stability operations. The Department of Defense will focus modernization on emerging threats and sustaining efforts to get rid of outdated Cold War-era systems so that we can invest in the capabilities we need for the future, including intelligence, surveillance and reconnaissance capabilities. My Administration will continue to enhance capabilities related to counterterrorism and countering weapons of mass destruction, and we will also maintain the ability to operate in environments where adversaries try to deny us access. And, we will keep faith with those who serve by giving priority to our wounded warriors, servicemembers' mental health, and the well-being of military families.

Adapting our forces to this new strategy will entail investing in high-priority programs, such as unmanned surveillance aircraft and upgraded tactical vehicles. It will mean terminating unnecessary and lower-priority programs such as the C-27 airlift aircraft and a new weather satellite and maintaining programs such as the Joint Strike Fighter at a reduced level. All told, reductions in the growth of defense spending will save $487 billion over the next 10 years. In addition, the end of our military activities in Iraq and the wind-down of operations in Afghanistan will mean that the country will spend 24 percent less on overseas contingency operations (OCO) this year than it did last year, saving $30 billion. I also am proposing a multi-year cap on OCO spending so that we fully realize the dividends of this change in policy.

Third, I believe that in our country, everyone must shoulder their fair share—especially those who have benefited the most from our economy. In the United States of America, a teacher, a nurse, or a construction worker who earns $50,000 a year should not pay taxes at a higher rate than somebody making $50 million. That is wrong. It is wrong for Warren Buffett's secretary to pay a higher tax rate than Warren Buffett. This is not about class warfare; this is about the Nation's welfare. This is about making fair choices that benefit not just the people who have done fantastically well over the last few decades, but that also benefit the middle class, those fighting to get into the middle class, and the economy as a whole.

In the Budget, I reiterate my opposition to permanently extending the Bush tax cuts for families making more than $250,000 a year and my opposition to a more generous estate tax than we had in 2009 benefiting only the very largest estates. These policies were unfair and unaffordable when they were passed, and they remain so today. I will push for their expiration in the coming year. I also propose to eliminate special tax breaks for oil and gas companies; preferred treatment for the purchase of corporate jets; tax rules that give a larger percentage deduction to the wealthiest two percent than to middle-class families for itemized deductions; and a loophole that allows some of the wealthiest money managers in the country to pay only 15 percent tax on the millions of dollars they earn. And I support tax reform that observes the "Buffett Rule" that no household making more than $1 million annually should pay a smaller share of its income taxes than middle-class families pay.

Fourth, to build on the work we have done to reduce health care costs through the Affordable Care Act, I am proposing more than $360 billion in reforms to Medicare, Medicaid, and other health programs over 10 years. The goal of these reforms is to make these critical programs more effective and efficient, and help make sure our health care system rewards high-quality medicine. What it does not do—and what I will not support—are efforts to turn Medicare into a voucher or Medicaid into a block grant. Doing so would weaken both programs and break the promise that we have made to American seniors, people with disabilities, and low-income families—a promise I am committed to keeping.

Finally, to address other looming, long-term challenges to our fiscal health, I have put forward a wide range of mandatory savings. These include reductions in agricultural subsidies, changes in Federal employee retirement and health benefits, reforms to the unemployment insurance system and the Postal Service, and new efforts to provide a better return to taxpayers from mineral development. Drawn from the plan I presented to the Joint Select Committee on Deficit Reduction, these mandatory proposals would save $217 billion over the next decade.

Reining in our deficits is not an end in and of itself. It is a necessary step to rebuilding a strong foundation so our economy can grow and create good jobs. That is our ultimate goal. And as we tighten our belts by cutting, consolidating, and reforming programs, we also must invest in the areas that will be critical to giving every American a fair shot at success and creating an economy that is built to last.

That starts with taking action now to strengthen our economy and boost job creation. We need to finish the work we started last year by extending the payroll tax cut and unemployment benefits for the rest of this year. We also need to take additional measures to put more people back to work. That is why I introduced the American Jobs Act last year, and why I will continue to put forward many of the ideas it contained, as well as additional measures, to put people back to work by rebuilding our infrastructure, providing businesses tax incentives to invest and hire, and giving States aid to rehire teachers and first responders.

We also know that education and lifelong learning will be critical for anyone trying to compete for the jobs of the future. That is why I will continue to make education a national mission. What one learns will have a big impact on what he or she earns: the unemployment rate for Americans with a college degree or more is only about half the national average, and the incomes of college graduates are twice as high as those without a high school diploma.

When I took office, I set the goal for America to have the highest proportion of college graduates in the world by 2020. To reach that goal, we increased the maximum annual Pell Grant by more than $900 to help nearly 10 million needy students afford a college education. The 2013 Budget continues that commitment and provides the necessary resources to sustain the maximum award of $5,635. In this Budget, I also propose a series of new proposals to help families with the costs of college including making permanent the American Opportunity Tax Credit, a partially refundable tax credit worth up to $10,000 per student over 4 years of college, and rewarding colleges and universities that act responsibly in setting tuition, providing the best value, and serving needy students well.

To help our students graduate with the skills they will need for the jobs of the future, we are continuing our effort to prepare 100,000 science and math teachers over the next decade. To improve our elementary and secondary schools, we are continuing our commitment to the Race to the Top initiative that rewards the most innovative and effective ways to raise standards, recruit and retain good teachers, and raise student achievement. My Budget invests $850 million in this effort, which already has been expanded to cover early learning and individual school districts.

And to prepare our workers for the jobs of tomorrow, we need to turn our unemployment system into a re-employment system. That includes giving more community colleges the resources they need to become community career centers—places that teach skills that businesses are looking for right now, from data management to high-tech manufacturing.

Once our students and workers gain the skills they need for the jobs of the future, we also need to make sure those jobs end up in America. In today's high-tech, global economy, that means the United States must be the best place in the world to take an idea from the drawing board to the factory floor to the store shelves. In this Budget, we are sustaining our level of investment in non-defense research and development (R&D) even as overall spending declines, thereby keeping us on track to double R&D funding in the key R&D agencies. We are supporting research at the National Institutes of Health that will accelerate the translation of new discoveries in biomedical science into new therapies and cures, along with initiatives at the Food and Drug Administration that will speed the approval of new medicines. We make important investments in the science and research needed to tackle the most important environmental challenges of our time, and we are investing in fields as varied as cyber-security, nano-technology, and advanced manufacturing. This Budget also puts an emphasis on the basic research that leads to the breakthroughs of tomorrow, which increasingly is no longer being conducted by the private sector, as well as helping inventors bring their innovations from laboratory to market.

This Budget reflects the importance of safeguarding our environment while strengthening our economy. We do not have to choose between having clean air and clean water and growing the economy.

By conserving iconic American landscapes, restoring significant ecosystems from the Everglades to the Great Lakes, and achieving measurable improvements in water and air quality, we are working with communities to protect the natural resources that serve as the engines of their local economies.

Moreover, this Budget continues my Administration's commitment to developing America's diverse, clean sources of energy. The Budget eliminates unwarranted tax breaks for oil companies, while extending key tax incentives to spur investment in clean energy manufacturing and renewable energy production. The Budget also invests in R&D to catalyze the next generation of clean energy technologies. These investments will help us achieve our goal of doubling the share of electricity from clean energy sources by 2035. By promoting American leadership in advanced vehicle manufacturing, including funding to encourage greater use of natural gas in the transportation sector, the Budget will help us reach our goal of reducing oil imports by one-third by 2025 and position the United States to become the first country to have one million electric vehicles on the road by 2015. We also are working to decrease the amount of energy used by commercial and industrial buildings by 20 percent to complement our ongoing efforts to improving the efficiency of the residential sector. And we will work with the private sector, utilities, and States to increase the energy productivity of American industries while investing in the innovative processes and materials that can dramatically reduce energy use.

It is also time for government to do its part to help make it easier for entrepreneurs, inventors, and workers to grow their businesses and thrive in the global economy. I am calling on Congress to immediately begin work on corporate tax reform that will close loopholes, lower the overall rate, encourage investment here at home, simplify taxes for America's small businesses, and not add a dime to the deficit. Moreover, to further assist these companies, we need a comprehensive reorganization of the parts of the Federal Government that help businesses grow and sell their products abroad. If given consolidation authority—which Presidents had for most of the 20th century—I will propose to consolidate six agencies into one Department, saving money, and making it easier for all companies—especially small businesses—get the help they need to thrive in the world economy.

Finally, this Budget advances the national security interests of the United States, including the security of the American people, the prosperity and trade that creates American jobs, and support for universal values around the world. It increases funding for the diplomatic efforts that strengthen the alliances and partnerships that improve international cooperation in meeting shared challenges, open new markets to American exports, and promote development. It invests in the intelligence and homeland security capabilities to detect, prevent, and defend against terrorist attacks against our country.

As we implement our new defense strategy, my Administration will invest in the systems and capabilities we need so that our Armed Forces are configured to meet the challenges of the coming decade. We will continue to invest in improving global health and food security so that we address the root causes of conflict and security threats. And we will keep faith with our men and women in uniform, their families, and veterans who have served their Nation.

These proposals will take us a long way towards strengthening the middle class and giving families the sense of security they have been missing for too long. But in the end, building an economy that works for everyone will require all of us to take responsibility. Parents will need to take greater responsibility for their children's education. Homeowners will have to take more responsibility when it comes to buying a house or taking out a loan. Businesses will have to take responsibility for doing right by their workers and our country. And those of us in public service will need to keep finding ways to make government more efficient and more effective.

Understanding and honoring the obligations we have to ourselves and each other is what has made this country great. We look out for each other, pull together, and do our part. But Americans also deserve to know that their hard work will be rewarded.

This Budget is a step in the right direction. And I hope it will help serve as a roadmap for how we can grow the economy, create jobs, and give Americans everywhere the security they deserve.

BARACK OBAMA

THE WHITE HOUSE,
      FEBRUARY 13, 2012.

BUILDING A STRONG ECONOMY

When the President took office, the economy was losing over 700,000 private sector jobs a month, and experiencing the worst two quarters of growth since the end of World War II. Due to swift action taken by the President shortly after taking office, the Nation avoided what could have been a second Great Depression—and has now experienced 22 consecutive months of private sector job growth, with 3.2 million jobs created. In just the first few months of 2009, the President's strong leadership produced a Recovery Act to bolster American families against the worst of the crisis, as well as a rescue of the auto industry and the stabilization of our financial system which, together, prevented our economy from spiraling into a deep depression.

At the beginning of 2011, our economy was gaining traction after enduring an historic recession and coming back from the brink of a depression. During the previous six quarters, real gross domestic product (GDP) had grown at an average annual rate of 3 percent and, over the previous 12 months, the private sector had created 1.3 million new jobs. The financial system was no longer in crisis. The credit and capital markets were functioning, and the cost of stabilizing the financial and automobile sectors was amounting to a fraction of initial estimates. We subsequently learned that the recession was deeper than many experts first thought: revised estimates showed that the economy contracted at an 8.9 percent annualized rate in the last quarter of 2008, from an original projection of 3.8 percent, the largest quarterly downward revision in history. A trio of world events then created strong headwinds

that challenged the economic expansion: uprisings in the Middle East that sent oil prices higher; an earthquake in Japan that prevented American auto and manufacturing companies from getting the supplies they needed to keep our factories producing; and widespread sovereign debt concerns in Europe that roiled markets across the globe. In addition, the willingness of Republicans in Congress to risk the first default in our Nation's history over the statutory debt ceiling and the subsequent downgrade by Standard & Poor's of the long-term sovereign rating of U.S. Treasuries and other debt tied to the U.S. credit rating kept financial markets on edge and appeared to rattle consumer confidence.

In the face of these headwinds, the policies enacted by the President played a key role in keeping the economy moving forward. Because of the policies that the President fought for, the typical working family received a $1,000 payroll tax cut in 2011, and millions of Americans pounding the pavement looking for jobs could continue to receive unemployment insurance (UI). This provided crucial insurance against headwinds buffeting our economy.

While concerns lingered over the financial developments in Europe and the risk they posed to the U.S. economy, the pace of real GDP growth increased in the second half of the year. Early in 2011, job growth picked up and the unemployment rate fell, but progress slowed in the spring and summer before picking up again in the fall. Overall, the unemployment rate fell over the course of the year, from 9.4 percent in December

2010 to 8.5 percent in December 2011, and the economy added 1.9 million private sector jobs in 2011. Over the last two months of 2011, consumer confidence jumped, nearing its high prior to the Japanese earthquake; housing starts were higher in November than they were in May; and after declining in August, the manufacturing Purchasing Managers Index (PMI) has now increased to 53.9, indicating an economic expansion.

Despite these encouraging signs, economic growth was not strong enough to create a sufficient number of good jobs for all of the Americans who wanted to work or robust enough to restore for the middle class the security and opportunity they deserved. At the same time, our country still faced the consequences of years of fiscal irresponsibility. When the President took office, he inherited an annual deficit of $1.3 trillion and projected deficits of trillions more in the years thereafter. Driving these deficits were decisions made over the previous eight years not to pay for two tax cuts and a Medicare prescription drug benefit. The deficits were then exacerbated by the recession: the sharp decline in receipts, steep increase in automatic outlays to help those in need, and efforts needed to jumpstart economic growth.

Recognizing the challenges still facing the economic recovery, the Administration believes that short-term efforts to boost economic growth and job creation plus comprehensive, balanced efforts to put the United States on the path toward fiscal stability were both needed. These are complementary policies: a growing economy is necessary for long-term deficit reduction, and likewise, long-term deficit reduction and fiscal sustainability is necessary to maintain and strengthen economic growth for years to come.

That is why the President pursued significant, balanced deficit reduction throughout calendar year 2011: first, in his 2012 Budget; then, in the Framework for Shared Prosperity and Shared Fiscal Responsibility released in April that built on the Budget to identify $4 trillion in deficit reduction; next, in a similarly sized plan presented to congressional Republicans during negotiations

over extending the debt ceiling during the summer; and finally in the President's Plan for Economic Growth and Deficit Reduction that was presented to the Joint Select Committee on Deficit Reduction in September. It also is why the President proposed the American Jobs Act (AJA) last September, a plan to put more people back to work, put more money in the pockets of working Americans, and do so without adding a dime to the deficit. This combination of tax cuts, infrastructure investments, and aid to those seeking work would give the economy a needed boost through this difficult time.

Unfortunately, at each step, partisan divides and unwillingness by Republicans in Congress to ask the wealthiest among us to pay their fair share through any revenue increases prevented a comprehensive deficit reduction agreement or measures in the AJA to boost demand from being enacted. Indeed, this lack of real progress on both the AJA and deficit reduction actually became a drag in and of itself on an economy already struggling to recover from a severe recession and battling significant headwinds from events around the globe.

As we look forward, the challenges of this past year persist: to build an economy that will grow robustly and create good jobs that pay well for years to come, and to put the country on a sustainable fiscal path through deficit reduction that is balanced and asks all Americans to pay their fair share. This Budget lays out the President's vision to accomplish both. It will take tough choices— cutting waste as well as some valuable programs that we would not cut if not for the fiscal situation. It will entail undertaking actions now to support and strengthen economic growth. And it will take reallocating resources to allow targeted investments so that we have an economy based not on speculation and bubbles, but one that is built on the solid foundation of an educated workforce, cutting-edge innovation, and world-class infrastructure.

MANAGING AND WINDING DOWN URGENT RECOVERY EFFORTS

When the President took office the economy was in free-fall. Real GDP was dropping at an annual rate of 6.7 percent in the first quarter of 2009, after falling at an annual rate of 8.9 percent the previous quarter. A seizure of credit markets in late 2008 caused companies to lay off workers and cut costs at an unprecedented rate. A steep decline in the stock market combined with falling home prices led to an enormous loss of household wealth. Between the third quarter of 2007 and the first quarter of 2009, the real net worth of American households declined by 27 percent—the equivalent of more than one year's GDP. Americans reacted to this massive loss of wealth by saving more instead of spending. The personal savings rate spiked at 6.2 percent in the second quarter of 2009, after averaging only 2 percent through the end of 2007. This had the effect of reducing consumer demand, a key driver of economic growth. The economy was in the worst downturn since the Great Depression, with significant risk that conditions could worsen. That is why the Administration took swift action to jumpstart economic growth and avoid a second Great Depression.

We now know that these efforts were even more critical to the recovery than it appeared at the time, as the decline we were in was deeper than anyone, at the time, knew. Now, as we work to build an economy that remains strong, stable and creating good jobs, the Administration is managing, and in some cases, winding down these critical recovery efforts.

The Recovery Act

Faced with the collapse of the economy, the Administration took decisive action to bolster macroeconomic demand and jumpstart economic activity, thus breaking the back of a recession that was spiraling out of control. The President moved rapidly, working with the Congress, and just 28 days after taking office, signed into law the Recovery Act to create and save jobs, as well as trans-

form the economy to compete in the 21st Century. Approximately one-third of the Act's funds were targeted to tax cuts for small businesses and 95 percent of working families. Another third was used for emergency relief for those who bore the brunt of the recession. For example, more than 17 million Americans benefited from extended or increased unemployment benefits, and health insurance was made 65 percent less expensive for laid-off workers and their families who relied on COBRA. The final third was invested in projects to create jobs, spur economic activity, and lay the foundation for future sustained growth. Aid to State and local governments helped to close budget shortfalls, supporting the jobs of more than 650,000 teachers, firefighters, and police officers. By the end of 2011, almost 95 percent of Recovery Act spending was obligated and 100 percent of the tax relief had been provided. Nearing the third anniversary of the Recovery Act, it is clear—and confirmed by independent analysts ranging from the Congressional Budget Office (CBO) to private-sector forecasters—that these swift and significant actions in the Recovery Act bolstered economic growth and created or preserved millions of jobs.

Progress has continued with sustained efforts by the Administration to ensure that Recovery Act funds continue to be spent expeditiously and in ways that create jobs and grow our economy, both now and in the future. In September 2011, the Administration directed Federal agencies to accelerate spending on the remaining Recovery Act funds for purposes that would create jobs right away, and is working closely with States, Tribes, local governments, and others on these efforts. Since this effort began, agencies have spent approximately $17 billion in additional discretionary funds, bringing the total amount of unspent discretionary funds down to less than $60 billion. In addition, 2011 saw investment and work begin in earnest on a number of long-term initiatives that were funded through the Recovery Act and are critical to creating a 21st Century economy and infrastructure. In particular, signature pieces of the Recovery Act dealing with high speed rail, broadband, clean energy, and health information technology began to ramp up, paving the way for long-term economic prosperity.

Reviewing the overall impact of the Recovery Act, the White House Council of Economic Advisers (CEA) estimates that the Recovery Act raised the level of GDP by the end of 2011, relative to what it would have been absent intervention, by between 2 and 2.9 percentage points. These estimates closely parallel those of a wide range of outside analysts, including CBO. The CEA also estimates that the Recovery Act raised employment relative to what it otherwise would have been by between 2.2 and 4.2 million jobs in the same time frame.

The Troubled Asset Relief Program

A central part of the response to the financial crisis was the implementation of the Troubled Asset Relief Program (TARP), which was established in the fall of 2008 under the Emergency Economic Stabilization Act of 2008. TARP succeeded in helping to stop widespread financial panic and helped prevent what could have been a devastating collapse of our financial system. The Government's authority to make new investments through the program expired on October 3, 2010, and TARP is now winding down. The U.S. Department of the Treasury (Treasury) has already recovered more than three-fourths of all the funds it disbursed, and the Government is now estimating the recovery of more funds for the taxpayers and at a faster rate than predicted at the inception of the program.

As of November 30, 2011, Treasury has received $318 billion in TARP repayments, interest, fees, and other income of the $413 billion disbursed. When it started, independent observers such as CBO estimated that TARP would cost $350 billion or more; CBO's December 2011 estimate is $34 billion, which assumes that $13 billion will be spent through the housing programs. The Administration now estimates the cost of the program will be $68 billion, assuming that the entire $45.6 billion set aside for housing initiatives is utilized. In short, the price of stabilizing our

financial system to prevent deep panic in every sector of our economy is now projected to be only one-fifth of the initially estimated cost.

The tasks ahead for TARP are to recover the remaining investments in the financial sector and auto industry in a manner that continues to promote financial stability while also maximizing the return for taxpayers. In addition, the Administration will continue to use TARP funds to assist homeowners seeking to avoid foreclosure.

The Automobile Industry

As a result of the President's aggressive and effective intervention, we are seeing a notable turnaround in the automobile industry at a lower cost than originally estimated. In late 2008, the combination of an historic recession and financial crisis pushed the American auto industry to the brink of collapse. Access to credit for car loans dried up and motor vehicle sales plunged 40 percent. Auto manufacturers and suppliers dramatically curtailed production. In the year before President Obama took office, the industry shed over 250,000 jobs. By late 2008, General Motors (GM) and Chrysler were on the brink of liquidation, which would have inflicted immediate and lasting damage to the country's manufacturing and industrial base. It also would have produced a significant rise in both regional and national unemployment, and would have further damaged the financial system since automobile financing is a significant portion of overall financial activity. Moreover, if these companies had gone out of business, the economy would have been forced deeper into recession and might have fallen into a depression. The President made a difficult decision to provide support to GM and Chrysler on the condition that they, and all of their stakeholders, make the sacrifices necessary to fundamentally restructure their businesses and commit to tough-minded plans to return to viability.

The President's decision to save GM and Chrysler was about more than those two companies. It was about standing behind the countless workers, families, communities, and businesses—large and small—that depend on the automotive industry. The success of this policy has been dramatic. Both companies restructured and emerged from bankruptcy, and since then, the auto industry has created more than 100,000 new jobs, and American automakers are in the midst of their strongest period of job growth in more than a decade. American workers are back at the assembly line manufacturing high-quality, fuel-efficient, American-made cars, capable of competing with manufacturers from around the world. In fact, General Motors is now once again the world's number one automaker. The impact of this resurgence goes beyond directly making cars and car parts, and affects the entire supply chain of goods and services that contribute to the world's largest manufacturing activity. Companies that make steel, tires, glass, aluminum products, machinery, and after-market products all rely on the continued success of the U.S. auto industry. Indeed, the resurgence of the American auto industry has been at the heart of a quiet improvement in the overall manufacturing sector—a key component of constructing an economy that is built to last and can create good jobs for years to come. Since December 2009, the United States has added 334,000 manufacturing jobs, the first time the manufacturing sector has had sustained job growth since 1998.

For taxpayers this means that the assistance extended to these companies is paying off. In May 2011, Chrysler repaid its outstanding loans to the U.S. Treasury—a full six years before their scheduled maturity. Chrysler was able to achieve this milestone by accessing the debt markets and raising capital on more favorable terms than the U.S. Government loans—another sign of its emerging strength as a private company. With that repayment, Chrysler had returned $11.1 billion to the U.S. Government, which represents nearly 90 percent of the Federal support committed to the company.

SUPPORTING AND PROTECTING MIDDLE-CLASS FAMILIES

The promise of America is that with hard work, Americans can provide a solid, middle-class life

for their families: find a good job, afford a home, send their children to good schools, receive high-quality and affordable health care, and enjoy a secure retirement in their later years. Americans' drive and ingenuity lie at the heart of this promise and a growing economy makes it possible to realize these aspirations. Also critical are rules of the road laid down to make our markets and free society work, and remove barriers so that no one has an unfair advantage and everyone can have a fair shot to go as far as their dreams and talents can take them. To that end, we have a responsibility to one another as neighbors and as Americans to make sure that the basic protections are in place to enable families and businesses to thrive. These include keeping our air and water healthy for our children, providing fairness in the workplace and supporting those looking for work, ensuring that products are safe and are represented honestly, and protecting Social Security and Medicare to provide for citizens in life's later years.

To add to this list, the Administration has undertaken two historic initiatives—health insurance and Wall Street reform—that will hold some of the largest companies in the country accountable and help give all Americans the security they need to ensure that an illness or ill-conceived financial decision made by a firm hundreds of miles away will not bankrupt them or prevent them from providing for their family. Over the past year, the Administration has worked diligently to implement these new reforms, and to protect them from efforts to undermine and defund them. In the appropriations negotiations both at the beginning and end of 2011, the Administration insisted on having the necessary funding to continue to implement health insurance and Wall Street reform, and stopped efforts to use policy riders to undermine both of these important initiatives, and their crucial protections for American consumers and families.

Health Insurance Reform

The President signed into law the Patient Protection and Affordable Care Act (ACA) on March 23, 2010, enacting comprehensive health insurance reforms that will hold insurance companies more accountable, lower health care costs, guarantee more health care choices, and enhance the quality of health care for all Americans. The ACA gives Americans the stability and security they need by ending many discriminatory and abusive insurance industry practices; expanding coverage to more than 30 million Americans who lack insurance; cutting waste and reforming health care delivery so that patients receive higher quality care; and doing it all without adding a dime to the deficit. In fact, the ACA will reduce the deficit by more than $1 trillion over the next two decades. Considering that rising health care costs are a major contributor to the deficit and hinder the Nation's overall competitiveness, the ACA puts in place much-needed deficit reduction.

Americans already are enjoying many of the protections put in place by the ACA. For instance, in the past, if a person became ill, insurance companies could rescind coverage and deny payments for health services by retroactively finding an error or other technical mistake on their previously accepted application; this is now illegal. Insurance companies are now prohibited from imposing lifetime dollar limits on benefits, such as hospital stays. Young adults under age 26 can now stay on their parents' policies. And because of the ACA, insurance companies can no longer deny coverage to children under the age of 19 due to a pre-existing condition. And all new private-market health insurance plans now must cover critical preventive care services such as mammograms and colonoscopies without charging a deductible, copay, or coinsurance.

Also, two important additions to coverage from the ACA for seniors went into effect. First, eligible Medicare beneficiaries are paying less for prescription drugs that are purchased in the Part D coverage gap starting with a 50 percent discount on covered brand-name prescription drugs in 2011; coverage will increase each year until the coverage gap is closed in 2020. Second, Medicare beneficiaries are now eligible for certain free preventive services, such as annual wellness visits and recommended cancer screenings.

More reforms also are taking effect. To ensure that dollars are going to patient care, the ACA requires insurance companies to spend at least 80 or 85 percent, depending on their market, of premium dollars on medical care and quality improvements, instead of administrative costs and profits. If they fail to meet these standards, insurance companies are required to provide a rebate to their customers. The first rebates will be paid out later this year. Additionally, the ACA brings an unprecedented level of scrutiny and transparency to health insurance rate increases. Large premium increases proposed by health insurance companies in the individual and small group markets will now be evaluated by experts to make sure they are based on reasonable cost assumptions and solid evidence, and insurance companies have to publicly justify unreasonable rate increases.

Beyond curbing the most egregious practices of the insurance industry, Americans have realized other benefits. Since ACA's passage, small businesses have been claiming tax credits to help them provide insurance benefits to their workers. Through 2013, this provision provides a credit worth up to 35 percent of employers' contributions to employees' health insurance; it rises to 50 percent for coverage purchased through Affordable Insurance Exchanges starting in 2014. For those individuals who have been uninsured for at least six months because of a pre-existing condition, there is now a Pre-Existing Condition Insurance Plan to provide them with affordable, comprehensive coverage options. This program serves as a bridge to 2014, when all discrimination against pre-existing conditions will be prohibited. Similarly, the Early Retiree Reinsurance Program provides temporary assistance to employers who had been struggling to maintain coverage for older workers who retired, but are not yet eligible for Medicare.

In addition, numerous ACA reforms aimed at improving quality, efficiency, and coordination of care will take effect over the next year. Hospital Value-Based Purchasing and the Hospital Readmissions Reduction Programs will both tie Medicare payments to hospitals to achievement of indicators of high-quality care. The Medicare Shared Savings Program will be launched nationwide, creating new opportunities for patient-centered, integrated care for Medicare beneficiaries. Further, the Administration is launching several initiatives to improve care for individuals eligible for both Medicare and Medicaid, including developing and testing new models designed to incentivize States to create efficiencies through integration of care and improved care coordination. And the ACA provided significant new tools and resources to crack down on waste and fraud in health care.

Finally, the Administration is committed to implementing the ACA swiftly, efficiently, and effectively, and will continue to work with the Congress to ensure that the resources are available to do just that. The need for resources is especially critical for establishing Affordable Insurance Exchanges, which will help ensure that every American can access high-quality, affordable health insurance coverage beginning in 2014. These competitive marketplaces will provide millions of Americans and small businesses with "one-stop shopping" for affordable coverage in every State. Since passage of the ACA, the Department of Health and Human Services (HHS) has provided grants to nearly all States to plan for and establish these State Exchanges.

Wall Street Reform

Curbing the abuses in the health insurance industry and beginning to bring down rising health care costs were long overdue steps toward addressing critical problems that affect Americans every day. The financial and economic crisis of 2008 also made it clear that the rules governing our financial system needed revision to provide a more stable foundation for the economy and to protect consumers, businesses, and families.

The American free market system is the most powerful engine of economic growth and job creation the world has known, and when it works, it helps ensure that the American middle class is strong and secure. But the free market was never meant to give the financial system free license to take irresponsible and reckless risks of such a size that they can harm our economy and leave taxpayers with the bill.

The recent recession was not just the result of a turn in the business cycle. Rather, it was the result of a perfect storm of excessive risk-taking, inadequate disclosure, non-existent or myopic oversight, individuals and firms who chose to leverage themselves beyond their means, and in some cases outright deceptive lending practices that led too many Americans to take on debt they could not afford. In sum, it was an abdication of responsibility from across many actors in the financial system.

To prevent this from happening again, the Administration set out to craft a financial reform package that filled the gaps in oversight, transparency, and restraint; put a check on predatory and abusive lending; and restored accountability to the system—especially for those who had operated outside the regulatory framework. The Administration's goal was to restore our financial system to its core mission: providing a safe and productive venue for private saving, helping entrepreneurs and businesses with the best ideas to create value and jobs, and enabling families to buy homes, finance college for their children, and secure a dignified retirement.

On July 21, 2010, after a long and difficult fight on Capitol Hill, the President signed into law the most far-reaching Wall Street reforms since the Great Depression—the Dodd-Frank Wall Street Reform and Consumer Protection Act (Wall Street Reform). This law takes the necessary steps to create a more stable and responsible financial system. The Act requires banks to hold more capital so that when they make a bad bet they pay for it, not taxpayers. It also prevents financial companies, like AIG, from posing such a risk to our economy that we have no choice but for taxpayers to bail them out. The Act does this by creating an orderly liquidation process for large financial firms that fail, and by requiring the largest and most systemically important financial firms to write "living wills" that detail how, if they fail, they will be wound down in a manner that does not leave taxpayers vulnerable. The Act also brings transparency to the $600 trillion derivatives market and prohibits banks from making risky bets with their customers' deposits. Finally, the Act holds CEOs accountable by taking back bonuses and compensation from failing CEOs, giving shareholders a voice on CEO pay, and protecting whistleblowers who speak out about wrong-doing on Wall Street.

In addition, Wall Street Reform puts in place sweeping reforms to protect American consumers. The Act created the Consumer Financial Protection Bureau (CFPB), an agency exclusively devoted to protecting consumers, in part by giving them the tools to make their own choices and find the most suitable financial products, even when a provider may have incentives to hide true costs. The CFPB is empowered to set high and uniform standards across the market; focus on improving financial literacy for all Americans; and help to end profits based on misleading sales pitches and hidden traps, forcing banks and non-bank financial institutions to compete vigorously for consumers on the basis of price and quality. It will help crack down on abusive practices in the mortgage industry, make financial contracts simpler, and end many of the hidden fees so that families know what they are signing when they buy a home. It also ensures that students who take out college loans will be provided clear and concise information about their obligations. It reinforces the Credit Card Accountability, Responsibility, and Disclosure Act passed in 2009 that bans unfair rate hikes, and ensures that banks cannot charge unwitting consumers overdraft fees when they sign up for a checking account. In total, these reforms put in place the strongest consumer financial protections in history.

Over the course of the last year, the Administration and independent regulators have been working to implement Wall Street Reform to achieve these goals. Regulators issued proposed regulations to implement the Volcker Rule to make sure that banks benefitting from Government protections—such as Federal Deposit Insurance Corporation (FDIC) insurance on customer deposits—are prohibited from making risky trading bets for their own accounts and face restrictions in investing in or sponsoring hedge funds or private equity funds. Regulators have also proposed new rules for higher capital standards to buffer against risk in the financial system. The FDIC has finalized new rules to resolve a failing financial firm without threatening the financial system or costing taxpayers.

To ensure that agencies and departments have the resources they need to implement Wall Street Reform, the Administration fought for and secured adequate funding levels for 2012, and continues this commitment in the 2013 Budget. And to ensure that consumers are protected, the President appointed Richard Cordray to head the CFPB. Without a Director, the CFPB could not fully supervise non-bank financial institutions such as independent payday lenders, non-bank mortgage lenders, non-bank mortgage servicers, debt collectors, credit reporting agencies, and private student lenders. This meant that tens of millions of Americans were left unprotected from falling prey to many of the harmful practices that contributed to the worst financial crisis since the Great Depression.

JUMPSTARTING ECONOMIC GROWTH AND JOB CREATION

By almost any measure, the economy this past year was stronger than it was in 2009 at the start of the Administration. However, too many Americans are still out of work, and our economy is not yet operating at its full potential. Part of this is due to the destructive nature of the recession that we went through, and part is due to a confluence of external world events that shook global markets as described earlier in this Chapter. The effect of these events on economic performance in the latter part of calendar year 2011 and, in turn, on the lives of millions of Americans in search of a good job and economic security led the Administration to propose the American Jobs Act in September 2011.

American Jobs Act

The purpose of the American Jobs Act (AJA) was simple: put more people back to work and put more money in the pockets of working Americans. Independent economists estimated that the Act would have added up to nearly 2 million jobs in 2012. The AJA included: tax cuts to help America's small businesses hire and grow; tax credits to spur hiring; investments in infrastructure improvements; new pathways back to work for Americans looking for jobs, including the most significant reforms to the Nation's unemployment system in 40 years to help those without jobs transition to the workplace; and tax cuts to put more money in the pockets of every American worker and family. Moreover, the AJA would not have added to the deficit. It included specific offsets that would, in combination, more than fully pay for its cost.

While the AJA was comprised of the kinds of ideas that had been embraced by Democrats and Republicans in the past, congressional intransigence prevented the AJA from becoming law. Nevertheless, the President kept fighting for measures to jumpstart economic growth and job creation. In November, the President won enactment of one plank of the AJA: a new tax credit for America's veterans, which provides up to $5,600 for hiring a veteran who is long-term unemployed and $9,600 for businesses that hire a veteran with a service-related disability.

And, in the waning days of the year, the President signed into law a short-term extension of the decrease in the payroll tax, an increase in UI benefits, and the prevention of a 27 percent cut to Medicare payments to physicians that was set to take effect at the end of the calendar year. To be clear, the President preferred a year-long extension of these critical growth measures, and expects the Congress to continue the short-term payroll tax and UI extension they approved in December for the rest of 2012, and avert the impending reduction in physician payments. The full-year extension of the payroll tax cut for 2012 would help 160 million American workers, pro-viding a typical worker with an additional $40 in each paycheck. The full-year extension of UI benefits for Americans pounding the pavement looking for work would save 5 million individuals from exhausting benefits this year, and would help to create nearly 500,000 jobs as these benefits are spent quickly in the economy. Finally, preventing a deep cut in Medicare physician payments is critical to seniors' access to care.

We need to finish the job because there are still too many Americans who want to work, but cannot find jobs. That is why the President is still calling for efforts to spur near-term economic growth and job creation. This includes many of the planks in the AJA that were not enacted, as well as measures not included in that legislation. Some of these job-creating proposals include:

- An upfront investment of $50 billion from the surface transportation reauthorization bill for roads, rails, and runways to create thousands of quality jobs in the short term.

- Aid to States and localities to retain and hire teachers and first responders.

- Extending UI benefits and undertaking major reforms to help the long-term unemployed find work and spur the creation of job opportunities for hundreds of thousands of the most-vulnerable Americans—low-income youth and adults. This includes reforms that require those receiving emergency Federal benefits to participate in Reemployment and Eligibility Assessments and be provided Reemployment Services, which have been proven to help put people back to work; that build on and improve innovative State programs where those who have been displaced take temporary, voluntary work or pursue on-the-job training; and that expand programs to allow those receiving UI to start their own businesses.

- The Better Buildings Initiative that seeks to make non-residential buildings 20 percent more energy efficient over the next decade by catalyzing private-sector investment through a series of incentives to upgrade offices, stores, universities, hospitals, and commercial buildings.

- Funds to modernize at least 35,000 schools to create jobs now and high-quality schools for the future.

- Reauthorization of Clean Energy Manufacturing Tax Credits to spur the creation of manufacturing jobs in the advanced energy technology sector.

- A new HomeStar program, which would encourage Americans to invest in energy and cost-saving home improvements, reducing families' energy bills over time and creating jobs for those who undertake and make these renovations.

- Continuing to allow businesses to write-off the full amount of new investments next year.

- Project Rebuild, a series of policies to help connect Americans looking for work in distressed communities with the work needed to repurpose residential and commercial properties.

We Can't Wait: Executive Actions to Boost the Economy

Recognizing the need for action in the face of congressional gridlock, the President believed that the American people could not wait for the Congress to act to spur economic growth and job creation. That is why, throughout the fall of 2011, the President waged a "We Can't Wait" campaign, a series of executive actions that he and his Cabinet took to help families hurt by the sluggish economic growth, boost economic activity, and spur job creation:

- *Housing Refinancing.* On October 24, the President announced steps to help respon-

sible borrowers with little or no equity in their homes take advantage of today's low mortgage rates.

- *Expanding Jobs for Veterans.* On October 25, HHS announced an initiative to challenge Community Health Centers to hire 8,000 veterans—approximately one veteran per health center site—over the next three years. The Administration also announced that it would work with health practitioner training programs to expand opportunities for returning service members with medical training to become physician assistants.

- *Creating New Opportunities for Improving College Affordability.* On October 26, the President announced "Pay as you Earn" to enable student loan borrowers to cap their student loan repayments at 10 percent of discretionary income beginning in fall 2012.

- *Helping Small Businesses Create Jobs.* On October 28, the White House issued two Presidential Memoranda to help small businesses create jobs. One memorandum directed agencies to take steps to speed up the transfer of Federal research from the laboratory to the marketplace. The other directed the creation of BusinessUSA, an online platform where businesses can access information about Federal programs that support small businesses and exports.

- *Preventing Drug Shortages.* On October 31, the President signed an Executive Order directing the Food and Drug Administration and the Department of Justice to take action to help further reduce and prevent shortages of critical drugs, protect consumers, and prevent price gouging.

- *Accelerating Transportation Projects.* On November 2, the President announced steps the Administration is taking to improve and expedite the process of reviewing and approving transportation projects. On December 15, as part of this effort, the Department of Transportation awarded $511 million in transportation grants as part of the Department's popular Transportation Investment Generating Economic Recovery (TIGER) program, months ahead of schedule.

- *Supporting Jobs for Veterans.* On November 7, the Administration announced three executive actions that will provide new resources for veterans to translate military experience to the private job market, give veterans additional career development support, and better identify firms looking to hire veterans.

- *Reforming Head Start.* On November 8, the President announced important steps to improve the quality of services and accountability at Head Start centers across the country.

- *Cutting Waste.* On November 9, the President signed an Executive Order that will cut waste and promote more efficient spending across the Federal Government. Overall spending in the areas covered by the Executive Order will be reduced by 20 percent, saving billions.

- *Creating Health Care Jobs.* On November 14, HHS announced a $1 billion Health Care Innovation Challenge, which will award grants to applicants who will implement the most compelling new ideas to deliver better care and lower costs to people enrolled in Medicare, Medicaid, and the Children's Health Insurance Program. This competition prioritizes projects that deploy the health care workforce in innovative ways.

- *Reducing Improper Payments.* On November 15, OMB and the Vice President announced that the Administration cut improper payments by nearly $18 billion in 2011, and that we are on track to meet the President's goal of cutting improper payments by $50 billion by the end of 2012. We also announced new actions to help further reduce Medicare and Medicaid waste, fraud, and abuse as well as a directive to agencies to step up their oversight of contractors and grant recipients.

- *Raising Fuel Economy Standards.* On November 16, the Department of Transportation and the Environmental Protection Agency formally unveiled their joint proposal to set stronger fuel economy and greenhouse gas pollution standards for Model Year 2017-2025 passenger cars and light duty trucks. This initiative will have net benefits of between $310 billion and $420 billion in fuel savings, slash oil consumption by 4 billion barrels, and reduce greenhouse gas emissions by 2 billion metric tons over the lifetimes of the vehicles sold those years. When combined with other steps we have taken to set standards for vehicles, this proposal will save Americans approximately $1.7 trillion at the pump, reduce America's dependence on oil by an estimated 12 billion barrels, and reduce greenhouse gas emissions by 6 billion metric tons over the life of the programs.

- *Modernizing Government Records.* On November 28, the Administration issued a Presidential Memorandum that directed agencies to move to a digital-based records keeping system. This action will save taxpayer dollars, promote accountability, and increase government transparency. This is one of the policy actions that open government advocates have sought for years.

- *Expanding Health Information Technology (IT).* On November 30, HHS announced at an event in Ohio that the number of physicians adopting electronic medical records has doubled since 2009, and set forth steps the agency is taking to make it easier for doctors and other health professionals to receive incentive payments for adopting and meaningfully using health IT.

- *Improving Energy Efficiency Through the "Better Building Initiative."* On December 2, with President Clinton, the President announced nearly $4 billion in combined Federal and private sector energy-efficiency upgrades to buildings over the next two years.

- *Expanding Advanced Biofuels.* In December, the Defense Logistics Agency signed a contract to purchase 450,000 gallons of advanced drop-in biofuel, the single largest purchase of biofuel in Government history.

- *Launching Small Business Innovation Fund.* On December 8, in conjunction with the first board meeting of the Startup America Partnership, the Small Business Administration announced that it is moving forward with launching a $1 billion Early Stage Innovation Fund that will provide matching capital to small business investment companies. The Administration also announced commitments from more than 50 private-sector partners to deliver over $1 billion in value to 100,000 startups over the next three years.

- *Extending Minimum Wage and Overtime Protections.* On December 15, the President announced new proposed rules to provide Federal minimum wage and overtime protections for nearly two million workers who provide in-home care services for the elderly and infirm.

If the Congress continues to block efforts to pass legislation that can spur economic growth and job creation, the President will undertake whatever executive actions he can to make sure that our economy continues its recovery.

Rejuvenating the Housing Market

As the financial crisis and recession was deepening in 2009, the Administration took immediate steps to help thousands of responsible homeowners who were facing foreclosure or were at risk of losing their homes. This began with the Administration's effort to establish a broad set of programs designed to stabilize the housing market and keep millions of Americans in their homes. The initiative included Treasury's mortgage-backed securities purchase program, which along with mortgage-backed securities purchases by the Federal Reserve, has helped to keep mortgage interest rates at historic lows and allowed

over 12 million homeowners to refinance since April 2009; the homebuyer tax credit, which helped millions of Americans to purchase homes, bolstering macroeconomic demand; the low-income housing tax credit and housing finance agency programs to support affordable housing; and the Home Affordable Modification Program (HAMP), which provides eligible homeowners the opportunity to significantly reduce their monthly mortgage payments, remain in their homes, and avoid foreclosures.

Although initially held back by implementation challenges and poor performance on the part of mortgage servicers, HAMP has provided 910,000 borrowers with a permanent modification and, equally importantly, established a template for the private market to provide more effective modifications for struggling homeowners. In total, since the Administration's housing programs took effect in 2009, there have been more than twice as many public and private mortgage modification offers made than foreclosures completed. The Administration has worked to expand and enhance the program—including introducing related programs for second lien modifications and short sales, and has increased servicer oversight and public reporting on servicer-specific performance.

While there are signs that the broader housing market is beginning to stabilize, too many Americans are still paying mortgage interest rates far above current market rates because home price declines made them ineligible for refinancing. To address this issue, the President announced last September that his economic team would work with Federal housing agencies and the Government-Sponsored Enterprises (GSEs) Fannie Mae and Freddie Mac to expand the Home Affordable Refinance Program (HARP), and in October specific changes were announced that will remove many of the barriers preventing GSE borrowers who have remained current on their mortgages from taking advantage of today's historically low mortgage rates.

While this is an important step, the Administration believes that more relief is needed.

Therefore, the Administration is calling on the Congress to take additional steps so virtually every family that has a standard mortgage and has been paying its bills on time will have the opportunity to refinance their mortgage at today's historically low rates. Specifically, this would be done by fully streamlining HARP to increase access and lower cost for borrowers and, more significantly, to provide those responsible Americans who happen not to have a loan guaranteed by the GSEs with access to a comparable streamlined refinance program through the Federal Housing Administration. Helping families refinance will help homeowners get into more sustainable loans, save each family on average $3,000, enable many people to stay in their homes, and give a jolt to local economies.

Opening Global Markets

The emergence of a global marketplace that includes the growing economies of China, India, Brazil, and other developing countries creates an opportunity for America to export our goods and services to new customers. With 95 percent of the world's customers as well as the globe's fastest-growing markets beyond our borders, we must compete aggressively to spur economic growth and job creation. That is why the President launched his National Export Initiative to marshal the full resources of the Federal Government behind America's businesses, especially small- and medium-sized enterprises, to best help them sell their goods, services, and ideas to the rest of the world and to reach the President's goal of doubling U.S. exports in five years' time (by the end of 2014).

The Administration is currently on pace to meet this target: through October 2011, exports of goods and services over the preceding 12 months totaled over $2 trillion, 32 percent above 2009 levels. Current GDP forecasts suggest that the ratio of exports to GDP will hit 14 percent in 2011, which would also be an historical record. To support international trade and the jobs that accompany it, the Administration has:

- *Signed Into Law Free Trade Agreements with Colombia, Panama, and Korea.* To help meet the President's export goal, the Administration completed negotiations for free trade agreements (FTAs) with Colombia, Panama, and Korea. The three trade agreements were passed in quick succession in the fall of 2011 and signed into law by the President, marking the biggest step forward in American trade liberalization in nearly two decades. These agreements are fair and were passed together with a renewed and strengthened trade adjustment assistance program for workers displaced by international trade. In particular, the Korea-United States FTA is expected to boost annual U.S. goods exports to Korea by as much as $11 billion and support more than 70,000 American jobs.

- *Promoted Business Investment in the U.S., Including Foreign Direct Investment (FDI).* The Obama Administration has taken unprecedented steps to facilitate and promote business investment in the United States. This includes establishing SelectUSA, a "one-stop shop" based in the Department of Commerce that facilitates investment in the United States from both foreign and domestic investors. This effort represents the first systematic Federal Government initiative to promote and facilitate business investment, a role that had historically been left to the States. In addition to increasing the level of FDI, SelectUSA also seeks to diversify our FDI beyond those countries that have historically been our largest trading partners. Within the United States, SelectUSA works across the Federal Government and partners with State and local economic development organizations to enable a coordinated approach to compete for business investment, an effort which the President is proposing to significantly expand in the 2013 Budget.

This year, the Administration will continue to vigorously enforce international and domestic trade laws and look for opportunities to level the playing field for American workers, businesses, ranchers, and farmers; pursue increased access to several foreign markets through the groundbreaking Trans-Pacific Partnership; implement the three FTAs passed in 2011; work with the Congress to pass legislation allowing the United States to benefit from Russia's accession to the World Trade Organization; and promote tourism and travel to the United States from the world's fastest growing economies by expanding visa processing in countries such as Brazil and China.

Pursuing Sensible Regulation

Administration is firmly committed to a regulatory strategy that promotes continued economic growth and job creation, while protecting the safety and health of all Americans. Smart, cost-effective regulations, crafted with input from stakeholders inside and outside of Government, can save lives and prevent harm while promoting growth and innovation. As the economy continues to recover and create new jobs, it is particularly critical for the Nation's regulatory strategy to enable American businesses to grow and innovate.

That is why the Administration carefully weighs the costs and benefits of rules—not by reducing difficult questions to problems of arithmetic, but by carefully weighing economic effects and also by taking into account qualitative factors, including fairness and human dignity. The Administration uses objective data to assess the impact of rules and to assess alternatives. Moreover, the Administration looks for areas where it can promote transparency and disclosure as a low-cost, high-impact regulatory tool. From automobile safety to energy efficiency and credit cards, this approach has been fruitful. In fact, in the Administration's first two years, the net benefits of regulation were estimated to exceed $35 billion—over 10 times the amount in the first two years of the George W. Bush Administration, and over three times the amount in the corresponding period in the Clinton Administration. In fact, fewer regulations were issued by Executive Agencies in the first three years of this Administration than in the first three years of the previous Administration.

To improve the regulatory process, the President issued a new Executive Order calling for attention to the best available evidence, careful consideration of costs and benefits, greater coordination among agencies, and selection of flexible and least burdensome alternatives, and has called on independent Federal regulators to follow suit in their rulemakings. The Executive Order also called for an unprecedented Government-wide review of existing rules. The review produced over 500 reform proposals across all Executive agencies. Already, we are on track to save more than $10 billion dollars in just the near term, with much more savings to come.

In the coming year, agencies will continue to pursue the regulatory reforms identified in the retrospective review process, producing billions more in savings by simplifying rules, eliminating redundancies, and identifying more cost-effective ways of doing things.

CUTTING WASTE, REDUCING THE DEFICIT, AND ASKING ALL TO PAY THEIR FAIR SHARE

To construct an economy that is built to last and creates good jobs that pay well for generations to come, it will take making investments in education, innovation, and infrastructure so that our entrepreneurs, scientists, and workers have the tools they need to succeed. To pay for those investments and free our economy from the burden of historic deficits and growing debt, we need to change how Washington does business, and restore responsibility for what we spend and accountability for how we spend it. For too long, Washington has spent money without identifying a way to pay for it. Indeed, the cost of the 2001 and 2003 tax cuts as well as the Medicare prescription drug benefit passed in the last administration contributed significantly to turning the surpluses of the 1990s into the record deficits of the following decade. The financial crisis and recession exacerbated our fiscal situation as revenue decreased and automatic Government outlays increased to counter the recession and cushion its impact. The result was that, upon taking office, the President faced an annual deficit of $1.3 trillion, or 9.2 percent of GDP, and a 10-year deficit of more than $8 trillion—and this figure grew even larger as the depth of the recession became clear. While the need to jump-start our economy through the Recovery Act and other measures added to the short-term deficit, these critical measures were temporary and did not have significant deficit effects beyond the recession.

In addition, for far too long, many Government programs have been allowed to continue or to grow even when their objectives are no longer clear and they lack rigorous assessment of whether the programs are achieving the desired goals. The result has been the profusion of programs that are duplicative, ineffective, or outdated—at a significant cost to taxpayers.

Since taking office the President has worked to restore accountability and fiscal responsibility. In his first Budget, the President directly confronted the unsustainable fiscal situation he inherited by making a commitment to restoring fiscal responsibility, while recognizing that increasing the deficit in the short term was necessary to arrest the economic freefall. He signed into law pay-as-you-go (PAYGO) legislation that returned the tough but disciplined budget rules of the 1990s to Washington. The principle behind PAYGO is simple: all new, non-emergency entitlement spending and revenue losses must be offset by savings or revenue increases, with no exception for new tax cuts. And, recognizing the role that rising health care costs play in our long-term fiscal future, the President advocated for and signed into law fiscally responsible health care reform that, according to the latest analysis, will reduce our deficit by more than $1 trillion over the next two decades, as well as fully pay for all new coverage. The President also convened the bipartisan National Commission on Fiscal Responsibility and Reform (the Fiscal Commission) whose work reset the debate about further deficit reduction, and who contributed many ideas that have been included in several deficit reduction plans to date.

Finally, the President pursued significant, balanced deficit reduction throughout last year: first, in February in his 2012 Budget; then, in April in the Framework for Shared Prosperity and Shared Fiscal Responsibility that built on the Budget to identify $4 trillion in deficit reduction; and next, in July, in a similarly sized plan presented to congressional Republicans during negotiations over extending the debt ceiling this summer. Unfortunately, an unwillingness by Republicans in Congress to ask the wealthiest among us to pay their fair share through any revenue increases prevented a comprehensive deficit reduction agreement from being enacted. Instead, the President signed into law the Budget Control Act of 2011 (BCA), which established discretionary spending caps that put into effect nearly $1 trillion of discretionary spending cuts. These caps impose very tight constraints on discretionary spending, and meeting them will take difficult decisions and trade-offs. In this Budget, the President has put forward a plan to meet these caps by making tough decisions that target resources toward priorities that will not undermine our ability to build a strong economy and that asks all to shoulder their fair share.

Discretionary spending is just one small part of the Budget, and the BCA also established a congressional process to cut at least $1.2 trillion more from the deficit. In August 2011, the President sent his Plan for Economic Growth and Deficit Reduction to the Joint Select Committee on Deficit Reduction, laying out how he would pay for the American Jobs Act and cut the deficit by an additional $3 trillion over the next decade.

In order to force the Congress to act and enact at least $1.2 trillion in deficit reduction, the BCA included an automatic sequester that would cut that same amount beginning in calendar year 2013 if the Joint Select Committee on Deficit Reduction failed. By design, the sequester is not good policy and is meant to force the Congress to take action: it would lead to significant cuts to critical domestic programs such as education and research and cuts to defense programs that could undermine our national security. Yet even this strong incentive to action was not enough for Republicans in Congress to agree to ask the wealthiest Americans to pay their fair share in revenue or to close special tax loopholes for large companies; thus, no action was taken, and the sequester was triggered and will take effect in January 2013 if no action is taken.

There is time for the Congress to pass a balanced, sensible plan to meet the deficit reduction goals of the BCA. And they should act to do so since cuts of this magnitude and done in an across-the-board fashion would be devastating both to defense and non-defense programs. Already, we have reduced spending on these programs, and further cuts would lead to an erosion of services that Americans would not want and undermine our national security in a way that we cannot allow. That is why in this Budget, the President again has put forward a plan that will, together with the deficit reduction enacted last year, cut the deficit by more than $4 trillion over the next decade. This would put our Nation on the right course toward a level of deficits of below 3 percent of GDP by the end of the decade. This is not an end in and of itself; rather, bringing our deficits to this level would mean that we are no longer adding to our deficits through additional spending; that debt is falling as a share of the economy; and that the country is headed in the right direction. To do this, we need to make tough choices: cutting waste where we can, reducing spending in areas that are not critical to long-term economic growth and job creation, and asking everyone to pay their fair share. Making these choices now is critical to building our economy on a solid foundation that can deliver for the middle class for years to come.

MAKING TOUGH CHOICES TO RESTORE FISCAL DISCIPLINE

To be competitive in the 21st Century, the United States cannot be weighed down by crippling budget deficits, ineffective programs that waste tax dollars, and Government spending that lacks accountability. As we move forward with the tough choices necessary to rein in our deficits and put the country on a sustainable fiscal path, we must balance those efforts with the investments and actions required to keep the economy growing and competing with other nations. We must look for cuts while protecting our core values. The Budget maintains and makes critical investments in areas important to growth and competitiveness while broadly sharing sacrifices to reduce the deficit. The Administration proposes to:

Reduce Discretionary Spending. In August 2011, the President signed into law the BCA, which put in place a down payment toward deficit reduction and a structure to accomplish even more. The BCA included a cap on discretionary spending that would achieve approximately $1 trillion in deficit reduction over the next decade. In 2012, the Congress worked in a bipartisan way to meet the caps that were agreed to in the BCA. As we turn to 2013, the caps, in combination with the drawdown in overseas contingency operations proposed in this Budget, would bring discretionary spending to its lowest level as a share of the economy since Dwight D. Eisenhower sat in the Oval Office. These are very tight caps; indeed, it would not be possible to go further and still meet the needs of the Nation. That is why achieving these cuts in discretionary spending is not easy and will take tough choices. Many programs are cut or consolidated where possible, and in some cases, only because of the demands of the fiscal situation. The Budget makes these cuts in a way that asks all to shoulder their fair share. In areas critical to building a strong, growing economy that can create good jobs that pay well, programs are not cut, but rather frozen or given small increases. In light of the caps on discretionary spending, these increases are significant.

Cut or Consolidate Programs. Allocating budgetary resources always involves a trade-off between what one wants to do and what one can afford to do. This is exacerbated when the imperative is to limit spending in order to reduce the drag of deficits and debt on our economic growth and competitiveness. In each of his first two budgets, the President put forward more than 120 terminations, reductions, and savings totaling approximately $20 billion in each year. In 2012, the Budget proposed more than 200 terminations, reductions, and savings, totaling approximately $30 billion in savings. This year, the Administration is proposing cuts and consolidations across the Government in order to live within the caps established by the BCA. To achieve these savings, we went through the Budget carefully to identify programs that were either ineffective, duplicative, or outdated and thus needed to be cut or consolidated. Other cuts were taken in programs whose mission the Administration cares deeply about, but that had to be reduced to meet our fiscal targets. A full list of these cuts and consolidations are detailed in the Budget volume, *Cuts, Consolidations, and Savings*. Furthermore, the President is pushing for the authority for even more substantial reorganizations, streamlining and consolidations—as discussed in detail below.

Implement the New Defense Strategy. Over the past three years, we have made historic investments in our troops and their capabilities, military families, and veterans. Now, we are at an inflection point after a decade of war: American troops have left Iraq; we are undergoing a transition in Afghanistan so Afghans can assume more responsibility for their security; and we have debilitated al Qaeda's leadership, putting that terrorist network on the path to defeat. At the same time, we have to renew our economic strength here at home, which is the foundation of our strength in the world, and that includes putting our fiscal house in order. That is why the President directed the Pentagon to undertake a comprehensive strategic review to ensure our defense budget is driven by a clear strategy that reflects our national interests. The key elements of the strategy are:

- Strengthening our presence in the Asia Pacific with a continued vigilance in the Middle East.

- Investing in our critical partnerships and alliances, including NATO, which has demonstrated time and again—most recently in Libya—that it is a force multiplier.

- Having ended our military commitment in Iraq and commenced a drawdown in Afghanistan, and as we look to future threats, we will no longer size our force for prolonged, large-scale stability operations. Instead, we will field smaller forces while focusing on modernization to address emerging threats.

- Continuing to get rid of outdated Cold War-era systems so that we can invest in the capabilities we need for the future, including intelligence, surveillance and reconnaissance; counterterrorism; countering weapons of mass destruction; and the ability to operate in environments where adversaries try to deny us access.

- Keeping faith with those who serve by prioritizing efforts that focus on wounded warriors, mental health, and the well-being of military families.

With this strategy as a guide, over the 10 years beginning in 2012, the Department of Defense (DOD) will spend $487 billion less than was planned in last year's Budget. The Department will realize these savings through targeted reductions in force structure; reprioritization of key missions and the requirements that support them; and continued reforms and efficiencies in acquisition, management, and other business practices. The overall defense budget, including overseas contingency operations reductions, will be down by 5 percent from the 2012 enacted level.

Establish a Budget Cap on Overseas Contingency Operations (OCO) Spending. The Budget also reflects the Administration's efforts to constrain OCO spending in the years beyond 2013. The BCA established year-by-year caps on discretionary spending for agencies' base budgets through 2021, reducing the 10-year budget deficit by about $1 trillion. However, the BCA did not limit OCO funding. Leaving OCO funding unconstrained could allow future Administrations and Congresses to use it as a convenient vehicle to evade the fiscal discipline that the BCA caps require elsewhere in the Budget. With the end of our military presence in Iraq, and as troops continue to draw down in Afghanistan, this Budget proposes a binding cap on OCO spending as well. From 2013 through 2021, the Budget limits OCO appropriations to $450 billion. Given the need for ample flexibility in budgeting for overseas contingencies, this is a multi-year total cap, rather than a series of year-by-year caps.

Require the Financial Services Industry to Pay Back Taxpayers. The Administration is calling for a Financial Crisis Responsibility Fee on the largest financial institutions to fully compensate taxpayers for the extraordinary support they provided to the financial sector, while discouraging excessive risk-taking. The assistance given to the largest financial firms represented an extraordinary step that no one wanted to take, but one that was necessary in order to stem a deeper financial crisis and set the economy on a path to recovery. The cost associated with the excessive risk-taking by the largest financial institutions continues to ripple through the economy. Furthermore, although many of the largest financial firms have repaid the Treasury for the direct Troubled Asset Relief Program (TARP) assistance they received, the entire financial system benefitted enormously from the support that TARP provided during a period of great economic upheaval. While the expected cost of the TARP program has fallen considerably from initial estimates to approximately $68 billion in the 2013 Budget, shared responsibility requires that the largest financial firms pay back the taxpayer for the extraordinary support they received as well as to discourage excessive risk taking. The fee will be restricted to financial firms with assets over $50 billion. The Administration's Financial Crisis Responsibility Fee meets the statutory requirement contained in the TARP legislation that requires the President to propose a way for the financial sector to pay back taxpayers so that not one penny of the Government's TARP-related debt is passed on to the next generation. It would extend beyond 2022 as necessary to achieve these ends, and to offset the cost of the President's new, broad-based mortgage refinancing program which is designed to help homeowners who are still suffering as a result of the financial crisis. The structure of this fee would be consistent with principles agreed to by the G-20 Leaders and similar to fees proposed by other countries. This fee will reduce the deficit by $61 billion over the first 10 years.

Restrain Increases in Federal Civilian Worker Pay. Putting the Nation back on a sustainable fiscal path will take some tough choices and sacrifices. The men and women who serve their fellow Americans as civilian Federal workers are patriots who work for the Nation often at great personal sacrifice; they deserve our respect and gratitude. But just as families and businesses across the country are tightening their belts, so too must the Federal Government. On his first day in office, the President froze salaries for all senior political appointees at the White House. In 2010, the President eliminated bonuses for all political appointees across the Administration and last year cut back on performance awards to all other employees. Starting in 2011, the President has proposed and the Congress enacted a two-year pay freeze for all civilian Federal workers, which has saved approximately $3 billion and is projected to save more than $60 billion over the next 10 years. A permanent pay freeze is neither sustainable nor desirable. However, in light of the fiscal constraints we are under, the Administration is proposing a 0.5 percent increase in civilian pay for 2013. Compared to the baseline, this slight increase in civilian pay would free up $2 billion in 2013 and $28 billion over 10 years to fund programs and services and is one of the measures the Administration proposes to help meet the discretionary caps.

Reform Federal Civilian Worker Retirement. In order to make reasonable changes to Federal worker retirement, while maintaining the ability to attract and retain highly qualified individuals, the Administration proposes to increase the employee contribution toward accruing retirement costs by 1.2 percent over three years beginning in 2013. While Federal agency contributions for currently accruing costs of employee pensions would decline, these Federal employers would pay an additional amount toward unfunded liabilities of the retirement system that would leave total agency contributions unchanged. Under the proposed plan, the amount of the employee pension would remain unchanged. We estimate this proposal will save $27 billion over 10 years. In addition, the Administration is proposing to eliminate the FERS Annuity Supplement for new employees. Overall, these changes are not expected to have a negative impact on the Administration's ability to manage its human resources, nor inhibit the Government's ability to serve the American people.

Modernize Federal Personnel Policies. To manage the complex work agencies perform today in order to meet the needs of the American people, Federal managers and employees need a modernized personnel system that reflects the reality of the 21st Century—where agencies offer compensation that reflects market competition for employees, facilitate career-development mobility across agencies and with the private sector, address poor performers consistently and fairly, develop staff, and motivate better performance using the best evidence-based public and private sector practices. To advance this effort, the Administration recommends that the Congress establish a Commission on Federal Public Service Reform comprised of Members of Congress, representatives from the President's Labor-Management Council, members of the private sector, and academic experts. The Commission would develop recommendations on reforms to modernize Federal personnel policies and practices within fiscal constraints. Such reforms could include but would not be limited to compensation, staff development and mobility, and personnel performance and motivation.

TAKING RESPONSIBILITY FOR LONG-TERM CHALLENGES TO OUR FISCAL HEALTH

In the BCA, the President signed into law a measure that will generate approximately $1 trillion in deficit reduction over the next decade through the use of discretionary spending caps. With discretionary spending projected to reach historically low levels, we cannot go any further and meet the needs and expectations of the American people. We need to look at other parts of the budget for deficit reduction. Mandatory programs, those that are not generally appropriated on an annual basis, are an important area to find savings. In some areas, these programs have not been updated or reformed for years. In others, parochial politics has allowed waste to pile up or programs to stray from their mission. In his submission to the Joint Select Committee on Deficit Reduction, the President put forward hundreds of billions of dollars in savings over 10 years in mandatory programs as well as guidelines to generate $1.5 trillion in revenue from tax reform. While the Committee was unsuccessful in its efforts to construct a bipartisan, balanced deficit reduction plan, the President is not deterred in his commitment to this goal. With a sequester poised to take effect in January 2013 that would inflict great damage on critical domestic priorities as well as the country's national security, it is especially important that the Congress come together and pass a balanced deficit reduction plan to replace this sequester and, also, go beyond its required deficit reduction.

That is why the President's Budget includes $517 billion in mandatory savings over the next 10 years and a plan for tax reform to raise more than $1.5 trillion. The President's proposal includes plans to:

Find Savings in the Agricultural Sector. A strong agricultural sector is important to maintaining a strong rural economy. The Administration is committed to a vital, robust farm economy. In recent years, we have had that: for the past decade farm income has been high and continues to increase, with net farm income forecast to be $100.9 billion in 2011, up $21.8 billion (28 percent) from the 2010 forecast—the second highest inflation-adjusted value for net farm income recorded in more than 35 years. The top five earnings years for the past three decades have occurred since 2004, attesting to the profitability of farming this decade. The Administration remains committed to a strong safety net for farmers, one that protects them from revenue losses that result from low yields or price declines, and strong crop insurance programs. But there are programs and places where current support is unnecessary or too generous. To reduce the deficit, the Administration proposes to eliminate or reduce those programs, while strengthening the safety net for those that need it most. The Administration is proposing to:

- *Eliminate Direct Payments to Farmers.* The direct payment program provides producers fixed annual income support payments for having historically planted crops that were supported by Government programs, regardless of whether the farmer is currently producing those crops—or producing any crop, for that matter. Direct payments do not vary with prices, yields, or producers' farm incomes. As a result, taxpayers continue to foot the bill for these payments to farmers who are experiencing record yields and prices; more than 50 percent of direct payments go to farmers with more than $100,000 in annual income. Eliminating these payments would save the Government roughly $23 billion over 10 years and build a better farm safety net.

- *Reduce Crop Insurance Subsidies.* Crop insurance is a foundation of our farm safety net. Yet, the program continues to be highly subsidized and costs the Government approximately $10 billion a year to run: $3 billion per year for the private insurance companies to administer and underwrite the program and $7 billion per year in premium subsidy to the farmers. A U.S. Department of Agriculture commissioned study found that, when compared to other private companies, crop insurance companies' rate of return on investment (ROI) should be around 12 percent, but that it is currently expected to be 14 percent. The Administration is proposing to lower the crop insurance companies' ROI to meet the 12 percent target, saving $1.2 billion over 10 years. In addition, the current cap on administrative expenses is based on the 2010 premiums, which were among the highest ever. A more appropriate level for the cap would be based on 2006 premiums, neutralizing the spike in commodity prices over the last four years, but not harming the delivery system. The Administration, therefore, proposes setting the cap at $0.9 billion adjusted annually for inflation, which would save $2.9 billion over 10 years. Finally, the Administration proposes to price more accurately the premium for catastrophic (CAT) coverage policies, which will slightly lower the reimbursement to crop insurance companies. The premium for CAT coverage is fully subsidized for the farmer, so the farmer is not impacted by the change. This change will save $225 million over 10 years.

In addition, the Administration is proposing to reduce producers' premium subsidy by 2 basis points for all but catastrophic crop insurance, where the subsidy is greater than 50 percent. This will have little impact on producers. Most producers pay only 40 percent of the cost of their crop insurance premium on average, with the Government paying for the remainder. This cost share arrangement was implemented in 2000, when very few producers participated in the program and "ad-hoc" agricultural disaster assistance bills were passed regularly. The Congress increased the subsidy for buy-up coverage by over 50 percent at the time to encourage greater participation. With current participation rates, the deep premium subsidies are no longer needed. This proposal is expected to save $3.3 billion over 10 years.

- *Better Target Agricultural Conservation Assistance.* The Administration has championed programs that create incentives for private lands conservation and has worked to leverage these resources with those of other Federal agencies toward greater landscape-scale conservation; however, the significant increases in conservation funding (roughly 200 percent since enactment of the Farm Security and Rural Investment Act of 2002) has led to redundancies among our agricultural conservation programs. At the same time, high crop prices have both strengthened market opportunities to expand agricultural production on the Nation's farmlands and decreased producer demand for certain agricultural conservation programs. To reduce the deficit, the Administration proposes to reduce conservation funding by $1.8 billion over 10 years by better targeting conservation funding to the most cost-effective and environmentally-beneficial programs and practices. Even under this proposal, conservation assistance is projected to grow by $60 billion over the next decade (assuming continuation of the current farm bill baseline).

Better Align Federal Worker and Military Retirement Programs. The men and women who serve their fellow Americans in the Armed Forces and civil service are patriots who work for the Nation often at great personal sacrifice. Just as families and businesses must tighten their belts to live within their means, so must the Federal Government. In addition to the proposed changes to civilian retirement noted above, one area to examine is the retirement and health benefits offered to the Federal military workforce—a group of benefits that has grown comparatively more generous than those offered in the private sector. The Administration is proposing a set of reforms to align these retirement programs better with the private sector, while still preserving the Federal Government's ability to recruit and retain the personnel that the American people need, including an adequately skilled and appropriately sized military force. The reductions sought in these retirement reforms are evenly split between civilian and military retirement programs. For military retirement reforms, the Administration proposes to:

- *Increase TRICARE Prime Enrollment Fees, Initiate Standard/Extra Annual Enrollment Fees, and Adjust Deductible and Catastrophic Caps.* DOD has implemented a variety of efficiencies within its medical program and continues to seek cost savings, but with increases in users, increased utilization, and expansion of benefits, defense health costs keep growing. In 2012, DOD implemented minor TRICARE Prime fee increases for new retiree enrollees. In 2013, DOD will phase in additional fee increases based on annual retirement pay and initiate Standard and Extra enrollment fees. Deductibles will be slightly increased and the current catastrophic cap adjusted. The Administration's proposal is estimated to save $12.1 billion in discretionary funds over 10 years.

- *Initiate Annual Fees for TRICARE-For-Life Enrollment (TFL).* Upon turning 65, military retirees and their families transition to Medicare coverage, with TFL becoming second payer. In the private sector, this type of "Medigap" policy would likely require premiums, deductibles, and copays. In 2009 the average annual premium for a Medigap policy was $2,100. By contrast, there are no premiums under the TFL programs. The Administration is proposing to introduce modest annual fees for the TFL program, based on retirement pay. This proposal is estimated to save approximately $5.9 billion in mandatory funds and $5.0 billion in discretionary funds over 10 years.

- *Make Targeted Increases to TRICARE Pharmacy Benefit Copayments.* Copayments for military members have lagged behind other Federal and private plans' copayments for prescription drugs. In an effort to slow the growth in DOD's health care costs, the President's 2012 Budget included minor pharmacy copay adjustments—which were supported by Congress. The new proposal would encourage the use of less expensive mail order and military treatment facility pharmacies. This option would have no impact on active duty members, but would affect active duty families and all military retirees regardless of the age of the beneficiary. The Administration's proposal is estimated to save $10.6 billion in mandatory funds and $17.4 billion in discretionary funds over 10 years.

- *Establish a Military Retirement Modernization Commission.* To recommend improvements to the military retirement system, the Administration is proposing to establish a Military Retirement Modernization Commission. Under the proposal, the President would appoint the Commissioners; DOD would transmit to the Commission initial recommendations to change the military retirement system; the Commission would hold hearings, make final recommendations, and draft legislation to implement its recommendations; the President would review and decide whether to transmit the Commission's

recommendations to the Congress; and Congress would vote "up or down" on the legislation. The Administration believes that any major military retirement reforms should include grandfathering provisions for current retirees and those currently serving in the military.

Reform the Aviation Passenger Security Fee to Reflect the Costs of Aviation Security More Accurately. Reflecting its commitment to keeping air travel and commerce safe, the Administration has invested heavily in personnel, technology, and infrastructure to mitigate the constantly-evolving risks to aviation security. As risk changes, however, so too must the way in which we fund our aviation security efforts. In 2001, the Aviation and Transportation Security Act created the Aviation Passenger Security Fee, which originally intended to recover the full costs of aviation security. Since its establishment, however, the fee has been statutorily limited to $2.50 per passenger enplanement with a maximum fee of $5.00 per one-way trip. This recovers only 43 percent of the Transportation Security Administration's aviation security costs, which have risen over the years while the fee has remained the same. The Administration proposes to replace the current "per-enplanement" fee structure with a "per one-way trip" fee structure so that passengers pay the fee only one time when travelling to their destination; remove the current statutory fee limit and replace it with a statutory fee minimum of $5.00, with annual incremental increases of 50 cents from 2014 to 2018, resulting in a fee of $7.50 in 2018 and thereafter; and allow the Secretary of Homeland Security to adjust the fee (to an amount equal to or greater than the new statutory fee minimum) through regulation when necessary. The proposed fee would collect an estimated $9 billion in additional fee revenue over five years, and $25.5 billion over 10 years. Of this amount, $18 billion will be deposited into the General Fund for debt reduction.

Share Payments More Equitably for Air Traffic Services. All flights that use controlled air space require a similar level of air traffic services. However, commercial and general aviation can pay very different aviation fees for those same air traffic services. To reduce the deficit and more equitably share the cost of air traffic services across the aviation user community, the Administration proposes to create a $100 per flight fee, payable to the Federal Aviation Administration, by aviation operators who fly in controlled airspace. All piston aircraft, military aircraft, public aircraft, air ambulances, aircraft operating outside of controlled airspace, and Canada-to-Canada flights would be exempted. This fee would generate an estimated $7.4 billion over 10 years. Assuming the enactment of the fee, total charges collected from aviation users would finance roughly three-fourths of airport investments and air traffic control system costs.

Provide Postal Service Financial Relief and Undertake Reform. The Administration recognizes the enormous value of the U.S. Postal Service (USPS) to the Nation's commerce and communications, as well as the urgent need for reform to ensure its future viability. USPS faces long-term, structural operating challenges that have been exacerbated by the precipitous drop in mail volume in the last few years due to the economic crisis and the continuing shift toward electronic communication. Bold action is needed to ensure that USPS can continue to operate in the short-run and achieve viability in the long-run. To that end, the President is proposing a comprehensive reform package that would: 1) restructure Retiree Health Benefit pre-funding in order to accelerate moving these Postal payments to an accruing cost basis and reduce near-year Postal payments; 2) provide USPS with a refund over two years of the $10.9 billion positive credit balance in Postal contributions to the FERS program; 3) reduce USPS operating costs by giving USPS authority, which it has said it will exercise, to reduce mail delivery from six days to five days starting in 2013; 4) allow USPS to increase collaboration with State and local governments; and 5) give USPS the ability to better align the costs of postage with the costs of mail delivery while still operating within the current price cap, and permit USPS to seek the balance of the modest one-time increase in postage rates it proposed in 2010. These reforms would provide USPS with

over $25 billion in cash relief over the next two years and in total would produce savings of $25 billion over 11 years.

Strengthen the Safety Net for Workers' Retirement Benefits. All Americans deserve a secure retirement. The Administration has proposed to create new opportunities to save for retirement by establishing a system of automatic workplace pensions and doubling the small employer pension plan start-up credit. In addition, the Administration has issued regulations that would increase 401(k) fee disclosure, so that businesses can better differentiate among retirement products and workers can make more informed choices about how to invest their retirement savings. The Pension Benefit Guaranty Corporation (PBGC), which protects the retirement security of 44 million workers in defined benefit pension plans, is also critical to the success of a robust pension system. When underfunded plans terminate, PBGC assumes responsibility for paying the insured benefits. PBGC is responsible for paying current and future retirement benefits to more than 1.5 million workers and retirees. PBGC receives no taxpayer financing and relies primarily on premiums paid by insured plans. PBGC premiums are currently much lower than what a private financial institution would charge for insuring the same risk and are insufficient for PBGC to meet its long-term obligations. As of the end of September 2011, PBGC faced a $26 billion deficit. The Administration proposes to encourage companies to fully fund their pension benefits and ensure PBGC's continued financial soundness by giving the PBGC Board the authority to adjust premiums to better account for the risk the agency is insuring. This proposal consists of two parts: a gradual increase in the single-employer flat-rate premium that will raise approximately $4 billion by 2022; and PBGC Board discretion to increase the single-employer variable-rate premium to raise $12 billion by 2022. This proposal would save $16 billion over the next decade.

Restore the Solvency and Financial Integrity of the Unemployment Insurance System by Helping Employers Now and Restoring State Fiscal Responsibility. Unemployment

Insurance (UI) provides a vital safety net for workers who are laid off. Over the past several years, UI benefits have kept many families afloat during tough financial times, and in 2010 these benefits prevented 3.2 million individuals—including nearly 1 million children—from falling into poverty. UI has among the highest "bang-for-the-buck" of any measure the Federal Government could take to support near-term economic growth—generating up to $2 of economic activity for every $1 spent. The President has strongly supported expanding this critical safety net and has called for an extension of unemployment benefits for another year, along with key reforms that would help connect long-term unemployed Americans with work.

At the same time, the combination of chronically underfunded reserves and the economic downturn has placed a considerable financial strain on States' UI operations. Currently, 28 States owe more than $37 billion to the Federal UI trust fund. As a result, employers in those States are now facing automatic Federal tax increases, and many States have little prospect of paying these loans back in the foreseeable future. State UI programs also have large improper payment rates—12 percent in fiscal year 2011. The Administration proposes to put the UI system back on the path to solvency and financial integrity by providing immediate relief to employers to encourage job creation now, reestablishing State fiscal responsibility going forward, and working closely with States to eliminate improper payments. Under this Budget proposal, employers in indebted States would receive tax relief for two years. To encourage State solvency, the proposal would also raise the minimum level of wages subject to unemployment taxes in 2015 to a level slightly lower in real terms than it was in 1983, after President Reagan signed into law the last wage base increase. The higher wage base will be offset by lower tax rates to avoid a Federal tax increase. Further, the Administration has taken a number of steps to address program integrity in States that have consistently failed to place enough emphasis on combating improper payments in their UI programs. The Administration's aggressive actions have given States a number of tools to prevent improper payments, and reducing State UI error rates remains an Administration priority.

Reform Abandoned Mine Lands (AML) Payments. The coal industry as a whole is currently held responsible for cleaning up abandoned coal mines by paying a fee that finances grants to States and Tribes for reclamation. This linkage was lost, however, when the Congress in 2006 authorized additional unrestricted payments to certain States and Tribes that had already completed their coal mine reclamation work. In addition, regular reclamation funds are not well targeted at the highest priority abandoned mine lands, because amounts are distributed by a production-based formula so that funding goes to the States with the most coal production, not the greatest reclamation needs. States can use their funding for a variety of purposes, including the reclamation of abandoned hardrock mines, for which there is no other source of Federal funding. The Administration proposes to reform the coal AML program to reduce unnecessary spending and ensure that the Nation's highest priority sites are reclaimed. First, the Administration proposes to terminate unrestricted payments to the States and Tribes that have been certified for completing their coal reclamation work, since these payments do not contribute to reclaiming abandoned coal mines. Second, the Administration proposes to reform the distribution process for the remaining funds to allocate available resources competitively to the highest priority coal AML sites. Through a competitive grant program, a new AML Advisory Council will review and rank the abandoned mine lands sites, so that the Department of the Interior, in coordination with States and Tribes, can distribute grants to reclaim the highest priority coal sites each year.

Mining for hardrock minerals (e.g., silver and gold) has also left a legacy of abandoned mines across the United States. The Administration proposes to create a parallel AML program for abandoned hardrock sites. Like the coal program, hardrock reclamation would be financed by a new AML fee on the production of hardrock minerals on both public and private lands. This would hold the hardrock mining industry responsible for cleaning up the hazards left by its predecessors. The funds would be distributed through a competitive grant program to reclaim the highest priority hardrock sites on Federal, State, tribal, and private lands. Altogether, this proposal will save $1.6 billion over the next 10 years. Equally important, it would focus available coal fees to better address the Nation's most dangerous abandoned coal mines and establish a new approach to cleaning up abandoned hardrock mines across the country.

Provide a Better Return to Taxpayers from Mineral Development. The public received about $10 billion in 2011 from fees, royalties, and other payments related to oil, gas, coal, and other mineral development on Federal lands and waters. A number of recent studies by the Government Accountability Office and the Department of the Interior's Inspector General have found that taxpayers could earn a better return through more rigorous oversight and policy changes, such as charging appropriate fees and reforming how royalties are set. The Budget proposes a number of actions to receive a fair return from the continued development of these vital U.S. mineral resources: charging a royalty on select hardrock minerals (such as silver, gold, and copper); extending net receipt sharing, where States with mineral revenue payments help defray the costs of managing the mineral leases that generate the revenue; charging user fees to oil companies for processing oil and gas drilling permits and inspecting operations on Federal lands and waters, which complement new and rigorous safety and environmental standards to make sure that these activities are done responsibly; establishing fees for new non-producing oil and gas leases (both onshore and offshore) to encourage more timely production; and making administrative changes to Federal oil and gas royalties, such as adjusting royalty rates and terminating the royalty-in-kind program. Together, these changes are expected to generate approximately $3 billion in savings over 10 years.

Health Savings

Health care comprises one-quarter of non-interest Federal spending, and is the major driver of future deficit growth. To help control these costs, the President signed into law the Patient Protection and Affordable Care Act (ACA) which, according to the Congressional Budget Office's latest analysis, will reduce the deficit by more than $1 trillion over the next two decades. Realizing this deficit reduction and efficiencies in the health care system that will reduce cost and improve quality will require effective implementation of the ACA, and the President is resolutely committed to implementing ACA fairly, efficiently, and swiftly. Repealing or failing to implement health care reform would return the Nation to a path of rapidly increasing health care costs, and add trillions to deficits over the long run. The President is putting forward $364 billion in health savings that build on the ACA to strengthen Medicare, Medicaid, and other health programs by reducing wasteful spending and erroneous payments, and supporting reforms that boost the quality of care. It accomplishes this in a way that does not shift significant risks onto the individuals they serve; slash benefits; or undermine the fundamental compact they represent to our Nation's seniors, people with disabilities, and low-income families. Included are savings that would:

Reduce Medicare Coverage of Bad Debts. Today, for most eligible provider types, Medicare generally reimburses 70 percent of bad debts resulting from beneficiaries' non-payment of deductibles and copayments after providers have made reasonable efforts to collect the unpaid amounts. Similar to a proposal made by the National Commission on Fiscal Responsibility and Reform (Fiscal Commission), the Budget proposes to align Medicare policy more closely with private sector standards by reducing bad debt payments to 25 percent for all eligible providers over three years starting in 2013. This proposal will save approximately $36 billion over 10 years.

Better Align Graduate Medical Education Payments With Patient Care Costs. Medicare compensates teaching hospitals for the indirect costs stemming from inefficiencies created from residents "learning by doing." The Medicare Payment Advisory Commission (MedPAC) has determined that these Indirect Medical Education (IME) add-on payments are significantly greater than the additional patient care costs that teaching hospitals experience, and the Fiscal Commission, among others, recommended reducing the IME adjustment. This proposal would reduce the IME adjustment by 10 percent beginning in 2014, and save approximately $10 billion over 10 years.

Better Align Payments to Rural Providers With the Cost of Care. Medicare makes a number of special payments to account for the unique challenges of delivering medical care to beneficiaries in rural areas. These payments continue to be important; however, in specific cases, the adjustments may be greater than necessary to ensure continued access to care. The Administration proposes to improve the consistency of payments across rural hospital types, provide incentives for efficient delivery of care, and eliminate higher than necessary reimbursement. To improve payment accuracy for Critical Access Hospitals (CAHs), the Administration proposes to reduce payments from 101 percent to 100 percent of reasonable costs, effective in 2013, and to eliminate the CAH designation for those that are fewer than 10 miles from the nearest hospital, effective in 2014. These changes will ensure that this unique payment system is better targeted to hospitals meeting the eligibility criteria and will save approximately $2 billion over 10 years.

Encourage Efficient Post-Acute Care. Medicare covers services in skilled nursing facilities (SNFs), long-term care hospitals (LTCHs), inpatient rehabilitation facilities (IRFs) and home health. Over the years, expenditures for post-acute care have increased dramatically, and payments in excess of the costs of providing high quality and efficient care place a drain on Medicare. Recognizing the importance of these services, the Administration supports policies that will save approximately $63 billion over 10 years and

improve the quality of care. These include adjusting payment updates for certain post-acute care providers, equalizing payments for certain conditions commonly treated in IRFs and SNFs; encouraging appropriate use of inpatient rehabilitation hospitals; and adjusting SNF payments to reduce unnecessary hospital readmissions.

Align Medicare Drug Payment Policies With Medicaid Policies for Low-Income Beneficiaries. Under current law, drug manufacturers are required to pay specified rebates for drugs dispensed to Medicaid beneficiaries. In contrast, Medicare Part D plan sponsors negotiate with manufacturers to obtain plan-specific rebates at unspecified levels. The Department of Health and Human Services' Inspector General has found substantial differences in rebate amounts and net prices paid for brand name drugs under the two programs, with Medicare receiving significantly lower rebates and paying higher prices than Medicaid. Moreover, Medicare per capita spending in Part D is growing significantly faster than that in Parts A or B under current law. This proposal would allow Medicare to benefit from the same rebates that Medicaid receives for brand name and generic drugs provided to beneficiaries who receive the Part D Low-Income Subsidy beginning 2013. Manufacturers previously paid Medicaid rebates for drugs provided to the dual eligible population prior to the establishment of Medicare Part D. The Fiscal Commission recommended a similar proposal to apply Medicaid rebates to dual eligibles for outpatient drugs covered under Part D. This proposal is estimated to save $156 billion over 10 years.

Increase Income-Related Premiums Under Medicare Parts B and D. Under Medicare Parts B and D, certain beneficiaries pay higher premiums as a result of their higher levels of income. Beginning in 2017, the Administration proposes to increase income-related premiums under Medicare Parts B and D by 15 percent and maintain the income thresholds associated with income-related premiums until 25 percent of beneficiaries under Parts B and D are subject to these premiums. This will help improve the financial stability of the Medicare program by reducing the Federal subsidy of Medicare costs for those beneficiaries who can most afford them. This proposal will save approximately $28 billion over 10 years.

Modify Part B Deductible for New Beneficiaries. Beneficiaries who are enrolled in Medicare Part B are required to pay an annual deductible. This deductible helps to share responsibility for payment of Medicare services between Medicare and beneficiaries. To strengthen program financing and encourage beneficiaries to seek high-value health care services, the Administration proposes to apply a $25 increase in the Part B deductible in 2017, 2019, and 2021 for new beneficiaries. Current beneficiaries or near retirees would not be subject to the revised deductible. This proposal will save approximately $2 billion over 10 years.

Introduce Home Health Copayments for New Beneficiaries. Medicare beneficiaries currently do not make copayments for Medicare home health services. This proposal would create a home health copayment of $100 per home health episode, applicable for episodes with five or more visits not preceded by a hospital or other inpatient post-acute care stay. This would apply to new beneficiaries beginning in 2017. This proposal is consistent with a MedPAC recommendation to establish a per episode copayment. MedPAC noted that "beneficiaries without a prior hospitalization account for a rising share of episodes" and that "adding beneficiary cost sharing for home health care could be an additional measure to encourage appropriate use of home health services." This proposal will save approximately $350 million over 10 years.

Introduce a Part B Premium Surcharge for New Beneficiaries That Purchase Near First-Dollar Medigap Coverage. Medigap policies sold by private insurance companies provide beneficiaries additional support for covering healthcare costs by covering most or all of the cost sharing Medicare requires. This protection, however, gives individuals less incentive to consider the costs of health care services and thus raises Medicare costs and Part B premiums. Of particular concern are Medigap plans that cover substantially all Medicare copayments, including even the modest copayments for routine care that most beneficiaries can afford to pay out of pocket. To encourage more efficient health care choices, the Administration proposes a Part B premium surcharge equivalent to about 15 percent of the average Medigap premium (or about 30 percent of the Part B premium) for new beneficiaries that purchase Medigap policies with particularly low cost-sharing requirements, starting in 2017. Current beneficiaries and near-retirees would not be subject to the surcharge. Other Medigap plans would be exempt from this requirement while still providing beneficiaries options for protection against high out-of-pocket costs. This proposal will save approximately $2.5 billion over 10 years.

Strengthen the Independent Payment Advisory Board (IPAB) to Reduce Long-Term Drivers of Medicare Cost Growth. Created by the ACA, IPAB has been highlighted by economists and health policy experts as a key contributor to Medicare's long term solvency. Under current law, if the projected Medicare per capita growth rate exceeds a predetermined target growth rate, IPAB recommends to the Congress policies to reduce the rate of Medicare growth to meet the target. IPAB recommendations are prohibited from increasing beneficiary premiums or cost-sharing, or restricting benefits. To further moderate the rate of Medicare growth, this proposal would lower the target rate from the GDP per capita growth rate plus 1 percent to plus 0.5 percent. Additionally, the proposal would give IPAB additional tools like the ability to consider value-based benefit design.

Cut Waste, Fraud, and Abuse in Medicare and Medicaid. In this fiscal environment, we cannot tolerate waste, fraud, and abuse in Medicare, Medicaid, and the Children's Health Insurance Program (CHIP)—or any Government program. That is why the Administration has introduced its Campaign to Cut Waste, together with long-standing efforts to boost program integrity and reduce improper payments (that is, payments made to the wrong person, in the wrong amount, or for the wrong reason).

The Administration is aggressively implementing the new tools for fraud prevention included in the ACA. Also, it is implementing the fraud prevention system, a predictive analytic model similar to those used by private sector experts. In addition, the Administration is proposing a series of policies to build on these ongoing efforts that will save nearly $5 billion over the next 10 years. Specifically, the Administration proposes to: create new initiatives to reduce improper payments in Medicare; dedicate penalties for failure to use electronic health records toward deficit reduction; update Medicare payments to more appropriately account for utilization of advanced imaging; require prior authorization for advanced imaging; direct States to track high prescribers and utilizers of prescription drugs in Medicaid to identify aberrant billing and prescribing patterns; and affirm Medicaid's position as a payer of last resort by removing exceptions to the requirement that State Medicaid agencies reject medical claims when another entity is legally liable to pay the claim. Additionally, the Budget would alleviate State program integrity reporting requirements by consolidating redundant error rate measurement programs to create a streamlined audit program with meaningful outcomes, while maintaining the Federal and State's government ability to identify and address improper Medicaid payments.

Phase Down the Medicaid Provider Tax Threshold Beginning in 2015. Many States impose taxes on health care providers to help finance the State share of Medicaid program costs. However, some States use those tax revenues to increase payments to those same providers and use that additional spending to increase their Federal Medicaid matching payments. The Administration proposes to limit these types of State financing practices that increase Federal Medicaid spending by phasing down the Medicaid provider tax threshold from the current law level of 6 percent in 2014, to 4.5 percent in 2015, 4 percent in 2016, and 3.5 percent in 2017 and beyond. By delaying the effective date until 2015, the proposal gives States more time to plan for the change. This proposal is projected to save $21.8 billion over 10 years.

Apply a Single Blended Matching Rate to Medicaid and CHIP Starting in 2017. Under current law, States face a patchwork of different Federal payment contributions for individuals eligible for Medicaid and CHIP. Specifically, State Medicaid expenditures are generally matched by the Federal Government using the Federal medical assistance percentage (FMAP); CHIP expenditures are matched with enhanced FMAP (eFMAP); and the ACA provides increased match for newly-eligible individuals and certain childless adults beginning in 2014. This proposal would replace these complicated formulas with a single matching rate specific to each State that automatically increases if a recession forces enrollment and State costs to rise beginning in 2017. This proposal is projected to save $17.9 billion over 10 years.

Limit Medicaid Reimbursement of Durable Medical Equipment (DME) Based on Medicare Rates. Under current law, States have experienced the same challenges in preventing overpayments for DME that previously confronted Medicare. The Medicare program is in the process of implementing innovative ways to increase efficiency for payment of DME through the DME Competitive Bidding Program, which is expected to save the Medicare program more than $25 billion and Medicare beneficiaries approximately $17 billion over 10 years. This proposal extends some of these efficiencies to Medicaid, starting in 2013, by limiting Federal reimbursement for a State's Medicaid spending on certain DME services to what Medicare would have paid in the same State for the same services. This proposal is projected to save $3.0 billion over 10 years.

Re-Base Medicaid Disproportionate Share Hospital (DSH) Allotments in 2021 and Beyond. This proposal continues the ACA policy to better align Medicaid DSH payments with reductions in the number of uninsured in 2021 and beyond. Supplemental DSH payments are intended to help support hospitals that provide care to disproportionate numbers of low-income and uninsured individuals. The ACA reduced State DSH allotments by $18.1 billion through 2020 to reflect the reduced need as a result of the increased coverage provided in the Act. The Administration proposes to compute 2021 State DSH allotments based on States' actual 2020 DSH allotments, better aligning future Medicaid supplemental payments to hospitals with reduced levels of uncompensated care. This proposal is projected to save $8.3 billion over 10 years.

Expand State Flexibility to Tailor Benefit Packages to Meet the Needs of Beneficiaries. This proposal would give States flexibility to require "benchmark" benefit plan coverage for non-elderly, non-disabled adults with incomes over 133 percent of the Federal poverty level. Currently, States have the option to provide certain populations "benchmark" or "benchmark equivalent" plans, or alternative benefit packages that may be offered in lieu of the benefits covered under a traditional Medicaid State plan.

Prohibit "Pay for Delay" Agreements to Increase the Availability of Generic Drugs and Biologics. The high cost of prescription drugs places a significant burden on Americans today, causing many to skip doses, split pills, or forgo needed medications altogether. The Administration proposes to increase the availability of generic drugs and biologics by authorizing the Federal Trade Commission to stop companies from entering into anti-competitive deals, known also as "pay for delay" agreements, intended to block consumer access to safe and effective generics. Such deals can cost consumers billions of dollars because generic drugs are typically priced significantly less than their branded counterparts. These agreements reduce competition and raise the cost of care for patients both directly, through higher drug and biologic prices, and indirectly through higher health care premiums. The Administration's proposal facilitates greater access to lower-cost generics and will generate $11 billion over 10 years in savings to Federal health programs including Medicare and Medicaid.

Modify the Length of Exclusivity to Facilitate Faster Development of Generic Biologics. Access to affordable lifesaving medicines is essential to improving the quality and efficiency of health care. The Administration's proposal ac-celerates access to affordable generic biologics by modifying the length of exclusivity on brand name biologics. Beginning in 2013, this proposal would award brand biologic manufacturers seven years of exclusivity rather than 12 years under current law and prohibit additional periods of exclusivity for brand biologics due to minor changes in product formulations, a practice often referred to as "evergreening." Reducing the exclusivity period increases the availability of generic biologics by encouraging faster development of generic biologics while retaining appropriate incentives for research and development for the innovation of breakthrough products. The Administration's proposal strikes a balance between promoting affordable access to medications and encouraging innovation to develop needed therapies. The proposal will result in $4 billion in savings over 10 years to Federal health programs including Medicare and Medicaid.

Tax Reform

The President is committed to reducing the deficit through a balanced approach—one that restrains spending across the Budget, including in the tax code; asks the wealthiest among us to contribute to deficit reduction; and lays the foundation for future growth. That is why the President is calling on the Congress to undertake comprehensive tax reform to cut rates, cut inefficient tax breaks, cut the deficit, and increase jobs and growth in the United States—while observing the "Buffett Rule" that people making over $1 million should not pay lower taxes than the middle class.

Tax reform is critical to rebuilding our economy to be stronger and more stable than in the past. Two of our biggest economic challenges— creating jobs and reducing long-term deficits— both depend on instituting a simpler, fairer, more progressive tax system than we have today. The Administration believes, like many others, that well-designed tax cuts can play an important role in job creation now. But the Administration believes that immediate, broad tax cuts for the middle class—rather than for only the wealthiest 1 or 2 percent of Americans—are far more effective at creating jobs and growing the economy. When millions of middle-class families across the country have more money in their bank accounts to spend in their communities, businesses large and small can grow, innovate, invest, and hire. The success of the American economy has long been built on the vibrancy of our middle class, and our efforts to create a tax system that is fairer, simpler, and more progressive reflect that reality.

Tax reform is also an important part of reducing our long-term deficits and placing our country on a fiscally sustainable path. We cannot address a deficit a decade in the making through spending cuts alone—that is, unless we, as a country, agree to cut every program in the entire budget by more than a quarter, including defense spending, Social Security payments, Medicare benefits, and veterans' benefits, along with everything else. The Administration believes in a balanced approach that cuts spending responsibly, but also asks the most well-off in society—many of whom, through loopholes and other exemptions, pay less in taxes than most middle-class families—to contribute their fair share toward reducing the deficit and invigorating our economy.

Unfortunately, the tax code has become increasingly complicated and unfair. Changes enacted during the previous Administration were skewed in favor of the wealthiest taxpayers and reduced the tax code's overall progressivity. Under today's tax laws, those who can afford expert advice can avoid paying their fair share and interests with the most connected lobbyists can get exemptions and special treatment written into our tax code. While many of the tax incentives serve important purposes, taken together the tax expenditures in the law are inefficient, unfair, duplicative, and often unnecessary. The corporate tax system provides special incentives for some industries, like oil and gas producers, yet fails to provide sufficient incentives for companies to invest in America. Because our corporate tax system is so riddled with special interest loopholes, our system has one of the highest statutory tax rates among developed countries to generate about the same amount of corporate tax revenue as our developed country

partners as a share of our economy; this, in turn, hurts our competitiveness in the world economy. In addition, a large fraction of the tax code is now temporary and expires periodically, adding uncertainty for households and businesses, and complicating the fiscal outlook.

The result is a tax code that neither serves the American people nor our economy. In September, the President announced five principles for tax reform. The President stands by those principles as elaborated upon below. Tax reform should:

- *Simplify the Tax Code and Lower Tax Rates.* The tax system should be simplified and work for all Americans with lower individual and corporate tax rates and fewer tax brackets.

- *Reform Inefficient and Unfair Tax Breaks— Eliminating Them for Millionaires While Making All Tax Breaks at Least as Good a Deal for the Middle Class as for Wealthy Americans.* Reform should cut and simplify tax breaks that are now inefficient, unfair, or both, so that wealthiest Americans cannot avoid their responsibilities by gaming the system, that middle class working Americans receive their fair share, and that Americans can spend less time and money each year filing taxes. That means eliminating tax subsidies for millionaires that they do not need; there is no reason that those making over $1 million should get any tax subsidies for housing, health care, retirement, and child care. And it means ensuring fair incentives for the middle class to buy a home or save for retirement, as opposed to allowing the most well-off to get two to three times as much.

- *Decrease the Deficit While Protecting Progressivity.* Reform should cut the deficit by $1.5 trillion over the next decade through tax reform, including the expiration of tax cuts for single taxpayers making over $200,000 and married couples making over $250,000. And it should do this while keeping the tax code at least as progressive as if the high-income

2001 and 2003 tax cuts were eliminated, as the President proposes.

- *Increase Job Creation and Growth in the United States.* The tax code should make America stronger at home and more competitive globally by increasing the incentive to work and invest in the United States. This includes fundamental corporate tax reform. That is why, in addition to these principles, the President is proposing a roadmap for corporate tax reform that will make America more competitive and create jobs here at home.

- *Observe the Buffett Rule.* No household making over $1 million annually should pay a smaller share of its income in taxes than middle-class families pay. As Warren Buffett has pointed out, his effective tax rate is lower than his secretary's. And, the President is now specifically proposing that in observance of the Buffett rule, those making over $1 million should pay no less than 30 percent of their income in taxes. The Administration will work to ensure that this rule is implemented in a way that is equitable, including not disadvantaging individuals who make large charitable contributions. And he is proposing that the Buffett rule should replace the Alternative Minimum Tax, which now burdens middle-class Americans rather than stopping the richest Americans from paying too little as was originally intended.

This will make our tax code simpler, fairer, and more efficient—and end a system that allows households making millions of dollars annually to pay lower tax rates than middle-class families.

To begin the national conversation about tax reform, the President is offering a detailed set of specific tax loophole closers and measures to broaden the tax base that, together with the expiration of the high-income tax cuts, would be more than sufficient to hit his $1.5 trillion target for tax reform, pay for tax cuts for the middle class, cut inefficient expenditures, and move the tax system closer to observing the Buffett rule. Included are measures that would:

Allow the 2001 and 2003 High-Income Tax Cuts to Expire and Return the Estate Tax to 2009 Parameters. The tax cuts for those with household income above $250,000 per year passed in the Bush Administration were unfair and unaffordable at the time they were enacted and remain so today. In December 2010, congressional Republicans insisted on extending them through 2012 and threatened to allow taxes to increase on middle-class families if the Administration did not agree. Not extending the middle-class tax cuts would have hurt our nascent economic recovery, and would have imposed an enormous burden on working families; as a result, the Administration agreed to extend them to 2012 as part of a deal that also included immediate support for the economy in the form of a payroll tax cut and an extension of unemployment insurance. The Administration remains opposed to the extension of these high-income tax cuts past 2012 and supports the return of the estate tax exemption and rates to 2009 levels. This would reduce the deficit by $968 billion over 10 years.

Reduce the Value of Itemized Deductions and Other Tax Preferences to 28 Percent for Families With Incomes Over $250,000. Currently, a millionaire who contributes to charity or deducts a dollar of mortgage interest, enjoys a deduction that is more than twice as generous as that for a middle-class family. The proposal would limit the tax rate at which high-income taxpayers can reduce their tax liability to a maximum of 28 percent, affecting only married taxpayers filing a joint return with income over $250,000 (at 2009 levels) and single taxpayers with income over $200,000. This limit would apply to: all itemized deductions; foreign excluded income; tax-exempt interest; employer sponsored health insurance; retirement contributions; and selected above-the-line deductions. The proposed limitation would return the deduction rate to the level it was at the end of the Reagan Administration. It would reduce the deficit by $584 billion over 10 years.

Tax Carried (Profits) Interests as Ordinary Income. Currently, many hedge fund managers, private equity partners, and other managers in partnerships are able to pay a 15 percent capital gains rate on their labor income (on income that is known as "carried interest"). This tax loophole is inappropriate and allows these financial managers to pay a lower tax rate on their income than other workers. The President proposes to eliminate the loophole for managers in investment services partnerships and to tax carried interest at ordinary income rates. This would reduce the deficit by $13 billion over 10 years.

Eliminate Special Depreciation Rules for Corporate Purchases of Aircraft. Under current law, airplanes used in commercial and contract carrying of passengers and freight can be depreciated over seven years. Airplanes not used in commercial or contract carrying of passengers or freight, for example corporate jets, are depreciated over five years. The proposal would change depreciation schedules for corporate planes that carry passengers to seven years to be consistent with the treatment of commercial aircraft. This would reduce the deficit by $2 billion over 10 years.

Eliminate Oil and Gas Tax Preferences. The tax code currently subsidizes oil and gas production through loopholes and tax expenditures that preference these industries over others. Current law provides a number of credits and deductions that are targeted toward certain oil and gas activities. In accordance with the President's agreement at the G-20 Summit in Pittsburgh in December 2009 to phase out subsidies for fossil fuels so that we can transition to a 21st Century energy economy, the President is proposing to repeal a number of tax preferences available for fossil fuels. Getting rid of these would reduce the deficit by $41 billion over 10 years.

CREATING A GOVERNMENT THAT IS EFFECTIVE AND EFFICIENT

Whether the Budget is in surplus or deficit, wasting taxpayer dollars on programs that are outdated, ineffective, or duplicative is wrong. With the tight discretionary caps implemented by the BCA, we have no choice but to redouble our efforts to scour the Budget for waste and to make tough decisions about reducing funding or ending programs that are laudable, but cannot be funded in this fiscal environment. This exercise is difficult, but builds on the efforts the Administration has undertaken since the President took office. As part of its Campaign to Cut Waste, the Administration has moved to cut wasteful spending and programs that do not work, strengthen and streamline what does work, leverage technology to transform Government operations to save money and improve performance, and make Government more open and responsive to the needs of the American people. As the President said in his 2011 State of the Union address, we cannot win the future with the government of the past. In order to win the future and better serve a more competitive America, we need a 21st Century government that is efficient, effective and accountable. To continue these efforts, the Administration proposes to:

Reorganize Government. We live and do business in the information age, but the organization of our Government has not kept pace, changing little since the days of black and white TV. Over the years, duplicative efforts sprang up that made it less effective, wasting taxpayer dollars, and making it harder for the American people to navigate their Government. To create an economy that is built to last, will take a private sector that has at its disposal all it needs to compete with firms and workers from around the world. That means re-organizing government so that it does more for less, and that it is best positioned to assist businesses and entrepreneurs grow and win in the world economy. That is why the President has asked the Congress to revive an authority that Presidents had for almost the entire period from 1932 through 1984: to submit proposals to reorganize the Executive Branch via a fast-track procedure. The Administration's proposal, the "Reforming and Consolidating Government Act of 2012," would enable the President to submit plans to consolidate and reorganize Executive Branch departments and agencies for fast track consideration by the Congress, but only so long as the result would be to reduce the size of Government or cut costs, the latter being a new requirement for this type of authority.

If given this authority, the President would submit a proposal to consolidate a number of agencies and programs into a new Department with a focused mission to foster economic growth and spur job creation. The proposal would consolidate the six primary business and trade agencies, as well as other related programs, integrating into one new Department the Government's core trade and competitiveness functions. Specifically, the new Department will absorb the Department of Commerce's core business and trade functions, the Small Business Administration, the Office of the U.S. Trade Representative, the Export-Import Bank, the Overseas Private Investment Corporation, and the U.S. Trade and Development Agency. It will also incorporate related programs from a number of other departments, including the Department of Agriculture's business development programs, the Department of the Treasury's Community Development Financial Institutions Fund program, the National Science Foundation's statistical agency and industry partnership programs, and the Bureau of Labor Statistics from the Department of Labor. Creating a department with a laser-focus on economic growth requires moving the National Oceanic and Atmospheric Administration to the Department of the Interior.

By bringing together the core tools to expand trade and investment, grow small businesses, and support innovation, the new Department could coordinate these resources to maximize the benefits for businesses and the economy. With more effectively aligned and deployed trade promotion resources, strengthened trade enforcement capacity, streamlined export finance programs, and enhanced focus on investment in the United States, the Government could better implement a strong, pro-growth trade policy. This reorganization would help American businesses compete more effectively in the global economy, expand exports, and create more jobs at home. Businesses will more easily and seamlessly be able to access services in support of exports, domestic competi-

tiveness, and job creation. The Administration expects these changes to generate approximately $1.5 billion in savings over the next 10 years by reducing overhead and consolidating offices and support functions, as well as additional, comparable savings through programmatic cuts once the synergies from consolidation are realized, for a total of $3 billion over the next 10 years.

Cut Improper Payments by $50 Billion. Each year, the Federal Government wastes billions of American taxpayers' dollars on improper payments to individuals, organizations, and contractors. These are payments made in the wrong amount, to the wrong person, or for the wrong reason. In the summer of 2010, the President set a goal of cutting improper payments by $50 billion between 2010 and 2012. The Administration is on track to meet or exceed this goal, having avoided more than $20 billion in improper payments in 2010 and 2011 combined. In 2011, the Government-wide improper payment rate declined to 4.69 percent, a sharp decrease from the 5.29 percent reported in 2010. Agencies also reported that they recaptured more than $1.2 billion in overpayments to contractors and vendors in 2011. This was the highest recapture amount reported in the eight years that agencies have reported results. In total, the Federal Government has recaptured $1.9 billion in 2010 and 2011 combined, and the Administration is less than $100 million away from meeting the President's goal to recapture $2 billion by the end of 2012.

Dispose of Excess or Under-Utilized Federal Property. With over 1.1 million buildings, structures, and land parcels, the Federal Government is the largest property owner and manager in the country. In 2010, agencies identified tens of thousands of excess and underutilized real property assets (both civilian and military assets) that represent hundreds of millions of taxpayer dollars spent annually on unnecessary operation and maintenance costs, as well as other opportunities for reforming the inventory that could create billions of dollars in savings through streamlined efficiencies and reduced operating costs. In June 2010, the President directed agencies to accelerate efforts to shed unneeded property and reduce operating costs in order to achieve $3 billion in non-defense savings by the end of 2012. To date, Federal agencies have achieved $1.5 billion in savings and identified enough savings opportunities to exceed the $3 billion goal for non-defense savings opportunities. In addition, the DOD has achieved roughly half of its $5 billion goal for Base Realignment and Closure (BRAC) related savings.

Despite these successes, there is bipartisan agreement that competing stakeholder interests and red tape continue to significantly hinder the disposal of Government property. There remain numerous high-value assets within the civilian real estate inventory that are no longer needed to support Federal agency missions and represent unnecessary costs to the taxpayer. Faced with similar challenges, DOD utilized BRAC, a streamlined process, to dispose of military properties and achieve billions of dollars of savings over the last 20 years. Building off the best practices of BRAC, the Administration proposed the Civilian Property Realignment Act (CPRA) in the 2012 Budget. The proposal would create an independent Board of experts to identify opportunities to consolidate, reduce, and realign the Federal footprint as well as expedite the disposal of properties. This proposal utilizes bundled recommendations, a fast-track congressional procedure, streamlined disposal and consolidation authorities, and a revolving fund replenished by proceeds to provide logistical and financial support to agencies, as a comprehensive solution to the key obstacles that prevent the Federal Government from effectively managing its real estate, and could make a significant contribution to deficit reduction. The Administration will continue to aggressively pursue the CPRA in 2013 so the Federal Government can cut through red tape and competing stakeholder interests to more quickly dispose and consolidate civilian properties and realize billions of dollars in savings for taxpayers.

Reduce Administrative Overhead. In his very first Cabinet meeting, the President asked his Cabinet to find at least $100 million in collective cuts to their administrative budgets, separate and apart from those identified in the Budget. They responded by identifying 77 cost-saving measures, amounting to $243 million in savings through 2010. Continuing that effort, the 2012 Budget included agency-specific, targeted cuts to administrative expenses such as travel, printing, supplies, and advisory contract services. The total administrative savings is estimated to be over $2 billion. Building upon that effort, the President issued an Executive Order to promote efficient spending in November 2011. The Executive Order called for agencies to make a 20 percent reduction in their spending on the administrative areas targeted in the 2012 Budget, as well as three additional areas: employee information technology devices, extraneous promotional items, and executive transportation. Overall, this will yield nearly $8 billion in savings in 2013 compared to 2010 spending on these administrative activities, which agencies are redirecting to higher priority programs.

Save Billions of Dollars in Contracting. The President's mandate to improve Federal procurement practices has stopped uncontrolled contract spending and put agencies on a path for achieving real and sustained improvement. After over a decade of dramatic increases in contract spending, contracting decreased in 2010 for the first time in 13 years—with agencies spending $80 billion less than what they would have, if contract costs had continued to grow at the same rate as they did from 2000 to 2008. In 2011, agencies maintained this lower level of spending by buying less, ending contracts that were unaffordable or no longer needed, improving the workforce's ability to negotiate better deals and hold contractors to their promise of delivering on time and on budget, and reducing the use of high-risk contracts, including time-and-materials contracts, where agencies reimburse contractors for the hours they work instead of the results they achieve. Agencies also increased their use of Government-wide contracts to leverage the Federal Government's buying power as the world's largest customer, saving taxpayers tens of millions of dollars for everyday needs, like office supplies and overnight delivery services.

In 2012, the Administration will continue its efforts to deliver better value to taxpayers. Agencies will reduce by 15 percent spending on management support service contracts, where contract spending has far outpaced the already fast growth in contracting generally and one that has been prone to risk, including the risk of overreliance on contractors. Agencies will also strengthen their suspension and debarment programs to better ensure that bad actors who put taxpayer dollars at risk of waste, fraud, and abuse are prohibited from doing work with Federal agencies. In addition, they will continue to build the capabilities of the acquisition workforce, by improving training and developing specialized cadres to better manage information technology procurements as well as centers of excellence to facilitate the rapid adoption of best practices for achieving stronger program outcomes.

Reform Military Acquisition. DOD contracts account for approximately 70 percent of all Federal procurement. Through its "Better Buying Power" acquisition reform initiative, DOD is charting a new path that will result in greater efficiency and productivity throughout the defense acquisition system. In particular, DOD is: 1) decreasing the use of high-risk contracts based on time-and-materials and labor-hours; 2) continuing to develop the acquisition workforce to provide needed oversight; 3) eliminating or restructuring lower-priority acquisitions; 4) reducing contract spending on management support services; 5) taking full advantage of contract vehicles that reflect the Government's buying leverage; 6) increasing the use of strategic sourcing; 7) increasing small business participation; and 8) improving financial management systems. In addition, DOD has instituted a number of acquisition management best practices: applying lessons learned from past acquisitions; establishing process teams to review qualifications of acquisition professionals; and instituting peer reviews to ensure affordability and effective competition. In a world of tight discretionary budget caps, these reforms will help free up resources that can be devoted to higher-priority programs.

Reduce Energy Costs for the Federal Government's Biggest Consumer. DOD consumes almost three-fourths of all Federal energy resources. To reduce consumption, the Budget includes approximately $1 billion for energy conservation investments at DOD—up from $400 million in 2010. These investments include making energy retrofits of existing buildings, meeting energy efficiency standards in new buildings, and developing renewable energy projects. DOD is steadily improving its installation energy performance by reducing the demand for traditional energy and by increasing the supply of renewable energy, currently 8.5 percent of DOD energy production and procurement. The request includes $150 million for the Energy Conservation Investment Program, which improves the energy efficiency of DOD facilities worldwide. In addition, the Budget provides $32 million, a 7 percent increase compared to 2012, for the Installation Energy Test Bed Program to demonstrate new energy technologies to reduce risk, overcome barriers to deployment, and facilitate wide-scale commercialization.

Harness Information Technology to Do More with Less. The American people expect the Government to use information technology (IT) to provide the same level of service they experience in their everyday lives. As part of the Accountable Government Initiative, the Administration is transforming how the Government uses IT to improve productivity, lower the cost of operations, and streamline service delivery, all while bolstering cyber security. By taking a hard look at Government IT projects through TechStats, over the last three years we have avoided project costs of nearly $4 billion—while also accelerating the time it takes to get usable products up and running. To reduce duplicative spending, the Administration has already shut down over 140 Government data centers and is on track to close nearly 1,100 by the end of 2015. Overall, the data center optimization efforts are expected to yield $3 to $5 billion in savings. And through the "Cloud First" policy, agencies are shifting from a capital-intensive model toward a more flexible operational model where they pay only for the services they use. The ultimate goal is to improve service to the American people. To do this, we must lower the barriers to interaction with the Government. That is why the Administration launched a one-stop, online portal for small businesses to find and access available programs, information, and other services from across the Government rather than having to waste time navigating the Federal bureaucracy. Going forward, the Administration will continue to harness the transformational power of IT to build the Government of the 21ˢᵗ Century and to help agencies deliver more effectively on their missions. By doing more with less, the Administration is driving savings across Government and using those savings to reinvest in information technology and services that benefit the American people.

The Federal Government is also improving how it acquires IT products and services through the use of early vendor engagement in complex and high-risk IT procurements and the development of specialized IT acquisition cadres that increase the chance of successful program outcomes.

Reduce Outdated and Duplicative Reporting. While the plans and reports that Congress requires of the Executive Branch often serve legislative decision-making, oversight and public transparency, they can become outdated, duplicative, or less useful than when originally mandated. Under the GPRA Modernization Act, the Congress instructed the Executive Branch to identify outdated or redundant reports to consolidate, streamline, or eliminate. Agencies identified more than 9,000 plans or reports currently produced for the Congress, with DOD responsible for approximately 70 percent of them. Of these, agencies proposed more than 450 low-priority plans and reports for the Congress to consider eliminating or consolidating. These reports currently take Federal employees approximately 200,000 hours to prepare and result in almost 30,000 pages. Concurrent with the Budget, the list of plans and reports identified for possible elimination or consolidation have been posted for public comment on *Performance.gov*. After collecting public comments, OMB will work with the Congress to eliminate or consolidate plans and reports that have become outdated or duplicative.

Adopt Performance-Based Reforms. Widely viewed as leveraging more change than any other competitive grant program in history, the Department of Education's Race to the Top (RTT) initiative spurred States across the Nation to bring together teachers, school leaders, and policymakers to achieve difficult yet fundamental improvements to our education system. By setting out clear standards that needed to be met to receive funds, RTT instigated change in States all across the Nation, including even those that ultimately did not receive RTT funds. By doing so, RTT has driven taxpayer dollars to be used more effectively. The RTT approach is being expanded to transform and improve lifelong learning from early childhood education through college and beyond; to allocate grants for transportation; to bring innovation to workforce training; and to accelerate advanced vehicle deployment.

Improve Outcomes with Better Evidence. In order to understand what works and what does not in the Federal Government, and thus better use taxpayer dollars, rigorous evaluations of results are critical. Agencies must establish a culture where they constantly ask, and try to answer, questions that help them find, implement, spread, and sustain effective programs and practices; find and fix or eliminate ineffective ones; test promising programs and practices to see if they are effective and can be replicated; and find lower-cost ways to achieve a positive impact. The Federal fiscal situation necessitates doing more with less, not only to reduce budget deficits, but to build confidence that Americans are receiving maximum value for their hard-earned tax dollars. It is therefore critical to apply an evidence-based approach to government management that utilizes rigorous methods appropriate to the situation, learns from experience, and is open to experimentation. Agencies are conducting evaluations across the Federal Government, and the Recovery Act launched a number of evaluations that are currently underway on such topics as the effects of different rent formulas on housing assistance recipients, the effects of electricity pricing treatments in combination with advanced metering infrastructure (including smart meters) on residential electricity usage, and the effects of extended unemployment insurance benefit programs on employment outcomes. In addition, the Administration is placing additional focus on agency evaluation budgets to ensure that those dollars are producing high quality evidence that informs key decisions.

Use Goals and Frequent Data-Driven Reviews to Achieve More Results for the Money. In these fiscal times, it is it more important than ever for Government agencies to use taxpayer money wisely to achieve greater program impact for the taxpayer's dollar. A careful review of past experience shows that government works better when leaders identify a limited number of clear, measurable, and ambitious goals and regularly review progress toward them. Building on these lessons from two prior years, senior agency leaders identified with their 2013 budget submissions a limited number of near-term Agency Priority Goals (formerly called High Priority Performance Goals) that require neither additional resources nor legislative action, but rather hinge on strong execution to be accomplished. They have also designated a senior accountable official, a "Goal Leader," responsible for driving progress on each goal. For the first time, as part of the 2013 Budget process, the Administration has also set a limited number of agency Federal Cross-Agency Priority Goals in areas where increased cross-agency coordination or learning, regular review, and designation of a goal leader are expected to accelerate progress. Agency and Cross-Agency 2013 Priority Goals have been set in a wide variety of areas. Some focus on increasing U.S. exports, broadband coverage, entrepreneurship opportunities, and the science and technology workforce. Others focus on reducing the cost of clean energy technologies, such as advanced vehicles and improving the energy efficiency of the Nation's homes and industries while reducing costs for families. Some seek to improve the well-being of the Nation's children and adults, especially veterans who served the Nation so well, while others seek to prevent bad things, such as fatalities and health-care associated infections, from happening and reduce their costs when they do. Several goals seek to cut the costs of delivery, while sustaining high quality customer service.

Pay for Success in Domestic Programs. Many traditional Government social programs fit one of two molds: prescriptive programs that stifle innovation by specifying eligible providers and activities, or flexible block grants that fail to focus on results. To ensure taxpayers get the best possible return on their investment, the Administration is testing a new program model—Pay for Success—in which the Government provides flexibility for how services are delivered and pays for results after they are achieved. The working capital for a Pay for Success project generally comes from private investors that bear the risk of failure, but receive a financial return if the project succeeds. Projects use and build evidence-based practices to improve the lives of vulnerable target populations, reducing their need for future Government services and cash assistance. Over the course of 2012, the Administration is launching a small number of Pay for Success pilots in criminal justice and workforce development. The President's 2013 Budget reserves a total of up to $109 million to test this new financing mechanism in a broader range of areas including education and homelessness. If successful, Pay for Success projects offer a cost-effective way to replicate effective practices and support continuing innovation as Federal resources become more constrained.

Empower Local Communities to Achieve Better Results. Inconsistent and overlapping Federal program requirements sometimes prevent States and localities from effectively coordinating services or using funding to support strategies that are likely to achieve the best outcomes. This is especially true for cross-cutting policy areas, such as disconnected youth and distressed neighborhoods, where multiple programs, each with its own requirements, all contribute to the same broad goals. Performance Partnership pilots provide a model for enabling leading edge States and localities to demonstrate better ways to use resources, by giving them flexibility to pool discretionary funds across multiple Federal programs in exchange for greater accountability for results. In 2013, the Administration proposes to establish a limited number of Performance Partnership pilots designed to improve outcomes for disconnected youth or to support the revitalization of distressed neighborhoods. All affected Federal agencies and the Director of the Office of Management and Budget would have to approve of the agreement and confirm that vulnerable populations would not be adversely affected, before a Performance Partnership pilot could be established.

INVESTING IN OUR FUTURE

Our economy is undergoing a transformation not seen since the move from an agrarian to an industrial economy at the turn of the 20th Century. Huge advances in technology—from computing power to communications—have allowed companies to boost productivity and realign their workforces. These technological advances, like earlier ones, raise our standard of living and create entire new industries. During the 20th Century, our economy was the envy of the rest of the world, in no small part because it was better at creating and harnessing new technologies, and more flexible in adapting to them.

Advances in technology also can require painful adjustments. Recent advances have allowed firms to search the world for the best place to make their products and deliver their services, and hire workers wherever they may find them. At first, this transition was felt most acutely by industrial workers; factories, plants, and mills have closed because fewer people were needed to run them or the operations were sent overseas. In recent years, white-collar workers have felt the effects of this transformation too. In some fields, technological advances have meant fewer workers were needed to perform a task. In others, advances in telecommunications have enabled the outsourcing of jobs to countries such as China or India.

The dislocations caused by these changes have been jarring and painful to many Americans and communities across our country. Moreover, their effects have been compounded by a belief among some policymakers that all that is needed to help our fellow Americans through this transformation is to cut regulations and reduce taxes for the wealthy. Prosperity and jobs will then trickle down to the vast majority of Americans. This approach has not worked. It contributed to years of income stagnation for middle-class families, helped produce a level of inequality that is a drag on overall economic growth, and helped create the deep rescission whose after-effects we are still grappling with. As a result, the rungs on the ladder of opportunity have grown farther apart, making it more difficult for people who work hard and play by the rules to provide a secure middle-class life for their family.

This is not a future that we can or should accept. Instead, we need to make sure that everyone gets a fair shot at success, does their fair share, and engages in fair play so that we, as a Nation, can grow and prosper. To do that, we must not race to the lowest global common denominator; instead, we must race to the top—to good jobs that pay well and offer middle-class security. In today's high-tech, interdependent economy, that means we must transform our economy from one that is too focused on speculation, spending, and borrowing to one that is educating, innovating, and building. We need to continue to construct a new foundation for long-term economic growth that has as its pillars what is needed to win in the world economy: an educated and skilled workforce; cutting-edge research leading to the innovations that will power the industries of tomorrow; and a modern, robust infrastructure that can support a growing, high-tech economy with the jobs that promote a growing middle class. With that as a base, we can out-compete any country and sustain a strong economy.

47

Putting the Nation on a sustainable fiscal path is critical to keeping the United States competitive in the global economy, and the Budget lays out a strategy to do that. At the same time, it also recognizes that we must go forward with investments that will fuel future economic growth, particularly since sustained and robust economic growth plays a very significant, long-term role in reducing deficits. To be sure, making these investments and re-tooling our Nation for this challenge is not an easy task. The discretionary budget caps put in place by the Budget Control Act of 2011 create tight limits, forcing us to make tough decisions about where to invest. In many areas, that means keeping funding level or cutting it; in some, it entails reforming programs to be more effective; in a small number, it means targeted increases. Overall, the Administration is pursuing a strategy in which the Budget identifies cuts and savings, asks for shared sacrifices across the board, and invests in areas critical to helping America win the race for the jobs and industries of the future.

Educating a Competitive Workforce

For decades, the strength of our schools and universities as well as our ability to provide a quality education to a large number of our people has been an engine for our economic growth. From the land-grant universities of the 19th Century to the GI Bill in the 20th, we have worked to open the doors of education to more and more of our people. Looking ahead, a highly-educated and skilled workforce will be critical to competing in the global economy and to creating jobs that pay well and offer middle-class security. The unemployment rate for Americans with a college degree or more is about half the national average, and their incomes are twice as high as those without a high-school diploma. Education needs to be a national mission in which we all—educators, government, businesses, parents, students, and communities—work together to give our children a world-class education. That is why the President has set an ambitious goal: by 2020, we will have the highest proportion of college graduates in the world. Meeting this goal will give us

a workforce that is second to none, and a steady stream of inventors and entrepreneurs to create the businesses and jobs of the future.

Our approach to investing in education is to direct significant resources to where they are needed and to ensure that those funds are being invested in programs that are effective in educating our children. Over the past three years, the Administration has funded evaluations and required greater use of evidence in grant competitions, so we can determine and fund what works. Central to this effort has been the Race to the Top (RTT) initiative for elementary and secondary education, which created a competition for funds that spurred States across the Nation to bring together teachers, school leaders, and policy makers to achieve difficult, yet fundamental improvements to our education system. By offering competitive funding, demanding significant reforms with deep support, requiring outcomes, and measuring success, the RTT competition fostered meaningful change even in States that ultimately did not win an award. This past year, a new RTT competition, called Race to the Top: Early Learning Challenge, also drove States to take major steps to focus systematically on improved quality and results in their early education programs. The 2013 Budget will extend the Race to the Top model to the realm of higher education, with a new competition that rewards States that keep public colleges affordable and adopt reforms that lead more students to complete their degrees on time.

To meet the President's goal on college access and completion, the Administration is proposing investments and reforms that touch every phase of a lifetime of learning. The Administration will:

Reform Elementary and Secondary School Funding by Setting High Standards, Encouraging Innovation, and Rewarding Success. The Administration has jump-started landmark reforms in our education system by rewarding excellence and promoting innovation. Early indications show impressive progress in helping children start school ready to succeed, raising academic standards, placing an effective teacher in every classroom, and turning around struggling schools. The Administration will work with the Congress on reauthorization legislation to restructure K-12 funding to continue to focus on these critical educational goals. In this reauthorization, we would encourage innovation by consolidating narrow authorities into broader programs. Key components of education reform reflected in the Budget include:

- *Race to the Top (RTT).* The Budget provides $850 million for RTT, a program that has enabled States to implement systemic reforms in five fundamental areas: implementing rigorous standards and assessments; using data to improve instruction and decision-making; recruiting and retaining effective teachers and principals; turning around the lowest-performing schools, and improving State systems of early learning and care. In 2011, the Department of Education launched the RTT Early Learning Challenge grant competition, a joint effort with the Department of Health and Human Services, designed to spur progress in States with the most ambitious plans to ensure that high-needs children from birth to age five enter kindergarten ready to succeed. In 2012, the Administration is building on the State-level progress of RTT by launching a district-level competition to support reforms best executed at the local level. In 2013, RTT will be poised to deepen our investments in these various areas, to address the unmet demand of States and districts that have demonstrated a commitment to implementing comprehensive and ambitious reforms. Additional resources also will be provided for Race to the Top: Early Learning Challenge, to be paired with new investments by the Department of Health and Human Services in improving child care quality and preparing children for success in school.

- *Promise Neighborhoods.* The Budget provides a considerable increase to Promise Neighborhoods, funding the program at $100 million. This initiative supports high-need communities who plan to integrate effective services for families combined with comprehensive reforms centered on high-quality schools, in an effort to improve educational and life outcomes for children and youth.

- *Investing in Innovation (i3).* The Budget continues robust investment in the i3 fund, to support evidence-based approaches that improve K-12 achievement and close achievement gaps, decrease dropout rates, increase high school graduation rates, and improve teacher and school leader effectiveness. A portion of i3 funds will also be used to support the development of breakthrough learning technologies through the Advanced Research Projects Agency for Education.

- *Flexibility in Exchange for Smart Reforms.* To build on the successful reforms leveraged by the first RTT competition, the Department of Education recently invited States to apply for Elementary and Secondary Education Act (ESEA) waivers in exchange for a commitment to continue to focus on closing achievement gaps and comprehensive reforms. The Budget maintains investments in key programs that States can use to advance these reforms. For example, States and districts will have new flexibility to use Title I funds that were previously required to be reserved for supplemental educational services, public school choice, and professional development to support locally-determined, rigorous interventions in schools.

- *Streamline and Consolidate Programs.* The Budget overhauls the Department of Education's ESEA programs by consolidating 38 program authorities into 11 competitive grant programs designed to allow States and districts more flexibility to use resources where they will have the greatest impact.

Open the Doors of College to More Americans. To boost the number of college graduates, we need to make it easier for students to afford a postsecondary education and increase the number of students who complete their degree. The Administration has already taken significant strides to improve access to college. Today, nearly 10 million students receive Pell Grants, and more than 12 million borrowers receive low-cost loans, with new affordable repayment options based on their income after leaving school. Just as investments over the past three years have transformed K-12 education, this Budget invests significant resources to reform higher education. Our goal is to reduce college costs, improve access, increase levels of completion, and better post-graduation outcomes. Key initiatives include:

* *Helping Students and Their Families Pay for College.* An educated and highly-skilled American workforce is essential to winning the future in today's global economy. Since 2008, the Administration has increased the maximum Pell Grant by $900, ensuring access to postsecondary education for nearly 10 million needy students. The Budget continues that commitment to Pell and provides the necessary resources to sustain the maximum award of $5,635 and, by generating savings elsewhere in higher education, to fund the maximum Pell award through the 2014-2015 award year. In addition, the Tax Relief, Unemployment Insurance Reauthorization, and Job Creation Act of 2010 extended for two years the new American Opportunity Tax Credit (AOTC)—a partially refundable tax credit worth up to $10,000 per student over four years of college. AOTC, which would be made permanent in the Budget, helps more than 9 million students and their families afford the cost of college.

* *Rewarding Colleges That Stay Affordable and Provide Good Value.* The Budget proposes Race to the Top: College Affordability and Completion to help make America's public colleges and universities more affordable and a better value, and to drive reforms that will help boost quality, productivity, and degree completion. In addition, the Budget proposes to reform the formula for distributing approximately $10 billion annually of Campus-Based Aid to reward colleges that act responsibly in setting tuition, providing the best value, and serving needy students

well. Finally, the Budget proposes a new $55 million First in the World Fund that introduces an evidence-based framework—modeled after the i3 initiative—to test, validate, and scale up effective strategies to improve higher education.

Prepare 100,000 STEM Teachers Over the Next Decade and Improve STEM Education. Students need to master science, technology, engineering, and mathematics (STEM) in order to thrive in the 21st Century economy. Steadily, we have seen other nations eclipse ours in preparing their children in these critical fields. That is why the President has set the ambitious goal of preparing 100,000 STEM teachers over the next decade, and recruiting 10,000 STEM teachers over the next two years. The Budget allocates $80 million within the Effective Teachers and Leaders State Grant program toward that goal, to expand promising and effective models of teacher preparation in STEM. The Budget also funds a jointly administered mathematics education initiative, with $30 million from the Department of Education and $30 million from the National Science Foundation to develop, validate, and scale up evidence-based approaches to improve student learning at the K-12 and undergraduate levels. These programs will be developed in conjunction with a Government-wide effort to improve the impact of Federal investments in math and science education by ensuring that all programs supporting K-12 and undergraduate education adhere to consistent standards of effectiveness.

Invest in Building the Skills of American Workers. As our economy continues to recover, millions of Americans are looking for ways to upgrade and hone their skills to prepare for emerging job opportunities. The Budget provides resources to connect these workers with job openings and skill-building opportunities. This includes a $12.5 billion Pathways Back to Work Fund, which will support summer and year-round jobs for low-income youth, and will help connect the long-term unemployed and low-income adults to subsidized employment and work-based training opportunities. To complement this short-run investment, the Budget continues to support a Workforce

Innovation Fund that, paired with broader waiver authority, will encourage States, regions, and localities to break down barriers among programs, test new ideas, and replicate proven strategies for delivering better employment and education results in a more cost-effective way. The Budget also funds a new initiative designed to improve access to job training across the Nation and provides $8 billion in the Departments of Education and Labor to support State and community college partnerships with businesses to build the skills of American workers.

Give Dislocated Workers the Help They Need to Find New Jobs. Nearly 7 million of the Americans who lost jobs in 2009 were displaced from jobs that are unlikely to come back, and those who do find reemployment, on average, suffer significant earnings losses. But our current system does not treat all workers who were dislocated because of economic shifts equally. Workers in trade-impacted industries are eligible for extensive income support, training, and reemployment services under the Trade Adjustment Assistance program, while those who lose their jobs for other reasons receive less generous assistance. In this increasingly global economy, it is increasingly difficult to distinguish between trade, technology, outsourcing, consumer trends, and other economic shifts that cause displacement. As part of the Administration's effort to reform and modernize the Nation's job training system so that individuals can quickly gain the training they need for the jobs created as our economy evolves, the Budget proposes a universal core set of services where the focus is on helping all dislocated workers find new jobs.

Prepare Young People for Jobs Through a Reformed Career and Technical Education Program. The President's Budget recommends reauthorization and reform of the Career and Technical Education (CTE) program, currently set to expire in 2013. The Administration's $1.1 billion reauthorization proposal would restructure CTE to align what students learn in school with the demands of 21st Century jobs. The Budget also invests in immediate job-creation measures to increase substantially the number of students enrolled in Career Academies, a particularly successful educational model for young people.

Reform Job Corps. The Administration strongly supports Job Corps, but believes the program could be more effective and efficient. The 2013 Budget launches a bold reform effort for Job Corps to improve program outcomes and strengthen accountability. Specifically, the Administration intends to fund Job Corps centers in every State, but close by program year 2013 the small number of Job Corps centers that are chronically low-performing, to be identified using criteria that will be published in advance. The Administration will also shift the program's focus toward the strategies that were proven most cost-effective in evaluations of Job Corps, strengthen the performance measurement system, and provide information to the public about each Job Corps center's performance in a more transparent way.

Investing in American Innovation

The world is shifting to an innovation economy, and no other country fosters innovation better than America. From Franklin to Edison, from Ford to Gates and Jobs, American inventors and entrepreneurs have transformed the world. Being daring and harnessing the talents of a diverse population are our Nation's strengths, and they match up with the demands of the economy today and in the decades to come.

To create jobs in the 21st Century economy, we need to create an environment where invention, innovation, and industry can flourish. We need to build a future in which our factories and workers are busy manufacturing the high-tech products that will define the century. We need an economy not built on bubbles and financial speculation, but one built on creating and selling throughout the world products that are stamped, "Made in America." Doing that starts with continuing investment in the basic science and engineering research and technology development from which new products, new businesses, and even new industries are formed. It means writing our rules, regulations, and laws in a way that promote growth and innovation and make it easier for scientists and inventors to bring their ideas to market and see those ideas become thriving businesses. And, we must focus our efforts in areas that show the most promise for job creation to compete with developing countries that are devoting more of their resources to these industries.

That is why the Budget continues to make a significant investment in clean energy technology. Whichever country leads in the global, clean energy economy will also take the lead in creating high-paying, highly-skilled jobs for its people. More than that, moving toward a clean energy economy will reduce our reliance on oil and on other energy sources that contribute to global warming. We are at the cusp of a future in which hundreds of thousands of vehicles that do not rely on a gasoline-powered engine will be on our roads, and where millions of homes will be powered by electricity from clean sources.

To continue to bring about this vision and to nurture the incalculable number of good ideas that one day will be ready to go from lab to market, we need to make the United States the world leader in innovation. The Budget proposes to:

Increase Investment in Research and Development (R&D). For many years, the United States has been a world leader in R&D. In order for the United States to thrive in today's innovation economy, we need to maintain a world-class commitment to science and research. The 2013 Budget does that by providing $140.8 billion for R&D overall, while targeting resources to those areas most likely to directly contribute to the creation of transformational technologies that can create the businesses and jobs of the future. Among the steps taken are:

• Increasing the level of investment in non-defense R&D by 5 percent from the 2011 and 2012 levels, even as overall budgets decline.

• Maintaining the President's commitment

to double the budgets of three key basic research agencies: the National Science Foundation (NSF), the Department of Energy's (DOE's)Office of Science, and the National Institute of Standards and Technology (NIST) labs. Basic research has been America's great strength, creating whole new industries and jobs. Especially as the private sector has reduced the amounts it dedicates to this type of research, it is critical that the Federal Government dedicates funds to it. Consequently, the Budget builds upon previous investments, including $13.1 billion in research programs and projects at these three agencies. Within these agencies, funds will be focused on basic research directed at priority areas, such as clean energy technologies, the bio-economy, advanced manufacturing technologies, "smart" infrastructure, wireless communications, and cybersecurity.

• Supporting biomedical research at the National Institutes of Health (NIH). Biomedical research contributes to improving the health of the American people as well as the economy. Tomorrow's advances in health care depend on today's investments in basic research on the fundamental causes and mechanisms of disease, new technologies to accelerate discoveries, innovations in clinical research, and a robust pipeline of creative and skillful biomedical researchers. Although there are very tight discretionary caps, the Budget provides $30.7 billion for NIH, the same amount as 2012.

• Providing $51 million at NSF for an interdisciplinary program to develop innovative approaches and technologies to enable more flexible and efficient access to the radio spectrum—an investment that reflects the large and growing importance of the wireless communications sector.

• Providing the National Aeronautics and Space Administration $1.3 billion to develop innovative aeronautics and space technologies that will keep the aerospace industry—one of the largest net export industries in the United States—at the cutting edge in the years to come.

Support the Long-Term Competitiveness of American Manufacturing. The Administration proposes $149 million, an increase of $39 million above the 2012 enacted level, for research at NSF targeted at developing revolutionary new manufacturing technologies in partnership with the private sector. This advanced manufacturing research is part of a larger $225 million research initiative aimed at transforming static systems, processes, and infrastructure into adaptive, pervasive "smart" systems with embedded computational intelligence that can sense, adapt, and react. The Administration also proposes $708 million, $86 million above the 2012 enacted level, for NIST labs to expand research in areas such as bio-manufacturing and nano-manufacturing, and $21 million for a new Advanced Manufacturing Technology Consortia program, a public-private partnership that will support road maps and research to address common manufacturing challenges faced by private sector businesses. In addition, the Administration proposes $290 million—more than double the amount in 2012 —for the Advanced Manufacturing Office at the DOE Office of Energy Efficiency and Renewable Energy. This Office will fund activities on innovative manufacturing processes and advanced industrial materials that will enable U.S. companies to cut the costs of manufacturing by using less energy, while improving product quality and accelerating product development. In total, the Budget provides $2.2 billion for Federal advanced manufacturing R&D, a 19 percent increase over 2012.

Accelerate Innovations from the Laboratory to the Market. One of the most difficult challenges facing an inventor or entrepreneur is taking a new idea from the laboratory or drawing board to market. While the knowledge gained from Government-supported basic and applied research frequently advances a particular field of science or engineering, some results also show immediate potential for broader applicability and impact in the business world. The Administration

proposes $19 million for the new public-private "Innovation Corps" program at NSF aimed at bringing together the technological, entrepreneurial, and business know-how necessary to bring discoveries ripe for innovation out of the university lab.

Bring About a Clean Energy Economy and Create the Jobs of the Future. Moving toward a clean energy economy will reduce air and water pollution and enhance our national security by reducing dependence on oil. Cleaner energy will play a crucial role in slowing global climate change, meeting the President's goals of cutting greenhouse gas emissions in the range of 17 percent below 2005 levels by 2020, and 83 percent by 2050. Just as important, ensuring that the Nation leads the world in the clean energy economy is an economic imperative. The clean energy industry, which was in its infancy just a few years ago, is now growing by leaps and bounds. Across the globe—from Europe to Asia to South America— countries are making significant investments in clean energy technologies. The Administration supports a range of investments and initiatives to help make the United States the leader in this industry and bring about a clean energy economy with its new companies and jobs:

- *Double the Share of Electricity from Clean Energy Sources by 2035.* The President's proposed Clean Energy Standard is the centerpiece of the Administration's strategy to ensure strong American leadership in the clean energy economy. To support this goal, the Budget increases funding for renewable energy research and development; supports advances in fossil energy technologies that reduce carbon emissions from coal-fired power plants; supports nuclear energy; and promotes the expansion and use of clean energy across the country including rural areas. The Budget also extends key tax incentives to encourage investment in wind energy and clean energy technology.

- *Put One Million Advanced Technology Vehicles on the Road by 2015.* In 2008, the President set an ambitious goal of having one million advanced technology vehicles on the road by 2015. To reach this goal and become the first in the world to do so, the Budget builds on Recovery Act investments and continues to support electric vehicle manufacturing and adoption in the United States through new consumer rebates, investments in R&D, and competitive programs to encourage investment in advanced vehicle infrastructure.

- *Save Manufacturers Money by Improving Energy Efficiency.* The President's Advanced Manufacturing Partnership invests in a national effort to develop and commercialize the emerging technologies that will create high quality manufacturing jobs and enhance our global competitiveness. By coordinating across Federal agencies and collaborating with the private sector, it will provide the platform for inventing new manufacturing technologies, speeding ideas from the drawing board to the manufacturing floor, scaling-up first-of-a-kind technologies, and developing the infrastructure and shared facilities to allow small and mid-sized manufacturers to innovate and compete.

- *Reduce Buildings' Energy Use by 20 Percent by 2020.* The 80 billion square feet of non-residential building space in the United States present an opportunity to realize large gains in energy efficiency. In 2010, commercial buildings consumed roughly 20 percent of all energy in the U.S. economy. The President's Better Buildings Initiative will, over the next 10 years, seek to make non-residential buildings 20 percent more energy efficient by catalyzing private sector investment through a series of incentives to upgrade offices, stores, universities, hospitals and commercial buildings. These programs build on the Administration's commitment to improving efficiency in residential and Government buildings, particularly through Recovery Act investments. The Budget proposes to encourage the use of the Small Business Administration's 504 Certified Development Company loan guarantee program to sup-

port energy efficiency retrofit investments in commercial buildings. The Administration continues to call on Congress to pass the HomeStar bill, which would create jobs by encouraging Americans to invest in energy saving home improvements. The Budget also supports increased R&D in innovative building efficiency technologies and the continued introduction of appliance efficiency standards that save consumers and companies money while improving performance.

- *Pursue Responsible Oil and Gas Production.* Even as we develop next generation energy technologies, we will continue to rely on oil and gas. As was underscored by the tragic 2010 explosion of the Deepwater Horizon and the oil spill that followed, we must take immediate steps to make production safer and more environmentally responsible. In the wake of the spill, the Administration focused on implementing more rigorous safety and environmental standards than ever before, and making structural reforms within the Department of the Interior to increase oversight of offshore drilling, including greater independence for the new environmental enforcement agency that has now been created through the restructuring. The Budget proposes $368 million to fund the two new bureaus that oversee offshore oil and gas development, the Bureau of Ocean Energy Management and the Bureau of Safety and Environmental Enforcement. These funds will be used to: hire new oil and gas inspectors, engineers, scientists, and other key staff to oversee industry operations; establish real-time monitoring of key drilling activities; conduct detailed engineering reviews of offshore drilling and production safety systems; and implement more aggressive reviews of company oil spill response plans. The Budget also includes $45 million for the Department of Energy, the Environmental Protection Agency, and the U.S. Geological Survey for a coordinated effort among these agencies to conduct an R&D program aimed at reducing the potential health, safety, and environmental risks of hydraulic fracturing for natural gas and oil production from shale formations.

Reform Our Tax Code to Create Jobs Here at Home and Foster Innovation and Competitiveness. Over the nearly three decades since the last comprehensive reform effort, the tax system has been loaded up with revenue-side spending such as special deductions, credits, and other tax expenditures that help well-connected special interests, but do little for middle-class families or our Nation's economic growth. Now more than ever, when we want to compete and win in the world economy, we cannot afford a tax code burdened with special interest tax breaks. Successful comprehensive tax reform is a long process, often taking several years, but even though it is a daunting task, we cannot afford to shirk from the work. In an increasingly competitive global economy, we need to ensure that our country remains the most attractive place for entrepreneurship and business growth. That is why this Budget proposes a number of measures to keep America competitive and to make sure that our tax system encourages jobs to be created here rather than abroad. In addition to these changes to the current tax code, the President is calling on the Congress to immediately begin work on corporate tax reform that will close loopholes, lower the overall rate, encourage investment here at home, and not add a dime to the deficit.

Improve the Patent System and Protect Intellectual Property. The Budget proposes to give the U.S. Patent and Trademark Office (USPTO) full access to its fee collections and strengthen USPTO's efforts to improve the speed and quality of patent examinations through reforms authorized by the America Invents Act. This will provide USPTO with more than $2.9 billion in resources in 2013. The Budget also supports strengthened intellectual property enforcement domestically and overseas as set out in the Intellectual Property Enforcement Coordinator's Joint Strategic Plan required by Prioritizing Resources and Organization for Intellectual Property Act of 2008 (Pro-IP).

Building a 21st Century Infrastructure

From the Erie Canal to the transcontinental railroad, from the interstate highway system to the Internet, infrastructure has been critical to the economic growth and competitiveness of the American economy. For too long, we have neglected our Nation's infrastructure, its roads, bridges, levees, ports and waterways, communications networks, and transit systems. To compete in the 21st Century, we need an infrastructure that keeps pace with the times and outpaces our rivals. Manufacturers and other companies are looking to expand in the places with the best infrastructure to ship their products, move their workers, and communicate with the rest of the world. To attract those businesses to the United States and grow them here at home, we need to invest today. That is why, in the Recovery Act, the Administration made the largest one-time investment in our Nation's infrastructure since President Eisenhower called for the creation of an interstate highway system. Now, we must build on those efforts, and we must do so responsibly by paying for what we build. We cannot strengthen our economy with a modern infrastructure if at the same time it weakens our fiscal standing. To build the infrastructure we need to compete in the 21st Century, the Budget proposes to:

Enact an Historic $476 Billion, Six-Year Surface Transportation Reauthorization and Better Allocate Those Dollars to Get Results. Recognizing the importance of a modern transportation infrastructure to the growth and competitiveness of the economy, the President proposes a $476 billion, six-year surface transportation reauthorization package—expanded to include inter-city passenger rail transportation. Together with an additional $50 billion investment in 2012 to jumpstart critical transportation infrastructure projects, the proposal is an increase of more than 80 percent above the inflation-adjusted levels in the previous six-year bill plus annual appropriated funding for passenger rail during those years. The proposal is not just a historic commitment of funds, but also seeks to reform how transportation dollars are spent so that they are directed to the most effective programs and projects. It will hold States and localities accountable for real results and make Federal funding decisions based on sounder and more inclusive transportation plans. It will complement steps the Administration is already taking to improve and expedite the process of reviewing and approving transportation projects. While we are committed to the user-financed principle that has guided surface transportation, we recognize that more funds will be needed to make these overdue investments. That is why the Administration is proposing to use savings from ending the war in Iraq and winding down operations in Afghanistan to pay for the difference. Specifically, the proposal seeks to:

- Build upon an immediate investment of $50 billion for roads, rails, and runways to create thousands of jobs in the short term with a robust, multi-year reauthorization proposal that will renew our decaying transportation infrastructure while deepening the economic recovery and spurring job creation.

- Provide 80 percent of Americans with convenient access to a passenger rail system, featuring high-speed service, within 25 years. The Budget provides $47 billion over six years, plus $6 billion in 2012, to fund the development of high-speed rail and other passenger rail programs as part of an integrated national strategy. This includes merging Amtrak's stand-alone subsidies into the high-speed rail program as part of a larger, competitive System Preservation Initiative.

- Bring more accountability, goal-driven performance, competition, and innovation to transportation funds through a competitive, Race to the Top-style grant program that also will create incentives for States and localities to adopt critical reforms in a variety of areas, including safety, livability, and demand management. Proposed funding for this program is nearly $20 billion over six years.

- Get the most out of taxpayer dollars with a new "fix-it-first" emphasis for highway and

transit formula grants and through the consolidation of 55 duplicative, often-earmarked highway programs into five streamlined programs.

Build a 21st Century Aviation System That Reduces Delays and Improves Safety. The Budget provides more than $1 billion for the Federal Aviation Administration for implementation of the Next Generation Air Transportation System, a multi-year, interagency effort to improve the efficiency, safety, and capacity of the aviation system. This will help the country move from a national, ground-based radar surveillance system to a more accurate satellite-based one, which will result in the development of more efficient routes through airspace. This, in turn, would allow more planes to fly, reduce delays, save fuel, and improve overall safety.

Establish a National Infrastructure Bank. To direct Federal resources for infrastructure to projects that demonstrate the most merit and may be difficult to fund under the current patchwork of Federal programs, the President has called for the creation of an independent, non-partisan National Infrastructure Bank (NIB), led by infrastructure and financial experts. The NIB would offer broad eligibility and merit-based selection for large-scale ($100 million minimum) transportation, water, and energy infrastructure projects. Projects would have a clear public benefit, meet rigorous economic, technical and environmental standards, and be backed by a dedicated revenue stream. Geographic, sector, and size considerations would also be taken into account. The NIB would issue loans and loan guarantees to eligible projects. Loans issued by the NIB could be extended up to 35 years, giving the NIB the ability to be a "patient" partner side-by-side with State, local, and private co-investors. To maximize leverage from Federal investments, the NIB would finance no more than 50 percent of the total costs of any project.

Bring Next-Generation, Wireless Broadband to All Parts of the Country. The advances in wireless technology and the adoption of and reliance on wireless devices in daily commercial and personal life have been dramatic. High-speed, wireless broadband is fast becoming a critical component of business operations and economic growth. The United States needs to lead the world in providing broad access to the fastest networks possible. To do that, however, requires freeing up of transmission rights to underutilized portions of the spectrum currently dedicated to other private and Federal uses. To that end, the Budget again proposes legislation to provide authority for "voluntary incentive auctions" that will enable spectrum licensees to auction the rights to transmit over their portion of the spectrum in return for a share of the proceeds. This step is critical for re-purposing use of the communications spectrum over the coming decade to greatly facilitate access for smart phones, portable computers, and innovative technologies that are on the horizon. Voluntary incentive auctions, along with other measures to enable more efficient spectrum management, will provide $10 billion in funds and reserved spectrum to help us build an interoperable wireless broadband network for public safety and allow for seamless use by first responders across the country; invest in spectrum innovation, including setting aside spectrum for unlicensed use; and reduce the deficit by $21 billion over the next 10 years.

Invest in Smart, Energy-Efficient, and Reliable Electricity Delivery Infrastructure. The Budget continues to support the modernization of the Nation's electrical grid, by investing in research, development, and demonstration of smart-grid technologies that will spur the transition to a smarter, more efficient, secure and reliable electrical system. The end result will promote energy- and cost-saving choices for consumers, reduce emissions, and foster the growth of renewable energy sources like wind and solar. In addition, the Budget supports the Power Marketing Administration to reliably operate, maintain, and rehabilitate the Federal hydropower and transmission systems.

Invest in High-Priority Water Resources Infrastructure. While there are a number of worthy water infrastructure projects, we cannot fund them all. In the 2013 Budget, the Admin-

istration gives priority for funding the operation and maintenance of the key infrastructure that is most important to the Nation, including navigation channels that serve our most heavily used coastal ports and inland waterways, such as the Mississippi and Ohio Rivers, and the Illinois Waterway. The Budget also emphasizes investing in projects that address a significant risk to life and public safety, and projects that will restore significant aquatic ecosystems. The Administration will also focus on ways to modernize Federal water resources development policies and programs to ensure their responsiveness, accountability, and operational oversight, and to improve performance of these programs to best meet current and future water resources challenges.

Opening Global Markets and Keeping America Safe

To thrive in the interdependent, global economy, U.S. businesses, farmers, and ranchers must have the ability to export the goods and services the world needs to consumers around the globe. Doing that will take a concerted effort to promote American exports and remove barriers that prevent American businesses, farmers, and ranchers from selling their goods and services in growing markets abroad. It will require working with our trading partners to ensure the aggressive enforcement of international trade rules and collaborating with other leading economies to keep the global economy growing.

It also will take security and stability in regions throughout the world. Just as modern technology makes it possible for commerce to happen across the planet, it also makes it possible for remote threats—such as terrorism, pandemics, and failed states—to affect us at home. That is why it is imperative that we continue to strengthen our alliances and America's standing in the world. American leadership is indispensable in marshaling the world against many of our shared threats, such as stopping the spread of nuclear weapons; disrupting, dismantling, and defeating al Qaeda; and improving the health of and enhancing food security for the world's poorest populations and the health systems of the nations where they live. To this end, the President charged the Department of Defense (DOD) to develop a new defense strategy to guide how the United States can respond to these and other challenges in a way that helps to put our country's fiscal house in order. Across the foreign affairs budget, the Administration has made many difficult decisions so investment in key areas that commit to keeping America engaged in the world to keep our people safe and our economy strong. The Administration proposes to:

Encourage Economic Growth Through Support for the National Export Initiative as well as Investment and Tourism Promotion. A critical component of building stronger and more durable domestic economic growth is ensuring that U.S. businesses, farmers, and ranchers can actively participate in international markets by increasing their exports of goods and services. In addition to securing passage of three new free trade agreements, the Administration launched the National Export Initiative (NEI) in January 2010 with the goal of doubling U.S. exports over five years while supporting millions of new jobs. The Administration is currently on pace to meet this target—through October 2011, exports of goods and services over the preceding 12 months totaled over $2 trillion, 32 percent above 2009 levels. The NEI helps achieve this goal by enforcing trade rules and removing trade barriers abroad, by helping firms—especially small businesses—overcome the hurdles to entering new export markets, by assisting with trade financing, and by pursuing a Government-wide approach to trade promotion and advocacy abroad. To that end, the Administration provides $430 million, an increase of $19 million over 2012 levels, for the Export-Import Bank, the U.S. Trade and Development Agency, the Office of the U.S. Trade Representative, the U.S. International Trade Commission, and the Overseas Private Investment Corporation (OPIC). The Budget also provides $517 million for the Department of Commerce's International Trade Administration (ITA), an increase of $61 million over 2012 levels, to strengthen its efforts to promote exports from small businesses; help enforce domestic and

international trade rules; fight to eliminate barriers on sales of U.S. goods and services; and improve the competitiveness of U.S. firms. Among the efforts that ITA will champion through its expanded funding is SelectUSA, the first Federal program to promote and facilitate business investment in the United States. Finally, the State Department's Bureau of Consular Affairs will promote tourism and travel by expanding visa processing to the United States from the world's fastest growing economies such as Brazil and China.

Facilitate Trade and Travel and Support Border Security. The safe, secure, and speedy flow of people and products across our borders is critical to international trade and the growth of our economy. The President's Budget includes funding to maintain 21,186 Customs and Border Protection officers and 21,370 Border Patrol agents, and continue the deployment of border surveillance technology along the Southwest border. These resources will reduce wait times at our Nation's ports of entry, enhance targeting and screening of cargo coming to the United States, increase seizures of unlawful items, and continue to strengthen the security of our borders.

Strengthen Immigration Verification. The Budget proposes $132 million to enhance immigration-related verification programs at U.S. Citizenship and Immigration Services and support the nationwide deployment of E-Verify Self Check. E-Verify Self-Check is a free service that empowers individuals to check their own employment eligibility status and allows workers to protect themselves from potential workplace discrimination. Additionally, the Budget supports continued enhancements to the Systematic Alien Verification for Entitlements (SAVE) program which assists Federal, State, and local benefit-granting agencies in determining eligibility for benefits by verifying applicants' immigration status. Both SAVE and E-Verify promote compliance with immigration laws and prevent individuals from obtaining benefits they are not eligible to receive.

Transform the Legal Immigration System to Work for Employers, Immigrants, and Their Families. The United States reaps numerous and significant economic rewards because we remain a magnet for the best, brightest, and most hardworking from across the globe. Many travel here in the hopes of being a part of an American culture of entrepreneurship and ingenuity, and in turn enhance that culture, resulting in jobs for American workers. From Goya to Google, immigrant entrepreneurs and their families have long helped America lead the world. The Administration is working to reform and streamline our legal immigration system so that employers, immigrants, and families can navigate the immigration system effectively. For example, the Budget continues the multi-year effort to transition U.S. Citizenship and Immigration Services from a paper-based filing service to a customer-focused, electronic filing service. The Budget also continues support for integration of new immigrants, proposing $11 million to promote citizenship through education and naturalization preparation programs, replication of promising practices in integration for use by communities across the Nation, and expansion of innovative English learning tools. Additionally, the President will continue to insist that Congress work with the Administration to fix the broken immigration system through legislation, which is the only way to change the law so that it meets America's 21st Century economic and security needs.

Implement the New Defense Strategy. The United States of America is the greatest force for freedom and security that the world has ever known. In no small measure, that is because we have built the best-trained, best-led, best-equipped military in history. The President, as Commander-in-Chief, is committed to keeping it that way. Over the past three years, the Administration has made historic investments in our troops and their capabilities, military families, and veterans. Now, we are at an inflection point after a decade of war: American troops have left Iraq; we are undergoing a transition in Afghanistan so Afghans can assume more responsibility; and we have debilitated al Qaeda's leadership, putting that terrorist network on the path to defeat. At the same time, we have to renew our economic strength here at home, which is the foundation of our strength in the world, and that includes putting our fiscal house in order. That is why the President directed DOD to undertake a comprehensive strategic review—to ensure our defense budget is driven by a clear strategy that reflects our national interests.

There are several key elements to this strategy. We will strengthen our presence in the Asia Pacific region and continue vigilance in the Middle East. The Administration will invest in critical partnerships and alliances, including NATO, which has demonstrated time and again—most recently in Libya—that it is a force multiplier. Looking past Iraq and Afghanistan to future threats, the force will no longer be sized for large-scale, prolonged stability operations. Instead, DOD will focus modernization on emerging threats, sustaining efforts to get rid of outdated Cold War-era systems so that we can invest in the capabilities we need for the future, including intelligence, surveillance and reconnaissance. The Administration will continue to enhance capabilities related to counterterrorism and countering weapons of mass destruction. We will also maintain the ability to operate in environments where adversaries try to deny us access. And, we will keep faith with those who serve by giving priority to our wounded warriors, servicemembers' mental health, and the well-being of military families. With this strategy as a guide, over the 10 years beginning in 2012, DOD will spend $486.9 billion less than was planned in last year's Budget. The Department will realize these savings through targeted reductions in force structure and modernization; reprioritization of key missions and the requirements that support them; and continued reforms and efficiencies in acquisition, management, and other business practices.

Re-prioritize Investments in Weapons Systems. The Administration is committed to providing our servicemembers with the necessary equipment and support to meet future modernization goals. The Budget reflects continued reevaluation of the magnitude and timing of planned modernization efforts to maintain the finest military in the world—a force capable of deterring conflict, projecting power, and winning wars. For example, expensive programs such as the Joint Strike Fighter, which are designed to counter the potential threat from a sophisticated adversary, will continue, but at a reduced level. In support of the new defense strategy, where possible, DOD will continue to rely on proven existing systems rather than developing new ones, and lower-priority programs will be terminated or reduced, including the C-27 airlift aircraft, High Mobility Multi-Purpose Wheeled Vehicle Recapitalization, and a new weather satellite. In addition, the Navy will truncate the Joint High Speed Vessel program after buying 10 ships, sufficient to meet its core requirement. The Administration is committed to maintaining a healthy industrial base and will work to mitigate adverse effects on workers and industry. As these reductions are implemented, the Administration will monitor and manage the industrial base to ensure that the Nation has the ability to develop and produce the future weapons systems it needs.

Work to Defeat al Qaeda and Prevent Terrorist Attacks. Building on recent successes against al Qaeda and its leadership, defeating al Qaeda and protecting the United States from terrorist attacks remains one of the Administration's highest national security priorities. As part of the *National Strategy for Counterterrorism*, the Administration continues to strengthen counterterrorism programs and develop partner capabilities to prevent terrorist attacks on the United States and other countries. The Budget protects resources in this high-priority area and makes necessary investments to protect the homeland, defeat al Qaeda and its affiliates, build partner capacity, and prevent the development, acquisition, and use of weapons of mass destruction by terrorists.

Modernize the Nation's Nuclear Deterrent. Even as we work to reduce the number and role of nuclear weapons in our national security strategy, the Administration remains committed to enhancing the reliability of the Nation's nuclear weapons complex and supporting the goals of the Nuclear Posture Review (NPR) as the United

States and Russia implement the New Strategic Arms Reduction Treaty. DOD and the National Nuclear Security Administration are working together to refine weapons system requirements so that these systems focus on the highest-priority capabilities. The Administration also continues its commitment to sustaining and modernizing U.S. strategic delivery systems, thus ensuring an effective deterrent in the face of evolving challenges and technological developments. Moreover, the Budget provides $9.7 billion for ballistic missile defense. The Administration is committed to developing and fielding proven capabilities to defend the United States from the threat of limited ballistic missile attack, and to defend against regional ballistic missile threats to U.S. forces, allies, and partners. The United States will continue to work with our allies and partners to this end as we continue to implement the European Phased Adaptive Approach.

Prepare for Emerging Threats, Including Cyber Attacks. There are a range of emerging threats for which the United States must be prepared, from chemical and biological weapons to cyber-attacks on the Nation's critical infrastructure and information technology networks that are integral to our economy and our society. The Budget invests in a host of initiatives to improve our ability to protect the United States from these emerging threats. These initiatives include a wide spectrum of chemical, biological, radiological, and high-yield explosive (CBRNE) response programs, supporting surveillance, training, research, and response to CBRNE threats. For example, the Budget provides $96 million for Medical Countermeasures Initiative activities, which span regulatory science, strategic investment in novel technologies, and the implementation of a concept acceleration program to improve the pipeline and approval of new countermeasures against CBRNE threats; $1.2 billion for biological, chemical, radiological and nuclear defense programs, including medical countermeasures; and $180 million for global disease surveillance. In the cyber domain, the Budget sustains and enhances all aspects of DOD's cybersecurity capabilities, including defensive and offensive operations in cyberspace as directed by the President, defense of national security-critical infrastructure, and leading-edge cybersecurity science and technology efforts. Moreover, the Administration proposes $769 million to support the operations of the National Cyber Security

Division of the Department of Homeland Security, which will further strengthen the defense of The Budget for Fiscal Year 2013 Federal civilian networks through the EINSTEIN program, improve continuous monitoring on Federal networks to more quickly respond to cyber threats, and support the cyber response capabilities of State and local governments and critical infrastructure owners and operators.

Support the Military-to-Civilian Transitions in Iraq and Afghanistan, Including Continued Support to Critical Coalition Partners. After a decade of war and consistent with the U.S.-Iraq Security Agreement, the withdrawal of U.S. military forces was completed by the end of December 2011. Success in Iraq and Afghanistan requires the seamless integration and optimal balance of military and civilian power. The Budget expands civilian operational capacity to secure our military's hard fought gains, and supports programs to build the Iraqi institutions necessary for long-term stability. This includes securing Embassy Baghdad and three regional consulates in Iraq, helping Iraq develop its energy sector in a self-supporting model, and supporting efforts to help Iraq build its civilian and military capabilities. Specifically, the Budget includes funding for: a diplomatic presence to strengthen our bilateral ties with the Iraqis; a police development and rule of law program to enhance the Iraqi police force and civilian ministries; and the Office of Security Cooperation-Iraq to manage security assistance and security cooperation activities, including cooperation on counterterrorism, counter-proliferation, maritime security, and air defense. In Afghanistan, the State Department and DOD have been integrating our civilian and military missions in readiness for the drawdown of military forces. In the critical year following the gradual drawdown, the Budget supports operations necessary to fulfill our security goals while strengthening our diplomatic presence and

strategically targeting our foreign assistance. Specifically, the Budget supports our mission in Afghanistan with funding for: military operations; incremental personnel costs; force protection; repair or replacement of damaged equipment; intelligence activities; support for coalition partners; training, equipping, and sustaining the Afghan National Army and Afghan National Police; expanded diplomatic presence; and targeted assistance to support the economic strategy for Afghanistan. Funding to build Afghan capacity is a key component of the joint U.S.-Afghan plan for transitioning full responsibility for security to the Afghan government by the end of 2014.

Assist Countries in Transition and Promote Reforms in the Middle East and North Africa. Building on the Administration's significant and continuing response to the transformative events in the Middle East and North Africa (MENA) region, the Budget provides over $800 million to support political and economic reform in the region. The Budget expands our bilateral economic support in countries such as Egypt, Tunisia, and Yemen where transitions are already underway. Consistent with the President's May 2011 speech, the Budget establishes a new $770 million MENA Incentive Fund, which will provide incentives for long-term economic, political, and trade reforms to countries in transition—and to countries prepared to make reforms proactively. This new Fund builds upon other recently announced programs in the region, including up to $2 billion in regional OPIC financing commitments, up to $1 billion in debt swaps for Egypt, and approximately $500 million in existing funds re-allocated to respond to regional developments in 2011.

Make Foreign Affairs Operations More Efficient and Effective. As with all Government resources, it is critical that foreign affairs investments maximize the impact of every dollar and that we ensure that money is not wasted on the unnecessary. The State Department budget reflects a program-by-program review that identified reductions and focused resources on high-priority areas. For instance, funding in the Assistance for Europe, Eurasia and Central Asia account has been shifted into other functional assistance accounts, reflecting the successful transition of many of these countries to market democracies. This has permitted the reallocation of funds to focus on regions with the greatest assistance needs. In concert with other domestic agencies, the State Department and the U.S. Agency for International Development (USAID) will reduce spending on administrative costs, such as travel and supplies, generating significant savings when compared to 2010. USAID has also launched a far-reaching initiative to improve overseas acquisitions and contracting processes through its Implementation of Procurement Reform Initiative and has instituted a new evaluation policy that will enable the agency to expand programs that demonstrate results and curtail those that are not performing. Within one of the largest international development programs, the Global Health Initiative, the costs of commodities and service delivery continue to fall dramatically; notably, the per patient cost to the United States of providing anti-retroviral treatment for AIDS patients has fallen by over 50 percent since 2008, enabling the President to increase the global treatment target by 50 percent without increasing funding levels.

Address Root Causes of Conflict and Security Threats. In our increasingly interdependent world, failed states or regional conflicts can quickly have effects all over the world. Intense poverty, pandemics, and food insecurity all can contribute to political instability and eventually conflict. Alleviating these conditions is the right thing to do, and it is also the smart thing to do as attacking these root causes of suffering can prevent future security threats. To that end, the Budget:

- *Supports Continued Progress in Global Health by Focusing on High-Impact Interventions.* The Administration is building on recent progress in the Global Health Initiative's fight against infectious diseases and child and maternal mortality, by focusing resources on interventions that have been proven effective and continuing to push for

more integrated and efficient programming. While fiscal constraints have meant that the Administration will not meet some of its most ambitious global health goals on its original timeline, dollars are focused on areas of critical importance. The Budget supports an aggressive effort to prevent HIV infections, including the President's goal of supporting 6 million HIV patients on anti-retroviral treatment in 2013, which research has shown also has a powerful preventive effect. The Budget continues efforts to reduce maternal and child deaths through proven malaria interventions and support for a basic set of effective interventions to address maternal and child health. In addition, the Budget fully funds the balance of the Administration's historic three-year, $4 billion pledge to the Global Fund to Fight AIDS, Tuberculosis, and Malaria, in recognition of this multilateral partner's key role in global health and its progress in instituting reform, and fully funds the Administration's pledge to the Global Alliance for Vaccines and Immunizations in order to expand access to child immunization globally.

- *Fights Hunger and Invests in Economic Stability and Growth by Improving Food Security.* The Administration continues funding for agriculture development and nutrition programs as part of a multi-year plan of strategic investments to address the root causes of hunger and poverty. These programs are intended to reduce extreme poverty, increase food security, and reduce malnutrition for millions of families by 2015. The 2011 famine in the Horn of Africa underscored the importance of targeted programs that help prevent future famines and instability in the Horn and elsewhere. The Administration also maintains strong support for food aid and other humanitarian assistance, including over $4 billion to help internally-displaced persons, refugees, and victims of armed conflict and natural disasters. The Budget provides funding through bilateral assistance and a multi-donor trust fund, the Global Agriculture and Food Security Program, directing funding to poor countries that commit to policy reforms and robust country-led strategies to address internal food security needs. Assistance helps countries increase agricultural productivity, improve agricultural research and development, and expand markets and trade, while monitoring and evaluating program performance.

- *Build Resilience to Climate-Related Events by Promoting Low-Emissions Economic Development.* The Administration will continue to fund support programs that build climate resilience in communities and countries most vulnerable to extreme weather and climate events. These efforts will enhance America's security by reducing the risk of instability caused by climate stresses, including drought, famine, and rising sea levels. In addition to building climate resilience, the Budget also addresses the drivers of climate change by promoting low-emissions economic development (helping to open up markets for American clean energy goods and services in the process) and sustainable land use, as well as helping countries develop the scientific and analytic capacity and sound governance necessary to reduce climate risk.

Foster the Creation of an Advanced, Interoperable Communications System for First Responders. Today's public safety agencies largely lack access to the level of wireless capabilities used by the military and large commercial enterprises. Federal, State, and local public safety agencies largely rely on their legacy land mobile radio systems, which only provide voice communications and are often not interoperable with other local and regional systems. This fragmented system of voice only communications has left public safety organizations with 1990's technology to face the problems of a 21st Century world. To support the creation of an interoperable, 4G wireless network for public safety, the Administration is calling for a total of over $10 billion toward this effort derived from the sale and reallocation of spectrum. Specifically, the Budget

again proposes to reallocate "D Block" spectrum valued at over $3.1 billion, which will be reserved for public safety and not auctioned as called for under existing law, and provides $7 billion to support the deployment of this network, including up to $300 million to fund R&D and support for standards and technologies to ensure the network capabilities meet the mission requirements of public safety.

Care for Wounded, Ill, and Injured Servicemembers. Caring for wounded, ill, and injured servicemembers is a critical priority of the Administration. The Budget includes $49.1 billion in base and Overseas Contingency Operations (OCO) funding for the DOD Unified Medical Budget to support the Military Health System, which provides medical care for over 9.6 million eligible beneficiaries, including active duty members, military retirees, family members, dependent survivors and eligible Reserve members and their families. The Budget funds a variety of strong programs to support wounded, ill and injured servicemembers and to help servicemembers transition into civilian life and the workforce. These programs include support for wounded warrior transition units and centers of excellence in vision, hearing, traumatic brain injury, as well as other areas to continuously improve the care provided to wounded, ill, and injured servicemembers. For example, the Budget provides $33.7 billion overall for medical care; $662 million to provide care for traumatic brain injury (TBI) and psychological health; and $771.3 million for continued support of wounded, ill, and injured medical research, including psychological health and TBI/Post Traumatic Stress Disorder.

Support Military Families. The President has made supporting military families a top priority. The Budget provides $8.5 billion to support military families, sustaining funding in this important area despite the challenges of the current budget environment. The Administration is committed to improving access to military family programs, integrating services to ensure the highest impact, and pursuing efficient innovations to increase capacity and capabilities to best meet the needs of military families. Key Administration priorities include enhancing the well-being and psychological health of the military family, ensuring excellence in military children's education and their development, developing career and educational opportunities for military spouses, and increasing child care availability and quality for the Armed Forces.

Help Veterans Transition to the Workforce. America faces a significant challenge of veteran unemployment. As of December 2011, there were more than 850,000 unemployed veterans, including nearly 250,000 unemployed post-9/11 veterans. At the same time, the Administration is planning to reduce the size of the military by more than 100,000 servicemembers, beyond the normal departures, over the next five years—including tens of thousands of young veterans under the age of 25. Already, the President has signed into law new tax credits to encourage businesses to hire post-9/11 veterans and disabled veterans; created resources to help veterans translate their military skills for the civilian workforce; built new online tools to help veterans and their spouses connect with jobs; and partnered with the private sector to make it easier to connect our veterans with companies that want to hire them. Yet more needs to be done. The Administration will take steps to help veterans make the transition back to work. These include the hiring of 279 additional vocational rehabilitation and employment counselors to support the Integrated Disability Evaluation System (IDES)

and VetSuccess on Campus initiatives. IDES and VetSuccess counselors ensure that veterans, especially wounded warriors and students, receive timely information about education opportunities, job counseling, and placement assistance to successfully transition from military to civilian life. The Budget also boosts funding for the Transition Assistance Program and grants for employment services to veterans by $8 million, 5 percent over 2012 levels.

Reduce Veteran Homelessness. The President's Budget invests $1.35 billion to provide Veterans Affairs services for homeless and at-risk veterans. These funds will continue to reduce veteran homelessness through collaborative partnerships with local governments, non-profit organizations, and the Departments of Housing and Urban Development, Justice, and Labor.

Continue Implementation of the Paperless Veteran Benefit Claims System to Boost Efficiency and Responsiveness. The President's Budget includes funding to support transformation initiatives, including the continued development of a digital, near-paperless environment that allows for great exchange of information and increased transparency for veterans. The goal of the Veterans Benefit Management System is to reduce the processing time and the claim backlog, facilitate quality improvements through rules-based tools, and automate claims tracking.

DEPARTMENT OF AGRICULTURE

Funding Highlights:

- Provides $23 billion in discretionary funding, a decrease of nearly 3 percent or almost $700 million, below the 2012 enacted level. Consistent with Administration priorities, targeted investments are made in renewable energy, housing, utilities, infrastructure, rural development, and key innovation research areas. Discretionary savings are achieved through ongoing efforts to streamline operations, reduce costs, and close offices, and these savings are redirected into critical activities in recognition of tighter budget constraints.

- Modernizes service by redirecting staff to areas of greatest need without reducing or disrupting service to customers.

- Reduces the deficit by $32 billion over 10 years by eliminating direct farm payments, decreasing subsidies to crop insurance companies, and better targeting conservation funding for high priority areas.

- Invests $6.1 billion in renewable and clean energy and environmental improvements to spur the creation of high-value jobs, make America more energy independent, and drive global competitiveness in the sector.

- Increases the 2012 funding level for the Agriculture and Food Research Initiative to $325 million and targets areas that are key to American scientific leadership: human nutrition and obesity reduction; food safety; sustainable bioenergy; global food security; and climate change.

- Contributes to the job creation and economic growth goals of the White House Rural Council by continuing to fund programs that effectively promote renewable energy, job training, infrastructure investment, access to capital, worker training, and green jobs throughout rural America.

- Leverages resources and works with Federal, State, and Tribal partners to accelerate voluntary adoption of agricultural conservation practices to improve water quality.

- Provides $7 billion for the Special Supplemental Nutrition Program for Women, Infants, and Children (WIC) for low-income and nutritionally at-risk pregnant and post-partum women, infants, and children up to age 5.

- Supports State, local, and Tribal efforts to serve healthy meals and snacks to schoolchildren.

- Preserves a strong Supplemental Nutrition Assistance Program to prevent hunger for millions of Americans.

- Conserves landscapes and promotes outdoor recreation in national forests and on working lands through the America's Great Outdoors initiative.

- Continues efforts to restore significant ecosystems such as the California Bay-Delta, Everglades, the Great Lakes, Chesapeake Bay, and the Gulf Coast, helping to promote their ecological sustainability and resilience.

The U.S. Department of Agriculture (USDA) provides leadership on issues related to food, agriculture, and natural resources, including energy, based on sound public policy, the best available science, and efficient management. USDA works to expand economic opportunity through innovation in research and provides financing needed to help expand job prospects and improve housing, utilities, and infrastructure in rural America. The Department also works to promote sustainable agricultural production to protect the long-term availability of food. USDA programs safeguard and protect America's food supply by reducing the incidence of food-borne hazards from farm to table and to improve nutrition and health through food assistance and nutrition education. Internationally, USDA supports agricultural and economic development through research and technical assistance to combat chronic hunger and achieve global food security. Finally, USDA manages and protects America's public and private lands by working cooperatively with other levels of government and the private sector to preserve and conserve our Nation's natural resources through restored forests, improved watersheds, and healthy private working lands. The President's 2013 Budget provides $23 billion to support this important mission, a decrease of almost $700 million from the 2012 enacted level. While investments are made in renewable en-

ergy, rural development, and key innovative research areas, the Budget makes tough choices to meet tight discretionary caps. Deficit reduction savings are achieved by eliminating direct farm payments, decreasing subsidies to crop insurance companies, and better targeting conservation funding.

Fosters Innovation, Job Creation, and Growth

Promotes Development of Rural Renewable Energy and Homegrown Biofuels. The Administration proposes $6.1 billion in loans to rural electric cooperatives and utilities that will support the transition to a clean-energy generation and the creation of high-value jobs in rural America. Specifically, this funding will be targeted to decrease America's reliance on fossil fuels and promote renewable and clean energy at electric generation, transmission, and distribution sites in rural communities. In addition, through the Rural Energy for America Program, this Budget provides $19 million in assistance to agricultural producers and rural small businesses to complete a variety of projects, including renewable energy systems, energy efficiency improvements, and renewable energy development. Finally, the Administration proposes over $200 million to continue support for the development of home-grown, advanced biofuels that have the potential to reduce America's dependence on foreign oil and to bolster our rural economies.

Spurs American Innovation by Advancing Priority Research. USDA research has played a key role in spurring innovation and advancing technology that has allowed American agriculture to increase in both efficiency and profitability. At the same time, the Administration recognizes that continued fiscal constraint requires trade-offs to focus resources on only the most important priorities. Therefore, the President's Budget proposes $325 million—a $60 million increase above the 2012 enacted level—for competitive research grants made through the Agriculture and Food Research Initiative. The Budget also increases in-house research in select areas such as crop protection, sustainable agriculture, and food safety by $75 million, and fully funds the Census of Agriculture. Consistent with Administration-wide efforts to create additional savings, the Agricultural Research Service is reallocating $70 million from lower priority projects.

Promotes Infrastructure and Community Development. The Budget supports economic growth in rural areas by funding loan programs that effectively promote infrastructure investment and access to capital throughout rural America. For instance, in order to provide support for projects in low income rural areas, the President's Budget includes a $700 million increase in the community facility program's direct loan level, a program that funds a wide array of rural projects, including schools, hospitals, day care facilities, and fire and police stations. In addition, the Budget also provides $24 billion in guaranteed single-family housing loans, which will support mortgage lending institutions in rural areas and boost home ownership among moderate-to low-income rural residents.

Prevents Hunger and Supports Healthy Eating

Prevents Hunger. At a time of continued need, the President's Budget provides $7.5 billion for discretionary nutrition program support. Funding supports the 9.1 million individuals expected to participate in the Special Supplemental Nutrition Program for Women, Infants, and Children (WIC), which is critical to the health of pregnant women, new mothers, and their infants. The Administration also reproposes to continue certain temporary Supplemental Nutrition Assistance Program (SNAP) benefits. SNAP is the cornerstone of our Nation's food assistance safety net and touches the lives of more than 46 million people. The Administration is committed to preventing hunger by preserving access to SNAP for all eligible participants.

Supports Healthy Eating. The Administration supports continued implementation of the Healthy, Hunger-Free Kids Act of 2010, strengthening the child nutrition programs and increasing children's access to healthy meals and snacks.

Makes Tough Choices with Targeted Reductions

Responsibly Reduces Farm Spending. Government payments to farmers are expected to total $10.6 billion in 2011. Roughly $4.7 billion—or 44 percent—of these payments are in the form of a "direct payment"—payments that do not vary with current prices or crop yields and for which a crop is not necessarily produced. As part of the strategy to confront our fiscal challenges in a thoughtful and responsible manner the Budget includes $32 billion in savings over 10 years by eliminating direct farm payments, providing disaster assistance, reducing subsidies to crop insurance companies, and better targeting conservation funding, consistent with the Administration's deficit reduction proposal. These proposals are sound policy and prudent steps that the Administration believes are necessary to put the country on a fiscally sustainable path.

Targets the Direct Single Family Housing Loan Program. The Budget proposes $653 million for the direct single family housing loan program, a significant reduction from an enacted amount of $900 million, and proposes to provide single family housing assistance primarily through loan guarantees. The reduced level represents a minimum level to allow targeted support for teachers in rural areas and beneficiaries of the mutual self-help housing program, along with other very-low and low income individuals in rural areas still needing mortgage credit assistance despite historically low interest rates.

Improves the Way Federal Dollars are Spent

Modernizes Service. Consistent with Administration-wide efforts, USDA agencies are reshaping the way that they do business, without sacrificing services to the public. In 2012, the Department began an effort to streamline operations and reduce cost, including closing about 260 offices. In some cases, staff will be redirected to areas of greatest need; in others, advances in technology have reduced the need for brick and mortar facilities. Building upon this effort, in 2013 the Forest Service proposes to create efficiencies and redirect savings toward more on-the-ground projects. Finally, the Department is further streamlining its staff through both Department-wide early retirement and targeted buyouts offered by more than 15 agencies and offices. As a result of these and other efficiencies the Budget proposes about 900 fewer staff positions for USDA than in 2012.

Improves Forest Conservation Outcomes by Using Landscape Scale Strategies. The President's Budget continues to emphasize the Forest Service's ability to restore our Nation's forests through landscape scale efforts. These efforts include: targeting scarce resources to on-the-ground activities; implementing a comprehensive approach to restoration and maintenance of sustainable landscapes; streamlining programs to improve forest management efficiency; reducing wildfire risk; and expanding efforts to maximize collaborative efforts including public-private partnerships. Together, these changes will make better use of available resources and increase the resilience and health of our Nation's forests.

Protects Communities and Ecosystems from Wildfire Damage. The Budget continues the long-standing practice of fully funding the 10-year average cost of wildland fire suppression operations. The Budget also continues the practice of targeting hazardous fuels reduction funding for activities near communities (known as the "wildland-urban interface") where they are most effective. Priority is given to projects in communities that have met "Firewise" standards (or the equivalent), identified acres to be treated, and invested in local solutions to protect against wildland fire.

Enhances Interagency Efforts to Improve Water Quality. The United States has made great strides in improving water quality; however, "nonpoint" source pollution remains a significant economic, environmental and public health challenge that requires policy attention and thoughtful new approaches. Key Federal partners, along with agricultural producer organizations, conservation districts, States, Tribes, non-governmental organizations and other local leaders will work together to identify areas where a focused and coordinated approach can achieve substantial improvements in water quality. The President's Budget builds upon the collaborative process already underway among Federal partners to demonstrate substantial improvements in water quality from conservation programs by ensuring that USDA's key investments through Farm Bill conservation programs and related efforts are appropriately leveraged by other Federal programs.

Department of Agriculture
(In millions of dollars)

	Actual 2011	Estimate	
		2012	2013
Spending			
Discretionary Budget Authority:			
Commodities and International	3,662	3,521	3,472
Rural Development	2,572	2,404	2,402
Forest Service	4,694	4,608	4,861
Conservation	898	851	827
Food and Nutrition Service	6,585	7,420	7,495
Research	2,361	2,536	2,604
Marketing and Regulatory Programs	2,001	1,945	1,879
Central Administration	494	509	589
Subtotal, Discretionary budget authority	23,267	23,794	24,129
Discretionary Changes in Mandatory Programs *(non-add in 2012)*[1]		−2,372	−906
Receipts and Collections:			
User Fees/Receipts	−103	−139	−266
Total, Discretionary budget authority[2]	23,164	23,655	22,957
Discretionary Cap Adjustment:[3]			
Disaster Relief	—	367	—
Total, Discretionary outlays	27,021	28,752	26,805
Mandatory Outlays:			
Food and Nutrition Service	94,689	104,660	102,731
Commodity Credit Corporation	10,276	10,009	12,055
Crop Insurance	6,387	3,753	9,162
Natural Resources Conservation Service	2,628	3,076	3,362
Agricultural Marketing Service	1,167	1,203	1,321
Forest Service	688	720	655
Rural Development liquidating accounts	−2,706	−1,236	−1,167
Receipts, reestimates and all other programs	−748	−251	−416
Total, Mandatory outlays	112,381	121,934	127,703
Total, Outlays	139,402	150,686	154,508

Department of Agriculture—Continued
(In millions of dollars)

	Actual 2011	Estimate	
		2012	2013
Credit activity			
Direct Loan Disbursements:			
Farm Loans	1,934	2,023	1,936
Commodity Credit Corporation	7,103	7,332	7,873
Rural Utilities Service	7,020	9,591	10,051
Rural Housing Service	2,144	2,250	2,111
All other programs	45	97	88
Total, Direct loan disbursements	18,246	21,293	22,059
Guaranteed Loan Disbursements by Private Lenders:			
Farm Loans	3,060	3,097	3,097
Commodity Credit Corporation	4,767	5,500	5,500
Rural Housing Service	15,295	24,433	24,149
Rural Business Service	1,820	1,385	1,292
All other programs	3	12	18
Total, Guaranteed loan disbursements by private lenders	24,945	34,427	34,056

[1] The 2012 amounts reflect OMB's scoring of the 2012 Appropriations acts (P.L. 112-55 and 112-74) as transmitted to the Congress. These amounts are displayed as non-add entries because they have been rebased as mandatory and are not included in any 2012 discretionary levels in the 2013 Budget.

[2] Includes funding for International Food Aid programs in the Department of Agriculture (Food for Peace Title II food aid and the McGovern-Dole International Food for Education and Child Nutrition). Funding for these programs are included in International Function 150, and are classified as Security pursuant to Title I of the Budget Control Act of 2011.

[3] The Balanced Budget and Emergency Deficit Control Act of 1985 (BBEDCA), as amended by the Budget Control Act of 2011, limits—or caps—budget authority available for discretionary programs each year through 2021. Section 251(b)(2) of BBEDCA authorizes certain adjustments to the caps after the enactment of appropriations.

DEPARTMENT OF COMMERCE

Funding Highlights:

- Provides $8 billion for Commerce programs through regular appropriations, an increase of 5 percent, or approximately $380 million above the 2012 level. This reflects continued strong support for key drivers of job creation, innovation, and the promotion of U.S. exports, as well as investments in critical satellite programs. Reductions are made to administrative costs and grant programs that overlap with activities funded elsewhere.

- Reduces administrative costs across bureaus to focus funding on core missions, and makes tough fiscal choices by reducing funding for public works and coastal habitat grants that overlap with other Federal programs.

- Enhances the competitiveness of U.S. manufacturers by providing $708 million for the National Institute of Standards and Technology laboratories, $128 million in the Hollings Manufacturing Extension Partnership, and $21 million for Advanced Manufacturing Technology Consortia, to develop measurements, standards, and technologies to support advanced manufacturing, robotics, nanotechnology, and cybersecurity.

- Increases resources for the U.S. Patent and Trademark Office, which will continue on its path to accelerate patent processing and improve patent quality.

- Promotes U.S. exports and export-related jobs by providing $517 million for the International Trade Administration, to better promote American exports in key markets abroad and improve trade enforcement; and for SelectUSA, to strengthen efforts to attract investment capital to the United States.

- Provides over $5 billion for the National Oceanic and Atmospheric Administration, an increase of approximately $160 million, to support critical weather and climate satellite programs and the agency's core responsibilities for environmental science and stewardship, including implementation of the National Ocean Policy.

- Provides over $10 billion of mandatory budget resources to help build an interoperable public safety broadband network that will strengthen economic growth and public safety, while benefitting from commercial innovation. These costs are fully offset by proceeds from auctioning spectrum that will be used to expand wireless broadband access and services.

- Invests in regional economic competitiveness by providing $220 million to the Economic Development Administration to support innovative planning, capacity building, and capital projects.

- Sustains critical economic and household data collection activities, such as the 2012 Economic Census and the American Community Survey, to inform private and public sector decision-making.

The Department of Commerce has a wide range of missions in the areas of international trade and domestic economic development; technology and innovation; demographic and economic statistics; and environmental science, stewardship and weather forecasting. As a group, these missions focus on expanding the American economy and job creation as well as providing critical environmental information. While there are tight constraints on discretionary spending, the President's 2013 Budget supports core functions in these areas by providing $8 billion for Commerce programs. This represents an increase of approximately $380 million from the 2012 level. Specifically, strong support is provided for critical satellite programs and public safety communications as well as trade promotion and enforcement. At the same time, to free up resources, reductions are made to administrative costs and grant programs that overlap with funding available elsewhere.

Invests in America's Long-Term Growth and Competitiveness

Enhances U.S. Competitiveness and Fosters Innovation. The Administration proposes $708 million for National Institute of Standards and Technology (NIST) laboratories as part of the President's Plan for Science and Innovation, $86 million above the 2012 enacted level. NIST's work in developing measurements and technologies supports U.S. industry's ability to innovate and develop new products. This funding will accelerate advances in a variety of important areas, ranging from next-generation robotics and smart manufacturing to nanotechnology and

cybersecurity. The Budget includes $21 million for a new Advanced Manufacturing Technology Consortia program, a public-private partnership that will support road maps and research to address common manufacturing challenges faced by private sector businesses. The Budget also proposes to provide the U.S. Patent and Trademark Office (USPTO) full access to its fee collections, which will support a program level of $2.95 billion or nearly $250 million more than in 2012, while strengthening USPTO's efforts to improve the speed and quality of patent examinations.

Promotes American Exports. The President has set the goal of doubling American exports by the end of 2014. To that end, the Administration proposes $517 million for the International Trade Administration (ITA) to continue to implement the National Export Initiative, a broad Federal strategy to increase U.S. exports and export related jobs. This funding will allow ITA's to increase its export promotion efforts in key, growing markets abroad, strengthen trade enforcement, and support the activities of SelectUSA, which helps attract investment capital to the United States that creates jobs.

Sustains Satellites Used for Weather Forecasting and Climate Monitoring. The Budget provides $1.8 billion to continue the development and acquisition of the National Oceanic and Atmospheric Administration's (NOAA's) polar-orbiting and geostationary weather satellite systems, as well as satellite-borne measurements of sea level and potentially damaging solar storms. These satellites are critical to NOAA's ability to provide accurate weather forecasts and warnings that help to protect lives and property.

Prioritizes Science and Stewardship Missions. The Budget provides an increase for NOAA's National Marine Fisheries Service and targets spending on data collection and stock assessments. Overfishing and resulting restrictions can be avoided with adequate stock assessments, and these funds will lead to more accurate data for our Nation's fisheries. The Budget will also improve the accuracy of regional projections of sea level rise and climate change and accelerate the implementation of the National Ocean Policy through multi-purpose integrated ecosystem assessments.

Invests Spectrum Proceeds to Build a Public Safety Broadband Network and Increase Wireless Access. As proposed in the American Jobs Act, the Budget supports a National Wireless Initiative that would provide $10 billion in total resources from spectrum auction proceeds to help build an interoperable public safety broadband network. The initiative includes $7 billion in funding for development and construction of the network, and additional spectrum valued at over $3 billion (the "D block" of spectrum in the 700 megahertz band) for public safety use. Within the $7 billion, up to $300 million will be provided for a Wireless Innovation Fund to develop technologies and a standards framework for interoperable first responder communications. Building upon the recommendations of the National Commission on Terrorist Attacks Upon the United States, this effort will enhance public safety by providing America's first responders modern and efficient communications capabilities while allowing the network to benefit from commercial innovation. The National Wireless Initiative also proposes to reallocate Federal agency and commercial spectrum bands to greatly increase wireless broadband access and innovation opportunities nationwide using auctions, and to authorize use of a spectrum license user fee for licenses not allocated via auctions to promote efficient utilization of spectrum. Together, these proposals are expected to reduce the deficit by $21 billion over the next 10 years.

Enhances Regional Economic Competitiveness. The Budget provides $220 million, a reduction of $38 million from the 2012 enacted level, to the Economic Development Administration (EDA). The Budget supports economic development planning and projects that catalyze entrepreneurship and innovation at the regional scale, but conserves resources by trimming the amount requested for traditional public works projects, which are often funded using tax-free bonds or other Federal programs.

Sustains Statistical Programs and Core Data Products. Commerce provides policymakers, businesses, and the public critical economic and household data to inform decision-making. The Budget proposes $970 million for the Census Bureau to implement activities including the 2012 Economic Census data collection; conduct the American Community Survey; and analyze the integrity of the 2010 Decennial Census and research improvements for the 2020 Census. Funding for the Bureau of Economic Analysis supports reliable and timely economic data, including Gross Domestic Product estimates that are among America's most closely-watched economic indicators.

Reforms the U.S. Export Control System. The Budget provides the Bureau of Industry and Security with $102 million to sustain export licensing and enforcement activities, including $6 million to meet its increased responsibilities under the Administration's Export Control Reform Initiative. Continued progress of the Reform Initiative will advance our national security and economic competitiveness by better focusing U.S. controls on transactions to destinations or end users of concern while facilitating secure trade for controlled items with U.S. allies and close partners.

Makes Tough Cuts

Terminates Non-Essential Programs. The Department supports a wide variety of programs aimed at spurring growth and competitiveness, and as our economy evolves, so must these programs. The Budget proposes to reduce funding for EDA grant programs, such as the Public Works program and the Global Climate Change Mitigation Incentive Fund, that overlap with programs in other agencies. The Budget reduces funding for conservation grants that are similar to programs in other agencies.

Cuts Administrative Costs. The Department will trim its administrative costs by at least $34 million through efficiencies in acquisitions, human capital, logistics, general administration, and information technology. This builds on savings of $142 million that the Department is implementing in 2012, for a total annual reduction of $176 million annually beginning in 2013.

Department of Commerce
(In millions of dollars)

	Actual 2011	Estimate 2012	Estimate 2013
Spending			
Discretionary Budget Authority:			
Departmental Management			
Salaries and Expenses	58	57	56
Steel Loan Program	−48	−1	—
HCHB Renovation	15	5	2
Office of the Inspector General	27	30	31
Subtotal, Departmental Management	52	91	89
Economic Development Administration (EDA)			
Salaries and Expenses	38	38	38
Economic Development Assistance Programs	246	220	182
Subtotal, EDA	284	258	220
Bureau of the Census			
Salaries and Expenses	258	253	259
Periodic Censuses and Programs	−894	689	711
Subtotal, Bureau of the Census	−686	887	970
Economics and Statistics Administration	97	96	100
International Trade Administration	444	455	517
Bureau of Industry and Security	103	101	102
Minority Business Development Agency	30	30	29

Department of Commerce—Continued
(In millions of dollars)

	Actual 2011	Estimate	
		2012	2013
National Oceanic and Atmospheric Administration			
Operations, Research and Facilities	3,245	3,131	3,161
Procurement, Acquisition and Construction	1,400	1,816	1,966
Other Accounts	82	67	52
Subtotal, National Oceanic and Atmospheric Administration	4,727	5,014	5,179
Patent and Trademark Office			
Program Level	2,016	2,705	2,951
Fees	−2,225	−2,706	−2,953
Subtotal, Patent and Trademark Office	−209	−1	−2
National Institute of Standards and Technology (NIST)			
Scientific and Technical Research Services	502	577	651
Industrial Technology Services	182	128	149
Advanced Manufacturing Technology Consortia (non-add)	—	—	*21*
Manufacturing Extension Partnership (non-add)	*128*	*128*	*128*
Construction of Research Facilities	70	56	60
Subtotal, NIST	754	761	860
National Telecommunications and Information Administration (NTIA)			
Salaries and Expenses	43	46	47
Rescissions	−5	−5	—
Subtotal, NTIA	38	41	47
Subtotal, Discretionary budget authority	5,629	7,726	8,109
Discretionary Changes in Mandatory Programs *(non-add in 2012):*[1]			
Promotion and Development of Fisheries		*−103*	−119
Digital Television and Public Safety Fund		*−4*	—
All other		*−6*	—
Subtotal, Discretionary changes in mandatory programs		*−113*	−119
Total, Discretionary budget authority	5,629	7,726	7,990
Discretionary Cap Adjustment:[2]			
Disaster Relief	—	200	—
Total, Discretionary outlays	9,579	10,856	9,533
Mandatory Outlays:			
Digital Television Transition and Public Safety Fund	334	309	5
National Wireless Initiative Legislative Proposal[3]			−923

Department of Commerce—Continued
(In millions of dollars)

	Actual 2011	Estimate	
		2012	2013
All other			
Existing law	28	162	172
Legislative proposal			208
Total, Mandatory outlays	362	471	−538
Total, Outlays	9,941	11,327	8,995
Credit activity			
Direct Loan Disbursements:			
Fisheries Finance Direct Loan Financing account	56	90	58
Total, Direct loan disbursements	56	90	58
Guaranteed Loan Disbursements by Private Lenders:			
Economic Development Assistance Programs account	—	65	39
Total, Guaranteed loan disbursements by private lenders	—	65	39

[1] The 2012 amounts reflect OMB's scoring of the 2012 Appropriations acts (P.L. 112-55 and 112-74) as transmitted to the Congress. These amounts are displayed as non-add entries because they have been rebased as mandatory and are not included in any 2012 discretionary levels in the 2013 Budget.
[2] The Balanced Budget and Emergency Deficit Control Act of 1985 (BBEDCA), as amended by the Budget Control Act of 2011, limits—or caps—budget authority available for discretionary programs each year through 2021. Section 251(b)(2) of BBEDCA authorizes certain adjustments to the caps after the enactment of appropriations.
[3] Outlays are negative for this initiative because incoming receipts are expected to be greater than outlays in 2013.

DEPARTMENT OF DEFENSE

Funding Highlights:

- Provides $525.4 billion in discretionary funding for the base Department of Defense budget, a decrease of 1 percent, or $5.1 billion, below the 2012 enacted level. This will provide the necessary resources to implement the President's new defense strategy, keep our military the finest in the world by investing in priorities, and help achieve $486.9 billion in savings by 2021.

- Reprioritizes investments in weapons programs to reflect the new strategy, provide service members with state of the art equipment, and maintain the industrial base. This includes making investments in high-priority programs, such as unmanned surveillance aircraft and upgraded tactical vehicles, while terminating unnecessary and lower-priority programs such as the C-27 airlift aircraft and a new weather satellite and maintaining programs such as the Joint Strike Fighter at a reduced level.

- Maintains ready forces for the full range of contingencies, including sustaining a robust counterterrorism capability, and continues to invest in our critical alliances, including NATO.

- Keeps faith with servicemembers by protecting well-deserved benefits for active duty personnel and their families, provides support for servicemembers returning from war, and at a time of tight discretionary caps, finds the resources to give the military the full pay increase as authorized by law.

- Continues strong support for servicemembers and military families—including access to medical care for over 9.6 million servicemembers, retirees, and their families—and takes steps to modernize military health and retirement systems.

- Enhances the Administration's commitment to maintain a reliable nuclear deterrent by increasing investments in the nuclear weapons complex and in weapon delivery technologies, and to nonproliferation by investing in securing, detecting, and neutralizing nuclear threats around the world.

- Reshapes and resizes military forces to ensure the size, balance, and flexibility to preserve core capabilities and meet future challenges.

- Continues to focus on acquisition reforms and management efficiencies, such as the consolidation of numerous data centers, to achieve savings.

- Invests in long-term scientific and technological innovation to ensure that the Nation has access to the best defense systems available in the world. High-priority research and development areas include: advanced manufacturing, cybersecurity, and autonomous systems.

The United States of America is the greatest force for freedom and security that the world has ever known. In no small measure, that is because we have built the best-trained, best-led, best-equipped military in history. The President, as Commander-in-Chief, is committed to keeping it that way. Over the past three years, we have made historic investments in our troops and their capabilities, military families, and veterans. Now, we are at an inflection point after a decade of war: American troops have left Iraq; we are undergoing a transition in Afghanistan so Afghans can assume more responsibility; and we have decimated al Qaeda's leadership, putting that terrorist network on the path to defeat.

At the same time, we have to renew our economic strength here at home, which is the foundation of our strength in the world, and that includes putting our fiscal house in order. That is why the President directed the Department of Defense (DOD) to undertake a comprehensive strategic review so that our defense budget is driven by a clear strategy that reflects our national interests.

There are several key elements to this strategy. To sustain a global presence, DOD will strengthen its presence in the Asia Pacific region and continue vigilance in the Middle East. The Administration will also invest in critical partnerships and alliances, including NATO, which has demonstrated time and again—most recently in Libya—that it is a force multiplier. Looking past Iraq and Afghanistan to future threats, the force will no longer be sized for large-scale, prolonged stability operations. Instead, DOD will focus modernization on emerging threats, sustaining efforts to get rid of outdated Cold War-era systems so that we can invest in

the capabilities we need for the future, including intelligence, surveillance and reconnaissance. The Administration will continue to enhance capabilities related to counterterrorism and countering weapons of mass destruction. We will also maintain the ability to operate in environments where adversaries try to deny us access. And, we will keep faith with those who serve by giving priority to our wounded warriors, servicemembers' mental health, and the well-being of military families.

With this strategy as a guide, over the 10 years beginning in 2012, DOD will spend $486.9 billion less than was planned in last year's Budget. The Department will realize these savings through targeted reductions in force structure and modernization; reprioritization of key missions and the requirements that support them; and continued reforms and efficiencies in acquisition, management, and other business practices. From the 2012 enacted level, base defense spending will fall by 1 percent to $525.4 billion in 2013, while DOD Overseas Contingency Operations funding will fall by 23 percent (these costs are addressed in a separate chapter). However, over the next 10 years, the base budget will grow modestly.

Invests in Critical Areas to Implement New Defense Strategy

Funds Military Readiness and Training. The Administration is committed to providing servicemembers with the equipment and resources they need to respond to the complex and often unconventional threats posed by today's security environment. The Budget provides $176.2 billion to support the operations, training, and maintenance needed for our troops to meet current and future threats.

Provides Needed Weapons Systems for Challenges of Today and Tomorrow. The Budget continues to invest in the weapons systems needed by our Armed Forces to meet the challenges laid out by the new defense strategy. For example, the Budget provides $3.7 billion to fund unmanned air surveillance systems, such as the Predator and Reaper, which provide critical and timely intelligence to our troops on the ground in Afghanistan and other operational areas. In addition, the Budget provides $2 billion for upgrading tactical vehicles including the newest and most effective version of armor protection, and $4.1 billion for the Virginia class submarine program that will improve the Navy's ability to operate in coastal waters and support special operations forces.

Secures Defense Information Networks from Intrusion. Preparing for emerging threats includes being able to operate across the full spectrum in cyberspace. The Budget sustains and enhances all aspects of DOD's cybersecurity capabilities. It also funds DOD's support for the Department of Homeland Security's (DHS's) cybersecurity efforts to protect the Federal Government's unclassified civilian information technology networks and improve the security of U.S. critical infrastructure. Funding allows DOD to invest in improving capabilities to implement the DOD Strategy for Operating in Cyberspace; conducting the full spectrum of operations, including defending the Nation's networks as directed by the President; and supporting the defense of infrastructure that is critical to national security.

The Budget sustains funding for U.S. Cyber Command to conduct its cyber mission and lead efforts to secure the Department's networks. The Budget also funds leading edge cybersecurity science and technology efforts, and cybersecurity pilot efforts (in partnership with DHS) to determine how best to protect critical information infrastructures owned and operated by the private sector.

Works to Defeat al Qaeda and Prevent Terrorist Attacks. Building on recent successes against al Qaeda and its leadership, protecting the United States from terrorist attacks and defeating al Qaeda remain the Administration's highest national security priorities. As part of the *National Strategy for Counterterrorism*, the Administration continues to strengthen counterterrorism programs and develop partner capabilities to prevent terrorist attacks on the United States and other countries. The Budget protects resources in this high-priority area and makes necessary investments to protect the homeland; defeat al Qaeda and its affiliates; build partner capacity; and prevent the development, acquisition, and use of weapons of mass destruction by terrorists.

Deters and Counters the Spread of Weapons of Mass Destruction. DOD continues to pursue a comprehensive strategy to reduce the risk of intentional nuclear, biological, chemical, and radiation related attacks. The Budget helps to counter the challenge of weapons of mass destruction by funding improved infrastructure and modernization of detection, neutralization, and treatment capabilities. Additionally, the Administration will enhance international stability by reducing the risks of global nuclear proliferation. The Budget continues the President's global lockdown initiative to secure nuclear materials worldwide within four years, detect and deter nuclear testing and smuggling, and support verification and implementation of international nonproliferation treaties.

Modernizes the Nation's Nuclear Deterrent. Even as we work to reduce the number and role of nuclear weapons in our national security strategy, the Administration remains committed to modernizing the Nation's nuclear weapons complex and supporting the goals of the Nuclear Posture Review (NPR) as the United States and Russia implement the New Strategic Arms Reduction Treaty. DOD and the National Nuclear Security Administration (NNSA) are working together to refine weapons system requirements so that these systems focus on the highest-priority capabilities. While still meeting the NPR goals, DOD and NNSA are reducing the scope and stretching out the schedule of several warhead weapons life extension programs, and are restructuring plans for maintaining plutonium capabilities to stay within the discretionary spending caps set in the Balanced Budget and Emergency Deficit Control Act of 1985, as amended by the Budget Control Act of 2011. Reflecting their close partnership and shared commitment, DOD has included in its outyear budget a portion of future funding for NNSA, with allocations to be made to NNSA within each budget year.

The Administration also continues its commitment to sustaining and modernizing U.S. strategic delivery systems, thus ensuring an effective deterrent in the face of evolving challenges and technological developments. This includes specific commitments to maintain continuous at-sea deployments of ballistic missile submarines in the Atlantic and Pacific Oceans, as well as the ability to surge additional submarines during crises; procure the lead ship for the OHIO Replacement program in 2021; sustain the Air Force's Minuteman III missile through 2030; and modernize the heavy bomber force so it can serve for the indefinite future.

Finally, the Budget includes $9.7 billion for ballistic missile defense. The Administration is committed to developing and fielding proven capabilities to defend the United States from the threat of limited ballistic missile attack, and to defend against regional ballistic missile threats to U.S. forces and U.S. allies and partners. These capabilities must be flexible enough to adapt as the ballistic missile threats change. In Europe, the United States is focused on addressing near-term threats from short- and medium-range ballistic missiles, and is working with our NATO allies to this end as we continue to implement the European Phased Adaptive Approach.

Cares for Servicemembers and Their Families. Keeping faith with servicemembers—which the President has called a "moral obligation"—is a key component of the new defense strategy. The high quality and readiness of our All-Volunteer Force is the Nation's most important military advantage, so it is critical that military members and their families receive the compensation and benefits that they deserve. The Budget provides a 1.7 percent increase to basic pay in calendar year 2013, the full increase authorized by current law.

The Administration prioritizes the care of servicemembers and their families by providing $48.7 billion for the DOD Unified Medical Budget to support the Military Health System, which provides medical care for over 9.6 million eligible beneficiaries. The Budget continues strong programs to support wounded, ill and injured servicemembers and to help servicemembers transition into civilian life and the workforce.

The Administration is committed to improving access to military family programs, integrating services to ensure the highest impact, and pursuing innovations to better reach and serve military families. Key Administration priorities include enhancing the well-being and psychological health of military families, ensuring excellence in military children's education, developing career and educational opportunities for military spouses, and ensuring child care availability and quality for the Armed Forces.

The Budget emphasizes our commitment to honor those who have served the Nation and to maintain the hallowed grounds where they are laid to rest. In 2013, the Army will provide $128 million for Arlington National Cemetery improvements. These funds will be combined with the $46 million requested directly for Arlington National Cemetery to almost quadruple support for planning and construction to extend burial availability, strengthen accounting and gravesite accountability systems, and improve service to families.

Funds Research and Development for the Military of the Future. The Administration will continue its strong commitment to funding the Nation's long-term scientific and technical needs, including those for national security. Accordingly, the Budget proposes $69.4 billion for research, development, test, and evaluation, including $11.9 billion for early-stage science and technology programs, focusing our efforts on those projects most likely to enhance our capability to respond to new threats. The Budget invests in the Defense Advanced Research Projects Agency and department-wide basic research slightly above the 2012 enacted levels. Such investments will allow the Nation to explore diverse scientific principles and technological applications, including bio-defense, cybersecurity, information access, and cleaner and more efficient energy use, robotics, and advanced computing. Funding in this area will also capitalize on the role that DOD plays in advanced manufacturing by establishing a number of public-private partnerships in targeted technologies to expedite their development and production. DOD-funded research provides future options for new defense systems, helps the Nation avoid a technological surprise by potential adversaries, results in cost savings by solving technical problems early in the life cycle of acquisition programs, and takes advantage of emerging technical opportunities. The funding proposed in the Budget will be awarded through competitive processes, with experts guiding the choices of research topics to be undertaken, and reviewing and selecting projects for funding based on proposals submitted by universities, non-profit organizations, for-profit companies, and Government laboratories.

Cuts and Reforms Spending to Reflect the New Defense Strategy

Resizes and Reshapes Military Forces. In response to the President's direction to conduct a fresh review of its roles, missions, and capabilities, DOD is resizing and reshaping U.S. military forces to meet future challenges and preserve core assets while retaining the ability to regenerate lower priority capabilities as necessary. The Administration is committed to supporting properly sized, balanced, and flexible forces that will continue to be the core of our dominant and capable military power. The Budget preserves core military capabilities and better integrates active and reserve forces to provide a smaller but more agile military force that will remain a strong deterrent against our adversaries. Re-

flecting this reduced end strength and the new defense strategy, DOD will eliminate several Brigade Combat Teams, as well as 130 transport aircraft and seven cruisers, over the next five years. At the same time, DOD will manage the force in ways that protect its ability to regenerate capabilities that may be needed to address emergent demands, sustaining the intellectual capital and rank structure to facilitate the expansion of key elements of the force if required.

Reassesses Base Structure. The force structure that emerges from the new defense strategy will require a properly aligned infrastructure from which to operate, deploy, and train. The Budget requests the authority for DOD to commence two additional rounds of base realignment and closure (BRAC) and to establish an independent Commission that will provide an objective, thorough, and non-partisan review and analysis of DOD's recommendations. While this is a difficult process, additional rounds of BRAC will enable DOD to align infrastructure to meet the needs of a leaner, more agile, and flexible force.

Adjusts Health Care Benefits and Initiates Retirement Review. DOD has implemented a variety of internal efficiencies within its medical program and continues to seek cost savings, but it is imperative to better manage the health benefit. The Budget introduces new TRICARE copays and fees to help constrain the cost of healthcare while continuing to provide high quality care. The Budget includes additional increases to TRICARE Prime enrollment fees, initiation of Standard/ Extra annual enrollment fees, and adjustments to deductibles and catastrophic caps. The Budget also modifies pharmacy copays to encourage the use of less expensive mail-order and military treatment facility pharmacies. Finally, the Budget includes modest annual fees for TRICARE beneficiaries over age 65 when they transition to Medicare coverage. These reforms will reduce DOD costs over five years by an estimated $12.9 billion in discretionary funding and $4.7 billion in mandatory savings in the Medicare-Eligible Retiree Health Care Fund.

The Budget also includes the Administration's proposal for a Military Retirement Modernization Commission, which, if enacted, will recommend improvements to the military retirement system. Under the proposal, the President would appoint the Commissioners; DOD would transmit to the Commission initial recommendations to change the military retirement system; the Commission would hold hearings, make final recommendations, and draft legislation to implement its recommendations; the President would review and decide whether to transmit the Commission's recommendations to the Congress; and Congress would vote "up or down" on the legislation. The Administration believes that any major military retirement reforms should include grandfathering for current retirees and those currently serving in the military.

Reprioritizes Investments in Weapons Systems. The Administration is committed to providing our servicemembers with the necessary equipment and support to meet future modernization goals. The Budget reflects continued reevaluation of the magnitude and timing of planned modernization efforts to maintain the finest military in the world—a force capable of deterring conflict, projecting power, and winning wars. For example, expensive programs such as the Joint Strike Fighter, which are designed to counter the potential threat from a sophisticated adversary, will continue but at a reduced level. In support of the new defense strategy, where possible, DOD will continue to rely on proven existing systems rather than developing new ones, and lower-priority programs will be terminated or reduced, including the C-27 airlift aircraft, High Mobility Multi-Purpose Wheeled Vehicle Recapitalization, and a new weather satellite. In addition, the Navy will truncate the Joint High Speed Vessel program after buying 10 ships, sufficient to meet its core requirement. The Administration is committed to maintaining a healthy industrial base and will work to mitigate adverse effects on workers and industry. As these reductions are implemented, the Administration will monitor and manage the industrial base to ensure that the Nation has the ability to develop and produce the future weapons systems it needs.

Reforms Acquisition. DOD contracts account for approximately 70 percent of all Federal procurement. The Budget requests $280 billion for DOD contracts in 2013. Through its "Better Buying Power" acquisition reform initiative, DOD is charting a new path that will result in greater efficiency and productivity throughout the defense acquisition system. In particular, DOD is: 1) decreasing the use of high-risk contracts based on time-and-materials and labor-hours; 2) continuing to develop the acquisition workforce to provide needed oversight; 3) eliminating or restructuring lower-priority acquisitions; 4) reducing contract spending on management support services; 5) taking full advantage of contract vehicles that reflect the Government's buying leverage; 6) increasing the use of strategic sourcing; 7) increasing small business participation; and 8) improving financial management systems. In addition, DOD has instituted a number of acquisition management best practices: applying lessons learned from past acquisitions; establishing process teams to review qualifications of acquisition professionals; and instituting peer reviews to ensure affordability and effective competition.

Improves Business Processes. The Budget supports DOD's ongoing efforts to upgrade its financial management business processes in several ways. First, to verify its ability to track spending and improve fiscal discipline, DOD will have Statements of Budgetary Resources for general funds "audit ready" by 2014, three years earlier than previously planned. This audit of the Department's Statement of Budgetary Resources will encompass a complete review of how the Department receives and spends its funds. Second, DOD continues to upgrade its logistics management business processes by pursuing initiatives designed to acquire, manage, and deliver cargo and personnel more efficiently and effectively. These Department-wide logistics initiatives build on previously successful business process re-engineering initiatives over many years. Overall, the Budget helps improve Departmental business processes and thus enables DOD to streamline the joint global distribution system, manage inventory in more efficient and cost effective ways, improve demand forecasting, speed movement of wounded warriors from the battlefield, and manage the return of equipment from Iraq and Afghanistan more responsibly.

Focuses on Management Efficiencies. The Budget creates a balanced approach to funding priorities within spending caps by freeing up resources from lower priorities, eliminating duplication, trimming overhead, and improving competition and management in operating and investment programs. For example, to reduce its information technology footprint—and in turn lower staffing and energy needs—the Department plans to continue consolidating its numerous data centers. In addition, across its global distribution system, DOD continues to pursue initiatives designed to acquire, manage, and deliver cargo and personnel more efficiently and effectively. Finally, as stated above, in lieu of costly new acquisition programs, DOD strives to upgrade existing equipment to provide equivalent capabilities wherever possible.

Conserves Energy. DOD consumes almost three-fourths of all Federal energy resources. To reduce consumption, the Budget includes approximately $1 billion for energy conservation investments—up from $400 million in 2010—increasing by two and one-half times the support of DOD's Priority Goal to Improve Energy Performance. These investments include energy retrofits of existing buildings, meeting energy efficiency standards for new buildings, and developing renewable energy projects. DOD is steadily improving its installation energy performance by reducing the demand for traditional energy and increasing the supply of renewable energy sources, currently at nearly 8.5 percent of DOD energy production and procurement. The request includes $150 million for the Energy Conservation Investment Program, which improves the energy efficiency of DOD facilities worldwide. In addition, the Budget provides $32 million, a 7 percent increase compared to 2012, for the Installation Energy Test Bed Program to demonstrate new energy technologies to reduce risk, overcome barriers to deployment, and facilitate wide-scale commercialization.

Department of Defense
(In millions of dollars)

	Actual 2011	Estimate 2012	Estimate 2013
Spending			
Discretionary Base Budget Authority:			
Military Personnel	137,046	141,819	135,113
Operation and Maintenance	192,649	197,198	208,744
Procurement	103,909	104,464	98,823
Research, Development, Test and Evaluation	75,733	71,375	69,408
Military Construction	14,768	11,367	9,572
Family Housing	1,819	1,683	1,651
Revolving and Management Funds	2,348	2,641	2,123
Subtotal, Discretionary base budget authority	528,272	530,547	525,434
Discretionary Cap Adjustment:[1]			
Overseas Contingency Operations (OCO)	158,753	115,083	88,482

Department of Defense—Continued
(In millions of dollars)

	Actual 2011	Estimate	
		2012	2013
Total, Discretionary budget authority (Base and OCO)	687,025	645,630	613,916
Total, Discretionary outlays (Base and OCO)	673,848	682,995	666,159
Total, Mandatory outlays	4,226	5,260	6,721
Total, Outlays	678,074	688,255	672,880

Credit activity

Direct Loan Disbursements:

Family Housing Improvement Direct Loan Financing Account	309	202	195
Total, Direct loan disbursements	309	202	195

[1] The Balanced Budget and Emergency Deficit Control Act of 1985 (BBEDCA), as amended by the Budget Control Act of 2011, limits—or caps—budget authority available for discretionary programs each year through 2021. Section 251(b)(2) of BBEDCA authorizes certain adjustments to the caps after the enactment of appropriations. Amounts in 2011 are not so designated but are shown for comparability purposes.

NATIONAL INTELLIGENCE PROGRAM

Funding Highlights:

- Provides $52.6 billion in discretionary funding. This funding supports our national security goals and reflects a deliberative process to focus funding on the most critical capabilities, curtail personnel growth, and invest in more efficient information technology solutions.

- Continues to better integrate intelligence to help policy officials make decisions informed by the latest and most accurate intelligence available.

- Strengthens global intelligence capabilities to disrupt terrorism and better understand extremist threats.

- Counters the proliferation of weapons of mass destruction by strengthening collection and analysis capabilities.

- Supports military operations in Afghanistan.

- Enhances cybersecurity capabilities to help protect Federal networks, critical infrastructure, and America's economy while improving the security of intelligence networks against intrusion and counterintelligence threats.

- Modernizes the Intelligence Community's information technology infrastructure to remove barriers to collaboration, information sharing, and efficiency.

- Reduces contractors and freezes Government personnel levels.

- Terminates or reduces lower priority operational and investment programs.

The National Intelligence Program (NIP) funds Intelligence Community (IC) activities in six Federal departments, the Central Intelligence Agency, and the Office of the Director of National Intelligence. The IC provides intelligence collection, the analysis of that intelligence, and the responsive dissemination of intelligence to those who need it—including the President, the heads of Executive Departments, military forces, and law enforcement agencies. The President's Budget advances the Administration's national security objectives and the National Intelligence Strategy and plays a critical role in protecting American citizens, safeguarding our economy and fostering continued economic growth. In addition, it represents a focused effort to address the most critical requirements while accepting and managing risk within a constrained fiscal environment. The Budget strikes a careful balance between addressing critical national security requirements and providing responsible management of taxpayer resources. Savings are achieved by curtailing personnel growth, eliminating legacy capabilities, scaling back operations against lower priority missions, reducing facilities, and implementing "cloud computing."

Reflecting the Administration's commitment to transparency and open government, the Budget continues the practice begun in the 2012 Budget and discloses the President's aggregate funding request for NIP. However, the details regarding the NIP budget remain classified; therefore, the President's Budget does not publicly disclose detailed funding requests for intelligence activities. This chapter highlights key NIP-funded activities without specific funding information.

Advances National Security Goals

Integrates Intelligence. The IC will continue to improve intelligence integration to harness more efficiently and effectively the strengths and capabilities that are spread across 17 organizations. Through National Intelligence Managers and their associated Unifying Intelligence Strategies, the Director of National Intelligence has drawn together the expertise required to accomplish the goals of the National Security Strategy and the National Intelligence Strategy, as guided by the National Intelligence Priorities Framework. The IC is working to ensure that integrated intelligence information flows anywhere and anytime it is required by any authorized user, from the President to our troops on the ground.

Strengthens Global Intelligence Capabilities to Disrupt Terrorism and Counter Weapons of Mass Destruction. The IC continues to make robust investments to combat terrorism and support the Administration's National Strategy for Counterterrorism. The IC will continue to lead operations to defeat al-Qaeda and other violent extremists and disrupt their capabilities; prevent the proliferation of weapons of mass destruction; penetrate and analyze the most difficult targets of interest to U.S. foreign policymakers; identify and disrupt counterintelligence threats; and provide strategic warning to policymakers on issues of geopolitical and economic concern. To protect our national security, the IC will strengthen its collection and analysis capabilities and promote responsible intelligence collaboration and information sharing. The Administration also remains committed to measuring performance to evaluate progress, ensure key intelligence gaps are closed, and create accountability for results across the entire NIP.

Supports Military Operations. The Budget supports the ability of the IC to play a key role in informing decision-makers at the strategic level and supporting the war fighter. Field commanders look to the IC for situational awareness, targeting support, and timely and actionable intelligence. Planners look to the IC for adversary plans, intentions, and capabilities. The Budget balances its focus between current, immediate needs for U.S. military forces engaged in operations with enduring intelligence requirements for potential future military and security needs.

Enhances Cybersecurity Capabilities and Safeguards Intelligence Networks. A secure U.S. information infrastructure—including IC telecommunications, computer networks and systems, and the data that reside on them—is critical to national security. Threats to information technology infrastructure endanger national and economic security and citizen privacy and are, therefore, an important policy focus of the Government. The NIP budget request supports Presidential cybersecurity priorities, including cybersecurity research and development. In addition, it supports the Senior Information Sharing and Safeguarding Steering Committee, which the President established by Executive Order 13587 to guide and prioritize Government-wide investments in classified networks. The Budget invests in the protection of these critical networks that facilitate the IC's information sharing and operational requirements.

Modernizes the Information Technology Infrastructure. The IC depends on robust information technology capabilities to support operations and allow for robust information sharing and collaboration with all customers. Management of this information and data is paramount to its usability; modernization of this infrastructure will develop efficient, interoperable solutions to the IC's storage and data handling challenges. The NIP budget request achieves significant savings by implementing the Administration's Cloud First policy and the Campaign to Cut Waste.

Makes Difficult Cuts and Reforms

Reduces Contractor Workforce and Freezes IC Hiring. Consistent with Administration-wide efforts to find savings in a tight fiscal environment, the Budget freezes IC Government personnel at 2012 levels and continues to reduce the IC contractor workforce. The Budget focuses on sustaining the skills in the current IC workforce that have been developed over the past decade.

Achieves Savings Through Reducing or Terminating Lower Priority Programs. Recognizing the challenges of this fiscal environment, the IC has undertaken a comprehensive review of its operational, investment, and infrastructure programs. The NIP budget reflects a deliberative process to ensure that the IC focuses on those programs that have the most significant return and terminates or reduces those considered lower priority or that are not performing.

OVERSEAS CONTINGENCY OPERATIONS

Funding Highlights:

- Provides $96.7 billion in unified Defense, State, and USAID funding for Overseas Contingency Operations (OCO), a reduction of 24 percent below the 2012 enacted level. This primarily reflects the savings from the end of military operations in Iraq and the drawdown of forces in Afghanistan.

- Maintains a unified approach to budgeting in conflict areas by continuing to integrate International Affairs resource requirements related to extraordinary and temporary national security needs with Department of Defense budget plans.

- Caps OCO spending through 2021 at $450 billion, which allows year-by-year flexibility for the Administration to respond effectively to changing circumstances on the ground, and which prevents the use of OCO funding as a way around discretionary caps.

- Addresses the military and civilian costs necessary to achieve U.S. national security goals in Afghanistan, Pakistan, and Iraq, including support for an entirely civilian-led mission in Iraq.

- Supports the security, diplomatic, and development requirements for successful military-to-civilian transitions in Iraq and Afghanistan, including continued support to critical coalition partners.

- Provides $88.5 billion for the Department of Defense, of which $85.6 billion is for Operation Enduring Freedom and $2.9 billion is for activities related to Iraq, primarily the repair and replacement of damaged equipment and the operation of the Office of Security Cooperation-Iraq.

- Reduces military spending at a rate consistent with the complete withdrawal of U.S. troops from Iraq and a 30 percent decline in the number of troops deployed to Afghanistan.

- Provides $8.2 billion for Department of State and USAID OCO activities, of which $3.3 billion is for Afghanistan, $1.0 billion is for Pakistan, and $4.0 billion is for Iraq.

- Promotes transparency and efficiency in the Budget by separating the costs of supporting OCO from those that are included in Department of Defense and Department of State and USAID base budgets.

For the second year, the President's Budget reflects a unified approach to budgeting for Department of Defense (DOD), Department of State, and U.S. Agency for International Development (USAID) operations in conflict areas. By aligning priority missions across these agencies, the Budget takes advantage of efficiencies, improves coordination, and reduces overall costs. Further, isolating the military and civilian costs related to temporary and extraordinary requirements in the OCO request promotes transparency and efficiency across the security agencies of the Federal Government. The President's 2013 Budget provides $96.7 billion for these operations, a reduction of 24 percent below the 2012 enacted level.

The Budget also reflects the Administration's efforts to constrain OCO spending in the years beyond 2013. The Budget Control Act of 2011 (BCA) established year-by-year caps on discretionary spending for agencies' base budgets through 2021, reducing the 10-year budget deficit by about $1 trillion. However, the BCA did not limit OCO funding. Leaving OCO funding unconstrained could allow future Administrations and Congresses to use it as a convenient vehicle to evade the fiscal discipline that the BCA caps require elsewhere in the Budget. With the end of our military presence in Iraq, and as troops continue to draw down in Afghanistan, the Budget proposes a binding cap on OCO spending, as well. From 2013 through 2021, the Budget limits OCO appropriations to $450 billion. Given the need for ample flexibility in budgeting for overseas contingencies, this is a multi-year total cap, rather than a series of year-by-year caps, and future Congresses may adjust it in the event of a national emergency requiring additional OCO spending.

Transitions from Military to Civilian-led Missions

The Budget funds several key efforts in the transition from military to civilian-led missions, including:

- Supporting a smaller number of U.S. forces in Afghanistan, down from about 100,000

at the beginning of 2012 to about 68,000 at the beginning of 2013.

- Supporting the continued development and professionalization of the Afghan National Security Forces (ANSF), enabling the ANSF to take increasing responsibility for the security of Afghanistan.

- Laying the groundwork to expand the civilian footprint in Afghanistan as U.S. forces draw down, while focusing civilian assistance on foundational investments in economic growth, reconciliation and reintegration, and capacity building.

- Reducing Iraq-related costs dramatically, reflecting the withdrawal of U.S. troops completed in December 2011.

- Strengthening the State Department's capacity to manage over 400 essential activities that it has taken over from DOD at Embassy Baghdad and three regional consulates in Iraq.

- Operating police and criminal justice hub facilities and security cooperation sites to continue enhancing Iraqi security forces and civilian ministries.

Reduces Defense Spending in Line with Troop Withdrawals. The Budget reflects a significant decrease in the OCO request for DOD, from $115.3 billion enacted in 2012 to $88.5 billion requested in 2013. This reflects the withdrawal of U.S. troops from Iraq and a 30 percent decline in the number of troops deployed to Afghanistan. Nearly all of these DOD funds support Operation Enduring Freedom (OEF), which is primarily conducted in Afghanistan. For OEF, the Budget funds military operations, incremental personnel costs, force protection, repair and replacement of damaged equipment, activities to counter and defeat improvised explosive devices, intelligence activities, support for coalition partners, and the training, equipping, and sustaining of the ANSF. To support implementation of the Nation's new defense strategy, the Budget funds, within the OCO request, the portion of the Army and Marine Corps end strength that DOD will remove from the force within the next five years. This end strength supports current operations in Afghanistan and elsewhere, but will not be required as troops withdraw.

The Budget provides $2.9 billion to support DOD's Iraq-related costs, including repair and replacement of equipment leaving the country, replenishment of munitions previously expended in combat, and the operation of the Office of Security Cooperation-Iraq (OSC-I). This is a reduction of about $7 billion from the 2012 enacted level for Iraq. Under the aegis of the U.S. diplomatic mission to Iraq, OSC-I is the cornerstone of the U.S.-Iraqi strategic security partnership and serves as the hub of both security assistance and security cooperation activities, including cooperation on counterterrorism, counterproliferation, maritime security, and air defense.

Provides Department of State and USAID Funding for Civilian-Led Missions. The Budget reflects the OCO costs associated with Department of State and USAID activities in Iraq, Afghanistan, and Pakistan. Overall, the 2013 request for OCO represents a decrease of $2.9 billion from the 2012 enacted level, and reflects a more conservative OCO definition that avoids the risk of inadequate base funding for enduring activities once OCO funding under the proposed cap is exhausted. These 2013 OCO costs are limited to certain near-term operational, security and development components of assistance programs related to stabilization and counterinsurgency operations, protection of civilian personnel, and oversight activities of the Special Inspector General for Afghanistan. In Iraq, these temporary operations and assistance programs are necessary to sustain a civilian-led mission; strengthen the capacity of the Iraqi government through police training, criminal justice programs, and military assistance; and ensure the Department and USAID have the necessary resources to support and secure the diplomatic mission. For Afghanistan and Pakistan, unique challenges require near-term stabilization and development assistance to support a responsible security transition in Afghanistan and support Pakistan's counterinsurgency programs. In Afghanistan, OCO funding will provide the initial infrastructure to maintain the diplomatic platform and security posture as Afghan forces take greater responsibility for security operations.

Overseas Contingency Operations (OCO)
(In millions of dollars)

	Actual 2011	Estimate	
		2012	2013
Spending Memorandum:[1]			
Discretionary Cap Adjustment:[2]			
Department of Defense			
Operation Enduring Freedom...	*113,963*	*105,737*	*85,627*
Operation New Dawn / Iraq...	*45,044*	*9,604*	*2,855*
Subtotal, Department of Defense [3]	*159,007*	*115,341*	*88,482*
Department of State and U.S. Agency for International Development (USAID) [4]			
Iraq...	*—*	*4,802*	*4,019*
Afghanistan	*—*	*3,636*	*3,267*
Pakistan and Other..	*297*	*2,750*	*959*
Subtotal, Department of State and USAID	*297*	*11,188*	*8,245*
Other International Agencies	*—*	*14*	*—*
Subtotal, Department of State, USAID, and Other International Agencies..	*297*	*11,203*	*8,245*
Department of Justice..	*101*	*—*	*—*
Total, Discretionary budget authority...	*159,405*	*126,544*	*96,727*

[1] OCO funding is included in the related agency chapter tables and is presented here as a non-add detail table.

[2] The Balanced Budget and Emergency Deficit Control Act of 1985 (BBEDCA), as amended by the Budget Control Act of 2011, limits—or caps—budget authority available for discretionary programs each year through 2021. Section 251(b)(2) of BBEDCA authorizes certain adjustments to the caps after the enactment of appropriations. Amounts in 2011 are not so designated but are shown for comparability purposes.

[3] For comparability purposes, the DOD totals include $254 million in 2011 and $258 million in 2012 that were requested in Defense but that Congress appropriated directly to the Department of Homeland Security (DHS), for Coast Guard operating expenses. The Budget requests $254 million in Defense that may be transferred to DHS for the same purpose in 2013.

[4] OCO funds were first appropriated to the Department of State, USAID, and Other International Programs in 2012. The 2011 OCO amount reflects a transfer from the Department of Defense to the Department of State.

DEPARTMENT OF EDUCATION

Funding Highlights:

- Provides $69.8 billion in discretionary spending, which is 2.5 percent, or $1.7 billion, above the 2012 enacted level. This request builds on the significant gains already made through Race to the Top and other Administration initiatives. It safeguards increases in major K-12 reform programs and funds new efforts to improve college access, affordability, and quality to help reach the President's college completion goal. To accommodate increases in these priority areas, the Budget makes targeted reductions and consolidations that help preserve resources for the highest priority investments.

- Spurs comprehensive reform at the State and local level by providing $850 million for Race to the Top and $100 million for Promise Neighborhoods, two signature reform initiatives.

- Overhauls the Department's Elementary and Secondary Act (ESEA) programs by consolidating 38 program authorities into 11 competitive grant programs designed to allow States and districts more flexibility to use resources where they will have the greatest impact.

- Sustains investments in programs that support States' efforts to implement rigorous and comprehensive reforms like the ones being developed in their ESEA flexibility plans.

- Invests $1.1 billion in a reauthorized Career and Technical Education program, that will prepare students for the future by aligning what they learn in school with the demands of 21st Century jobs. The Budget also provides support for establishing new highly-effective career academies.

- Prepares America's students for the 21st Century workplace by providing $260 million in funding for science, technology, engineering, and mathematics (STEM) programs, including a new $30 million evidence-based math education initiative to be jointly administered with a comparable program at the National Science Foundation, and $80 million to help reach the President's goal of recruiting and preparing 100,000 high-quality STEM teachers over the next 10 years.

- Continues the Administration's commitment to keep college affordable for students and their families by making the American Opportunity Tax Credit permanent, suspending an increase in student loan interest rates, and helping to secure the future of the Pell Grant program. The

Budget provides sufficient funding for a $5,635 maximum Pell Grant award, $900 above the 2008 level which ensures access to postsecondary education for nearly 10 million needy students. The Budget also provides over 12 million borrowers with low-cost loans to attend college.

- Invests significant new resources to reform higher education through Race to the Top: College Affordability and Completion, reforms to the Campus-Based Aid program, and a new First in the World competition.

- Builds the knowledge base of effective educational interventions and helps translate research into practice through an additional $12 million for Institute of Education Sciences' research and development and sustained funding for Investing in Innovation.

- Supports new interagency efforts to break down administrative barriers to coordinating services for disadvantaged children and disconnected youth.

- Makes targeted reductions to a handful of programs to ensure that funds are spent only on the most effective and essential activities.

In its first three years, the Administration has combined unprecedented financial support for education with extraordinary success in pursuing and achieving fundamental reforms that will benefit students of all ages and help build a globally competitive workforce. Central to this effort has been the Race to the Top (RTT) initiative for elementary and secondary education, a competition that spurred States across the Nation to bring together teachers, school leaders, and policy makers to achieve difficult, yet fundamental improvements to our education system. By offering competitive funding, supporting systemic reforms, requiring outcomes, and measuring success, the RTT competition fostered meaningful change even in States that ultimately did not win an award. This past year, a new RTT competition, called the Race to the Top: Early Learning Challenge, also drove States to take major steps to improve the quality of their early childhood programs.

The President's 2013 Budget builds on this success with a request of $69.8 billion for the Department of Education, a $1.7 billion increase above 2012 levels. In addition to sustaining and building on investments in improving early learning and elementary and secondary education, the Budget places a heightened emphasis on postsecondary education reform with efforts to tackle college costs while improving outcomes for students. The Budget also continues strong support for increasing access to college by maintaining historic increases for Pell Grants, which are critical to creating future generations that are well-educated and globally-competitive.

Invests in an Educated, Competitive America

Sustains Successful K-12 Reform. The Department of Education has jump-started landmark reforms in our education system by rewarding excellence and promoting innovation. Early indications show impressive progress in helping children start school ready to succeed, raising academic standards, placing an effective teacher in every classroom, and turning around struggling schools. The Budget continues to build on these reforms with new and sustained investments:

- *Race to the Top (RTT).* The Budget provides $850 million for RTT, a program that has enabled States to implement systemic reforms in five fundamental areas: implementing rigorous standards and assessments; using data to improve instruction and decision-making; recruiting and retaining effective teachers and principals; turning around the lowest-performing schools; and improving State systems of early learning and care. In 2011, the Department of Education launched the RTT Early Learning Challenge grant competition, a joint effort with the Department of Health and Human Services, designed to support the States with the most ambitious plans to ensure that high-need children from birth to age five enter kindergarten ready to succeed. In 2012, the Administration is building on the State-level progress of RTT by launching a district-level competition to support reforms best executed at the local level. In 2013, RTT will be poised to deepen the Administration's investments in these various areas, and address the unmet demand of States and districts that have demonstrated a commitment to implementing comprehensive and ambitious reforms. Additional resources will be provided for the Race to the Top: Early Learning Challenge, to be paired with new investments by the Department of Health and Human Services in improving child care quality and preparing children for success in school.

- *Promise Neighborhoods.* The Budget provides a considerable increase to Promise Neighborhoods, funding the program at $100 million. This initiative supports high-need communities who plan to combine effective services for families with comprehensive reforms centered on high-quality schools, in an effort to improve educational and life outcomes for children and youth.

- *Investing in Innovation (i3).* The Budget continues robust investment in the i3 fund, providing $150 million, to support evidence-based approaches that improve K-12 achievement and close achievement gaps, decrease dropout rates, increase high school graduation rates, and improve teacher and school leader effectiveness. A portion of i3 funds will also be used to support the development of breakthrough learning technologies through the Advanced Research Projects Agency for Education.

- *School Turnaround Grants.* The Budget provides $534 million for School Turnaround Grants to support the Administration's commitment to helping States and districts turn around America's lowest-performing schools.

- *Flexibility in Exchange for Smart Reforms.* To build on the successful reforms leveraged by the first RTT competition, the Department recently invited States to apply for Elementary and Secondary Education Act (ESEA) waivers in exchange for a commitment to implement comprehensive reforms. The Budget maintains investments in key programs that States can use to advance these reforms. For example, States and districts will have new flexibility to use Title I funds that were previously required to be reserved for supplemental educational services, public school choice, and professional development to support locally determined, rigorous interventions in schools.

- *Support for Teachers and Schools.* Districts will continue to receive the vital resources needed to pay teacher salaries and fund other educational interventions needed to help disadvantaged students and students with disabilities succeed through sustained investments in Title I and Individuals with Disabilities Education Act (IDEA) Grants to States of $14.5 billion and $11.6 billion, respectively.

- *Strengthens the Teaching Profession.* The Budget makes a number of investments to help ensure that an effective teacher is in every classroom, including a 25 percent set-aside within the new Effective Teachers and Leaders State Grants program to build evidence on ways to best recruit, prepare and support effective teachers and principals. The Budget also invests $400 million in the Teacher and Leader Innovation Fund to transform teacher and leader evaluation and compensation to reward strong teaching and support improvement.

Delivers a Quality, Affordable College Education to Millions of Americans. To strengthen our Nation's competitiveness and to be first in the world in the proportion of college graduates, the Nation must open the doors of college to more Americans and make sure that students can complete their degrees. The Administration has already taken significant strides to make college more affordable. Today, nearly 10 million students receive Pell Grants, and more than 12 million borrowers receive low-cost loans, with new affordable repayment options based on their income after leaving school. This Budget builds on that progress by continuing to invest in student aid. Just as the Administration's investments over the past three years have transformed K-12 education, this Budget contains new initiatives to reform higher education by addressing rising tuition and improving outcomes. Our goal is reduced college costs, improved access, increased levels of completion, and better post-graduation outcomes—all at an affordable cost to students. Key initiatives include:

- *Tackling College Costs and Raising Completion Levels.* Rising college tuition has stymied recent efforts to make college more affordable through investments in Pell Grants, student financial aid, and higher education tax credits. Students are still struggling to pay their tuition bills and are leaving school with significant debt that they are having difficulty repaying. This path is not sustainable. Institutions of higher education have to do their part to rein in costs and deliver a high-value education, and States must halt their disinvestment in higher education and pursue reforms that will stabilize their systems in the long run. Our goal is reduced college costs, improved access, increased levels of completion, and better post-graduation outcomes. To this end, the Budget proposes a new Race to the Top: College Affordability and Completion, reforms to the Campus-Based Aid program, and a new First in the World competition.

- *Support for Community Colleges.* The Budget also funds a new initiative designed to improve access to job training across the nation and provides $8 billion in the Departments of Education and Labor to support State and community college partnerships with businesses to build the skills of American workers.

- *Maintaining a Strong Pell Grant Program.* Since 2008, the Administration has increased the maximum Pell Grant by more than $900, to $5,635. The Budget continues the Administration's strong commitment to the Pell Grant program and to preserving the maximum award, and includes measures that ensure full program funding through the 2014–2015 academic year. The Administration believes that action must be taken this year to keep the Pell Grant program on a sound footing, and that reforms such as those included in the Budget are necessary to maintain this critical investment in opening the doors of opportunity to all Americans and strengthening our Nation's competiveness.

- *Making the American Opportunity Tax Credit Permanent.* The Tax Relief, Unemployment Insurance Reauthorization and Job Creation Act of 2010 extended for two years the new American Opportunity Tax Credit (AOTC)— a partially refundable tax credit worth up to $2,500 per student per year. AOTC, which would be made permanent in the Budget, helps more than 9 million taxpayers afford the cost of college.

- *Suspending an Increase in Student Loan Interest Rates.* Under current law, interest rates on subsidized Stafford loans are slated to rise this summer from 3.4 percent to 6.8 percent. At a time when the economy is still recovering and market interest rates remain low, it makes no sense to double rates on student loans. The Budget suspends the scheduled increase for the coming year, so that rates will remain at 3.4 percent.

- *Improving the Quality of Postsecondary Outcome Data.* Informed decision-making by students and families is critical to improving value and quality in higher education. Better data can also help institutions make more informed decisions that will improve both programs and outcomes. The Budget provides resources to invest in improving the quality of postsecondary data and making information on education and employment outcomes available to the public. This will drive smarter decision-making, by showing which higher education programs lead to good results.

Prepares 100,000 STEM Teachers and Improves STEM Education. Students need to master science, technology, engineering, and mathematics (STEM) in order to thrive in the 21st Century economy. Steadily, we have seen other nations eclipse ours in preparing their children in these critical fields. That is why the President has set the ambitious goal of preparing 100,000 STEM teachers over the next decade. The Budget invests $80 million within the Effective Teachers and Leaders State Grants program toward that goal, to expand promising and effective models of teacher preparation in STEM. The Budget also funds a jointly administered mathematics education initiative, with $30 million from the Department of Education and $30 million from the National Science Foundation (NSF). This new evidence-based math initiative will combine the strength in mathematics education research at NSF with the Department of Education's State

and school district connections and program scale-up expertise. These programs will be developed in conjunction with a Government-wide effort to improve the impact of Federal investments in math and science education by ensuring that all programs supporting K-12 and undergraduate education adhere to consistent standards of effectiveness.

Prepares Young People for Jobs Through a Reformed Career and Technical Education Program. The President's Budget recommends reauthorization and reform of the Career and Technical Education (CTE) program, currently set to expire in 2013. The Administration's $1.1 billion reauthorization proposal would restructure CTE to align what students learn in school with the demands of 21st Century jobs and create better quality programs for students. The Budget also provides new funding to scale up career academies.

Uses Resources More Effectively for Better Results

Helps States and Districts Make Better Choices by Identifying Proven Strategies. In a time of fiscal constraint, it is crucial that we understand which interventions and strategies are effective at improving student outcomes. The President's Budget maintains a commitment to building a rich evidence base of what works so that districts and schools can make informed decisions about how to best educate their students. The Budget sustains support for the i3 program and provides new funds for a CTE innovation and transformation fund and First in the World, which will contribute to our evidence base by requiring rigorous evaluations of promising and proven education interventions and solutions. The Budget also provides an increase of $12 million for the Institute of Education Sciences Research and Development program to support rigorous research and evaluation and new strategies to make this evidence accessible to education practitioners.

Creates Efficiencies and Encourages Interagency Coordination. When the Administration outlined its reauthorization of ESEA in the 2011 Budget, it proposed to overhaul the Department's K-12 program structure by consolidating 38 existing authorities into 11 new programs that would give communities more choices in implementing activities and allow for the use of rigorous evidence to fund what works. In the past two years, Congress eliminated the funding for 22 of the 38 programs, but failed to replace these eliminations with the improved program structure, funding only two (RTT and i3) of the 11 new programs. Eliminating programs alone will not enable the Department to drive the reform that is needed in the nation's schools. That is why the 2013 Budget seeks funding for all 11 of the proposed programs and continues to consolidate the 38 existing program authorities, including the 16 programs still operating, into this new program structure.

The Budget also provides investments and flexibility to coordinate Federal, State, tribal, and local services and improve outcomes for disadvantaged children and disconnected youth. It continues to support the Promoting Readiness of Minors in the Supplemental Security Income Program (PROMISE) pilot—a joint effort between the Social Security Administration and the Department of Education, with input from the Departments of Labor and Health and Human Services. The Budget also includes new resources dedicated to disconnected youth that will build knowledge about the most effective programs, provide flexible funding, and improve coordination across levels of government.

Reduces Funding in Select Areas to Focus Resources on Core Activities. Consistent with Administration-wide efforts to achieve savings where possible, the Budget makes targeted reductions to some programs, including the National Assessment of Educational Progress and the National Institute on Disability and Rehabilitation Research, and generates savings by ending Impact Aid for school districts where the presence of Federal property does not affect enrollment.

Department of Education
(In millions of dollars)

	Actual 2011	Estimate 2012	Estimate 2013
Spending			
Discretionary Budget Authority:			
Legislative proposal, Elementary and Secondary Education Act:			
College and Career Ready Students (program level)	14,443	14,516	14,516
School Turnaround Grants	535	534	534
Race to the Top	699	549	850
Investing in Innovation	150	149	150
English Learner Education	734	732	732
Effective Teaching and Learning for a Complete Education	305	362	427
College Pathways and Accelerated Learning	92	76	81
Excellent Instructional Teams (program level)	2,977	2,864	2,941
Supporting Student Success	1,441	1,407	1,448
Expanding Educational Options	281	255	255
Special Education State Grants (program level)	12,278	12,393	12,413

Department of Education—Continued
(In millions of dollars)

	Actual 2011	Estimate	
		2012	2013
Career and Technical Education State Grants and National Activities (program level)	1,130	1,131	1,131
Adult Education State Grants and National Activities	607	606	606
Federal Student Aid:			
Supplemental Educational Opportunity Grants	736	735	735
Federal Work Study	979	977	1,127
Race to the Top: College Affordability and Completion	—	—	1,000
Higher Education:			
Minority Serving Institutions—Discretionary funding	562	541	541
Minority Serving Institutions—Mandatory funding (non-add)	*278*	*278*	*278*
TRIO programs—Discretionary funding	827	840	840
TRIO programs—Mandatory funding (non-add)	*57*	*—*	*—*
GEAR UP	303	302	302
Student Aid Administration	992	1,043	1,129
Institute of Education Sciences	609	594	621
All other	4,670	4,683	4,698
Subtotal, Discretionary budget authority, excluding Pell Grants	45,349	45,288	47,076
Federal Pell Grants	22,956	22,824	22,824
Subtotal, Discretionary budget authority (program level)	68,305	68,112	69,900
Discretionary Changes in Mandatory Programs *(non-add in 2012):*[1]			
Pell Grants		*−124*	*—*
VR State Grants (Change from baseline)		*—*	*−63*
Subtotal, Discretionary changes in mandatory programs		*−124*	*−63*
Changes in Advance Appropriations[2]	41	−732	—
Total, Discretionary budget authority	68,346	67,381	69,837
Total, Discretionary outlays	89,360	79,102	67,712
Mandatory Outlays:			
Legislative proposal, Federal Pell Grants	14,242	15,323	13,553
Legislative proposal, Perkins Loans			−648
Legislative proposal, Federal Student Loan Programs	−47,295	−34,315	−32,190
Legislative proposal, Teacher Education Assistance	12	38	19
Legislative proposal, American Jobs Act		30,517	19,577
Education Jobs Fund	5,056	3,712	—
Academic Competitiveness and SMART Grants	820	10	—

Department of Education—Continued
(In millions of dollars)

	Actual 2011	Estimate	
		2012	2013
Vocational Rehabilitation (VR) State Grants	2,795	3,512	3,278
All other	524	588	625
Total, Mandatory outlays	−23,846	19,385	4,214
Total, Outlays	65,514	98,487	71,926

Credit activity

Direct Loan Disbursements:

Historically Black College and University Capital Financing	137	186	186
Federal Direct Student Loans (FDSL)	132,804	176,266	147,282
Consolidation Loans (non-add)	*24,038*	*63,446*	*28,382*
TEACH Grants	127	149	120
Student Loan Acquisition	3,147	907	704
Federal Perkins Loans	—	—	2,226
Total, Direct loan disbursements	136,215	177,508	150,518

[1] The 2012 amounts reflect OMB's scoring of the 2012 Appropriations acts (P.L. 112–55 and 112–74) as transmitted to the Congress. These amounts are displayed as non-add entries because they have been rebased as mandatory and are not included in any 2012 discretionary levels in the 2013 Budget.

[2] Reflects the cumulative changes in Department of Education advance appropriations in four accounts: College and Career Ready Students; Excellent Instructional Teams; Special Education; and Career, Technical, and Adult Education. The Budget Appendix includes, for each account, a Summary of Program Level table that shows the change in advance appropriations in each year. These advance appropriations are also discussed in the Analytical Perspectives volume's "Budget Process" chapter.

DEPARTMENT OF ENERGY

Funding Highlights:

- Provides $27.2 billion in discretionary funds, a 3.2 percent increase above the 2012 enacted level. This request includes increased funding for priority areas such as clean energy, research and development to spur innovation, and advanced manufacturing. Savings and efficiencies are achieved through cuts to inefficient and outdated fossil fuel subsidies, low-priority and low-performing programs, and by concentrating resources on full utilization of existing facilities and infrastructure.

- Increases funding for applied research, development, and demonstration in the Office of Energy Efficiency and Renewable Energy. The Budget also maintains and expands funding for the Advanced Research Projects Agency-Energy. These investments in high-performing programs will help position the United States as a world leader in the clean energy economy, and create the foundation for new industries and new jobs.

- Improves the competitiveness of U.S. industries by more than doubling research and development on advanced manufacturing processes and advanced industrial materials, enabling companies to cut costs by using less energy while improving product quality.

- Works through the President's Better Building Initiative to make non-residential buildings more energy efficient by catalyzing private sector investment. Creates jobs through mandatory funding for HomeStar incentives to consumers to make their homes more energy efficient.

- Promotes basic research through $5 billion in funding to the Office of Science.

- Positions the Environmental Management program to meet its legally enforceable cleanup commitments at sites across the country.

- Continues investments to maintain a safe, secure, and effective nuclear weapons stockpile in support of the planned decrease in deployed U.S. and Russian weapons under the New Strategic Arms Reduction Treaty.

- Strengthens national security through funding for securing, disposing of, and detecting nuclear and radiological material worldwide.

> • Eliminates $4 billion annually in inefficient and outdated fossil fuel subsidies.

The Department of Energy (DOE) is charged with advancing the national, economic, and energy security of the United States; promoting scientific and technological innovation in support of that mission; maintaining the Nation's nuclear weapons and reducing nuclear dangers; and ensuring the environmental cleanup of the national nuclear weapons complex. It facilitates some of the President's highest priorities: clean energy and innovation, which are critical to job creation, long-term economic stability, and national security. The President's 2013 Budget provides $27.2 billion in discretionary funds for DOE to support this mission, a 3.2 percent increase above the 2012 enacted level. In light of the tight discretionary spending caps, this increase in funding is significant and a testament to the importance of innovation and clean energy to the country's economic future. While the Budget includes funding increases in these critical areas, the Administration has identified areas for savings and efficiency, such as pursuing alternative approaches to the Pit Disassembly and Conversion project and restructuring plans for maintaining the necessary plutonium capabilities for the nuclear stockpile, transitioning the Second Line of Defense program to a sustainment phase, and concentrating funds on fully utilizing our investments in scientific facilities.

Invests in Clean Energy, Innovation, and Jobs of the Future

Funds Clean Energy Research, Development, and Deployment to Keep America Competitive. To lead in the industries of tomorrow, it is critical that we invest in research and development (R&D) today. The Budget includes $2.3 billion for the Office of Energy Efficiency and Renewable Energy (EERE). These funds are part of a broad energy strategy that emphasizes priorities in clean energy and advanced manufacturing, through grants, financing assistance, and tax incentives that accelerate fundamental research, technology development, and commercialization. Within EERE, the Budget increases funding by nearly 80 percent for energy efficiency activities to improve the energy productivity and competitiveness of our industries and businesses. It increases funding for the development of the next generation of advanced vehicles and biofuels, and it maintains crucial support for research, development, and demonstration of renewable electricity generation, including: $310 million for the SunShot Initiative to make solar energy cost-competitive nationwide without subsidies by the end of the decade; $95 million for wind energy, including off-shore wind technologies; and $65 million for geothermal energy and enhanced geothermal systems. The Budget also provides $770 million for the Office of Nuclear Energy, which includes funding for advanced small modular reactors R&D. Other priority activities include R&D on storage, transportation, and disposal of nuclear waste that supports the implementation of recommendations put forward by the Blue Ribbon Commission on America's Nuclear Future. The Budget includes funding to maintain and expand the deployment of new models of energy research pioneered in the last several years, including $350 million for the Advanced Research Projects Agency–Energy, a program that seeks to fund transformative energy research.

Supports Critical Natural Gas Research Initiative. As part of an overall investment of $421 million in fossil energy R&D, the Budget includes $12 million to fund a multi-year research initiative aimed at advancing technology and methods to safely and responsibly develop America's natural gas resources. Specifically, DOE, in collaboration with the Environmental Protection Agency and the U.S. Geological Survey, will focus on understanding and reducing the environmental, health, and safety risks of natural gas and oil production from hydraulic fracturing in shale and other geologic formations.

Saves Manufacturers Money by Improving Energy Efficiency. The President's Advanced Manufacturing Partnership invests in a national effort to develop and commercialize the emerging technologies that will create high quality manufacturing jobs and enhance our global competitiveness. By coordinating across Federal agencies and collaborating with the private sector, it will provide the platform for inventing new manufacturing technologies, speeding ideas from the drawing board to the manufacturing floor, scaling-up first-of-a-kind technologies, and developing the infrastructure and shared facilities to allow small and mid-sized manufacturers to innovate and compete. As an integral part of this initiative, the Budget provides DOE with $290 million to expand R&D on innovative manufacturing processes and advanced industrial materials that will enable U.S. companies to cut the costs of manufacturing by using less energy, while improving product quality and accelerating product development. The Budget also continues to support the development of competitive new manufacturing processes for advanced vehicles, biofuels, solar energy, and other new clean energy technology, to help ensure that the technologies invented here are manufactured here. The Budget also helps consumers save money through the continued introduction of appliance efficiency standards.

Invests in Long-Range R&D to Keep America Competitive. The Office of Science, the largest civilian source of physical sciences research funding, will receive $5 billion to continue cutting-edge R&D that is the foundation of the U.S. economic competitiveness. This also funds investments in critical national assets, such as national supercomputers, which are essential to competing in the global economy and to maintaining our national security. The Office of Science funds research grants and scientific activities in key areas of science, including physics, materials, and chemistry. In addition, the Office of Science operates U.S. light sources that are used by both biologists and physical scientists to understand the molecular structure of materials and the processes of chemical reactions.

Cuts Wasteful Spending and Improves Efficiency

Eliminates Inefficient Fossil Fuel Subsidies. As we continue to pursue clean energy technologies that will support future economic growth, we should not devote scarce resources to subsidizing the use of fossil fuels produced by some of the largest, most profitable companies in the world. That is why the Budget eliminates inefficient fossil fuel subsidies that impede investment in clean energy sources and undermine efforts to address the threat of climate change. The Budget proposes to repeal over $4 billion per year in tax subsidies to oil, gas, and other fossil fuel producers.

Reduces Buildings' Energy Use. The 80 billion square feet of non-residential building space in the United States present an opportunity to realize large gains in energy efficiency. In 2010, commercial buildings consumed roughly 20 percent of all energy in the U.S. economy. The Administration continues to call on the Congress to pass the HomeStar bill, or other mandatory funding legislation aimed at creating jobs by encouraging Americans to invest in energy saving home improvements. The Budget also supports increased R&D on innovative building efficiency technologies and the continued introduction of appliance efficiency standards that save consumers and companies' money while improving performance. Through the Federal Energy Management Program, DOE will help other Federal agencies improve the energy efficiency of all Federal buildings (representing over 3 billion square feet) with agencies' total investment to exceed $2 billion through performance-based contracts over the next two years, all at no net cost to the taxpayer. This is achieved through contracts that provide enough savings in energy to more than pay for the investments.

Protects Americans from the Threat of Nuclear Harm and Pollution

Maintains a Safe, Secure, and Effective Nuclear Deterrent. The Administration proposes $7.6 billion for Weapons Activities, an increase of $363 million or 5 percent above the 2012 enacted level, to maintain a safe, secure, and effective nuclear deterrent as described in the Administration's Nuclear Posture Review (NPR) of 2010. This Budget meets the goals of the NPR by continuing nuclear weapon life extension programs—such as upgrades to the W76 and B61 nuclear weapons—by improving and replacing aging facilities —such as increasing investments in funding for the Uranium Processing Facility—and by sustaining the existing stockpile through underlying science, surveillance, and other support programs. However, to meet the NPR goals, but still stay within the discretionary spending caps, the National Nuclear Security Administration (NNSA) and the Department of Defense are reducing and stretching out the schedule of several weapons life extension programs and are restructuring plans for maintaining plutonium capabilities. As a result, the 2013 Budget provides $372 million less for Weapons Activities than the Administration projected in last year's request and reported to the Congress in the "Section 1251 Report" on nuclear weapons plans.

The Administration also proposes $1.1 billion, a $9 million increase above the 2012 enacted level, to support work on naval reactors, including continued operational support of nuclear-powered submarines and aircraft carriers, and reactor development for a replacement to the OHIO class ballistic missile submarine.

Finally, reflecting their close partnership and shared commitment, the Budget assumes that a portion of future funding for NNSA will continue to be included in the Department of Defense's budget, with allocations made to NNSA each budget year.

Protects the Public from Harmful Exposure to Radioactive Waste and Nuclear Materials. The Budget includes $5.65 billion to ensure our Nation's legacy of nuclear wastes from the production of weapons during the Cold War are processed, secured, and safely disposed of in a timely manner. The Environmental Management program continues to clean up waste and contamination, focusing on its legally enforceable regulatory commitments. The program's cleanup actions include removing radioactive wastes from underground storage tanks, decontaminating and decommissioning old production facilities, and installing groundwater monitoring wells primarily at sites in Washington, South Carolina, Idaho, Tennessee, Kentucky, Ohio, and New Mexico.

Reduces the Proliferation of Nuclear Material and Weapons. The Budget includes $2.5 billion, a $163 million or 7 percent increase above the 2012 enacted level, which reflects completion of accelerated efforts to secure vulnerable nuclear materials within four years, the President's stated timeframe. This proposal fully funds Administration priorities to secure and dispose of nuclear material, to develop technologies to prevent, deter, or detect nuclear proliferation, and to implement international nonproliferation treaties, regulatory controls, and safeguards. DOE will have removed more than 4,300 kilograms—over 170 nuclear warheads worth—of vulnerable nuclear material from sites around the world by the end of 2013. The savings that make it possible to fund these priorities come from restructuring the Pit Disassembly and Conversion project and transitioning the Second Line of Defense (SLD) program to a sustainment phase. By the end of 2012, SLD will have exceeded its original goals, having installed radiation detection equipment at almost 500 foreign ports or crossing sites, including all 383 customs sites in Russia. SLD will continue its efforts to improve deployed capabilities and continue to provide foreign partners with mobile detection equipment.

Department of Energy
(In millions of dollars)

	Actual 2011	Estimate	
		2012	2013
Spending			
Discretionary Budget Authority:			
National Defense:			
National Nuclear Security Administration...	10,504	11,000	11,536
Other Defense Activities..	796	823	736
Energy Resources	3,613	3,666	4,307
Science	4,897	4,874	4,992
Environmental Management...	5,665	5,711	5,650
Corporate Management..	134	168	166
Power Marketing Administration	107	85	85
Offsetting receipts...	–23	–26	–26
Subtotal, Discretionary budget authority...	25,693	26,301	27,446
Discretionary Changes in Mandatory Programs *(non-add in 2012):[1]*			
Strategic Petroleum Reserve		*–500*	–291
Northeast Home Heating Oil Reserve		*–100*	—
Subtotal, Discretionary changes in mandatory programs		*–600*	–291
Total, Discretionary budget authority...	25,693	26,301	27,155
Total, Discretionary outlays	37,970	42,308	35,563
Mandatory Outlays:			
Existing law..	–5,231	–1,747	–1,080
Legislative proposals:			
Ultradeep Water, Oil, and Gas Research and Development			30
Home Energy Retrofit Rebate Program (HomeStar)............................			300
Advanced Vehicles, Community Development Challenge....................			150
Total, Mandatory outlays	–5,231	–1,747	–600
Total, Outlays	32,739	40,561	34,963
Credit activity			
Direct Loan Disbursements:			
Title 17 Innovative Technology Direct Loan Financing Account [2]...............	1,544	8,888	10,862
Advanced Technology Vehicles Manufacturing Direct Loan Financing Account	2,452	18,713	1,368
Total, Direct loan disbursements..	3,996	27,601	12,230

Department of Energy—Continued
(In millions of dollars)

	Actual 2011	Estimate	
		2012	2013
Guaranteed Loan Disbursements by Private Lenders:			
Title 17 Innovative Technology Guarantee Loans Financing Account [2]	1,670	2,116	1,177
Total, Guaranteed loan disbursements by private lenders.............................	1,670	2,116	1,177

[1] The 2012 amounts reflect OMB's scoring of the 2012 Appropriations acts (P.L. 112–55 and 112–74) as transmitted to the Congress. These amounts are displayed as non-add entries because they have been rebased as mandatory and are not included in any 2012 discretionary levels in the 2013 Budget.

[2] The commitments noted here include disbursements of loan guarantee commitments by the government, not "conditional commitments" under Title XVII which are legally contingent on the satisfaction of various conditions precedent.

DEPARTMENT OF HEALTH AND HUMAN SERVICES

Funding Highlights:

- Provides $76.4 billion, or $0.3 billion above the 2012 funding level. The Budget maintains investments in Administration priorities such as Affordable Care Act implementation and Head Start. Savings are achieved through difficult trade-offs, such as the consolidation of environmental health and substance abuse prevention grant programs.

- Supports innovative medical research by maintaining funding for the National Institutes of Health at $31 billion while implementing new grant management policies to increase the number of new research grants awarded and continue to focus resources for first-time grantees.

- Consolidates funding for disease-specific chronic diseases with common risk factors into a comprehensive program to improve public health outcomes for the leading chronic disease causes of death and disability and enhance efficiency.

- Eliminates the Preventive Health and Health Service Block Grant because the activities it supports can be more effectively implemented through the Consolidated Chronic Disease Program and Prevention and Public Health Fund investments.

- Supports implementation of the Affordable Care Act's health insurance coverage improvements in 2014 by helping States establish Affordable Insurance Exchanges and developing the infrastructure to provide cost sharing and premium assistance to make coverage affordable.

- Strengthens Medicare, Medicaid, and other health programs by implementing payment innovations and other reforms that encourage high-quality and efficient care, improve program integrity, and preserve the fundamental compact with seniors, individuals with disabilities, and low-income Americans these programs represent. These improvements will save approximately $364 billion over the next decade.

- Accelerates research on the discovery and development of new therapeutic interventions through the National Center for Advancing Translational Sciences.

- Improves access to health care services for American Indians and Alaska Natives.

- Invests approximately $3.3 billion for discretionary HIV/AIDS prevention and treatment activities across the Department to expand access to affordable health care, prevention, and treatment services and align activities with the National HIV/AIDS Strategy.

- Bolsters food and medical product safety activities by increasing the Food and Drug Administration's total resources by $654 million above the 2012 level and supports a new effort to improve food and drug import safety.

- Strengthens national preparedness for all threats to public health, including naturally occurring threats and deliberate attacks, through funding the advanced development of next generation medical countermeasures against chemical, biological, radiological, nuclear threats, and pandemic influenza.

- Invests in high-quality early childhood programs, with increased funding in Child Care and Head Start to improve outcomes for America's children and prepare them for the future. To make sure that every Head Start dollar is used to provide high quality services, the Budget also supports the implementation of new regulations to strengthen Head Start by requiring low-performing grantees to compete for continued funding.

- Supports the President's fatherhood agenda by modernizing the child support program to promote stronger family relationships and increase the payment of child support.

- Adjusts the Low Income Home Energy Assistance Program to reflect rising winter costs, particularly in areas of the country that rely on heating oil.

- Reforms foster care to improve outcomes for children including promoting their social and emotional well-being.

The Department of Health and Human Services (HHS) is the principal Federal agency charged with protecting the health of all Americans and providing essential human services. The President's Budget includes $76.4 billion to support HHS's mission. Within this level, the Department is carrying out significant responsibilities such as implementing the Affordable Care Act and strengthening program integrity across major entitlement programs. The Budget also invests in Head Start and health care services for American Indians and Alaska Natives. These increases are offset by tough cuts to worthy programs like the Community Services Block Grant as well as through new grants management policies at the National Institutes of Health (NIH) and the consolidation of various public health funding streams.

Improves Health Care Access and Quality of Service

Implements the Affordable Care Act. The Affordable Care Act (ACA) will ensure that every American can access high-quality, affordable coverage, providing health insurance to 34 million Americans who would otherwise be uninsured. The ACA does this by establishing State-based Affordable Insurance Exchanges, competitive marketplaces that will provide millions of Americans and small businesses with "one-stop shopping" for affordable coverage beginning in 2014. It also provides premium assistance to make coverage affordable for low-income Americans. Efficiently and effectively implementing these coverage expansions is one of the Administration's highest priorities. The Budget provides resources in support of these efforts, such as building capacity and creating infrastructure to establish exchanges, including the Federally-facilitated Exchange, and develops systems to help individuals enroll in the right health insurance coverage option.

Accelerates the Issuance of State Innovation Waivers. This proposal empowers States to develop their own innovation strategies to ensure their residents have access to high quality, affordable health insurance, achieving the same outcomes as the ACA. Similar to legislation previously introduced in the Senate and endorsed by the President, it would make "State Innovation Waivers" available starting in 2014, three years earlier than under current law. These State strategies would need to provide affordable insurance coverage to at least as many residents as those without the waiver and must not increase the federal deficit. The Administration is committed to the budget neutrality of these waivers.

Strengthens the Health Workforce. Strengthening the primary care workforce is critical to reforming America's health care system. Increasing access to primary care health providers can help prevent disease and illness, ensure all Americans have access to high-quality care, and reduce costs by decreasing the need for more invasive treatment that could have been prevented through early care. To increase access, the Administration provides increased resources for primary care training programs and support for health care providers who choose to train and practice in medically underserved areas. In total, the Budget initiates investments that will help train more than 2,800 additional primary care providers estimated to enter the workforce over the next five years.

Continues Funding for Health Centers. Health centers are a key component of the Nation's health care safety net. These clinics offer comprehensive, high quality, primary and preventive health care services to all Americans regardless of their ability to pay. Health centers will continue to be a critical element of the health system as the United States expands insurance coverage through the ACA, largely because they can provide an accessible and dependable source of primary care services in underserved communities. The ACA provides the Health Center Program with $7.3 billion over the 2013–2015 period. These resources complement the funding that the program receives annually through the discretionary appropriations process. To ensure that health centers continue to provide critical access and services to millions of Americans in 2013 and for many years to come, the Budget promotes a policy of steady and sustainable health center growth by distributing ACA resources over the long term, including in years after 2015. This policy safeguards resources for existing health centers to continue services and avoids the funding shortfall that would otherwise occur when the ACA funding ends in 2015. In addition, the Budget provides sufficient funding to open new health centers in areas in the country where they do not currently exist, through 2015 and beyond. In total, the Budget invests $3.1 billion for health center services in 2013 to support the creation of more than 25 new health center sites across the country. In 2013, health centers are estimated to serve nearly 21 million patients.

Maintains Continuity of Coverage for Low-income Individuals. The Budget continues to fund transitional medical assistance, which provides continued Medicaid eligibility for low-income adults transitioning to work. It also maintains funding for the qualified individuals program, which pays Medicare Part B premiums for qualified low-income seniors.

Supports Biomedical Research at NIH. Biomedical research contributes to improving the health of the American people as well as the economy. The Budget includes $31 billion for NIH to support research on-campus and at academic and independent research institutions across the country. Tomorrow's advances in health care depend on today's investments in basic research on the fundamental causes and mechanisms of disease, new technologies to accelerate discoveries, advancing translational sciences, and encouraging new investigators and new ideas. In 2013, NIH will implement new grants management policies to increase the number of new research grants awarded and continue to focus on resources for new investigators.

Improves Access to Health Care for American Indians and Alaska Natives (AI/ANS). The Budget includes $5.5 billion for the Indian Health Service (IHS) to strengthen Federal, tribal, and urban programs that serve two million AI/ANS at over 650 facilities in 35 States. The Budget provides increased resources for contract Health Services to purchase health care services provided outside of the Indian health system when services are not available at IHS-funded facilities. In addition, the Budget funds construction of new hospitals and health clinics and staff and operating costs at new facilities to increase access to health care services and improve the Indian health system.

Expands Access to HIV/AIDS Treatment, Care, and Prevention. The Budget expands access to HIV/AIDS prevention and treatment activities and supports the goals of the national HIV/AIDS Strategy to reduce HIV incidence; increases access to care and optimizing health outcomes for people living with HIV; and reduces HIV-related health disparities. The Budget includes $2.4 billion, an increase of $75 million, for the Health Resources and Services Administration's Ryan White program to expand access to care for persons living with HIV/AIDS who are otherwise unable to afford health care and related support services. The Budget also includes $1 billion for the AIDS Drug Assistance Program (ADAP), an increase of $67 million, to expand access to lifesaving HIV-related medications for uninsured and underinsured individuals living with HIV/AIDS and help distressed State ADAP programs eliminate waiting lists. The Budget includes an increase of $30 million for Centers for Disease Control and Prevention (CDC) HIV/AIDS prevention activities. The Budget also allows CDC and States to transfer up to 10 percent of total funding across HIV/AIDS, tuberculosis, sexually transmitted diseases, and hepatitis programs to improve coordination and integration.

Strengthens the Safety of U.S. Food and Medicines. The Budget includes $2.5 billion in budget authority and $4.5 billion in total program resources for the Food and Drug Administration (FDA). This includes $10 million in new resources to improve food safety and medical product imports to the United States through a greater FDA presence in foreign countries such as China. The Budget also includes new user fee programs to support implementation of key elements of the Food Safety Modernization Act, and to bring more safe, effective, and affordable generic drugs and generic biologics, also known as biosimilars, to the American public. To better protect public health in response to natural or intentional threats, the Administration also invests in FDA's efforts to advance regulatory science and support the review of new medical countermeasures for chemical, radiological, biomedical, and nuclear threats.

Strengthens National Preparedness for All Hazards, Including Naturally Occurring Threats and Intentional Attacks. The Budget includes $547 million to enhance the advanced development of next generation medical countermeasures against chemical, biological, radiological and nuclear threats. In addition, the Budget includes $50 million to establish the Strategic Investor, an independent venture capital entity in the Office of the Assistant Secretary for Preparedness and Response, and continues funding for the NIH Concept Acceleration Program to assist investigators with developing promising new countermeasures, and the FDA's Medical Countermeasures Regulatory Science Initiatives. The Department has invested $6.9 billion since 2005 to enhance America's ability to rapidly respond to an influenza pandemic. In 2013, HHS plans to use remaining pandemic influenza resources to support the new U.S.-based advanced development and manufacturing facilities for vaccines and other biologics.

Targets Funding for Mental Health and Substance Abuse Prevention Efforts. Within the Substance Abuse and Mental Health Services Administration (SAMHSA), the Budget requests $460 million for prevention services targeting early risk factors that can improve behavioral health outcomes for children and young adults.

The Budget proposes to merge SAMHSA prevention programs to enhance efficiency and improve efforts to prevent substance abuse and mental health disorders. The Budget also includes $140 million for behavioral health supportive services for homeless individuals and for families with mental and substance abuse disorders, to help them transition into permanent supportive housing.

Makes Tough Choices While Continuing to Serve Vulnerable Populations

Cuts and Reforms the Community Services Block Grant (CSBG). CSBG provides funding for the important work of community action agencies, but the program's current structure does too little to hold these agencies accountable for outcomes. The Budget provides $350 million and proposes to use competition to target the funds to high-performing agencies that are most successful in meeting important community needs.

Continues Strong Support for High-Quality Early Childhood Programs. Research has shown that effective early childhood programs help children succeed in school and beyond. Increasing Federal investments in high quality early education is a key part of a broader education agenda that will strengthen the Nation's competiveness and help every child reach his or her potential. The Budget includes over $8 billion for Head Start and Early Head Start to serve approximately 962,000 children and families, maintaining the historic expansion undertaken in 2009–2010. The Budget supports the implementation of new regulations to strengthen Head Start by requiring low-performing grantees to compete for continued funding for the first time in the program's history. The Budget also includes an additional $7 billion over the next 10 years to support low-income children with child care subsidies. Finally, the Budget supports critical reforms to the Child Care Development Block Grant and provides an additional $300 million for States to improve child care quality, and ultimately help children succeed in school.

Supports Responsible Fatherhood. The Budget modernizes the child support program, which touches the lives of more than half of poor children as well as many middle-class families. These policy changes, which will encourage fathers to take responsibility for their children include: increasing financial support for States that pass through child support payments to families rather than retaining them; ending the Federal expectation of reimbursement for payments that are distributed to families receiving assistance through the Temporary Assistance for Needy Families program; and encouraging States to provide access and visitation services that can improve a father's relationship with his family.

Adjusts LIHEAP for Rising Winter Fuel Costs. The President's Budget provides $3 billion for the Low Income Home Energy Assistance Program (LIHEAP) to help struggling families make ends meet by offsetting some of their home heating and cooling costs. While the costs of fuels used by most LIHEAP households remain low, the price of heating oil has been on the rise. In response, the Budget provides an additional $450 million over the 2012 request, and targets funds to States with vulnerable households facing high home heating costs for winter 2012–2013.

Reforms Foster Care to Improve Outcomes for Abused and Neglected Children. The Administration proposes $2.5 billion over 10 years in new mandatory funding for incentive payments to States that demonstrate real, meaningful improvements on measures of child outcomes, including child abuse and neglect, and service quality. These incentives would help States finance innovative services and encourage continuous improvement in the foster care system.

Improves the Way Federal Dollars are Spent and Strengthens Long-Term Viability of Current Programs

Reduces Waste, Fraud, and Abuse in Medicare, Medicaid, and the Children's Health Insurance Program (CHIP). Significant progress has been made in achieving the President's goal of reducing the Medicare fee-for-service improper payment rate in half by 2012 and in implementing the ACA's anti-fraud provisions. The Budget builds on this progress through a robust set of proposals to strengthen Medicare, Medicaid, and CHIP program integrity. The Budget invests $610 million in discretionary program integrity funding to implement activities that reduce payment error rates, prevent fraud and abuse, target high risk services and supplies, and enhance civil and criminal enforcement for Medicare, Medicaid, and CHIP. For example, the Budget proposes to authorize civil monetary penalties or other intermediate sanctions for providers who do not update enrollment records and permits exclusion of individuals affiliated with entities sanctioned for fraudulent or other prohibited actions from Federal health care programs. The Budget also affirms Medicaid's position as a payer of last resort when another entity is legally liable to pay claims for beneficiaries. These new resources and authorities will better enable the Administration to minimize improper payments and provide greater value for program expenditures to beneficiaries and taxpayers.

Supports Permanent, Fiscally Responsible Reform to Medicare's Payments to Physicians. Medicare payments to physicians are determined under a formula, commonly referred to as the "sustainable growth rate" (SGR). This formula has called for reductions in physician payment rates since 2002, which the Congress has consistently overridden for nearly 10 years. Under the SGR, physician payment rates would be reduced by nearly 28 percent later this year. The Administration is committed to working with the Congress to fix the SGR, providing predictable Medicare physician payments that incentivize quality and efficiency in a fiscally responsible way. Failing to do so masks the long-run deficit.

Improves Medicare's and Medicaid's Sustainability by Encouraging High-Quality, Efficient Care. The Budget contains several proposals that build on initiatives included in the ACA to help extend Medicare's solvency while encouraging provider efficiencies and improved patient care. Specifically, the Budget modifies

payments to certain providers, to address payments that exceed patient care costs. It also reduces Medicare's payments to providers for beneficiaries' non-payment of their deductibles and copayments. The Budget also aligns Medicare drug payment policies with Medicaid policies for low-income beneficiaries. These, along with other Medicare proposals, would extend the solvency of the Hospital Insurance trust fund for an estimated two years.

Encourages Beneficiaries to Seek High-Value Services. The Budget includes structural changes that will help encourage Medicare beneficiaries to seek high-value health care services. To help improve the financial stability of the Medicare program, the Budget reduces the Federal subsidy of Medicare costs for those beneficiaries who can most afford them, and also introduces a modified Part B deductible for new beneficiaries beginning in 2017. To encourage appropriate use of home health services that are not preceded by inpatient care, new beneficiaries beginning in 2017 would be responsible for a modest copayment for home health services in certain cases. Research indicates that beneficiaries with Medigap plans that provide first dollar or near-first dollar coverage have less incentive to consider the costs of health care services, thus raising Medicare costs and Part B premiums for all beneficiaries. The Budget applies a premium surcharge for new beneficiaries beginning in 2017 if they choose such Medigap coverage. In addition, it strengthens the Independent Payment Advisory Board to reduce long-term drivers of Medicare cost growth.

Establishes a More Flexible and Accountable Medicaid Program. Medicaid is critically important to providing health care to the poorest in our country, including children, seniors, and individuals with disabilities. The Administration opposes efforts to turn it into a block grant and slash its funding. Instead, the Budget seeks to make Medicaid more efficient by streamlining financing and reimbursement policies. Specifically, the Budget proposes to reduce the Medicaid provider tax threshold beginning in 2015 to promote integrity of Federal-State financing. The

Administration also proposes a single blended matching rate for Medicaid and CHIP spending to replace the current complicated patchwork of matching formulas starting in 2017. In addition, the Budget would implement more efficient reimbursement rates for durable medical equipment based on Medicare rates. Finally, the Budget better aligns Medicaid supplemental hospital payments by rebasing Disproportionate Share Hospital allotments in 2021. These Medicaid proposals are projected to save approximately $51 billion over 10 years.

Prioritizes Effective Prevention and Public Health Programs. The Budget promotes wellness and focuses on reducing the national burden of chronic disease by allocating $1.25 billion from the Prevention and Public Health Fund (Fund) for activities to help improve health outcomes and reduce health care costs, such as immunizations, and activities to reduce health-care associated infections. The Fund was authorized and funded by the ACA. The Budget also proposes a new lab consolidation program to region-alize our public health lab system and produce long-term cost savings by improving efficiencies across labs. The Budget includes $39 million for CDC activities to reduce health care associated infections (HAIS) and expand reporting of HAIS in hospitals and nursing homes. The Budget also includes a Comprehensive Chronic Disease Prevention Program that combines select chronic disease programs into one main program. This will provide States with additional flexibility to address the leading causes of chronic disease and disability, while increasing accountability and improving health outcomes through performance incentives. CDC's Consolidated Chronic Disease Program along with investments from the Prevention Public Health Fund, will also support some of the activities previously funded through the Preventive Health and Health Services Block Grant. The Budget includes an increase of $15 million to eradicate polio within India and reduce transmission of the wild polio virus in Pakistan, Afghanistan and Nigeria by the end of 2013.

Department of Health and Human Services
(In millions of dollars)

	Actual 2011	Estimate	
		2012	2013
Spending			
Discretionary Budget Authority:			
Food and Drug Administration [1]	2,403	2,506	2,517
Program Level (non-add)	*3,636*	*3,832*	*4,486*
Health Resources and Services Administration	6,284	6,228	6,088
Indian Health Service	4,069	4,307	4,422
Centers for Disease Control and Prevention	5,726	5,732	5,068
National Institutes of Health	30,470	30,702	30,702
Substance Abuse and Mental Health Services Administration	3,380	3,347	3,152
Agency for Healthcare Research and Quality			
Program Level (non-add)	*392*	*405*	*409*
Centers for Medicare and Medicaid Services (CMS) [2]	3,537	3,828	4,821
Discretionary Health Care Fraud and Abuse Control	310	311	311

Department of Health and Human Services—Continued
(In millions of dollars)

	Actual 2011	Estimate	
		2012	2013
Administration on Children and Families (ACF) [3]	17,210	16,489	16,194
Administration on Aging	1,497	1,471	1,978
General Departmental Management	655	474	306
Office of Civil Rights	41	41	39
Office of the National Coordinator for Health Information Technology	42	16	26
Program Level (non-add)	*61*	*61*	*66*
Office of Medicare Hearing and Appeals	70	72	84
Public Health and Social Services Emergency Fund	675	568	642
Office of Inspector General	50	50	59
All other	51	43	37
Subtotal, Discretionary budget authority [4]	76,472	76,186	76,446
Discretionary Changes in Mandatory Programs *(non-add in 2012):* [5]			
Children's Health Insurance Program Reauthorization Act of 2009—Performance Bonuses		*−6,368*	*−6,706*
Consumer Operated and Oriented Plan (CO-OP) Program		*−400*	—
High Risk Pool		*44*	—
ACF		—	*−13*
Subtotal, Discretionary changes in mandatory programs		*−6,724*	*−6,719*
Total, Discretionary budget authority	76,472	76,186	69,727
Discretionary Cap Adjustment:[6]			
Program Integrity	—	270	299
Rescission of Balances of Funds Provided by P.L. 111–32	−1,259	—	—
Total, Discretionary outlays [2]	86,528	84,160	80,605
Mandatory Outlays:			
Medicare			
Baseline Outlays [7]	480,202	479,338	528,556
Legislative proposal		215	−4,807
Medicaid and Children's Health Insurance Program (CHIP)			
Existing law	283,597	265,011	292,856
Legislative proposal		155	190
All other [8]			
Existing law	41,007	43,057	42,901
Legislative proposal		1	639
Total, Mandatory outlays	804,806	787,777	860,335

Department of Health and Human Services—Continued
(In millions of dollars)

	Actual 2011	Estimate	
		2012	2013
Total, Outlays	891,334	871,937	940,940
Credit activity			
Direct Loan Disbursements:			
CO-OP Financing..	—	225	1,844
Total, Direct loan disbursements..		225	1,844
Guaranteed Loan Disbursements by Private Lenders:			
Health Center Guaranteed Loan Finance...	25	13	10
Total, Guaranteed loan disbursements by private lenders............................	25	13	10

[1] FDA budget authority reported to Treasury for 2011 is $54 million lower than actual available budget authority due to the timing of FDA user fee collections.

[2] The CMS budget authority and outlay total for 2011 includes approximately $129 million that is misclassified as discretionary rather than mandatory.

[3] ACF's BA as displayed here in 2013 is $13 million higher than the actual BA, reflecting the repurposing of $13 million in Abstinence Education Funds, displayed here as a discretionary change in a mandatory program (CHIMP).

[4] Amounts, approximately $2 billion each year, appropriated to the Social Security Administration (SSA) from the Hospital Insurance and Supplementary Medical Insurance accounts are included in the corresponding table in the SSA chapter.

[5] The 2012 amounts reflect OMB's scoring of the 2012 Appropriations acts (P.L. 112–55 and 112–74) as transmitted to the Congress. These amounts are displayed as non-add entries because they have been rebased as mandatory and are not included in any 2012 discretionary levels in the 2013 Budget.

[6] The Balanced Budget and Emergency Deficit Control Act of 1985 (BBEDCA), as amended by the Budget Control Act of 2011, limits—or caps—budget authority available for discretionary programs each year through 2021. Section 251(b)(2) of BBEDCA authorizes certain adjustments to the caps after the enactment of appropriations. Amounts in 2011 are not so designated but are shown for comparability purposes.

[7] Includes $280 million in 2011, $1,501 million in 2011, and $368 million in 2012 of CMS Program Management mandatory funding. SSA funding from the Medicare Improvements for Patients and Providers Act is included in the corresponding table of the SSA chapter.

[8] Funding for the Centers for Medicare and Medicaid Innovation is included with all other mandatory outlays.

DEPARTMENT OF HOMELAND SECURITY

Funding Highlights:

- Provides $39.5 billion, a decrease of 0.5 percent or $191 million, below the 2012 enacted level. The Budget continues strong investments in core homeland security functions such as the prevention of terrorist attacks, border security, aviation security, disaster preparedness, and cybersecurity. Savings are created through cuts in administrative costs and the elimination of duplicative programs. The Budget also supports disaster relief through a cap adjustment, consistent with the Budget Control Act.

- Makes $853 million in cuts to administrative categories including travel, overtime, and fleet management, and eliminates duplicative and low-priority programs.

- Maintains front-line homeland security operations, supporting 21,186 Customs and Border Protection officers and 21,370 Border Patrol agents to facilitate legitimate travel and the movement of goods while strengthening border security.

- Supports the recovery of States and communities that have been devastated by disasters and emergencies with $6.1 billion for FEMA's Disaster Relief Fund, which includes $5.5 billion in disaster relief cap adjustments pursuant to the designation established in the Budget Control Act.

- Strengthens Government cybersecurity by providing $769 million to improve security of Federal civilian information technology networks while enhancing outreach to State and local governments and critical infrastructure sectors.

- Promotes innovation and economic growth by providing $650 million to fund important research and development advances in cybersecurity, explosives detection, and chemical/ biological response systems.

- Eliminates duplicative, stand-alone FEMA grant programs, consolidating them into a new National Preparedness Grant Program to better develop, sustain, and leverage core capabilities across the country while supporting national preparedness and response.

- Aligns resources with risk in immigration detention by focusing on criminal aliens, repeat immigration law violators, recent border entrants, immigration fugitives, and other priorities, and expanding resources for electronic monitoring and intensive supervision.

- Initiates acquisition of a new polar icebreaker and continues recapitalization of Coast Guard assets, including $658 million to construct the sixth National Security Cutter.

The Department of Homeland Security's (DHS's) mission is to ensure a homeland that is safe, secure, and resilient against terrorism and other hazards. DHS does this by securing and managing America's borders, enforcing and administering immigration laws, safeguarding and securing cyberspace, and ensuring resilience to disasters. The President's 2013 Budget includes $39.5 billion to support these missions, $191 million less than the 2012 enacted level. Tough choices were made to meet the discretionary targets in place. Savings are realized through cuts to administrative areas including travel, overtime, fleet management, the elimination of duplicative and low-priority programs, and strategic sourcing and acquisition reform initiatives. These savings help enable increased funding for core homeland security functions such as cybersecurity, border protection, and aviation security.

Protects the Homeland

Enhances Aviation Security with New Technology. The Budget includes $117 million in funding to support new explosives detection systems in U.S. airports. The Administration also proposes $58 million to continue to modernize and streamline transportation security vetting and credentialing for individuals who require access to America's transportation infrastructure, which will reduce redundant Transportation Security Administration processes and systems. The Budget provides resources to implement risk-based screening initiatives and focuses on enhanced targeting and information sharing efforts to interdict threats and dangerous people at the earliest point possible.

Supports Border Security and Facilitates Trade and Travel. The Budget includes funding to support 21,186 Customs and Border Protection officers, and 21,370 Border Patrol agents, and to continue deployment of border surveillance technology along the Southwest border. These resources will reduce wait times at our Nation's ports of entry, increase seizures of unlawful items, and continue to strengthen the security of our borders.

Invests in Cybersecurity. The Administration proposes $769 million to support the operations of the National Cyber Security Division, which protects Federal computer systems and sustains efforts under the Comprehensive National Cybersecurity Initiative to protect U.S. information networks from the threat of cyber-attacks or disruptions. The benefits of this investment extend beyond the Federal sphere and will help strengthen State and local governments' and the private sector's capabilities to address cyber threats.

Establishes an Effective Response to Disasters. The Administration also supports disaster response and resilience efforts by funding the Disaster Relief Fund (DRF) at $6.1 billion, including disaster-related adjustments to the Budget Control Act's discretionary caps. The DRF is used by the Federal Emergency Management Agency (FEMA), in the event of a presidentially-declared disaster or emergency, to assist State and local governments in response, recovery, and mitigation.

Sustains Essential Fire and Emergency Response Coverage. To retain an acceptable level of fire and emergency response coverage in the current constrained budgetary environment, the Budget anticipates $1 billion in immediate assistance for the retention, rehiring, and hiring of firefighters in 2012, as requested by the President in the American Jobs Act. In addition, departments will gain a preference for implementing programs and policies that focus on the recruitment of post–9/11 veterans for firefighter positions.

Improves Immigration Verification Programs. The President's Budget proposes $132 million for verification programs at U.S. Citizenship and Immigration Services and supports the nationwide deployment of E-Verify Self Check. E-Verify Self Check is a free service that empowers individuals to check their own employment eligibility status and allows workers to protect themselves from potential workplace discrimination. Additionally, the Budget supports enhancements to the Systematic Alien Verification for Entitlements (SAVE) program, which assists Federal, State, and local benefit-granting agencies in determining eligibility for benefits by verifying applicants' immigration status. E-Verify Self Check and the SAVE program both promote compliance with immigration laws while preventing individuals from obtaining benefits they are not eligible to receive.

Promotes Citizenship and Integration. The Administration continues support for integrating new immigrants into our American family, proposing $11 million to promote citizenship through education and preparation programs, the replication of promising practices in integration for use by communities across the country, and the expansion of innovative English-language learning tools.

Funds Critical Scientific Research Efforts. Research and Development (R&D) programs are critical to improving homeland security through state-of-the-art solutions and technology. DHS relies on R&D investments to discover, develop, and demonstrate high-payoff and game changing technologies. The Administration proposes $650 million to equip DHS and its State and local partners with tools to effectively and efficiently

prevent, protect against, respond to, and recover from all hazards and homeland security threats.

Invests in Upgrading the Coast Guard Fleet. The Budget includes $658 million to construct the sixth Coast Guard National Security Cutter and $8 million for the Coast Guard to initiate acquisition of a new polar icebreaker. These new assets will replace aging vessels that are well past their service life and will provide stronger platforms for the execution of Coast Guard missions.

Makes Tough Choices

Consolidates and Restructures Duplicative FEMA Grant Programs While Accelerating Expenditure of Already-Awarded Grants. Americans rely on first responders to help them through crises, from natural disasters to terrorist attacks. Accordingly, the Budget provides $2.9 billion for State and local programs to equip, train, exercise, and hire first responders. To better target these funds, the Budget proposes eliminating duplicative, stand-alone grant programs, and consolidating them into the National Preparedness Grant Program. This new initiative is designed to build, sustain, and leverage core capabilities as established in the National Preparedness Goal. Using a competitive risk-based model, the National Preparedness Grant Program will use a comprehensive process for identifying and prioritizing deployable capabilities; limit periods of performance to put funding to work quickly; and require grantees to regularly report progress in the acquisition and development of these capabilities.

While the Budget's proposed consolidated grant structure will strengthen State and local capabilities through smarter regional investments, accelerating the expenditure of already-awarded grant funds will improve first responders' capabilities and grow the economy now. The Administration will implement a series of measures to put the $9 billion of grant funding currently in the pipeline to work immediately. Similar to the successful effort that accelerated the American Recovery and

Reinvestment Act spending, the Administration has planned strong incentives to speed up spending of State and local grant balances by providing additional flexibility to grantees, waiving some administrative requirements, and proposing regulatory reforms to further reduce the backlog of unspent grants. Simultaneously, the Administration will set and enforce aggressive expiration dates for awarded grant funds, designating unexpended balances as "use or lose" to ensure first responders receive the support they need as quickly as possible.

Improves the Way Federal Dollars are Spent

Aligns Resources with Risk in Immigration Detention. Under this Administration, U.S. Immigration and Customs Enforcement (ICE) has focused its immigration enforcement efforts on identifying and removing criminal aliens and those who fall into other priority categories, including repeat immigration law violators, recent border entrants, and immigration fugitives. As ICE continues to focus on criminal and other priority cases, it expects to reduce the time removable aliens spend in detention custody. To ensure the most cost effective use of Federal dol-

lars, the Budget includes flexibility to transfer funding between jail detention and other forms of detention such as electronic monitoring and intensive supervision, commensurate with the level of risk a detainee presents. Consistent with its stated enforcement priorities and recent policy guidance, ICE will continue to focus resources on those individuals who have criminal convictions or fall under other priority categories. For low risk individuals, ICE will work to enhance the effectiveness of Alternatives to Detention, which costs significantly less than detention.

Cuts Administrative Costs and Eliminates Duplicative Programs. In order to focus limited resources on the highest priorities, the Budget cuts more than $853 million from administrative categories such as travel, overtime, and fleet management. It also eliminates duplicative and low-priority programs. These reductions result from the Secretary of Homeland Security's department-wide Efficiency Review and the government-wide Campaign to Cut Waste. These cost savings allow DHS to prioritize mission operations that safeguard the traveling public, strengthen the border, and prioritize the removal of criminal aliens to secure our communities.

Department of Homeland Security
(In millions of dollars)

	Actual 2011	Estimate	
		2012	2013
Spending			
Discretionary Budget Authority:			
Departmental Management and Operations	1,169	1,135	1,135
Office of the Inspector General	130	141	144
Office of Health Affairs	140	167	166
Citizenship and Immigration Services	131	101	143
United States Secret Service	1,527	1,665	1,601
Immigration and Customs Enforcement	5,482	5,526	5,333
Customs and Border Protection	9,613	10,145	10,353

Department of Homeland Security—Continued

(In millions of dollars)

	Actual 2011	Estimate	
		2012	2013
Transportation Security Administration	5,384	5,425	5,106
Federal Law Enforcement Training Center	270	271	258
National Protection and Programs Directorate	1,165	1,214	1,217
United States Coast Guard	8,622	8,656	8,319
Federal Emergency Management Agency	7,155	4,246	4,528
Science and Technology	767	668	831
Domestic Nuclear Detection Office	330	289	328
Subtotal, Discretionary budget authority	41,885	39,649	39,462
Discretionary Changes in Mandatory Programs *(non-add in 2012):*[1]			
Citizenship and Immigration Services		−4	−4
Total, Discretionary budget authority	41,885	39,649	39,458
Discretionary Cap Adjustment:[2]			
Disaster Relief	—	6,400	5,481
Overseas Contingency Operations	254	258	—
Total, Discretionary outlays	47,474	58,845	54,884
Mandatory Outlays:			
Citizenship and Immigration Services	2,386	2,928	3,059
Customs and Border Protection	1,017	1,659	1,634
United States Coast Guard	1,838	1,465	1,694
Federal Emergency Management Agency	−1,296	1,398	36
All other	−5,653	−5,840	−5,950
Total, Mandatory outlays	−1,708	1,610	473
Total, Outlays	45,766	60,455	55,357
Credit activity			
Direct Loan Disbursements:			
Disaster Assistance	18	12	18
Total, Direct loan disbursements	18	12	18

[1] The 2012 amounts reflect OMB's scoring of the 2012 Appropriations acts (P.L. 112–55 and 112–74) as transmitted to the Congress. These amounts are displayed as non-add entries because they have been rebased as mandatory and are not included in any 2012 discretionary levels in the 2013 Budget.
[2] The Balanced Budget and Emergency Deficit Control Act of 1985 (BBEDCA), as amended by the Budget Control Act of 2011, limits—or caps—budget authority available for discretionary programs each year through 2021. Section 251(b)(2) of BBEDCA authorizes certain adjustments to the caps after the enactment of appropriations. Amounts in 2011 are not so designated but are shown for comparability purposes.

DEPARTMENT OF HOUSING AND URBAN DEVELOPMENT

Funding Highlights:

- Provides $44.8 billion, an increase of 3.2 percent, or $1.4 billion, above the 2012 program funding level. Increases are made to protect vulnerable families, revitalize distressed neighborhoods, and advance investments in sustainable development. Savings are created through measured reforms to the Department's rental assistance programs without reducing the number of families served.

- Invests $2.3 billion to continue progress toward the Administration's goal to end chronic homelessness and homelessness among veterans and families, implementing an innovative, multi-agency strategic plan.

- Increases support for housing counseling services, including assistance for families in danger of foreclosure, and continues to offer loss mitigation solutions for FHA-insured borrowers similarly at risk.

- Revitalizes affordable rental housing and surrounding neighborhoods by providing $150 million to continue the Department's transformative investments in high-poverty neighborhoods where distressed HUD-assisted public and privately owned housing is located.

- Restores the 2011 funding level of $100 million for the Sustainable Communities Initiative to create incentives for more communities to develop comprehensive housing and transportation plans that result in sustainable development, increased transit-accessible housing, lower energy costs for consumers, and reduced air pollution that impacts public health and the climate.

- Preserves funding for the Community Development Block Grant and HOME Investment Partnerships programs at 2012 levels to enable State and local governments to continue to address infrastructure, affordable housing, and economic development needs in their communities.

- Provides $34.8 billion to preserve rental housing assistance to 4.7 million low-income families, $154 million to expand the supply of affordable housing to seniors and persons with disabilities, and $650 million to address the housing needs of Native American Tribes. The Budget also provides $1 billion to capitalize the Housing Trust Fund to expand the supply of housing targeted to very-low income families.

123

- Reduces Project-Based Rental Assistance by $640 million below 2012 without affecting families served and increases minimum rents across-the-board to $75 per month for all HUD-assisted households, a rate comparable to the minimum rent enacted in 1998 when adjusted for inflation.

- Increases employment opportunities for over 30,000 Public Housing residents by providing up to $50 million to pilot an expansion of the successful Jobs-Plus demonstration, and expands local flexibility to use HUD funding to connect residents to supportive services.

- Simplifies and improves the Public Housing program by converting it to a single subsidy stream, and proposes changes to the Housing Opportunities for Persons with AIDS program to target funds to areas with the highest needs.

The Department of Housing and Urban Development (HUD) supports home ownership, access to affordable housing free from discrimination, and community development. Affordable housing and a healthy mortgage market are especially critical to America's continued recovery and long-term economic health and are a central part of the American dream to which middle-class families aspire. The President's 2013 Budget provides $44.8 billion for HUD programs to support these efforts, an increase of $1.4 billion over 2012. The constrained fiscal environment forced difficult choices, including a reduction of $640 million in Project-Based Rental Assistance, which will not affect families served by the program, and an increase in the minimum rent charged to HUD-assisted households. Consistent with Administration priorities, funding increases were provided to protect the homeless and other vulnerable families, revitalize distressed neighborhoods, and support sustainable community development.

Supports the Housing Sector and Delivers on Administration Priorities

Supports the Mortgage Market and Helps Borrowers Who are at Risk of Foreclosure. The Administration projects that the Federal Housing Administration (FHA) will insure $149 billion in mortgage loans in 2013, supporting new home purchases and re-financed mortgages that significantly reduce borrower payments.

FHA financing was used for 37 percent of home purchase loans in 2010, with 60 percent of African American and 59 percent of Hispanic borrowers who purchased homes using FHA. It also is an important financing source for first-time homeowners, 56 percent of whom used FHA insured financing in 2009 and 2010. FHA also provides vital assistance to homeowners facing foreclosure. FHA's loss mitigation program minimizes the risk of financially struggling borrowers going into foreclosure, and since the start of the mortgage crisis, it has helped more than a million homeowners stay in their homes. The Budget includes the recently enacted increases in FHA premium levels. These will boost FHA's capital reserves—to better protect taxpayers against the risk of credit losses by the program— and increase Federal revenues. The Budget also includes $141 million for housing and homeowner counseling through HUD and the Neighborhood Reinvestment Corporation (NeighborWorks). Over half of these funds are dedicated to foreclosure assistance. NeighborWorks' National Foreclosure Mitigation Counseling program has assisted over one million households since its inception in 2008.

Funds the Federal Strategic Plan to End Homelessness. The President's Budget continues the Administration's commitment to the goals laid out in the Federal Strategic Plan to Prevent and End Homelessness. The Budget requests $2.2 billion for Homeless Assistance Grants to maintain existing units and expand prevention, rapid re-housing, and permanent supportive housing. The Budget also provides $75 million in new housing vouchers set aside for homeless veterans that are paired with health care and other services from the Department of Veterans Affairs. These investments will make further progress toward the goals laid out in the Federal Strategic Plan.

Rehabilitates and Transforms HUD-Assisted Housing and Distressed Neighborhoods. The Budget provides $150 million for the Choice Neighborhoods Initiative to continue transformative investments in high-poverty neighborhoods where distressed HUD-assisted public and privately-owned housing is located. The Budget will reach four to six neighborhoods with implementation grants that primarily fund the preservation, rehabilitation and transformation of HUD-assisted public and privately-owned multifamily housing, and will also engage local governments, nonprofits, and for-profit developers in partnerships to improve the economic conditions in their surrounding communities. This initiative is a central element of the Administration's inter-agency, place-based strategy to support local communities in developing the tools they need to revitalize neighborhoods of concentrated poverty into neighborhoods of opportunity.

Restores Funding for Sustainable Communities and Innovative Infrastructure Planning. The Budget supports the multi-agency Partnership for Sustainable Communities, an Administration initiative that integrates resources and expertise from HUD, the Department of Transportation, and the Environmental Protection Agency. In particular, the Budget restores $100 million for the Sustainable Communities Initiative, which creates incentives for communities to develop comprehensive housing and transportation plans to achieve sustainable development, reduce energy consumption and greenhouse gas emissions, and increase affordable housing near public transit. This includes $46 million to fund about 20 additional regional planning grants to help enable communities to align public and private investments in housing, transportation, and infrastructure to strategical-

ly integrate goals for mobility, regional housing choices and economic development. In addition, $46 million will be invested in neighborhoods and communities to update building codes, zoning, and local planning efforts as complementary strategies to the regional grants.

Preserves HUD's Major Block Grant Programs for Community Development and Housing. The Budget provides $3 billion for the Community Development Block Grant (CDBG) formula program and $1 billion for the HOME Investment Partnerships program, both equal to 2012 funding. These funding levels for CDBG and HOME reflect the Administration's commitment in a constrained Federal budget to supporting municipalities and States as they navigate through their challenging fiscal climate. CDBG funding will allow over 1,200 State and local governments to invest in needed public infrastructure improvements, rehabilitate affordable housing, and create and retain jobs. The Budget request for HOME will provide funding to about 645 State and local governments to increase the supply of affordable housing for low-income families.

Makes Tough Choices

Reforms Rental Assistance Programs While Maintaining the Number of Families Served. The Budget includes a menu of reforms to HUD rental assistance programs that save over $500 million in 2013 without reducing the number of families served. In the Project-Based Rental Assistance program, savings are achieved by improving oversight of market rent studies used to set subsidy payment levels, capping annual subsidy increases for certain properties, and using excess reserves to offset HUD payments to landlords. The Budget also aligns policy across rental assistance programs and reduces costs by increasing the minimum rent to $75 per month for all HUD-assisted households, which is comparable to the minimum rent enacted in 1998, adjusted for inflation. Recognizing the potential burden that this higher minimum rent may impose, the Budget maintains the current exemption for families facing financial hardship.

In addition, the Budget reduces costs by simplifying administration of the medical expense deduction, better targeting rental assistance to the working poor, and setting Public Housing flat rents closer to market levels.

Reduces Upfront Funding for Some Project-Based Rental Assistance (PBRA) Contracts. The Budget provides $8.7 billion for PBRA, which is $640 million below 2012. The PBRA program provides critically-needed affordable housing to 1.2 million low-income households through contracts between HUD and private landlords. These savings in 2013 are generated by providing less than 12 months of funding upfront on some PBRA contracts that straddle fiscal years. This change will not reduce or delay payments to landlords nor impact the number of families served by the program.

Improves the Way Federal Dollars are Spent

Consolidates the Public Housing Operating and Capital Funds. The Budget proposes to combine the separate Operating Fund and Capital Fund programs into a single Public Housing subsidy stream. The current structure presents restrictions that are difficult to implement and regulate, and underscores the isolation of Public Housing properties from mainstream real estate financing and management practices. This proposed merger will simplify the program and reduce the administrative burden on State and local public housing authorities (PHAs) that own and manage these properties. As a first step toward consolidation, the Budget provides all PHAs with full flexibility to use their operating and capital funds for any eligible capital or operating expense. The Budget requests a total of $6.6 billion for Public Housing, a critical investment that will help 1.1 million extremely low- to low-income households to obtain or retain decent, safe and sanitary housing. In addition, the Budget provides up to $50 million to pilot the expansion of

the successful Jobs-Plus demonstration to over 30,000 Public Housing residents.

Provides Flexibility for PHAs to Improve Supportive Services for Assisted Households. The Budget proposes streamlining and flexibility measures to help PHAs improve supportive services for assisted families. The Family Self-Sufficiency (FSS) program will be consolidated and aligned to enable PHAs to more uniformly serve both Housing Choice Voucher and Public Housing residents. This program, which the Budget also expands to residents of PBRA housing, aims to connect residents to resources and services to find and retain jobs that lead to economic independence and self-sufficiency. In addition, the Budget authorizes PHAs to use a portion of their Public Housing and Housing Voucher funding to augment case management and supportive services provided through FSS or provide other supportive services to increase opportunities for residents.

Modernizes the Housing Opportunities for Persons with AIDS (HOPWA) Program. The Budget proposes to update the HOPWA program to better reflect the current understanding of HIV/AIDS and ensure that funds are directed in a more equitable and effective manner. This modernization includes a new formula that will distribute HOPWA funds based on the current population of HIV-positive individuals, fair market rents, and poverty rates in order to target funds to areas with the most need. It also makes the program more flexible, giving local communities more options to provide targeted, timely, and cost-effective interventions. The Budget's $330 million investment in HOPWA, in combination with the proposed modernization, will assist local communities in keeping individuals with HIV/AIDS housed, making it easier for them to stay in therapy, and therefore improving health outcomes for this vulnerable population.

Provides Housing Opportunities

Preserves Affordable Rental Opportunities. The President's Budget requests $19 billion for the Housing Choice Voucher program to help more than two million extremely low- to low-income families afford decent housing in neighborhoods of their choice. The Budget funds all existing mainstream vouchers and provides 10,000 new vouchers targeted to homeless veterans. The Administration remains committed to working with the Congress to improve the management and budgeting for the Housing Choice Voucher program, including reducing inefficiencies, and re-allocating PHA reserves to high performers. In addition, the Budget provides $1 billion in mandatory funding in 2013 for the Housing Trust Fund to finance the development, rehabilitation, and preservation of affordable housing for extremely-low income families.

Expands the Supply of Supportive Housing for Seniors and Persons with Disabilities. The Budget provides a total of $625 million for the Housing for the Elderly and Housing for Persons with Disabilities programs, which includes $154 million to support 5,300 additional supportive housing units. Doing more with less, the Budget proposes reforms to the Housing for the Elderly program to target resources to help those most in need, reduce the up-front cost of new awards, and better connect residents with the supportive services they need to age in place and live independently.

Addresses the Housing Needs of Native American Tribes. The Budget provides $650 million for the Native American Housing Block Grant program, which will provide much-needed funds to over 550 Tribes to help mitigate severe housing needs and overcrowding on reservations. This program is the primary source for housing on tribal lands and provides funding for vital housing activities such as construction, rehabilitation, and operations. In addition, the Budget provides $60 million in Indian Community Development Block Grant funding that Tribes use to improve their housing stock, create community facilities, make infrastructure improvements, and expand job opportunities.

Department of Housing and Urban Development
(In millions of dollars)

	Actual 2011	Estimate	
		2012	2013
Spending			
Discretionary Budget Authority:			
Community Development Fund	3,501	3,308	3,143
Sustainable Housing and Communities (non-add)	100	—	100
HOME Investment Partnerships Program	1,607	1,000	1,000
Homeless Assistance Grants	1,901	1,901	2,231
Housing Opportunities for Persons with AIDS	334	332	330
Tenant-based Rental Assistance	18,371	18,264	19,074
Project-based Rental Assistance	9,257	9,340	8,700
Public Housing Operating Fund	4,617	3,962	4,524
Public Housing Capital Fund	2,040	1,875	2,070

Department of Housing and Urban Development—Continued
(In millions of dollars)

	Actual 2011	Estimate 2012	Estimate 2013
Jobs-Plus Pilot (non-add)..	—	—	*50*
Choice Neighborhoods	65	120	150
Native American Housing Block Grant...	649	650	650
Housing for the Elderly..	399	375	475
Housing for Persons with Disabilities...	150	165	150
Housing Counseling..	—	45	55
Federal Housing Administration (FHA)	207	207	215
Fair Housing..	72	71	68
Lead Hazard Reduction	120	120	120
Policy Development and Research	48	46	52
Salaries and Expenses...	1,326	1,351	1,370
Office of the Inspector General..	125	124	126
All other...	468	133	256
Subtotal, Discretionary budget authority..	45,257	43,389	44,759
Receipts and Other Program Level Adjustments:			
Federal Housing Administration (FHA)	−7,231	−4,333	−8,776
Government National Mortgage Association (GNMA)...........................	−841	−653	−636
Other Adjustments	−41	−232	—
Total, Discretionary budget authority..	37,144	38,171	35,347
Discretionary Cap Adjustment:[1]			
Disaster Relief...	—	100	—
Total, Discretionary outlays...	46,602	47,890	41,091
Mandatory Outlays:			
FHA...	8,818	7,797	−40
GNMA..	726	164	197
Neighborhood Stabilization Program	1,123	1,013	898
Project Rebuild..	—	50	4,650
Housing Trust Fund..	—	—	10
All other programs...	−267	−126	−523
Total, Mandatory outlays...	10,400	8,898	5,192
Total, Outlays	57,002	56,788	46,283

Department of Housing and Urban Development—Continued
(In millions of dollars)

	Actual 2011	Estimate	
		2012	2013
Credit activity			
Direct Loan Disbursements:			
Emergency Homeowners' Relief	—	210	—
FHA	—	50	50
GNMA	—	9	9
Green Retrofit Program for Multifamily Housing	27	—	—
Total, Direct loan disbursements	27	269	59
Guaranteed Loan Disbursements by Private Lenders:			
FHA	245,956	251,244	237,942
GNMA	350,398	291,000	239,000
All other	793	616	1,158
Total, Guaranteed loan disbursements by private lenders	597,147	542,860	478,100

[1] The Balanced Budget and Emergency Deficit Control Act of 1985 (BBEDCA), as amended by the Budget Control Act of 2011, limits—or caps—budget authority available for discretionary programs each year through 2021. Section 251(b)(2) of BBEDCA authorizes certain adjustments to the caps after the enactment of appropriations.

DEPARTMENT OF THE INTERIOR

Funding Highlights:

- Provides $11.4 billion in discretionary funding, an increase of about one percent above the 2012 enacted level. This reflects an ongoing commitment to critical landscapes and infrastructure, as well as savings achieved through administrative efficiencies and reductions in construction funding to focus on projects necessary for health and safety.

- Invests in the safety, reliability, and efficiency of America's water infrastructure and in the protection and restoration of fragile aquatic ecosystems.

- Conserves landscapes and promotes outdoor recreation in national parks, refuges, and on other public lands through the America's Great Outdoors initiative.

- Invests $386 million to strengthen oversight of offshore oil and gas operations so that energy development can proceed in a safe and sustainable manner.

- Supports tribal priorities in Indian Country by increasing funding for public safety and justice, natural resources, and compensation to Tribes that assume responsibility for managing Federal programs.

- Reforms mining oversight and reduces the environmental impacts of coal and hardrock mining by dedicating and prioritizing funds to reclaim abandoned mines and by evaluating integration of activities between bureaus.

- Continues the Administration's commitment to land conservation by providing $450 million for the Land and Water Conservation Fund.

- Improves the return to taxpayers from mineral production on Federal lands and waters through royalty reforms and industry fees.

- Saves over $200 million from 2010 levels through administrative efficiencies and reduced spending in travel, printing, supplies, and advisory services.

- Reduces construction funding by $49.4 million, or 16 percent.

- Continues efforts to restore significant ecosystems such as the California Bay-Delta, the Everglades, the Great Lakes, Chesapeake Bay, and the Gulf Coast, helping to promote their ecological sustainability and resilience.

The Department of the Interior's (DOI's) mission is to protect and manage America's natural resources and cultural heritage; provide scientific and other information about those resources; and honor its trust responsibilities and special commitments to American Indians, Alaska Natives, and Insular areas. In support of this mission, the President's 2013 Budget provides $11.4 billion for DOI, about a one percent increase over the 2012 enacted level. This is close to the average for the past five years, and in light of the tight discretionary budget caps, a sign of the Administration's commitment to these priorities. To free up resources, the Budget also includes legislative proposals that would save a net total of approximately $2 billion over 10 years, including reforms to fees, royalties, and other payments related to oil, gas, coal, and other mineral development on Federal lands and waters.

Promotes Economic Growth by Investing in Our Natural Heritage and Energy Resources

Protects and Restores Water Resources and Infrastructure. The Budget invests in the safety, reliability, and efficiency of our water infrastructure, to ensure the continued delivery of water and power to millions of customers and serve as a foundation for a healthy economy, especially in the arid West. The Budget continues investments in the protection and restoration of fragile aquatic ecosystems, such as California's Bay-Delta, to ensure that such environmental treasures are available for future generations. These investments are made possible by making difficult choices elsewhere, finding savings and consolidations, and reaping the benefits of smart choices made in previous years. Both study of

new projects and construction of ongoing projects have been severely curtailed; the Budget proposes to merge the Central Utah Project Completion Act Office (CUPCA) with the Bureau of Reclamation; and water reuse, recycling and conservation programs are emphasized over new construction.

Makes Public Lands Available for Private Investments for the Development of Clean Energy. To enhance energy security and create green jobs in new industries, the Administration proposes key funding increases for renewable energy development and Federal natural resource stewardship. The Budget includes $86 million to maintain capacity to review and permit new renewable energy projects on Federal lands and waters, with the goal of permitting 11,000 megawatts of new solar, wind, and geothermal electricity generation capacity on DOI-managed lands by the end of 2013.

Funds Development of the Nation's Offshore Oil and Gas Resources. The Administration proposes $164 million and $222 million, respectively, to fund the new Bureau of Ocean Energy Management (BOEM) and Bureau of Safety and Environmental Enforcement (BSEE). Together, BOEM and BSEE will work to aggressively—but responsibly—conduct the remaining Gulf of Mexico lease sale pursuant to the 2007-2012 Outer Continental Shelf Five-Year Oil and Gas Leasing Program. In addition, the Bureaus will work to finalize and begin implementation of the Administration's proposed 2012-2017 leasing program, which would make more than 75 percent of undiscovered technically recoverable oil and gas resources estimated on the Outer Continental Shelf (OCS) available for development.

Conserves Landscapes, Creates Jobs, and Promotes Outdoor Recreation. The America's Great Outdoors (AGO) initiative supports Federal, State, local, and tribal conservation efforts while reconnecting Americans, particularly young people, to the outdoors. Investments for AGO programs support conservation and outdoor recreation activities nationwide that create millions of jobs, generate hundreds of millions of dollars in tax revenue, and spur billions in total national economic activity. These programs include operating national parks, refuges, and public lands, which are critical for conserving natural and cultural resources; protecting wildlife; and drawing recreational tourists from across the country and the world. They also include grant programs that assist States, Tribes, local governments, landowners, and private groups (such as sportsmen) in preserving wildlife habitat, wetlands, historic battlefields, regional parks, and the countless other sites that form the mosaic of our cultural and natural legacy. The Budget provides $450 million for the Land and Water Conservation Fund (LWCF), programs in the Departments of the Interior and Agriculture. Of this amount, $270 million is proposed to conserve lands within national parks public lands, refuges, and forests, including $109 million in collaborative funds for Interior and the U.S. Forest Service to jointly and strategically conserve the most critical landscapes. In addition, reauthorization of the Federal Land Transaction Facilitation Act would allow DOI to use proceeds from the sale of low-conservation value lands to acquire additional high-priority conservation lands.

Protects Communities and Ecosystems from Wildfire Damage. The Budget continues the long-standing practice of fully funding the 10-year average cost of wildland fire suppression operations. The Budget also continues the practice of targeting hazardous fuels reduction funding for activities near communities (known as the "wildland-urban interface") where they are most effective. Priority is given to projects in communities that have met "Firewise" standards (or the equivalent), identified acres to be treated, and invested in local solutions to protect against wildland fire.

Strengthens Tribal Nations. The Administration supports the principle of tribal self-determination and improved outcomes with a $9 million increase to compensate Tribes when they manage Federal programs themselves under self-determination contracts and self-governance compacts. Administration efforts to combat crime in Indian Country through cooperation among Federal, State and tribal entities are making progress, as demonstrated by a pilot program to reduce violent crime on selected reservations. The Budget builds on this progress with increased funds for operating tribal courts, staffing new detention centers, and coordinating community policing programs to reduce crime. The Budget also includes increases to meet the needs due to growing enrollment in tribal colleges and to protect natural resources in Indian Country.

Improves Oversight and the Use of Federal Dollars

Reorganizes and Reforms the Management and Oversight of Offshore Drilling. In the wake of the Deepwater Horizon disaster and subsequent oil spill, the Administration has initiated comprehensive reforms to the management of offshore oil and gas drilling on the OCS. In addition to establishing greater independence for safety regulators through the creation of a separate Bureau of Safety and Environmental Enforcement, the Administration is aggressively implementing management reforms to strengthen oversight of OCS oil and gas operations. These investments are consistent with recommendations for stronger oversight made by the National Commission on the BP Deepwater Horizon Oil Spill and Offshore Drilling in its January 2011 report. The Budget includes $386 million, a $28 million increase over the 2012 enacted level, to complete reforms to the two bureaus that now oversee offshore oil and gas development. This includes funding to hire new oil and gas inspectors, engineers, scientists, and other staff to oversee industry operations; establish real-time monitoring of key drilling activities; conduct detailed engineering reviews of offshore drilling and production safety systems; improve oil spill research and development activities; and implement more aggressive reviews of company oil spill response plans. These reforms will also facilitate the timely review of offshore oil and gas permits.

Reforms Mining Operations and Reduces the Environmental Impacts of Mining. The Budget addresses the environmental impacts of past mining by dedicating and prioritizing funds to clean up abandoned mines. Currently, DOI charges the coal industry an abandoned mine lands (AML) fee and allocates receipts to States based on production, rather than on the most pressing needs for cleaning up abandoned mines. The Administration proposes to target these coal AML fee receipts at the most hazardous sites through a new competitive allocation process with State participation. It also proposes to establish a new AML fee on hardrock mining, with receipts allocated through a competitive process to reclaim abandoned hardrock mines, so that the hardrock mining industry is held responsible in the same manner as the coal mining industry. The Administration is also evaluating a better alignment of mining oversight and cleanup operations by integrating certain functions of the Office of Surface Mining and Bureau of Land Management. A new organizational structure would allow the two bureaus to gain efficiencies through shared administrative costs, while building on their respective strengths.

Provides a Better Return to Taxpayers from Mineral Development. The public received above $10 billion in 2011 from fees, royalties, and other payments related to oil, gas, coal, and other mineral development on Federal lands and waters. A number of recent studies by the Government Accountability Office and DOI's Inspector General have found that taxpayers could earn a better return through more rigorous oversight and policy changes, such as charging appropriate fees and reforming how royalties are set. The Budget proposes a number of actions to ensure that taxpayers receive a fair return from the development of U.S. mineral resources:

- Charging a royalty on select hardrock minerals (such as silver, gold and copper);

- Terminating unwarranted payments to coal-producing States and Tribes that no longer need funds to clean up abandoned coal mines;

- Extending net receipts sharing, where States receiving mineral revenue payments help defray the costs of managing the mineral leases that generate the revenue;

- Charging user fees to oil companies for processing oil and gas drilling permits and inspecting operations on Federal lands and waters;

- Establishing fees for new non-producing oil and gas leases (both onshore and offshore) to encourage more timely production; and

- Making administrative changes to Federal oil and gas royalties, such as adjusting royalty rates and terminating the royalty-in-kind program.

Department of the Interior
(In millions of dollars)

	Actual 2011	Estimate 2012	Estimate 2013
Spending			
Discretionary Budget Authority:			
Bureau of Land Management (BLM)...	1,100	1,098	1,146
Bureau of Ocean Energy Management	161	161	164
Bureau of Safety and Environmental Enforcement (BSEE)......................	145	197	222
Office of Surface Mining..	162	150	141
Bureau of Reclamation/CUPCA...	1,045	1,024	994
U.S. Geological Survey	1,084	1,068	1,102
Fish and Wildlife Service..	1,505	1,476	1,548
National Park Service	2,641	2,610	2,609
Bureau of Indian Affairs	2,594	2,531	2,527
Office of the Special Trustee	161	152	146
Wildland Fire...	779	575	818
All other...	472	500	502
Subtotal, Discretionary budget authority...	11,849	11,542	11,919
Discretionary Changes in Mandatory Programs *(non-add in 2012):*[1]			
LWCF Contract Authority		*−30*	*−30*
Coastal Impact Assistance Program Balances		*—*	*−200*
Net Receipts Sharing...		*−42*	*−40*
Palau Compact Extension...		*14*	*—*
Subtotal, Discretionary changes in mandatory programs.............................		*−58*	*−270*
Receipts and Collections:			
Offsetting OCS Collections (rents/cost recovery)	−155	−160	−162
OCS Inspection Fees (BSEE)...	−10	−62	−65
Onshore Oil and Gas Inspection Fees (BLM)	—	—	−48
Total, Discretionary budget authority...	11,684	11,320	11,374
Total, Discretionary outlays	13,121	12,416	12,258
Mandatory Outlays:			
Existing law	558	−1,101	938
Legislative proposals		29	254
Total, Mandatory outlays...	558	−1,072	1,192
Total, Outlays	13,679	11,344	13,450

Department of the Interior—Continued
(In millions of dollars)

	Actual 2011	Estimate	
		2012	2013
Credit activity			
Guaranteed Loan Disbursements by Private Lenders:			
Indian Guaranteed Loan Program	84	73	73
Total, Guaranteed loan disbursements by private lenders...............................	84	73	73

[1] The 2012 amounts reflect OMB's scoring of the 2012 Appropriations acts (P.L. 112–55 and 112–74) as transmitted to the Congress. These amounts are displayed as non-add entries because they have been rebased as mandatory and are not included in any 2012 discretionary levels in the 2013 Budget.

DEPARTMENT OF JUSTICE

Funding Highlights:

- Provides $27.1 billion in discretionary funding, a decrease of 0.4 percent below the 2012 level. Savings are achieved by prioritizing uniquely Federal responsibilities and streamlining programs and operations. Core Federal programs including law enforcement, litigation, and prisons and detention, however, are funded at 1.2 percent above 2012 levels.

- Invests more than $700 million to investigate and prosecute financial crimes, an increase of $55 million over 2012. The Budget provides funding for additional FBI agents, criminal prosecutors, civil litigators, in-house investigators, and forensic accountants to improve the Department's capacity to investigate and prosecute the full spectrum of financial fraud.

- Supports the Department's national security mission by fully funding the National Security Division and providing for FBI programs critical to mitigating and countering terrorism threats.

- Finances efforts to combat transnational criminal organizations and maintain the security of the Southwest border with new investments in intelligence capabilities and nearly $2 billion in Southwest border enforcement spending.

- Increases funding for the investigation and deterrence of intellectual property crime by $5 million for additional attorneys and FBI agents, bringing total spending to nearly $40 million annually.

- Maintains safe and secure capacity in Federal prisons and detention facilities and continues activation of completed but not yet occupied prisons to address population growth.

- Prioritizes uniquely Federal responsibilities, streamlines programs, and redirects funding to improve the capabilities of the Department of Justice law enforcement agencies.

- Consistent with Administration-wide efforts to help States maximize effective activities, the Budget continues to assist State and local criminal justice programs with more than $2 billion in program assistance for police hiring, general purpose criminal justice assistance, violence against women programs, and Second Chance Act grants; the same as in 2012.

The Department of Justice (DOJ) is responsible for enforcing laws and defending the interests of the United States; ensuring public safety against foreign and domestic threats; providing Federal leadership in preventing and controlling crime; punishing those guilty of unlawful behavior; and ensuring fair and impartial administration of justice for all Americans. On April 25, 2011, the Attorney General laid out four priorities to guide and focus the Department's future work: protecting Americans from terrorism; protecting Americans from violent crime; protecting Americans from financial fraud; and protecting the most vulnerable members of our society. The President's Budget supports these priorities and protects the progress that has already been made in key programs, including civil rights enforcement. The Budget also reflects the need to operate within tight fiscal constraints while continuing to support ongoing requirements such as keeping pace with the continuing growth in the Federal prison population.

Enforces Laws and Protects U.S. Interests

Combats Financial Fraud. Honest and fair competition, based on transparent rules equally applied, is the cornerstone of our economy and our competitiveness. To continue its aggressive efforts to combat financial, mortgage, and other fraud, the Administration proposes more than $700 million, an increase of $55 million over the 2012 enacted level. These funds will support the Department's investigation and prosecution of the broad range of crimes that fall under the definition of financial fraud, including securities and commodities fraud, investment scams, mortgage foreclosure schemes, and efforts to defraud economic recovery programs. The Department also plays a leading role in coordinating referrals of cases from other agencies and will work to improve capacity Government-wide to respond to fraud. Additional resources will allow the agencies, as well as different DOJ components, to better assist each other in the investigation and litigation efforts. In 2011, these efforts led to the recovery of more than $5.6 billion in fines and penalties, an increase of more than 167 percent since 2008.

Counters the Threat of Terrorism and Strengthens National Security. Combating the threat of terrorism remains a top priority for DOJ—not only for the safety of our citizens, but also the security of our economy and information infrastructure, which are critical to America's global competitiveness. The Budget therefore maintains recent increases related to intelligence gathering and surveillance capabilities. Funding is preserved for the Comprehensive National Cybersecurity Initiative, the High-Value Detainee Interrogation Group, the Joint Terrorism Task Forces, as well as other critical counterterrorism and counterintelligence programs.

Combats Transnational Organized Crime and Maintains the Security of the Southwest Border. The Budget provides enhancements for the International Organized Crime Intelligence and Operations Center and efforts to disrupt and dismantle the most significant drug trafficking organizations and their related entities. Working cooperatively, DOJ components and other law enforcement agencies develop a list of Consolidated Priority Targets. These targets become the focus for investigative and prosecutorial resources. The Administration is also making a concerted effort to combat crime along the Southwest border and provides nearly $2 billion in funding support for the Administration's Southwest border security priorities; including those priorities started with the passage of the 2010 Southwest Border Security Supplemental Appropriations Act, (Public Law 111–230).

Promotes Innovation by Protecting Intellectual Property Rights. Recent technological advances, particularly in methods of manufacturing and distribution, have created new opportunities for businesses of all sizes to innovate and grow. These advancements, however, have also created new vulnerabilities, which tech-savvy criminals are eager to exploit. As a result, there has been an alarming rise in intellectual property (IP) crimes, illegal activities that not only devastate individual lives and legitimate businesses, but undermine our financial stability and prosperity. Therefore, the Administration is devoting nearly $40 million to identify and defeat intellectual property criminals, an increase of $5 million over 2012. The Administration's efforts have already resulted in shutting down 350 websites engaged in the illegal sale and distribution of counterfeit goods and copyrighted works. Additionally, international partnerships and joint initiatives have enabled experts to train or educate in IP protection more than 2,500 foreign judges, prosecutors, investigators, and other officials from over 30 countries.

Maintains Safe and Secure Prison Capacity. The Budget proposes $8.5 billion, a 4 percent increase over 2012, for Federal prisons and detention facilities. These funds are provided to staff and operate recently completed prisons as well as address additional capacity requirements due to projected growth in the Federal detainee population. An additional $13 million is provided to expand inmate re-entry programs that help ensure inmates are well prepared to re-enter society and become positive and productive members of their communities. The Administration will also continue to explore opportunities to reduce the prison population, with a focus on non-violent offenders.

Improves the Way Federal Dollars are Spent

Explores Improvements to the Prosecution of Criminals. The Administration is committed to a smarter allocation of resources for crime prevention and public safety; one that utilizes Federal resources more efficiently and effectively to address the wide range of criminal justice and national security threats facing the country. The U.S. Attorneys will continue to lead efforts to ensure that law enforcement investigations are conducted in a manner that leads to strong case presentation and results in effective and successful prosecutions, thereby improving the effectiveness of all the Department's law enforcement activities.

Strategically Invests in Law Enforcement by Streamlining Activities and Reducing Duplication. DOJ's law enforcement components have grown 106 percent from 2001 to 2012 and now encompass more than 50 percent of the Department's total budget. Recognizing this, the Administration proposes to strategically align the Department's law enforcement resources and invest $12.4 billion in the FBI, the Drug Enforcement Administration, the Bureau of Alcohol, Tobacco, Firearms and Explosives, and the U.S. Marshals. Although this funding is slightly below the 2012 enacted level, the Administration is encouraged by the continuing downward trend in violent crime rates. Despite these improvements, however, the Administration remains vigilant and understands that for progress to continue, Federal law enforcement must be aligned with today's criminal justice challenges. As such, the Department is focusing its law enforcement resources foremost on preventing, protecting against, and mitigating terrorist threats; disrupting and dismantling organized and sophisticated criminal enterprises; defending against the penetration of the Nation's critical information infrastructure; and ensuring the safety of those most at risk. In addition, the Department has identified $138 million in savings and administrative efficiencies. For example, task forces with similar missions and geographic commonality will be considered for consolidation or elimination; offices, facilities, and information technology systems will be restructured and condensed; and gang and drug intelligence and operations will be streamlined, reduced, or eliminated.

Makes Targeted Investments for State and Local Assistance Initiatives

Provides Funding for Juvenile Justice and Child Safety Programs. The Budget provides $312 million for Juvenile Justice and Child Safety programs that assist States with their juvenile justice systems. Research indicates that more than 60 percent of children have been exposed to violence, crime, and abuse. This problem has significant consequences for individuals, families, and communities at-large, which makes these Juvenile Justice and Child Safety programs an essential part of the State and local assistance portfolio. The Budget also provides $20 million for the Adam Walsh Act implementation.

Invests in First Responders. The Budget provides $257 million to support America's first responders and the hiring and retention of police officers and sheriffs' deputies across the country, and includes a preference for the hiring of post–9/11 veterans. This funding builds on the $166 million in COPS Hiring Grants funding enacted in 2012. These investments assist in building capacity to enable State and local law enforcement partners to make the most of their resources and encourage their most promising and effective public safety efforts. The Budget includes $4 billion in immediate assistance for the retention, rehiring, and hiring of police officers in 2012, as requested by the President in the American Jobs Act. States and localities will gain a preference for implementing programs and policies that focus on the recruitment of post–9/11 veterans for law enforcement positions.

Reinforces Efforts to Combat Violence Against Women. The Budget provides $413 million to continue efforts to combat the hundreds of thousands of violent crimes against women that are committed each year. Violence Against Women Act funding plays a critical role in building a coordinated community response. In turn, this response has changed the civil and criminal justice systems for the better—encouraging victims to file complaints, improving prosecution of sexual assault and domestic violence cases, and increasing the issuance and enforcement of protection orders. The increased availability of legal services for victims seeking protection orders has made it easier to obtain such orders when they are needed, and has helped reduce domestic violence and improve their quality of life.

Invests in Jail Diversion Programs. The Budget provides $153 million in prisoner re-entry and jail diversion programs, including $80 million for the Second Chance Act programs and $52 million for problem-solving grants supporting drug courts, mentally ill offender assistance, and other problem-solving approaches. With 2.3 million people in U.S. prisons and 1 in 32 American adults under some kind of correctional supervision, these programs aim to divert individuals from incarceration, reduce recidivism, and achieve public safety in a more sensible way.

Supports Neighborhood Revitalization Initiative. The Budget provides $20 million for the Byrne Criminal Justice Innovation Program, which supports the Administration's multi-agency Neighborhood Revitalization Initiative by directing resources where they are needed in higher-risk neighborhoods, integrating public safety, housing services, and other investments.

Department of Justice
(In millions of dollars)

	Actual 2011	Estimate	
		2012	2013
Spending			
Discretionary Budget Authority:			
Federal Bureau of Investigation	7,822	8,108	8,070
Federal Prison System	6,381	6,596	6,844
Drug Enforcement Administration	2,053	2,037	2,035
United States Attorneys	1,931	1,960	1,974
Federal Prisoner Detention	1,516	1,580	1,668

Department of Justice—Continued
(In millions of dollars)

	Actual 2011	Estimate	
		2012	2013
Office of Justice Programs, Office of Community Oriented Policing Services, Office on Violence Against Women	2,695	2,053	1,675
United States Marshals Service	1,143	1,185	1,199
Bureau of Alcohol, Tobacco, Firearms, and Explosives	1,113	1,152	1,140
General Legal Activities	866	862	904
Organized Crime and Drug Enforcement Task Forces	527	527	525
National Security Division	88	87	90
All other	1,117	1,059	980
Subtotal, Discretionary budget authority	27,252	27,206	27,104
Discretionary Changes in Mandatory Programs *(non-add in 2012):*[1]			
Less Crime Victims' Fund discretionary offset		*–7,113*	*–8,125*
Less Assets Forfeiture Fund cancellation		*–675*	*–675*
Subtotal, Discretionary changes in mandatory programs		*–7,788*	*–8,800*
Less Hart-Scott-Rodino Antitrust Premerger Filing Fee Receipts	–96	–110	–118
Less U.S. Trustee Fee Receipts and Interest on U.S. Securities	–267	–267	–267
Total, Discretionary budget authority	26,889	26,829	17,919
Discretionary Cap Adjustment:[2]			
Overseas Contingency Operations	101	—	—
Total, Discretionary outlays	28,547	28,795	23,861
Mandatory Outlays:			
Existing law	1,978	3,369	10,967
Legislative proposal		2,400	1,700
Total, Mandatory outlays	1,978	5,769	12,667
Total, Outlays	30,525	34,564	36,528

[1] The 2012 amounts reflect OMB's scoring of the 2012 Appropriations acts (P.L. 112–55 and 112–74) as transmitted to the Congress. These amounts are displayed as non-add entries because they have been rebased as mandatory and are not included in any 2012 discretionary levels in the 2013 Budget.
[2] The Balanced Budget and Emergency Deficit Control Act of 1985 (BBEDCA), as amended by the Budget Control Act of 2011, limits—or caps—budget authority available for discretionary programs each year through 2021. Section 251(b)(2) of BBEDCA authorizes certain adjustments to the caps after the enactment of appropriations. Amounts in 2011 are not so designated but are shown for comparability purposes.

DEPARTMENT OF LABOR

Funding Highlights:

- Provides $12 billion in discretionary funding, a slight reduction from the comparable 2012 level. The Budget continues critical investments in job training and resources for job seekers. It also includes savings from administrative efficiencies, consolidation of regional offices, and the elimination of overlapping job training programs.

- Preserves a strong Unemployment Insurance safety net, ensuring that all Americans who have lost their jobs have the help they need to improve their skills and return to the workforce, and creates subsidized employment opportunities for long-term unemployed and low-income adults and youth. To improve program integrity and cost-effectiveness, the Budget also works to reduce improper payments in the Unemployment Insurance program.

- Improves access to services for workers and job-seekers and invests $125 million in a competitive Workforce Innovation Fund in the Departments of Labor and Education to engage States and localities in identifying better ways of delivering services, breaking down program silos, and paying providers for success.

- Introduces bold reforms to strengthen Job Corps by improving its outcomes and cost-effectiveness.

- Provides improved re-employment services to newly separated veterans.

- Increases support for agencies that protect workers' wages, benefits, health, and safety and invests in preventing and detecting the inappropriate misclassification of employees as independent contractors.

- Safeguards workers' pensions by encouraging companies to fully fund their employees' promised pension benefits and assuring the long-term solvency of the Federal pension insurance system.

- Creates new opportunities for Americans to save for retirement by establishing a system of automatic workplace pensions and doubling the small employer pension plan start-up credit.

- Assists workers who need to take time off to care for a child or other family member by helping States launch paid leave programs.

The Department of Labor (DOL) is charged with promoting the welfare of American workers, job seekers, and retirees, which is critical to America's continued economic recovery and long-term competitiveness. To support this mission, the Budget provides almost $12 billion in discretionary funding for DOL, a small reduction from the comparable 2012 level. This funding level makes substantial investments and introduces significant reforms to better help workers gain skills, regain their footing after a job loss, and find new employment opportunities. Investments are also made for the enforcement of critical wage and hour, whistleblower, and worker safety laws. The Budget achieves savings through the consolidation of several DOL regional offices, and the elimination of duplicative programs.

Invests in a Competitive Workforce and Protects American Workers

Preserves a Strong Unemployment Insurance Safety Net and Gives All Dislocated and Low-Income Workers the Help They Need to Find New Jobs. Particularly during this time of high unemployment, the Administration believes it is critical to provide both a helping hand and a viable path back to employment. Over the past several years, unemployment insurance (UI) benefits have helped American families stay afloat, keeping 3.2 million individuals—including nearly 1 million children—from falling into poverty in 2010. The American Jobs Act proposed an extension of federally funded benefits as well as the Reemployment NOW program, which includes a number of reforms to help UI claimants get back to work quickly. The Budget continues this support for extending federally funded benefits through December 2012 and instituting innovative approaches to better connect UI claimants with job opportunities.

Nearly 7 million of the Americans who lost jobs in 2009 were displaced from jobs that are unlikely to come back, and those who do find reemployment, on average, suffer significant earnings losses. As part of the Administration's effort to reform and modernize the Nation's job

training system so that individuals can quickly gain the training they need for the jobs created as our economy evolves, the Budget proposes a universal core set of services where the focus is on helping all dislocated workers find new jobs.

Building on successful Recovery Act programs that provided job opportunities for long-term unemployed and low-income adults and youths, the Budget also includes a $12.5 billion Pathways Back to Work Fund to make it easier for workers to remain connected to the workforce and gain new skills for long-term employment. This initiative will include support for summer- and year-round jobs for low-income youth, subsidized employment opportunities for unemployed and low-income adults, and other promising strategies designed to lead to employment.

Promotes New Approaches to Job Training. As the economy changes, training and employment programs that help Americans navigate those changes must continuously adapt to remain effective. To spur job training innovation among States and localities, the Budget provides $125 million in the Departments of Labor and Education for the Workforce Innovation Fund (Fund). Paired with broader waiver authority, the Fund will test new ideas and replicate proven strategies for delivering better employment and education results at a lower cost. Both agencies will jointly administer the Fund, in consultation with other agencies that fund employment services, such as the Department of Health and Human Services. The initiative will fund a competition among States and regions to implement bold systemic reforms that break down barriers between programs and provide rewards based on outcomes, particularly in serving disadvantaged populations. Within the Fund, $10 million is dedicated to building knowledge of what interventions are most effective with disconnected youth. Like DOL's existing Trade Adjustment Assistance Community College and Career Training Grants, the Fund will create incentives for grantees to consider evidence in designing their programs, collect better data to know what is working well and what is not, and find ways to make program dollars stretch further.

The Budget also funds a new initiative designed to improve access to job training and employment services across the Nation and provide $8 billion in the Departments of Labor and Education to support State and community college partnerships with businesses to build the skills of American workers.

Reforms Job Corps. The Administration strongly supports Job Corps and, with the planned addition of centers in New Hampshire and Wyoming, is committed to having a Job Corps center in every State to reach disadvantaged youth across the country. However, the Administration also believes the program could be more effective and efficient. The 2013 Budget launches a bold reform effort for Job Corps to improve program outcomes and strengthen accountability. Specifically, the Administration proposes to close by program year 2013 the small number of Job Corps centers that are chronically low-performing, which will be identified using criteria the Administration will publish in advance. The program will also shift its focus toward the strategies that were proven most cost-effective in evaluations of the Job Corps model. The Administration also plans to undertake other efforts to improve the program, including changes to strengthen the performance measurement system and report center-level performance in a more transparent way.

Improves Career Transitions for Newly-Separated Veterans. The President places a high priority on delivering effective education, employment, and other transition services that enable newly separated veterans to move successfully into civilian careers. The Administration has created resources to help veterans translate their military skills to the civilian workforce, built new online tools to help veterans and their family connect with jobs, and partnered with the private sector to make it easier to connect veterans with employers that want to hire them. The VOW to Hire Heroes Act, signed into law by the President on November 21, 2011, expands tax credits to encourage the hiring of veterans, and expands access to the

Transition Assistance Program (TAP) workshops that are offered to separating servicemembers. The Budget builds on these efforts by boosting funding for the Department's TAP program and grants for employment services to veterans by $8 million, or 34 percent, over 2012 levels.

Maintains Strong Support for Worker Protection. The Budget includes nearly $1.8 billion for the Department's worker protection agencies, putting them on sound footing to meet their responsibilities to protect the health, safety, wages, working conditions, and retirement security of American workers. In doing so, the Budget preserves recent investments in rebuilding the Department's enforcement capacity and makes strategic choices to ensure funding is used for the highest priority activities.

- *Protect the Health and Safety of America's Miners.* The Budget maintains funding within DOL and the Federal Mine Safety and Health Review Commission (FMSHRC) to continue efforts to address FMSHRC's large case backlog. It also preserves funding to allow the Mine Safety and Health Administration (MSHA) to effectively enforce safety and health laws, while achieving efficiencies and reallocating resources from lower priority activities into coal and metal/non-metal enforcement. The Administration continues to support legislation that would provide MSHA with stronger enforcement tools to ensure mine operators meet their responsibility to protect their workers.

- *Enhance Protections for Whistleblowers.* The Budget includes an additional $5 million over the 2012 level to bolster the Occupational Safety and Health Administration's (OSHA's) enforcement of the nearly 20 laws that protect workers and others who are retaliated against for reporting unsafe and unscrupulous practices. These resources will be paired with administrative efforts to improve the transparency and effectiveness of the program.

- *Increase Enforcement of Worker Protection Laws.* The Budget provides an increase of $6 million for the Wage and Hour Division for increased enforcement of the Fair Labor Standards Act and the Family and Medical Leave Act, which ensure that workers receive appropriate wages, overtime pay, and the right to take job-protected leave for family and medical purposes.

- *Detect and Deter the Misclassification of Workers as Independent Contractors.* When employees are misclassified as independent contractors, they are deprived of benefits and protections to which they are legally entitled, such as overtime and unemployment benefits. Misclassification also costs taxpayers money in lost funds for the Treasury and in the Social Security, Medicare, and Unemployment Insurance Trust Funds. The Budget includes $14 million to combat misclassification, including $10 million for grants to States to identify misclassification and recover unpaid taxes and $4 million for personnel at the Wage and Hour Division to investigate misclassification.

Makes Tough Cuts and Consolidations

Ends Overlapping Training Programs. In a constrained environment, we must make difficult choices to preserve core functions. The 2013 Budget ends funding for Women in Apprenticeship in Non-Traditional Occupations, whose mission of expanding apprenticeship opportunities for women can be met through DOL's work to expand registered apprenticeships and ensure equal access to apprenticeship programs. The Budget also ends the Veterans Workforce Investment Program, instead supporting service delivery innovations through the Workforce Innovation Fund.

Consolidates Regional Offices to Increase Efficiency. Consistent with Administration-wide efforts to improve efficiency and find savings, the Budget proposes to streamline agency operations by reforming the Department's regional office structure. While regional offices allow the Department to provide services to citizens at the local level, several DOL components have more regional offices than they need to be effective. The Budget proposes adopting a leaner, more efficient approach for five offices within the Department: the Women's Bureau, OSHA, the Office of the Solicitor, the Employee Benefits Security Administration, and the Office of Public Affairs. In 2013, each of these components will consolidate their regional offices to ensure that they are strategically placed to perform DOL's key functions across the country while eliminating unnecessary administrative costs.

Increases Efficiency, and Reduces Future Liabilities

Strengthens the UI Safety Net and Improves Program Integrity. The combination of chronically underfunded reserves and the economic downturn has placed a considerable financial strain on States' UI operations. Currently, 28 States owe more than $37 billion to the Federal UI trust fund. As a result, employers in those States are now facing automatic Federal tax increases, and many States have little prospect of paying these loans back in the foreseeable future. At the same time, State UI programs have large improper payment rates—12 percent in fiscal year 2011. The Administration proposes to put the UI system back on the path to solvency and financial integrity by providing immediate relief to employers to encourage job creation now, reestablishing State fiscal responsibility going forward, and working closely with States to eliminate improper payments. Under this Budget proposal, employers in indebted States would receive tax relief for two years. To encourage State solvency, the proposal would also raise the minimum level of wages subject to unemployment taxes in 2015 to a level slightly less in real terms that it was in 1983, after President Reagan signed into law the last wage base increase. The higher wage base will be offset by lower tax rates to avoid a Federal tax increase. Further, the Administration has taken a number of steps to address program integrity in States that have consistently failed to place enough emphasis on combating improper payments in their UI programs. The Administration's aggressive actions have given States a number of tools to prevent improper payments, and reducing State UI error rates remains an Administration priority.

Shores Up the Pension Benefit Guaranty Corporation to Protect Worker Pensions. The Pension Benefit Guaranty Corporation (PBGC) acts as a backstop to protect pension payments for workers whose companies have failed. Currently, the PBGC's pension insurance system is itself underfunded, and the PBGC's liabilities exceed its assets. The PBGC receives no taxpayer funds and its premiums are currently much lower than what a private financial institution would charge for insuring the same risk. The Budget proposes to give the PBGC Board the authority to adjust premiums and directs PBGC to take into account the risks that different sponsors pose to their retirees and to PBGC. This will both encourage companies to fully fund their pension benefits and ensure the continued financial soundness of PBGC. In order to ensure that these reforms are undertaken responsibly during challenging economic times, the Budget would require a year of study and public comment before any implementation and the gradual phasing-in of any premium increases. This proposal is estimated to save $16 billion over the next decade.

Provides Greater Security for American Workers and Retirees

Establishes Automatic Workplace Pensions and Expands the Small Employer Pension Plan Startup Credit. Currently, 78 million working Americans—roughly half the workforce—lack employer-based retirement plans. The Budget proposes a system of automatic workplace pensions that will expand access to tens of millions of workers who currently lack pensions. Under the proposal, employers who do not currently offer a retirement plan will be required to enroll their employees in a direct-deposit IRA account that is compatible with existing direct-deposit payroll systems. Employees may opt-out if they choose. To minimize burdens on small businesses, those with ten and fewer employees would be exempt. Employers would also be entitled to an additional credit of $25 per participating employee—up to a total of $250 per year—for six years.

To make it easier for small employers to offer pensions to their workers in connection with the automatic IRA proposal, the Budget will increase the maximum tax credit available for small employers establishing or administering a new retirement plan from $500 to $1,000 per year. This credit would be available for four years.

Encourages State Establishment of Family Leave Initiatives. Too many American workers must make the painful choice between the care of their families and a paycheck they desperately need. While the Family and Medical Leave Act allows workers to take job-protected unpaid time off, millions of families cannot afford to use unpaid leave. A handful of States have enacted policies to offer paid family leave, but more States should have the chance to follow their example. The Budget supports a $5 million State Paid Leave Fund within DOL to provide technical assistance and support to States that are considering paid-leave programs.

Department of Labor
(In millions of dollars)

	Actual 2011	Estimate 2012	Estimate 2013
Spending			
Discretionary Budget Authority:			
Training and Employment Services	3,216	3,189	3,232
Unemployment Insurance Administration	3,250	3,236	3,001
Employment Service/One-Stop Career Centers	787	785	868
Office of Job Corps[1]	1,630	2,393	1,650
Community Service Employment for Older Americans[2]	449	448	—
Bureau of Labor Statistics	610	609	618
Occupational Safety and Health Administration	559	565	565
Mine Safety and Health Administration	362	373	372
Wage and Hour Division	227	227	238
Office of Federal Contract Compliance Programs	105	105	106
Office of Labor-Management Standards	41	41	42
Office of Workers' Compensation Programs	118	118	122
Employee Benefits Security Administration	159	183	183
Veterans Employment and Training	256	264	259
Bureau of International Labor Affairs	92	92	95
Office of the Solicitor	119	129	131
Foreign Labor Certification	66	65	66
Office of Disability Employment Policy	39	39	39
State Paid Leave Fund	—	—	5
Office of the Inspector General	84	84	85
All other	285	293	293
Subtotal, Discretionary budget authority	12,456	13,240	11,970
Proposed Cancellations			−10
Total, Discretionary budget authority	12,456	13,240	11,960
Discretionary Cap Adjustment:[3]			
Program Integrity	—	—	15
Total, Discretionary outlays	14,599	14,043	13,244
Mandatory Outlays:			
Unemployment Insurance Benefits:			
Existing law	116,466	84,433	55,235
Legislative proposal	—	21,295	19,273
Trade Adjustment Assistance	770	1,133	1,637
Pension Benefit Guaranty Corporation:			
Existing law [4]	−1,166	−237	−1,575

Department of Labor—Continued
(In millions of dollars)

	Actual 2011	Estimate	
		2012	2013
Legislative proposal[5]	—	—	—
Black Lung Benefits Program...	297	302	309
Federal Employees' Compensation Act:			
Existing law	191	347	393
Legislative proposal	—	—	−13
Energy Employees Occupational Illness Compensation Program Act.......	1,249	1,302	1,260
American Jobs Act:			
Legislative proposal	—	5,062	12,147
All other...	809	−498	−221
Total, Mandatory outlays[4]..	118,616	113,139	88,445
Total, Outlays	133,215	127,182	101,689

[1] In a departure from historic practice the 2012 Appropriations Act funded program year 2012 entirely with regular 2012 appropriations rather than funding $691 million of these costs in 2013 via an advance appropriation. Job Corps' program year 2013 level reflects a $53 million (3 percent) reduction from program year 2012.

[2] The 2013 Budget proposes to transfer this program to the Department of Health and Human Services.

[3] The Balanced Budget and Emergency Deficit Control Act of 1985 (BBEDCA), as amended by the Budget Control Act of 2011, limits—or caps—budget authority available for discretionary programs each year through 2021. Section 251(b)(2) of BBEDCA authorizes certain adjustments to the caps after the enactment of appropriations.

[4] Net mandatory outlays are negative when offsetting collections exceed outlays.

[5] The Budget proposal that would increase PBGC premiums would have no outlay effects until 2014.

DEPARTMENT OF STATE AND OTHER INTERNATIONAL PROGRAMS

Funding Highlights:

- Provides $51.6 billion in discretionary funding for the Department of State and U.S. Agency for International Development (USAID), an increase of 1.6 percent, or $0.8 billion over the 2012 enacted level when including Overseas Contingency Operations (OCO) resources. Within tightly capped budget constraints, the Budget makes investments in key priorities including the Middle East, Iraq, Afghanistan and Pakistan, plus continues funding for critical initiatives such as global health, climate change and food security.

- State Department and USAID OCO programs are described along with Department of Defense OCO programs in a separate chapter on OCO resources. OCO funding is also shown in this chapter in order to provide a more complete picture of total State Department and USAID resources.

- Responds to the Arab Spring by supporting the aspirations of people in the Middle East and North Africa, with more than $800 million to assist countries in transition and create incentives for long-term economic, political, and trade reforms.

- Advances the President's aggressive HIV-prevention goal, including his plan to support 6 million HIV patients on antiretroviral treatment by the end of 2013 through a $7.9 billion investment in the President's Global Health Initiative. This builds on the Initiative's strong progress in fighting infectious disease and child and maternal mortality.

- Fully funds the Administration's historic pledges to the Global Fund to Fight AIDS, Tuberculosis, and Malaria and the Global Alliance for Vaccines and Immunizations.

- Continues a multi-year plan to make strategic investments to address the root causes of hunger and poverty and to help prevent crises such as the 2011 famine in the Horn of Africa.

- Provides $2.9 billion to the Department of the Treasury for U.S. international commitments to the multilateral development banks and bilateral debt relief, supporting poverty reduction, economic growth, and U.S. national security. The Administration's request prioritizes the most important commitments, while pursuing a multi-year strategy designed to promote U.S. leadership in multilateral institutions and leverage other donors' resources.

- Provides $432 million to strengthen efforts at five international trade-related agencies to promote and enforce international trade, and meet the goals of the National Export Initiative.

- Separate from the term-limited and extraordinary level of transition expenses in OCO, base budget funding strengthens core diplomatic, development and security activities in Iraq, Afghanistan, and Pakistan to ensure ongoing activities in military to civilian operations.

- Makes significant investments to support the Administration's new National Strategy for Counterterrorism.

- Makes strategic investments to encourage climate-resilient development, investment from the private sector in clean energy and low carbon infrastructure, and meaningful reductions in greenhouse gas and national emissions trajectories.

- Rationalizes assistance to Europe, Eurasia, and Central Asia by transitioning funds into other assistance accounts, recognizing the successes of transition in the region.

- Reduces operational costs through administrative savings and procurement reform.

The Department of State, the U.S. Agency for International Development (USAID), and other international programs advance the national security interests of the United States through global engagement, partnerships with nations and their people, and the promotion of universal values. By investing in civilian diplomacy and development, we foster stability around the world to protect our national security and make conflicts less likely. This work also supports economic development in the United States, opening new markets for U.S. businesses and increasing trade to create jobs at home.

The President's 2013 Budget proposes $51.6 billion for the Department of State and USAID, including costs for OCO, a 1.6 percent increase from 2012. The Budget provides the necessary base resources to sustain critical diplomatic and development efforts around the world. To support the Administration's ongoing programs in key regions in transition, significant levels of funding are continued for diplomatic operations and assistance in Iraq, Afghanistan, and Pakistan. The Budget also makes a substantial investment in economic and political reform in the Middle East and North Africa in the wake of the Arab

Spring. The Administration continues to prioritize funding for food security to reduce hunger and to help prevent political instability; for climate change to promote low-emission growth; and for global health to reduce the incidence of disease and strengthen local health systems. At the same time, the Department of State and US-AID are committed to finding efficiencies, cutting waste, and focusing on key priorities. Accordingly, savings are created by focusing resources on the highest priorities worldwide and reducing operational and administrative costs.

Maintains U.S. Global Leadership

Assists Countries in Transition and Promotes Reforms in the Middle East and North Africa. Building on the Administration's significant and continuing response to the transformative events in the Middle East and North Africa region, the Budget provides over $800 million to support political and economic reform in the region. The Budget expands our bilateral economic support in countries such as Tunisia and Yemen where transitions are already underway. Consistent with the President's May 2011 speech, the Budget establishes a new $770 million Middle East and North Africa Incentive Fund, which will provide incentives for long-term economic, political, and trade reforms to countries in transition—and to countries prepared to make reforms proactively. This new Fund builds upon other recently announced programs in the region, including up to $2 billion in regional Overseas Private Investment Corporation (OPIC) financing, up to $1 billion in debt swaps for Egypt, and approximately $500 million in existing funds re-allocated to respond to regional developments in 2011.

Invests in Long-Term Partnerships in Iraq, Afghanistan, and Pakistan. The Budget continues significant levels of funding for operations and assistance in Iraq, Afghanistan, and Pakistan within the base budget, while extraordinary and temporary costs are requested as OCO funding. Base resources requested to support strong, long-term partnerships with these countries include core diplomatic and development operational support funding, as well as economic development, health, education, governance, security, and other assistance programs necessary to reinforce development progress and promote stability.

Maintains Counterterrorism Capabilities. The Department continues to make significant investments to support the Administration's National Strategy for Counterterrorism. The Administration remains committed to improving U.S. Government programs and developing partner capabilities to prevent terrorist attacks on the United States and other countries. The Budget protects resources in this high-priority area, including the establishment of a new Counterterrorism Bureau overseeing investments to protect the homeland, defeat al Qaeda and its affiliates, counter violent extremism, build partner capacity, and prevent the development, acquisition, trafficking, and use of weapons of mass destruction by terrorists.

Supports Global Health by Focusing on High-Impact Interventions. The Administration is building on recent progress in the Global Health Initiative's fight against infectious diseases and child and maternal mortality by focusing resources on interventions that have been proven effective and by pushing for more integrated and efficient programming. The Budget supports an aggressive effort to prevent HIV infections, including the President's goal of supporting 6 million HIV patients on antiretroviral treatment by the end of 2013. The Budget continues efforts to reduce maternal and child deaths through proven malaria interventions and support for a basic set of effective interventions to address maternal and child health. The Budget fully funds the balance of the Administration's historic three-year, $4 billion pledge to the Global Fund to Fight AIDS, Tuberculosis, and Malaria, in recognition of this multilateral partner's key role in global health and its progress in instituting reform. In addition, the Budget fully funds the Administration's pledge to the Global Alliance for Vaccines and Immunizations in order to expand access to immunization for children globally.

Fights Hunger by Improving Food Security. As part of a multi-year plan to address the root causes of hunger and poverty, the Administration continues funding for agriculture development and nutrition programs. The 2011 famine in the Horn of Africa has underscored the need for targeted programs to help prevent future famines and crises in the Horn and elsewhere. Therefore, Administration programs are intended to reduce extreme poverty, increase food security, and reduce malnutrition for millions of families by 2015. The Administration provides funding through the President's Feed the Future Initiative and the multi-donor Global Agriculture and Food Security Program, directing funding to poor countries that commit to policy reforms and robust country-led strategies to address internal food security needs. Assistance helps countries increase agricultural productivity, improve agricultural research and development, and expand markets and trade, while monitoring and evaluating program performance. The Administration also maintains strong support for food aid and other humanitarian assistance, including over $4 billion to help internally displaced persons, refugees, and victims of armed conflict and natural disasters.

Combats Global Climate Change by Promoting Low-Emission, Climate-Resilient Economic Growth. The Administration continues to promote global reductions in greenhouse gas emissions and reduce vulnerabilities in key sectors to climate-related events by supporting clean energy, combating deforestation, and building climate-resilience in developing countries. The Administration is working in partnership with national and local governments, and the private sector, to make effective investments in three key programmatic areas: 1) multilateral institutions and bilateral activities that focus on energy efficiency, renewable energy, and energy sector reforms; 2) sustainable land use to combat unsustainable forest clearing for agriculture and illegal logging, and promote forest governance; and 3) programs to build resilience of the most vulnerable communities and countries to climate change, and reduce the risk of damage, loss of life, and broader instability that can result from extreme weather and climate events.

Leverages International Organizations to Support Cooperation and Security. The Administration will advance the President's vision of robust multilateral engagement as a crucial tool in advancing U.S. national interests, accomplished through our contributions to the United Nations, peacekeeping operations and international organizations. Our contributions enable U.S. participation in over 40 international organizations that maintain peace and security, promote economic growth, and advance human rights around the world. Peacekeeping assessments fund peacekeeping activities directed to the maintenance or restoration of international peace and security, and promote the peaceful resolution of conflict.

Prioritizes Poverty Reduction, Economic Growth, and U.S. National Security. The Budget provides $2.9 billion to the Department of the Treasury for our international commitments to multilateral development banks (MDBs) and bilateral debt relief. The MDBs are a key international forum for advancing U.S. foreign policy objectives in economic development, climate change, and food security. U.S.-supported MDB activities help developing nations grow, opening new markets for American companies and fostering stability in regions critical to U.S. national security. By fully funding the current round of General Capital Increases and replenishments of concessional lending facilities, the Administration makes essential contributions to global development priorities, while pursuing a multi-year strategy to meet our commitments, promote U.S. leadership in multilateral institutions, and leverage other donors' resources. The Budget also provides for bilateral debt relief to Sudan, in support of the commitments made in the Comprehensive Peace Agreement.

Encourages Economic Growth Through Support for the National Export Initiative and Tourism Promotion. A critical component of stimulating domestic economic growth is ensuring that U.S. businesses can actively participate in international markets by increasing their exports of goods and services. The Administration launched the National Export Initiative (NEI) in 2010 to improve the private sector's ability to export American goods and services. The NEI advances the Administration's goal of doubling exports over five years by working to remove trade barriers abroad, helping firms—especially small businesses—overcome the hurdles to entering new export markets, assisting with trade financing, and pursuing a Government-wide approach to export advocacy abroad. To that end, the Administration provides $432 million, an increase of $19 million over 2012 levels, for the Export-Import Bank, U.S. Trade and Development Agency, the U.S. Trade Representative, U.S. International Trade Commission, and OPIC. These investments will strengthen international trade promotion and enforcement efforts. In parallel with the NEI, the State Department Bureau of Consular Affairs will promote tourism and travel to the United States from the world's fastest growing economies by expanding visa processing capacity in emerging economies such as Brazil and China.

Reduces Costs and Improves Efficiency

Rationalizes the Foreign Assistance Funding Structure for Europe, Eurasia, and Central Asia. The Administration proposes to transition programs funded through the Assistance for Europe, Eurasia, and Central Asia (AEECA) account into the Economic Support Fund, International Narcotics Control and Law Enforcement, and Global Health Programs accounts. The normalization of the AEECA assistance structure, which was established in the immediate aftermath of the fall of the Iron Curtain and the collapse of the Soviet Union, reflects the need to be able to focus resources on the highest global priorities. While the United States remains deeply engaged in the region, using its diplomatic and assistance resources to advance national security interests and address difficult development challenges, the successful transition of a number of countries over time to market democracies has also enabled us to reduce the levels of assistance.

Improves Efficiency of Foreign Affairs Operations. The Department of State and USAID will continue to reduce administrative costs, building on the Administrative Efficiency Initiative to increase the efficiency of operations. The agencies will reduce travel, printing supplies, and other costs below 2010 levels by increasing the use of phone, web-based and digital video conferencing; reducing unnecessary or duplicative reports and publishing critical reports online; and streamlining purchasing of equipment and supplies. The agencies will also seek to reduce the use of contractors for management support services by reducing contract spending on these services by up to 15 percent below 2010 levels.

Reforms Contract Procurement. USAID will continue to increase the efficiency of U.S. foreign assistance through the Implementation and Procurement Reform Initiative, which streamlines procurement policies, procedures, and processes; increases the use of small business and host country systems; and strengthens the local capacity of partner countries.

Department of State and Other International Programs
(In millions of dollars)

	Actual 2011	Estimate 2012	Estimate 2013
Spending			
Discretionary Budget Authority, State and USAID:			
Administration of Foreign Affairs	11,228	8,859	9,589
International Organizations and Peacekeeping	3,463	3,278	3,669
Economic Support, Democracy, and Development Assistance	9,171	6,256	7,374
Global Health Programs	7,830	8,168	7,854
Middle East and North Africa Incentive Fund	—	—	770
International Narcotics Control and Law Enforcement	1,659	1,061	1,457
Migration and Refugee Programs	1,745	1,673	1,675
Non-proliferation, Anti-terrorism, Demining Programs	739	590	636
Foreign Military Financing	5,374	5,210	5,472
USAID Operations	1,528	1,269	1,448
Other State and USAID programs	2,319	1,928	2,033
Overseas Contingency Operations [1]	297	11,188	8,245
Rescissions of Unobligated Balances	−371	−114	—
USDA Food for Peace Title II (non-add in total line)	*1,497*	*1,466*	*1,400*
Subtotal, Department of State and USAID (including Food for Peace)	46,479	50,832	51,622

Department of State and Other International Programs—Continued
(In millions of dollars)

	Actual 2011	Estimate 2012	Estimate 2013
Discretionary Budget Authority, Other International Programs:			
Treasury International Programs	2,028	2,660	2,901
Millennium Challenge Corporation	898	898	898
Peace Corps	374	375	375
Broadcasting Board of Governors	748	747	720
Export-Import Bank	2	−266	−359
Overseas Private Investment Corporation	−198	−197	−192
Other International Programs	271	266	274
Overseas Contingency Operations	—	14	—
Rescissions of Unobligated Balances	−275	−400	—
Total, Discretionary budget authority [2]	48,830	53,463	54,839
Discretionary Cap Adjustment (included in totals above):[3]			
Overseas Contingency Operations	297	11,203	8,245
Total, Discretionary outlays	47,108	53,406	56,093
Total, Mandatory outlays	−1,882	2,552	3,420
Total, Outlays	45,226	55,958	59,513
Credit activity			
Direct Loan Disbursements:			
Export-Import Bank	2,590	25	25
All other	2,460	5,399	5,402
Total, Direct loan disbursements	5,050	5,424	5,427
Guaranteed Loan Disbursements by Private Lenders:			
Export-Import Bank	17,892	21,500	26,750
All other	964	5,234	963
Total, Guaranteed loan disbursements by private lenders	18,856	26,734	27,713

[1] Overseas Contingency Operations (OCO) funds were first appropriated to the Department of State, USAID, and Other International Programs in 2012. In 2011, OCO reflects a transfer from the Department of Defense to the Department of State.

[2] Funding for International Food Aid programs in the Department of Agriculture (Food for Peace Title II food aid and the McGovern-Dole International Food for Education and Child Nutrition) are not included in the totals above. Funding for these programs are included in International Function 150, and are classified as Security pursuant to Title I of the Budget Control Act of 2011.

[3] The Balanced Budget and Emergency Deficit Control Act of 1985 (BBEDCA), as amended by the Budget Control Act of 2011, limits—or caps—budget authority available for discretionary programs each year through 2021. Section 251(b)(2) of BBEDCA authorizes certain adjustments to the caps after the enactment of appropriations. Amounts in 2011 are not so designated but are shown for comparability purposes.

DEPARTMENT OF TRANSPORTATION

Funding Highlights:

- Invests a total of $74 billion in discretionary and mandatory budgetary resources for the Department of Transportation, an increase of 2 percent, or $1.4 billion, above the 2012 enacted level. This includes job-creating infrastructure investments as well as savings from reductions to grant programs for larger airports.

- Jump starts job creation in 2012 with $50 billion in immediate investments to support critical infrastructure projects, improving America's roads, bridges, transit systems, border crossings, railways, and runways.

- Proposes an urgently needed six-year, $476 billion surface reauthorization plan to modernize the country's transportation infrastructure, and pave the way for long-term economic growth.

- Pays for these investments with the "peace dividend" from ramping down overseas military operations. Because rebuilding the Nation's transportation infrastructure is an immediate need, the Budget uses near-term savings from reduced overseas operations to support increased investments in the reauthorization proposal.

- Provides $2.7 billion in 2013 and $47 billion over six years to develop high-speed passenger rail corridors and improve intercity passenger rail service to significantly enhance the national rail network.

- Supports a more robust, rigorous, and data-driven pipeline safety program to ensure the highest level of safety for America's pipeline system.

- Invests over $1 billion for 2013 in the Next Generation Air Transportation System, a revolutionary modernization of our aviation system.

- Initiates Transportation Leadership Awards, which will encourage innovation by allowing States to compete for grants to pursue critical transportation policy reforms.

- Reduces funding for airport grants by over $900 million, focusing Federal support on smaller airports, while giving larger airports additional flexibility to raise their own resources.

A well-functioning transportation system is critical to America's economic future. Whether it is by road, transit, aviation, rail, pipeline, or waterway, we rely on our transportation system to move people and goods safely, facilitate commerce, attract and retain businesses, and support jobs. The President's 2013 Budget provides a total of $74 billion in discretionary and mandatory funding plus an additional $50 billion above what has been provided to date in 2012 to jump-start economic growth and job creation. Recognizing the fiscal realities, the Budget again proposes significant reforms to surface transportation programs, including a consolidation of over 55 duplicative, often earmarked highway programs into five streamlined ones.

Invests in Infrastructure Critical for Long-Term Growth. Much of the country's transportation infrastructure was built decades ago and is in desperate need of repairs and upgrades to meet current economic demands. The President's Budget again includes a multi-year reauthorization proposal for critical highway, transit, highway safety, passenger rail, and multi-modal programs. This proposal would provide $476 billion over six years, which together with the additional $50 billion requested in 2012, represents an increase of approximately 80 percent above the previous surface transportation reauthorization, plus annual appropriated funding for passenger rail funding in those years. This proposal seeks not only to fill a long overdue funding gap, but also to reform how Federal dollars are spent to ensure that they are directed to the most effective programs. It reflects a need to balance fiscal discipline with efforts to expedite our economic recovery and job creation. It emphasizes fixing existing assets, moving toward cost-benefit analysis of large transportation projects, and consolidating duplicative, often-earmarked highway programs. Consistent with Administration policy, this proposal does not contain earmarks. Additionally, the reauthorization proposal will not add to the deficit as the Budget proposes to use the "peace dividend" from ramping down military operations overseas to offset all costs. After the six-year reauthorization period, the Administration

is committed to working with the Congress on a financing mechanism.

Creates Jobs Now. To spur job growth and allow States to initiate sound multi-year investments, the Budget assumes enactment of an additional $50 billion in transportation investments in 2012. Although infrastructure projects take time to get underway, these investments would generate hundreds of thousands of jobs in the first few years—and in industries suffering from protracted unemployment. Not only will job markets and municipal transportation programs access much-needed support in the near-term, but Federal taxpayers will reap the benefits of historically competitive pricing in construction. To help these funds flow into our communities without delay, key Federal agencies have been directed to find ways to expedite permitting and approvals for infrastructure projects.

Provides Dedicated Funding for High Speed Rail Investments. The Budget provides $47 billion over six years to fund the development of high-speed rail and other passenger rail programs as part of an integrated national strategy. This system will provide 80 percent of Americans with convenient access to a passenger rail system, featuring high-speed service, within 25 years. The proposal includes merging Amtrak's stand-alone subsidies into the high-speed rail program as part of a larger, competitive System Preservation initiative.

Helps Communities Become More Livable and Sustainable. Fostering livable communities—places where coordinated transportation, housing, and commercial development gives people access to affordable and environmentally sustainable transportation—is a transformational policy shift. The Administration's reauthorization proposal adopts a multi-pronged approach to help communities achieve this goal. For example, the Administration proposes to permanently authorize the Transportation Investment Generating Economic Recovery (TIGER) program, which has supported projects like multi-modal transportation hubs (where different forms of transportation converge) and streets that accommodate pedestrian, bicycle, and transit access. The proposal also seeks to harmonize State and local planning requirements and facilitate more cooperation—and includes competitive grant funding ($200 million in 2012 and $1.2 billion over six years) to improve those entities' ability to deliver sound, data-driven, and collaboratively-developed transportation plans. The Budget also includes $108 billion for transit programs over six years, more than doubling the commitment to transit in the prior reauthorization for both existing capacity and capacity expansion. This unprecedented increase for buses, subways, and other systems of public transportation will help improve and expand travel options, cut energy use, and help make our communities more livable.

Enhances Pipeline Safety. In order to ensure the highest safety standards for the U.S. pipeline system, the Budget proposes to both enhance and revamp the Department's Pipeline Safety program. The Budget increases the size of the State Pipeline Safety Grant program by 50 percent and institutes several reforms to the Federal program. It funds the first phase of a three-year effort to more than double the number of Federal pipeline safety inspectors to make certain that more pipelines are inspected on a regular basis. In addition, the Budget modernizes pipeline data collection and analysis, improves Federal investigation of pipeline accidents of all sizes, and expands the public education and outreach program.

Modernizes the Air Traffic Control System. The Budget provides over $1 billion for 2013, an increase of more than $99 million from the 2012 enacted level, for the Next Generation Air Transportation System (NextGen). NextGen is the Federal Aviation Administration's multi-year effort to improve the efficiency, safety, capacity, and environmental performance of the aviation system. These funds would continue to support the transformation from a ground-based radar surveillance system to a more accurate satellite-based surveillance system; the development of 21st Century data communications capability between air traffic control and aircraft

to improve efficiency; and the improvement of aviation weather information.

Enhances Roadway Safety Research, Data Collection and Data Analysis. The Budget creates an Integrated Highway Safety Program Office to enable best practices in highway safety, and to streamline highway safety research and data collection and analysis, in order to reduce the paperwork burden of grantees and to enhance the Department's approach to safety. In addition, the Budget continues to support a performance-based program to advance commercial motor vehicle safety. It also expands research and development in vehicle safety technology, with a focus on electronic systems, to continue progress towards safer vehicles and safer transportation.

Improves the Way Federal Funds Are Spent

Encourages Innovative Solutions Through Competition. The Administration's six-year reauthorization plan would dedicate approximately $20 billion for a competitive grant program designed to create incentives for State and local partners to adopt critical reforms in variety of areas, including safety, livability, and demand management. Federally-inspired safety reforms such as seat belt and drunk driving laws saved thousands of American lives and avoided billions in property losses. This initiative will seek to repeat the successes of the past across the complete spectrum of transportation policy priorities. Specifically, the Department will work with States and localities to set ambitious goals in different areas—for example, passing measures to continue our successes in distracted driving (safety) or modifying transportation plans to include mass transit, bike, and pedestrian options (livability)—and to tie resources to goal achievement.

Adopts a "Fix It First" Approach for Highway and Transit Grants. Too many elements of the U.S. surface transportation infrastructure—our highways, bridges, and transit assets—fall short of a state of good repair. This can impact the capacity, performance, and safety of our transportation system. At the same time, States and localities have incentives to emphasize new investments over improving the condition of the existing infrastructure. The Administration's re-authorization proposal will underscore the importance of preserving and improving existing assets, encouraging its government and industry partners to make optimal use of current capacity, and minimizing life cycle costs through sound asset management principles. Accountability is a key element of this system: States and localities will be required to report on highway condition and performance measures.

Consolidates Highway Programs. The Administration's proposal would consolidate over 55 duplicative, often earmarked highway programs into five streamlined programs. This would give States and localities greater flexibility to direct resources to their highest priorities. In the interest of taxpayer value and accountability, that flexibility will come with reformed requirements on States to establish and meet performance targets tied to national goals and to move toward rigorous cost-benefit analyses of major new projects before they are initiated.

Pays for the Six-Year Reauthorization Plan Using Real Savings. The President is committed to working with the Congress to ensure that funding increases for surface transportation do not increase the deficit. Because rebuilding our transportation infrastructure is an urgent need, the Budget uses savings from ramping down overseas military operations to fully offset the President's six-year surface transportation proposal. The Budget also proposes closing loopholes in budgetary treatment to make sure that surface transportation programs are transparently reflected in the budget and paid for in both the short- and the long-term. Beyond the reauthorization window, the Budget assumes that the President and the Congress will work together to develop other fiscally responsible solutions.

Reduces Funding in Targeted Areas. In support of the President's call for spending restraint, the Budget lowers funding for the airport grants program to $2.4 billion, a reduction of $926 million, by eliminating guaranteed funding for large and medium hub airports. The Budget focuses Federal grants to support smaller commercial and general aviation airports that do not have access to additional revenue or other outside sources of capital. At the same time, the Budget would allow larger airports to increase non-Federal passenger facility charges, thereby giving larger airports greater flexibility to generate their own revenue. Also, given difficult fiscal circumstances, the Budget reduces the annual grant to the Washington Metropolitan Area Transit Authority by $15 million. The President's surface transportation plan would substantially increase overall transit funding and would benefit both the Washington area and transit systems nationwide.

Department of Transportation
(In millions of dollars)

	Actual 2011	Estimate	
		2012	2013
Spending			
Discretionary Budgetary Authority:			
Federal Aviation Administration	12,417	12,553	12,748
Federal Motor Carrier Safety Administration	—	1	—
National Highway Traffic Safety Administration [1]	3	—	—
Federal Railroad Administration [1]	223	214	152
Federal Transit Administration [1]	150	150	134

Department of Transportation—Continued
(In millions of dollars)

	Actual 2011	Estimate 2012	Estimate 2013
Maritime Administration	366	314	344
Office of the Secretary [1]	295	295	284
Pipeline and Hazardous Materials Safety Administration	167	172	248
Pipeline Fee Offsetting Collections	−90	−91	−167
Proposed Cancellations of Unobligated Balances	—	—	−135
All other	137	140	147
Total, Discretionary budgetary authority	13,668	13,748	13,755
Discretionary Changes in Mandatory Programs *(non-add in 2012):* [2]			
Federal Motor Carrier Safety Administration		*−1*	—
Discretionary Obligation Limitations/Mandatory Budget Authority:			
Federal Aviation Administration	3,515	3,350	2,424
Surface Transportation Reauthorization [3,4]			
Federal Highway Administration [5]	41,846	39,883	42,569
Federal Motor Carrier Safety Administration	551	554	580
National Highway Traffic Safety Administration	869	800	981
Federal Railroad Administration	1,084	1,418	2,546
Federal Transit Administration	9,865	10,400	10,701
Office of the Secretary	527	500	500
Total, Discretionary obligation limitations/mandatory budget authority	58,257	56,905	60,301
Total, Other mandatory budget authority (incl. 2012 immediate investments)	253	50,253	278
Total, Budget Resources, excluding 2012 immediate investments	72,178	70,906	74,334
Total, Budget Resources, including 2012 immediate investments	72,178	120,906	74,334
Discretionary Cap Adjustment: [6]			
Disaster Relief	—	1,662	—
Total, Discretionary outlays [7]	29,124	25,551	23,987
Mandatory Outlays:			
Federal Aviation Administration	−204	−183	−194
Federal Highway Administration	36,085	38,956	41,484
Federal Motor Carrier Safety Administration	494	571	583
National Highway Traffic Safety Administration	817	905	946
Federal Railroad Administration	1,569	1,670	1,562

Department of Transportation—Continued
(In millions of dollars)

	Actual 2011	Estimate	
		2012	2013
Federal Transit Administration	9,283	10,788	11,361
Office of the Secretary	94	158	400
Immediate Transportation Investments	—	5,690	18,280
All other	40	29	114
Total, Mandatory outlays [7]	48,178	58,584	74,536
Total, Outlays	77,302	84,135	98,523

Credit activity

Direct Loan Disbursements:

	Actual 2011	Estimate 2012	2013
Transportation Infrastructure Financing and Innovation Program	1,310	1,188	1,935
Railroad Rehabilitation and Improvement Financing Program	107	600	600
Total, Direct loan disbursements	1,417	1,788	2,535

Guaranteed Loan Disbursements by Private Lenders:

	Actual 2011	Estimate 2012	2013
Transportation Infrastructure Financing and Innovation Program	—	40	251
Railroad Rehabilitation and Improvement Financing Program	—	100	100
Minority Business Resource Centers	4	18	22
Maritime Guaranteed Loans	—	1,168	—
Total, Guaranteed loan disbursements by private lenders	4	1,326	373

[1] The 2013 Budget reflects enactment of the Administration's six-year (2013–2018) surface transportation reauthorization proposal, under which a number of General Fund programs are moved into the Transportation Trust Fund. For comparability purposes, 2011 and 2012 budget authority for certain programs in these bureaus have been reclassified as mandatory, and listed in the Obligation Limitation/Mandatory Budget Authority totals.

[2] The 2012 amounts reflect OMB's scoring of the 2012 Appropriations acts (P.L. 112–55 and 112–74) as transmitted to the Congress. These amounts are displayed as non-add entries because they have been rebased as mandatory and are not included in any 2012 discretionary levels in the 2013 Budget.

[3] Amounts include $3.3 billion in 2011 and $4.1 billion in 2012 in rebased mandatory BA for rail, transit, highway safety, and TIGER grant programs.

[4] Requested discretionary obligation limitations for 2012 are equal to Contract Authority proposed in the surface transportation reauthorization bill.

[5] Includes $739 million in contract authority that is exempt from obligation limitations.

[6] The Balanced Budget and Emergency Deficit Control Act of 1985 (BBEDCA), as amended by the Budget Control Act of 2011, limits—or caps—budget authority available for discretionary programs each year through 2021. Section 251(b)(2) of BBEDCA authorizes certain adjustments to the caps after the enactment of appropriations.

[7] The Administration proposes to reclassify all surface transportation outlays as mandatory, consistent with the recommendations of the National Commission on Fiscal Responsibility and Reform. This reclassification includes outlays from General Fund programs being shifted into the Transportation Trust Fund, as well as outlays from prior obligation limitations. New outlays in 2013 are also classified as mandatory, derived from contract authority.

DEPARTMENT OF THE TREASURY

Funding Highlights:

- Provides $14 billion in total budgetary resources, including program integrity funding, for Treasury programs, a reduction of 2.7 percent below the 2012 enacted level when IRS funding is excluded. Overall, the Department's budget increases by 6.9 percent, including investments in robust IRS tax enforcement and compliance initiatives that can return $5 for each dollar spent.

- Saves over $100 million through reduced administrative costs and efficiency initiatives.

- Improves market transparency, protects consumers, and increases financial competitiveness by supporting implementation of the Dodd-Frank Wall Street Reform and Consumer Protection Act.

- Supports small business lending and protects vulnerable homeowners, while responsibly winding-down the Troubled Asset Relief Program.

- Promotes community development through capital, credit, and financial services to low-income communities.

- Proposes debt collection legislative reforms to increase collections over the next 10 years from individuals and businesses that have failed to pay taxes or repay Government loans.

- Consolidates the Bureau of the Public Debt and the Financial Management Service to streamline and modernize operations.

- Builds on the Treasury Secretary's December 2011 action to stop the overproduction of $1 coins with an initiative to reduce the cost of producing pennies and nickels.

- Increases funding for the Healthy Food Financing Initiative, which helps make healthy foods more affordable and accessible to underserved communities.

The Department of the Treasury supports a strong U.S. economy by promoting economic growth, building a comprehensive financial regulatory framework, and identifying domestic and international economic threats. The Department also carries out many functions that are essential to the financial integrity of the Government, such as collecting revenue, managing Federal finances, distributing payments, and producing currency. To support this mission, the President's Budget provides $14 billion in total budgetary resources, including program integrity funding, for the Department, 6.9 percent above the 2012 enacted level. The increase is largely due to investments that strengthen the Internal Revenue Service's (IRS) tax enforcement activities, which are critical to a fair and cost-effective tax system and which significantly reduce the deficit. The Budget also provides funding to continue implementing the Dodd-Frank Wall Street Reform and Consumer Protection Act (Wall Street Reform) and the Affordable Care Act (ACA). Wall Street Reform establishes a transparent, competitive, and fair financial system, and ACA expands health care access to millions of Americans.

Excluding the IRS, Treasury's budget decreases by 2.7 percent compared to the 2012 enacted level. Savings are achieved through program reductions and administrative reforms like information technology consolidations, telework expansions, and efficiency initiatives.

Strengthens Financial Market Stability, Promotes Economic Growth, and Supports Homeowners

Protects Consumers and Supports Continued Implementation of Wall Street Reform. Over one year after the enactment of Wall Street Reform, the Administration continues to support financial regulators' efforts to effectively implement the requirements of the Act in order to improve market transparency and operations, financial competitiveness, and consumer fairness. Through the Financial Stability Oversight Council chaired by the Treasury Secretary, the Administration supports efforts to identify, monitor, and respond to emerging threats to U.S. financial stability. The Administration also continues to vigorously support the protection of American consumers, and on July 21, 2011, Treasury successfully completed its role in standing up the Consumer Financial Protection Bureau (CFPB).

The CFPB is now exercising its full regulatory powers as an independent bureau in the Federal Reserve System.

Encourages Small Business Lending. The Small Business Lending Fund (SBLF) and the State Small Business Credit Initiative (SSBCI), both created by the Small Business Jobs Act of 2010, have committed over $5 billion to facilitate the restoration of credit markets and financing options for small businesses for years to come. The SBLF has provided over $4 billion to 332 banks across the country, providing low-cost capital to small and community banks to enable them to increase their small business lending. As of January 1, 2012, the $1.5 billion SSBCI, which boosts State-sponsored small business loan funds, has approved funding for 47 States, 3 territories, and the District of Columbia, and is expected to spur at least $15 billion in new lending. Treasury is working with the State funds to maximize the effectiveness of this assistance to small businesses.

Supports Struggling Homeowners. The Administration continues to actively implement ongoing Troubled Asset Relief Program (TARP) activities targeted to assist homeowners threatened by foreclosure, including unemployed homeowners and those with negative home equity. As of December 31, 2011, nearly 910,000 borrowers have received permanent modifications through the Home Affordable Modification Program (HAMP), which amounts to an estimated $10 billion in realized aggregate savings for these homeowners. The Administration's TARP housing programs have also been a catalyst for private sector modifications. Between April 2009 and the end of October 2011, HAMP and the private-sector HOPE NOW alliance initiated more than 5.5 million mortgage modifications, which is more than double the number of foreclosure completions that were executed in the same period. Furthermore, through the HFA Hardest Hit Fund, the Administration has allocated $7.6 billion to eligible States to implement innovative housing programs to bring stability to local housing markets and meet the unique needs of their communities.

Responsibly Winds Down TARP. The Treasury's authority to enter into new financial commitments through the TARP program ended on October 3, 2010. The President's Budget continues to support the effective, transparent, and accountable winding down of TARP programs that have helped stabilize the financial system, preserve jobs in the American automotive industry, and restart markets critical to financing American households and businesses. Moreover, TARP's banking programs have generated a positive return for taxpayers—with almost $258 billion recovered as of December 31, 2011 compared to the $245 billion originally invested in banks. The progressing economic recovery and the Administration's prudent management of TARP have also resulted in an estimated overall TARP cost of $68 billion, significantly lower than the $341 billion cost estimated for the program in its first year.

Requires Wall Street to Pay Back the American Taxpayer. The President's Budget proposes a $61 billion Financial Crisis Responsibility Fee to be imposed on the largest financial firms in order to compensate the American people for the extraordinary assistance they provided to Wall Street, as well as to discourage excessive risk-taking. Many of the largest financial firms contributed to the financial crisis through the risks they took, and all of the largest firms benefited enormously from the extraordinary actions taken to stabilize the financial system. The Budget asks these firms to compensate Americans for benefits they received from these actions and to recoup TARP costs.

Invests in Community Development. The Budget maintains robust funding for Community Development Financial Institutions, including for the Healthy Food Financing Initiative, which promotes the development of healthy food outlets in underserved communities. The Budget also includes funding for the Bank on USA program to facilitate access to affordable, high quality financial services for individuals and families that may not have bank accounts or other fundamental financial services.

Makes Necessary Cuts in a Constrained Fiscal Environment

Cuts Administrative Overhead. The Administration proposes over $100 million in reduced Treasury Department administrative costs through information technology consolidations, teleworking implementation, efficiency initiatives, and other overhead reductions that are consistent with the President's Campaign to Cut Waste. In particular, the Budget includes consolidation of Treasury data centers and a Paperless Treasury initiative that will save an estimated $500 million over five years. As part of its Paperless Treasury initiative, the Department is using electronic payments rather than paper Social Security checks for new beneficiaries, such as millions of baby boomers and others applying for Federal benefits.

Modernizes U.S. Currency. Treasury has increased the use of electronic financial transactions to meet the needs of commerce while working to ensure efficient and secure currency and coin production. In December 2011, the Treasury Secretary suspended production of circulating Presidential $1 Coins in light of the Federal Reserve Banks' inventories of 1.4 billion in $1 coins. This measure will reduce the U.S. Mint's expenses by $50 million annually. In addition, the Budget proposes legislation to provide the Secretary flexibility to change the composition of coins to more cost-effective materials, given that the current cost of making the penny is 2.4 cents and the nickel is 11.2 cents. Treasury is also taking additional actions to improve the efficiency of the coin and currency production efforts, including more than $75 million in savings proposed in the 2013 Budget.

Saves Taxpayer Money

Invests in and Modernizes Tax Administration to Prevent Evasion and Cheating. The Budget funds the IRS at nearly $12.8 billion, roughly $950 million above the 2012 enacted level. About $700 million of this total is provided through a "program integrity" adjustment to the discretionary caps that recognizes the benefit to taxpayers of a strong tax enforcement program that can return $5 for each additional IRS dollar spent. The Budget also continues significant investment in the IRS Business Systems Modernization program, which will yield substantial benefits to both taxpayers and the IRS by bringing tax data onto a fully modernized technology platform. Driven by up-to-date and comprehensive tax data, this modernized platform will revolutionize the efficiency and effectiveness with which the IRS serves taxpayers.

Improves Efforts to Collect Debt. The Budget proposes common sense debt collection reforms that will significantly increase Federal collections from individuals and businesses that have failed to pay taxes or repay Government loans, and help States collect a portion of the sizable State income tax debt owed by former residents. These proposals will help enforce a fairer tax system in which everyone pays their share. These reforms will increase collections by more than $2 billion over the next 10 years, a significant portion of which is owed to States and will be passed through to them.

Streamlines Core Operations Through Bureau Consolidation. The Budget supports a full consolidation by 2014 of the Bureau of the Public Debt and the Financial Management Service into the Fiscal Service. This allows Treasury to adopt more innovative strategies and streamline its core functions. The consolidation also strengthens Treasury's leadership of Federal financial management issues, reduces costs, and enhances efficiencies by further modernizing Federal financial management processes.

Department of the Treasury
(In millions of dollars)

	Actual 2011	Estimate	
		2012	2013
Spending			
Discretionary Budget Authority:			
Internal Revenue Service	12,150	11,816	12,070
Fiscal Service	411	384	360
Departmental Offices	316	308	308
Department and IRS Inspectors General	181	182	183
Special Inspector General for Troubled Asset Relief Program (TARP)	36	42	40
Alcohol and Tobacco Tax and Trade Bureau	101	100	97
Financial Crimes Enforcement Network	111	111	102
Community Development Financial Institutions Fund	228	221	221
All other	−85	—	—
Subtotal, Discretionary budget authority	13,449	13,164	13,381
Discretionary Changes in Mandatory Programs *(non-add in 2012):*[1]			
Treasury Forfeiture Fund		*−950*	−830
Total, Discretionary budget authority	13,449	13,164	12,551

Department of the Treasury—Continued
(In millions of dollars)

	Actual 2011	Estimate	
		2012	2013
Discretionary Cap Adjustment:[2]			
Program Integrity	—	—	691
Total, Discretionary outlays	13,113	13,486	14,054
Mandatory Outlays:			
Tax Expenditure programs	108,383	87,473	87,891
Legislative proposals		139	3,889
Government Sponsored Enterprise (GSE), Mortgage-Backed Securities (MBS) and Housing Finance Agencies (HFA) purchases	12,633	12,317	−10,458
Troubled Asset Relief Program (TARP)	24,148	40,152	12,193
TARP Housing (non-add)	*1,935*	*13,619*	*12,148*
TARP Equity (non-add)	*20,656*	*18,675*	*45*
TARP Direct Loans (non-add)	*1,557*	*7,858*	*—*
TARP Downward Reestimate of Subsidies	−60,355	−5,206	—
TARP Equity (non-add)	*−52,148*	*−3,567*	*—*
TARP Direct Loans (non-add)	*−8,207*	*−1,639*	*—*
Office of Financial Stability	352	457	291
Special Inspector General for TARP	5	7	7
Internal Revenue Collections for Puerto Rico	452	390	370
Legislative proposal		97	96
Terrorism Insurance Program	2	105	245
State Small Business Credit Initiative	366	859	251
Financial Research Fund (Office of Financial Research and FSOC)	4	120	154
All other	5,783	11,801	1,294
Total, Mandatory outlays	91,773	148,711	96,223
Total, Outlays	104,886	162,197	110,277

Credit activity

	Actual 2011	Estimate	
		2012	2013
Direct Loan Disbursements:			
HFA Purchases	—	102	3,452
Troubled Asset Relief Program	23,840	3,389	615
Small Business Lending Fund	4,028	—	—
Community Development Financial Institutions Fund	—	10	8
Total, Direct loan disbursements	27,868	3,501	4,075

Department of the Treasury—Continued
(In millions of dollars)

	Actual 2011	Estimate	
		2012	2013
Guaranteed Loan Disbursements by Private Lenders:			
Troubled Asset Relief Program	73	51,862	51,862
Total, Guaranteed loan disbursements by private lenders	73	51,862	51,862

[1] The 2012 amounts reflect OMB's scoring of the 2012 Appropriations acts (P.L. 112–55 and 112–74) as transmitted to the Congress. These amounts are displayed as non-add entries because they have been rebased as mandatory and are not included in any 2012 discretionary levels in the 2013 Budget.
[2] The Balanced Budget and Emergency Deficit Control Act of 1985 (BBEDCA), as amended by the Budget Control Act of 2011, limits—or caps—budget authority available for discretionary programs each year through 2021. Section 251(b)(2) of BBEDCA authorizes certain adjustments to the caps after the enactment of appropriations.

DEPARTMENT OF VETERANS AFFAIRS

Funding Highlights:

- Continues historic levels of support to veterans and their families by providing $64 billion, a 4.5 percent increase over the 2012 enacted level, to allow the Department to deliver on its promise to care for veterans and their families while working to improve efficiency in a constrained fiscal environment.

- Prioritizes care for veterans and their families, including medical care for special conditions—such as Post Traumatic Stress Disorder and Traumatic Brain Injury—long-term care, and benefits for veterans' caregivers.

- Continues the Administration's ongoing efforts to combat veteran homelessness.

- Recognizes and supports the unique needs of veterans who reside in rural areas.

- Provides $32.7 million to help provide veterans a seamless transition from active duty to civilian life, through veteran employment and education counselors.

- Provides $792 million to ensure timely activation of new and renovated medical facilities already under construction.

- Invests $583 million for medical and prosthetic research efforts to advance the care and quality of life for veterans.

- Improves Department of Veterans Affairs efficiency and responsiveness by continuing the implementation of the paperless system and transformation efforts that will provide faster and more accurate benefits claims processing and improve veterans' access to benefits information.

- Requests $54.5 billion in 2014 advance appropriations for medical care programs, to ensure adequate resources across fiscal years for medical care of veterans.

Our Nation has a solemn obligation to take care of our veterans as well as they took care of us. To deliver on this commitment, the President's 2013 Budget provides $64 billion in discretionary funding, a 4.5 percent increase above 2012 levels. This increase will continue to drive improvements in efficiency and responsiveness in the Department of Veterans

Affairs (VA), enabling the Department to better serve veterans and their families at a time when much is being asked of our men and women in uniform. The Budget simplifies access to these benefits; ensures that we are meeting the needs of today's veteran population; and invests in the continued modernization of the VA to meet 21st Century challenges.

Sustains and Strengthens Services for Veterans

Supports Veteran Employment and Education Transition. To help our newest veterans transition to civilian life and find good jobs, the Budget provides $32.7 million to fund 279 additional vocational rehabilitation and employment counselors to support the Integrated Disability Evaluation System (IDES) and VetSuccess on Campus initiatives. IDES and VetSuccess counselors ensure that veterans, especially wounded warriors and students, receive timely information about education opportunities, job counseling, and placement.

Activates New and Improved Health Care Facilities. The Budget includes $792 million to help VA provide the best possible specialized care for veterans in new or renovated facilities. These funds will support the staff and equipment at VA facilities across the country, including new major medical centers already under construction in Las Vegas, Denver, and Orlando.

Supports Medical and Prosthetic Research. As part of the largest integrated health care system in the United States, the VA research program benefits from clinical care and research occurring together, allowing discoveries to be directly coordinated with the care of veterans. In particular, the Budget includes $583 million in funds for medical and prosthetic research.

Combats Veterans Homelessness. The Budget invests over $1 billion to provide VA services for homeless and at-risk veterans. These funds will help combat veteran homelessness through collaborative partnerships with local governments, non-profit organizations, and the Departments of Housing and Urban Development, Justice, and Labor.

Serves Rural Veterans. The President's Budget continues the historic funding level of $250 million to improve access and quality of care for enrolled veterans residing in rural areas by supporting their unique needs. In addition, the Budget supports a new initiative to enable the National Cemetery Administration to purchase small parcels in existing local cemeteries and establish a national cemetery presence in previously underserved rural areas.

Improves Efficiency in Benefits Delivery

Continues Implementation of the Paperless Claims System to Boost Efficiency and Responsiveness. The Budget includes funding to support transformation initiatives, including the continued development of a digital, near-paperless environment that allows for greater exchange of information and increased transparency for veterans. Specifically, the request includes $128 million for the Veterans Benefit Management System, designed to reduce the processing time and the claim backlog, facilitate quality improvements through rules-based tools, and automate claims tracking.

Improves Efficiency and Access to Comprehensive Services and Benefits. The Budget continues support for VA efforts to ensure consistent, personalized, and accurate information about services and benefits, especially in the delivery of compensation and pension claims processing, in order to improve the speed, effectiveness, and efficiency of service delivery of benefits.

Effectively Utilizes Multi-Year Funding to Manage VA Medical Care. The Administration proposes $54.5 billion in advance appropriations for the VA medical care program in 2014, which enables timely and predictable funding for VA's medical care to prevent our veterans from being adversely affected by budget delays.

Department of Veterans Affairs
(In millions of dollars)

	Actual 2011	Estimate	
		2012	2013
Spending			
Discretionary Budget Authority:			
Medical Care	48,137	50,633	52,721
Medical Collections (non-add)	*2,772*	*2,767*	*2,966*
Total Medical Care including collections (non-add)	*50,909*	*53,400*	*55,687*
Medical and Prosthetic Research	580	581	583
Information Technology	2,992	3,104	3,327
Construction	1,672	1,203	1,270
Veterans Benefits Administration	2,133	2,019	2,164
General Administration	397	417	417
Housing and Other Credit	166	156	159
National Cemetery Administration	249	251	258
Office of Inspector General	109	112	113
Total, Discretionary budget authority	56,434	58,476	61,012
Total, Discretionary outlays	56,567	58,819	60,384
Mandatory Outlays:			
Disability Compensation and Pensions	57,578	56,193	64,521
Education Benefits	9,908	11,166	12,633
Vocational Rehabilitation and Employment:			
Existing law	797	949	1,067
Legislative proposals			16
Housing (credit):			
Existing law	1,383	1,667	179
Legislative proposals			1
Insurance	82	100	105
All other	609	299	842
Total, Mandatory outlays	70,357	70,374	79,354
Total, Outlays	126,924	129,193	139,748
Credit activity			
Direct Loan Disbursements:			
Vendee and Acquired Loans	258	1,140	1,325
All other programs	10	14	14
Total, Direct loan disbursements	268	1,154	1,339

Department of Veterans Affairs—Continued
(In millions of dollars)

	Actual 2011	Estimate	
		2012	2013
Guaranteed Loan Disbursements by Private Lenders:			
Veterans Home Loans	71,931	63,941	49,640
Total, Guaranteed loan disbursements by private lenders..........................	71,931	63,941	49,640

CORPS OF ENGINEERS—CIVIL WORKS

Funding Highlights:

- Provides $4.7 billion, a 5.4 percent decrease from the 2012 enacted level. The Budget achieves savings by prioritizing investments that will yield high economic and environmental returns or address a significant risk to public safety.

- Continues efforts to restore significant ecosystems such as the California Bay-Delta, the Everglades, the Great Lakes, Chesapeake Bay, and the Gulf Coast, helping to promote their ecological sustainability and resilience.

- Supports a high level of investment in maintenance and related activities at the most heavily used commercial harbors in the Nation and other high performing projects, such as navigation in the Mississippi and Ohio Rivers and the Illinois Waterway.

- Reforms financing of capital investments in inland waterways that support economic growth by establishing a new user fee.

- Invests in improvements to the Corps Regulatory Program that will provide greater certainty for businesses and more protection to our wetlands and small streams.

- Supports the modernization of Federal water resources infrastructure processes to address 21st Century water resources needs through improvements to policies and procedures that govern Federal water resources development and strategies for both managing the Nation's aging infrastructure and restoring aquatic ecosystem functions affected by past investments.

- Increases the organizational efficiency and improves the management, oversight, and performance of ongoing programs to meet water resources needs and achieve additional savings.

The Army Corps of Engineers civil works program (Corps) develops, manages, restores, and protects water resources primarily through construction of projects, operation and maintenance, studies of potential projects, and its regulatory program. Working with other Federal agencies, the Corps also helps communities respond to and recover from floods and other natural disasters. To support this work, the President's 2013 Budget provides $4.7 billion, a $271 million decrease from the 2012 enacted level. In light of the tight discretionary constraints, the Budget focuses on the highest priority work within the agency's three main missions: flood and storm damage reduction, commercial navigation, and aquatic ecosystem restoration.

Invests in Our Water Resources to Spur Economic Growth and Protect the Environment

Emphasizes Investments with High Economic and Environmental Returns While Addressing Public Safety. The Administration proposes about $1.6 billion in total for high-return construction projects in the three main mission areas of the Corps: flood and storm damage reduction, commercial navigation, and aquatic ecosystem restoration. For example, the Budget emphasizes funding for dam safety work and for projects to address a significant risk to public safety. The Administration will establish a White House-led Navigation Task Force to develop a Federal strategy for future navigation investments.

Restores High-Priority Aquatic Ecosystems. The Administration proposes funding to restore significant aquatic ecosystems based on sound science, criteria grounded in research and development, and adaptive management. Funds are provided for work on priority ecosystems, including the California Bay-Delta, Chesapeake Bay, Everglades, Great Lakes, and Gulf Coast. Funding is also provided for other ecosystem efforts, such as restoring Puget Sound and improving aquatic ecosystem restoration outcomes in the Upper Mississippi River, Missouri River, and Columbia River.

Invests in the Reliability and Safety of Water Resources Infrastructure. The Administration prioritizes funding for the operation and maintenance of key infrastructure, including navigation channels that serve our largest coastal ports and the inland waterways with the most commercial use (such as the Mississippi and Ohio Rivers and the Illinois Waterway). The Budget focuses on improving the reliability and operation of existing infrastructure rather than starting new projects that require additional Federal dollars and resources.

Increases Revenue and Flexibility

Reforms the Inland Waterways Funding Process. The Administration has proposed legislation to reform the laws governing the Inland Waterways Trust Fund, including increasing the revenue paid by commercial navigation users sufficiently to meet their share of the costs of activities financed from this fund. This proposal will provide an additional source of financing for major new investments in the inland waterways to support economic growth.

Modernizes Federal Water Resources Management. The Administration has already proposed several major actions to modernize the policies and procedures of the Corps and other Federal water resources agencies, to allow the Federal Government, working with its non-Federal partners, to make better use of water resources to generate economic growth, environmental improvements, and social benefits. These actions include revising the 25-year old principles and guidelines for planning water resources projects, proposing a user fee to help finance inland waterways capital investments, and establishing an Infrastructure Bank that would help finance port deepening projects, levees, and other major water resources development activities. The Administration is also considering proposals to improve the ability of the Corps to invest in and manage its assets and to enhance non-Federal leadership in water resources, including removing unnecessary obstacles and streamlining procedures for non-Federal parties to move forward on their own with important water resources activities, while ensuring appropriate Federal interests are maintained.

Improves Operational Oversight and Management

Improves the Corps Regulatory Program. The Budget increases funding for the Regulatory Program by 6 percent above the 2012 enacted level, allowing support for sustainable economic development. This funding will enable the Corps to provide greater protection to our wetlands and small streams, to reduce an ongoing loss of wetlands and other aquatic resources. This will support a transparent and timely permit review process, helping to bring greater certainty to business planning while protecting environmental, social, and economic benefits provided to the American public by clean water.

Increases Organizational Efficiency. The Administration will also focus on ways to improve the responsiveness, accountability, and operational oversight of the civil works program in order to best meet current and future water resources challenges. This effort will improve performance and free up resources for other uses and deficit reduction.

Corps of Engineers—Civil Works
(In millions of dollars)

	Actual 2011	Estimate	
		2012	2013
Spending			
Discretionary Budget Authority:			
Construction	1,612	1,694	1,471
Operation and Maintenance	2,460	2,412	2,398
Mississippi River and Tributaries	242	252	234
Flood Control and Coastal Emergencies	—	27	30
Investigations	122	125	102
Regulatory Program	190	193	205
Expenses	185	185	182
Office of Assistant Secretary of the Army for Civil Works	5	5	5
Formerly Utilized Sites Remedial Action Program	130	109	104
Total, Discretionary budget authority	4,946	5,001	4,731
Discretionary Cap Adjustment:[1]			
Disaster Relief	—	1,724	—
Total, Discretionary outlays	10,298	9,261	8,165
Mandatory Outlays:			
Existing Law	−140	−56	−7
Total, Mandatory outlays	−140	−56	−7
Total, Outlays	10,158	9,205	8,158

[1] The Balanced Budget and Emergency Deficit Control Act of 1985 (BBEDCA), as amended by the Budget Control Act of 2011, limits—or caps—budget authority available for discretionary programs each year through 2021. Section 251(b)(2) of BBEDCA authorizes certain adjustments to the caps after the enactment of appropriations.

ENVIRONMENTAL PROTECTION AGENCY

Funding Highlights:

- Provides $8.3 billion, a decrease of 1.2 percent, or $105 million, below the 2012 enacted level. Funding is increased for priorities, such as the agency's operating budget, which includes funds for the enforcement of environmental and public health protections, and for grants to States and Tribes.

- Achieves savings largely through reductions in the Drinking Water and Clean Water State Revolving Funds and Superfund Remedial activities, and the elimination of outdated, underperforming, and overlapping programs within EPA.

- Increases support to States and Tribes by approximately $93 million for implementation of delegated air quality management and water pollution control programs.

- Invests in 21st Century technology to establish electronic reporting for the National Pollutant Discharge Elimination System, which will improve oversight and reduce burdens on business. The Budget will also allow EPA to increase the number and frequency of inspections at high-risk oil and chemical facilities.

- Supports upgrades to the National Vehicle and Fuel Emissions Laboratory to implement the Renewable Fuel Standard and the light-duty and heavy-duty mobile source greenhouse gas standards. The Administration's national program of greenhouse gas and fuel economy standards for light duty vehicles alone will save approximately 12 billion barrels of oil and prevent 6 billion metric tons of greenhouse gas emissions over the lifetimes of the vehicles sold through model year 2025.

- Stimulates economic growth in local communities with abandoned industrial properties by integrating sustainable development with environmental remediation activities for the restoration of these areas.

- Enhances EPA and USDA coordination to reduce nonpoint source pollution, the largest cause of impaired waters, to achieve measurable improvements in water quality and ecosystem health by targeting resources and helping landowners implement voluntary stewardship practices.

- Continues efforts to restore significant ecosystems such as the Great Lakes, Chesapeake Bay, California Bay-Delta, Everglades, and the Gulf Coast, helping to promote their ecological sustainability and resilience.

The Environmental Protection Agency's (EPA) mission is to protect human health and the environment. Because of the tight fiscal environment, the President's 2013 Budget includes $8.3 billion to continue to deliver on this mission, a decrease of $105 million from 2012 enacted levels. Funding is increased for core priorities, such as the agency's operating budget which includes funds for the enforcement of environmental and public health protections, and for grants to support State and tribal implementation of delegated environmental programs. The Budget decreases the State Revolving Funds (SRFs) by $359 million, in part because of the continuing constrained fiscal environment. The reduced Federal contribution to the SRFs will still allow robust financing by State programs. The Budget also reduces the Hazardous Substance Superfund Remedial program by $33 million and eliminates $50 million in outdated, underperforming, and overlapping programs.

Prepares the United States to be a Global Leader in the Clean Energy Economy

Supports Efforts to Mitigate Climate Change and the Transition to a Clean Energy Economy. The President has called on the Congress to enact forward-looking legislation that would spur U.S. development of advanced, clean energy technologies to reduce U.S. dependence on oil, strengthen energy and national security, create new jobs, and restore America's position as a global leader in efforts to mitigate climate change and address its consequences. The Administration continues to support greenhouse gas emissions reductions in the U.S. in the range of 17 percent below 2005 levels by 2020 and 83 percent by 2050.

Implements Historic Fuel Economy Standards to Reduce Dependence on Oil and Save Consumers Money at the Pump. EPA will continue to collaborate with Federal and State agencies as well as regulated sources of greenhouse gas (GHG) emissions to seek cost-effective emissions reductions strategies. In 2013, EPA will continue to implement a national program to reduce GHGs from light-duty and heavy-duty mobile sources. The Administration's national program of fuel economy and greenhouse gas standards for light duty vehicles alone will save approximately 12 billion barrels of oil and prevent 6 billion metric tons of GHG emissions over the lifetimes of the vehicles sold through model year 2025. Additionally, EPA will continue to develop regulatory strategies to control GHG emissions from major stationary sources. The Administration also maintains funding levels for partnership and voluntary programs like Energy Star, which help conserve energy and cut utility bills.

Revitalizes Communities and Ecosystems

Promotes Economic Growth with Funding for Brownfields Projects Grants and Urban Waters Partnership. Brownfields are lightly contaminated sites—many in economically hard-hit areas—where the presence or potential presence of contamination may keep these sites from being used productively. As part of the Strong Cities, Strong Communities and the America's Great Outdoors initiatives, the President's Budget maintains an adequate level of funding within the Brownfields program and urban waters partnership for technical assistance and grants to local communities to promote sustainable development.

Works to Restore the Gulf Coast Ecosystem. The Administration remains committed to restoring and protecting the Gulf Coast ecosystem following the BP Deepwater Horizon oil spill. The Federal and State Gulf Coast Ecosystem Restoration Task Force, which the President established last year by Executive Order, recently released its restoration strategy. As Chair of the Gulf Coast Ecosystem Restoration Task Force, the EPA Administrator will help lead environmental recovery efforts in the region in support of the strategy. Additionally, the Administration continues to support dedicating a significant amount of the Clean Water Act civil penalties resulting from the Deepwater Horizon oil spill for Gulf recovery.

Continues to Fund the Great Lakes Restoration Initiative. The Administration proposes maintaining funding for the Great Lakes Restoration Initiative at $300 million, which will allow for continued ecosystem restoration efforts while exercising fiscal restraint. This EPA-led interagency effort to restore the Great Lakes focuses on priority environmental issues such as cleaning up contaminated sediments and toxics, reducing non-point source pollution, mitigating habitat degradation and loss, and addressing invasive species.

Supports Restoration of the Chesapeake Bay. The Budget increases funding for Chesapeake Bay restoration by $15 million to support Bay watershed States as they implement their plans to reduce nutrient and sediment pollution in an unprecedented effort to restore this economically important ecosystem. EPA and Federal partners will continue to coordinate with States, Tribes, municipalities, and industry to restore the integrity of this national treasure.

Supports State and Tribal Environmental Programs. The Administration proposes $1.2 billion for grants to support State and tribal implementation of delegated environmental programs. Among other changes, the support includes $302 million in State grant funding for air programs, an increase of $66 million to assist States in addressing additional responsibilities associated with achieving more stringent air quality standards, and $265 million in State water pollution control grants, a $27 million increase including $15 million to address nutrient loadings. The Administration also determined not to repropose the Multi-Media Tribal Implementation grant program in favor of a $29 million increase in funding to the Tribal General Assistance Program (Tribal GAP). Tribal GAP funding builds tribal capacity and assists Tribes in leveraging other EPA and Federal funding to contribute toward a higher level of environmental and health protection.

Enhances Interagency Efforts to Improve Water Quality. The United States has made great strides in improving water quality; however, "nonpoint" source pollution remains a significant economic, environmental, and public health challenge that requires policy attention and thoughtful new approaches. Key Federal partners, along with agricultural producer organizations, conservation districts, States, Tribes, non-governmental organizations, and other local leaders will work together to identify areas where a focused and coordinated approach can achieve decreases in water pollution. The President's Budget builds upon the collaborative process already underway among Federal partners to demonstrate substantial improvements in water quality from conservation programs by coordinating efforts between U.S. Department of Agriculture (USDA) and EPA programs such as EPA's Nonpoint Source Grants and Water Pollution Control Grants and USDA's Farm Bill conservation programs. This coordination will allow for more effective, targeted investments at the Federal and State level during a time of constrained budgets, and will ensure continued improvements in water quality.

Makes Tough Cuts

Makes Targeted Reductions to the Hazardous Substance Superfund Account. The Administration reduces funding for the Hazardous Substance Superfund Remedial program by $33 million. In order to ensure that this reduction does not negatively impact public health, the Administration maintains the funding level necessary for EPA to be prepared to respond to emergency releases of hazardous substances and circumstances that place the public at imminent risk of exposure and harm. Reductions will therefore be targeted largely to non-time critical activities that address long-term remediation goals.

Reduces Funding for State Revolving Funds (SRFs). The Administration requests a combined $2 billion for federal capitalization of the SRFs. This will allow the SRFs to finance over $6 billion in wastewater and drinking water infrastructure projects annually. The

Administration has strongly supported the SRFs, having received and/or requested funding totaling over $18 billion since 2009; since their inception, over $52 billion has been provided for the SRFs. EPA will work to target assistance to small and underserved communities with limited ability to repay loans, while maintaining State program integrity. Additionally, a number of systems could have access to capital through the Administration's proposed Infrastructure Bank.

Improves the Way Federal Dollars are Spent

Improves Compliance and Oversight to Increase Efficiency and Reduce Burdens. The Administration proposes a $36 million investment to upgrade compliance reporting and oversight activities with new technologies for detecting violations and reporting emissions electronically. After initially piloting this strategy through the National Pollutant Discharge Elimination System, EPA plans to expand the use of electronic reporting of data on permits and compliance as a means of increasing efficiency, reducing burdens on businesses, and increasing transparency for the public. Additionally, the Budget provides $5 million to increase the frequency of compliance inspections at high-risk

oil and chemical facilities, from the current 20 year frequency to a 7- to 10-year cycle.

Eliminates Outdated, Underperforming, and Overlapping Programs. Reducing duplicative, overlapping, or underperforming activities across governments is essential to ensure that taxpayer dollars are spent efficiently. For 2013, the Administration terminates $50 million in EPA programs, including programs that overlap other Federal agency missions (e.g., the Clean Automotive Technologies program), are underperforming, or can be implemented through other Federal or State efforts (e.g., the Radon and Beaches grant programs).

Redirects Funding to Advance Sustainable Practices for Electronic Waste Management. To ensure America remains a global leader in developing new sustainable electronics materials management practices, the Administration redirected resources from well-established legacy recycling efforts and launched the National Strategy for Electronics Stewardship in July 2011. EPA is leveraging its national leadership role to engage industry, producers, and consumers to advance the framework set forth in the strategy and address the growing need for responsible electronics design, purchasing, management, and recycling.

Environmental Protection Agency
(In millions of dollars)

	Actual 2011	Estimate	
		2012	2013
Spending			
Discretionary Budget Authority:			
Operating Budget[1]	3,669	3,569	3,738
State and Tribal Assistance Grants	1,103	1,089	1,202
Clean Water State Revolving Fund	1,522	1,466	1,175
Drinking Water State Revolving Fund	963	918	850
Brownfields Assessment and Cleanup	100	95	93
Clean Diesel Grants	50	30	15
Targeted Water Infrastructure	20	15	20

Environmental Protection Agency—Continued
(In millions of dollars)

	Actual 2011	Estimate	
		2012	2013
Superfund	1,281	1,214	1,176
Leaking Underground Storage Tanks..	113	104	104
Cancellation of unobligated balances	−140	−50	−30
Total, Discretionary budget authority	8,681	8,450	8,344
Total, Discretionary outlays...	10,900	9,500	9,151
Mandatory Outlays:			
Existing law...	−128	−148	−139
Legislative proposals, Pesticide and PMN user fees			−77
Total, Mandatory outlays	−128	−148	−216
Total, Outlays	10,772	9,352	8,935

[1] Includes funding for the Great Lakes Initiative.

NATIONAL AERONAUTICS AND SPACE ADMINISTRATION

Funding Highlights:

- Provides $17.7 billion, a decrease of 0.3 percent, or $59 million, below the 2012 enacted level. While making difficult choices, the Budget builds on our existing space infrastructure, continues efforts to streamline agency operations, and preserves innovative capabilities and technologies to sustain American leadership in space.

- Implements a lower cost program of robotic exploration of Mars that will advance science and will also help lay the foundation for future human exploration.

- Invests in new space technologies, such as laser communications and zero-gravity propellant transfer, which can improve America's ability to access and operate in space and enhance the competitiveness of the U.S. space industry.

- Leverages a Federal investment of $830 million and private sector investment and ingenuity to develop a U.S. capability to transport crews into space, thereby eliminating our dependence on foreign capabilities in this area.

- Provides continued robust funding for the development of a new heavy-lift rocket and crew capsule that will take America deeper into space than ever before, create American jobs, ensure continued U.S. leadership in space exploration, and inspire people around the world.

- Provides $1.8 billion for research and a robust fleet of Earth observation spacecraft to strengthen U.S. leadership in the field, better understand climate change, improve future disaster predictions, and provide vital environmental data to Federal, State, and local policymakers.

- Funds the highest priority astronomical observatories and robotic solar system explorers, including a successor to the Hubble telescope and a mission to return samples from an asteroid, while delaying unaffordable new missions.

- Continues the effort to turn NASA's former Space Shuttle launch facilities at the Kennedy Space Center in Florida into a 21st Century launch complex so that they can efficiently support programs like the Space Launch System and commercial operators.

- Streamlines agency operations, resulting in over $200 million in savings.

The President's 2013 Budget provides $17.7 billion to support the National Aeronautics and Space Administration (NASA) in its mission to drive advances in science, technology, and exploration to enhance knowledge, education, innovation, economic vitality, and stewardship of the Earth. Key investments are made in programs that will ensure American leadership in space science and exploration, support the development of new space capabilities, make air travel safer and more affordable, and answer important scientific questions about the Earth, the solar system, and the universe.

Invests in American Innovation

Expands Human Exploration of the Solar System. After three decades of learning how to live and work in orbit, including the ongoing operation and use of the International Space Station national laboratory, NASA is now investing almost $3 billion in 2013 to continue development of new systems for deep space crewed missions: the Space Launch System (SLS) heavy-lift rocket and the Multi-Purpose Crew Vehicle crew capsule. These programs will leverage NASA's skilled workforce and contractor teams to expand human exploration into the solar system, with a key initial goal of visiting an asteroid next decade.

Supports U.S. Jobs and Industry Growth. Recognizing the need to find a more efficient means to transport people and cargo to locations like the International Space Station, NASA is working with American industry to develop innovative, lower-cost, and safe approaches to human spaceflight through a combination of Government and industry investment. This program reduces America's reliance on Russian capabilities for supporting the International Space Station, keeps jobs here in the United States, and also accelerates the growth of the American commercial spaceflight industry.

Promotes Innovation and Advances Our Understanding of the Universe. NASA operates satellites and aircraft to better understand the Earth and improve our ability to forecast climate change and natural disasters.

NASA's science program also supports telescopes and space probes to advance our understanding of the cosmos. The Administration's proposal supports research grants and operating satellites, telescopes, and space probes to study the solar system as well as projects in development and important new efforts. Following a thorough management and technical review, the Budget funds the James Webb Space Telescope, the successor to the Hubble, to enable a launch later this decade. This decade also will see the launch of a new robotic mission to visit an asteroid and return with samples—helping us understand how our solar system formed and how life began—and paving the way for human missions to an asteroid. Some important, but currently unaffordable missions are deferred, such as large-scale missions to study the expansion of the universe and to return samples from Mars.

Fosters R&D Breakthroughs in Innovative Technologies. From ongoing demonstrations of human-robotic systems on the International Space Station to supporting the early-stage ideas that will revolutionize the technologies used in next decades' missions, NASA continues to expand the limits of the Nation's activities in space. For example, development of in-space propellant transfer and storage technologies could decrease the number of rocket launches needed for future exploration missions, and might have valuable application to other commercial and Government space activities. The Budget supports a broad spectrum of space and aviation technology research grants and demonstrations of high-priority technologies, from laser space communications to unmanned aerial systems to in-space transportation. The Administration's commitment to enhance NASA's role in aerospace technology development aims to create the innovations necessary to keep the Aerospace Industry—one of the largest net export industries in the United States—on the cutting edge for years to come.

Maximizes Resources

Boosts Efficiency of NASA Facilities and Property. NASA owns or leases more than 45 million square feet of property. Consistent with Administration waste-cutting efforts, the Budget supports a number of initiatives to help NASA operate more efficiently. Today, over 80 percent of NASA buildings are beyond their design life. The Budget continues to enable NASA to replace or modernize inefficient buildings, providing jobs to the local communities and leading to increasingly efficient use of taxpayer dollars. In addition, the Budget moves aggressively to dispose of NASA's excess properties and make more efficient and effective use of remaining assets. NASA's 21st Century Launch Complex and Exploration Ground Systems programs, for example, are upgrading NASA's former Shuttle launch facilities to support programs like the SLS and commercial operators.

Cuts Costs by Streamlining Operations. The President's 2013 Budget saves over $200 million in administrative costs by streamlining NASA's operations in areas such as travel, printing, information technology devices, and support contracts.

National Aeronautics and Space Administration
(In millions of dollars)

	Actual 2011	Estimate 2012	Estimate 2013
Spending			
Discretionary Budget Authority:			
Science	4,919	5,074	4,911
Exploration	3,928	3,721	3,933
Aeronautics	534	569	552
Space Operations	5,321	4,196	4,013
Space Technology	—	548	699
Education	146	136	100
Cross Agency Support	3,130	3,003	2,848
Construction and Environmental Compliance and Restoration	433	486	619
Inspector General	36	38	37
Mission Support	—	—	—
Subtotal, Discretionary budget authority	18,447	17,770	17,712
Total, Discretionary outlays	17,633	17,656	17,825
Total, Mandatory outlays	−15	−19	−19
Total, Outlays	17,618	17,637	17,806

NATIONAL SCIENCE FOUNDATION

Funding Highlights:

- Provides $7.4 billion for the National Science Foundation, which is $340 million above the 2012 enacted level. Investments are made in research priorities and savings of $66 million are realized through terminations and reductions in lower-priority programs.

- Maintains the President's commitment to double funding for key basic research agencies, including a robust 5 percent increase over the 2012 enacted level for NSF.

- Fosters the development of a clean energy economy by providing $203 million for a cross-agency sustainability research effort focused on renewable energy technologies and complex environmental- and climate-system processes.

- Supports future job creation in advanced manufacturing and emerging technologies with $414 million for multidisciplinary research targeted at new materials, wireless communications, cyberinfrastructure, "smart" infrastructure, and robotics technologies.

- Protects the Nation's critical information technology infrastructure with $57 million for a coordinated cybersecurity research initiative.

- Develops the next generation of scientific leaders with $459 million for the prestigious graduate fellowship and early career faculty programs.

- Advances evidence-based reforms in K-16 science and math education, including improved undergraduate instruction at research universities and a joint math education initiative with the Department of Education.

- Makes tough reductions and terminations to lower-priority education, outreach, and research programs, which will save over $66 million.

- Cuts administrative expenses, which will save an additional $19 million.

The National Science Foundation (NSF) is the key Federal grant-making agency responsible for supporting the full breadth of non-biomedical science and engineering research at the Nation's universities and colleges. NSF's research programs and high-tech workforce development programs help drive future economic growth, global competitiveness, and the creation of high-wage jobs for American workers. NSF plays a critical role in the implementation of the President's Plan for Science and Innovation. To support this important mission and underscore the priority the Administration places on innovation, the President's 2013 Budget provides $7.4 billion for NSF, 5 percent above the 2012 enacted level, and focuses on cross-cutting research priorities in advanced manufacturing, clean energy, wireless communications, and science and mathematics education. Consistent with Administration-wide efforts to reduce spending in a tight fiscal environment, the Budget realizes savings by reducing administrative costs and eliminating funding for lower priority education and research programs that lack evidence of impact or do not align well with NSF's core mission responsibilities.

Invests in American Competitiveness

Supports the Fundamental Research that Underpins Progress in Science, Technology, and Innovation. The Administration proposes $3.2 billion for the core fundamental research grant programs at NSF. The Budget also provides $63 million for the second year of an interdisciplinary research and education initiative that is changing the way the agency solicits and funds innovative cross-disciplinary proposals that may not have fared well under the standard peer review process.

Lays the Groundwork for the Industries and Jobs of the Future. NSF focuses on linking the results of fundamental research to societal needs, including building human capacity through educating tomorrow's science, technology, engineering, and mathematics (STEM)

workforce. To encourage interdisciplinary research for a future bio-economy, the Budget provides $30 million for innovative proposals at the interface of biology, mathematics, the physical sciences, and engineering. The Administration proposes $106 million, an increase of $28 million above the 2012 enacted level, for the second year of a cyberinfrastructure initiative that will accelerate the pace of discovery in all research disciplines. Given the large and growing importance of the wireless communication sector, the Budget also provides $51 million for an interdisciplinary program to develop innovative approaches and technologies to enable more flexible and efficient access to the radio spectrum.

Supports the Long-Term Competitiveness of American Manufacturing. The Administration proposes $149 million, an increase of $39 million above the 2012 enacted level, for basic research targeted at developing revolutionary new manufacturing technologies in partnership with other Federal agencies and the private sector. This advanced manufacturing research is part of a larger $257 million research initiative aimed at transforming static systems, processes, and infrastructure into adaptive, pervasive "smart" systems with embedded computational intelligence that can sense, adapt, and react. This larger research initiative also provides $28 million for NSF's contribution to the National Robotics Initiative, which will accelerate the development and use of robots in the United States.

Supports the Long Term Development of a Clean Energy Economy. The Administration proposes $355 million, an increase of $14 million above the 2012 enacted level, for research that is directly relevant to future clean energy technologies such as solar power generation and energy efficiency. In coordination with other Federal agencies, this clean energy research is a key component of an integrated approach to increasing U.S. energy independence, enhancing environmental stewardship, reducing energy and carbon intensity, and generating sustainable economic growth.

Accelerates Innovations from the Laboratory to the Market. While the knowledge gained from NSF-supported basic research frequently advances a particular field of science or engineering, some results also show immediate potential for broader applicability and impact in the business world. The Administration proposes $19 million for the new public-private "Innovation Corps" program at NSF aimed at bringing together the technological, entrepreneurial, and business know-how necessary to bring discoveries ripe for innovation out of the university lab.

Develops the Next Generation of Scientific Leaders. The Administration proposes $459 million, an increase of $55 over the 2012 enacted level, for two prestigious agency-wide science and engineering workforce development programs: the graduate research fellowship program and the faculty early career development program. These two programs recognize and support the best and brightest scientists and engineers at the formative stages of their careers. The Budget will also provide $49 million for a new effort within NSF to integrate and leverage STEM education research to improve learning in science and engineering disciplines and to capitalize on the scientific assets across NSF to enhance outcomes in learning and education programs.

Promotes a Secure and Reliable Cyberspace. The Administration proposes $110 million for a basic research initiative at NSF aimed at protecting the Nation's critical information technology infrastructure, including the Internet, from a wide range of threats that challenge its security, reliability, availability, and overall trustworthiness. This initiative will be managed in partnership with other Federal agencies consistent with the Administration's strategic plan for cybersecurity research and development.

Builds and Operates a Cutting-Edge Suite of Major Scientific Research Facilities. The Administration proposes $196 million to continue the construction of four cutting-edge research projects: the world's largest solar telescope, a fundamental gravitational physics experiment, an ecological observation network that spans the United States, and an unprecedented set of ocean observatories. The operation of NSF's existing research facilities—such as the academic research fleet, the Cornell synchrotron source, and the South Pole Station—is equally important, so the Administration proposes $843 million to maintain this unique suite of facilities.

Increases the Number and Quality of STEM Graduates

Improves Undergraduate Math and Science Instruction. The Administration proposes $20 million for the second year of a teacher-training research and development program for undergraduate teachers. This new program will transform the way science, engineering, and math is taught to undergraduate students. Competitive proposals will target the teaching of all undergraduate courses and the teaching practices of all faculty members in a department for all, or most, of the relevant departments at an institution. This program will support research on how to achieve widespread sustainable implementation of improved STEM undergraduate teaching practices and student outcomes at major universities, particularly for future K-12 STEM teachers. The Administration also proposes $61 million, an increase of 56 percent over 2012 enacted, for NSF's Transforming Undergraduate Education in STEM program. This increase will provide targeted research and development funds to design, test, and implement more effective educational materials, curriculum, and methods to improve undergraduate learning and completion rates in STEM for a diverse population.

Improves K-16 Math Education and Knowledge Building. The Administration proposes $30 million at NSF (in combination with $30 million at the Department of Education) for a jointly administered mathematics education initiative. This new program will create a multi-agency STEM tiered evidence initiative on K-16 mathematics that will combine the strength in mathematics education research at NSF with the Department of Education's State and school district connections and program scale up expertise. The program would provide grants to researchers, or programs with the greatest potential for transformational impact, and provide incentives for State, local, and institutional decision makers to infuse proven practices into math education programs. The program will lead to the creation of a knowledge-building infrastructure and model a new approach to grantmaking that systematically takes educational programs from early research through widespread effective use. This program is a pilot for a model that will be implemented more widely as part of the Federal STEM education strategic plan.

Makes Tough Choices

Reduces Administrative Expenses and Terminates Low-Priority Programs. The Administration proposes to terminate or reduce several research and public affairs programs that have achieved their original goals, are no longer innovative, or are tangential to the agency's core mission. NSF will also promote efficiency and effectiveness through improved business processes and the use of technology. The Administration proposes to repurpose the savings from these administrative efficiencies and low-priority program terminations to provide programmatic increases for high priority areas of basic research, innovation, workforce development, and science education.

National Science Foundation
(In millions of dollars)

	Actual 2011	Estimate	
		2012	2013
Discretionary Budget Authority:			
Research and Related Activities	5,510	5,689	5,983
Education and Human Resources	861	829	876
Major Research Equipment and Facilities Construction	117	197	196
Agency Operations and Award Management	299	299	299
Office of the Inspector General	14	14	14
Office of the National Science Board	5	4	4
Total, Discretionary budget authority	6,806	7,032	7,372
Total, Discretionary outlays	7,050	8,045	7,368
Mandatory Outlays:			
H-1B Visa Fee Programs	115	152	150
Donations and Receipts	−19	84	10
Total, Mandatory outlays	96	236	160
Total, Outlays	7,146	8,281	7,528

SMALL BUSINESS ADMINISTRATION

Funding Highlights:

- Provides $949 million, an increase of 3 percent, or $32 million, above the 2012 enacted level. The Budget includes increased funding for initiatives that will create jobs in America's small businesses, while making tough choices that achieve savings in reductions to select technical assistance activities. In addition, $167 million is provided for the Disaster Loans Program that will be designated as being for disaster relief under the Budget Control Act's cap adjustment.

- Supports $26 billion in loan guarantees for small businesses to enable them to invest, expand, and create jobs.

- Supports equity investments in underserved markets and helps innovative small businesses obtain early-stage financing, including expanding financing available for Small Business Investment Companies.

- Fully implements a one-stop shop for business-related information through BusinessUSA, which will help small businesses gain access to resources to grow their businesses.

- Expands entrepreneurship training opportunities for transitioning veterans.

- Supports over $1 billion in long-term disaster recovery loans for homeowners, renters, and businesses of all sizes.

- Makes tough choices in a difficult fiscal environment by reducing overall funding for non-credit technical assistance programs by approximately 8 percent from the 2012 enacted level.

- Strengthens SBA's lender and procurement program oversight to protect taxpayer dollars.

- Supports the transition to a cloud-based computing model to improve information technology flexibility, maximize capacity utilization, and increase innovation.

Small businesses play a vital role in job creation, economic recovery, global competitiveness, and the ability of millions of Americans to lead or gain a middle-class life. The Small Business Administration's (SBA's) mission is to help Americans start, build, and grow businesses. To deliver on this promise, the Administration proposes $949 million through regular appropriations and $167 million of disaster funding, a $199 million increase in aggregate from 2012 enacted funding. Small business loan guarantees are provided at levels above historical demand, and increased Federal funding is provided in order to avoid increasing loan fees on borrowers and lenders. Consistent with the Administration's commitment to make tough cuts in a constrained fiscal environment, funding for some technical assistance programs is reduced.

Invests in America's Businesses to Foster Economic Growth and Competitiveness

Spurs Job Creation by Enhancing Small Business Access to Credit. Because small businesses are a major engine of economic growth and job creation, the Budget provides $349 million in subsidy for SBA's 7(a) and 504 business loan programs. This funding supports $16 billion in 7(a) loan guarantees, (including $2 billion in revolving lines of credit that support $46 billion in total economic activity) which help small businesses operate and expand, as well as $6 billion in guaranteed lending under the 504 program to finance small businesses' commercial real estate development and heavy machinery purchases. In addition, the Small Business Investment Company (SBIC) program will provide up to $4 billion in guaranteed lending to enable SBICs to invest in high-growth small businesses, through expanded funding authorities.

Promotes Impact Investment in Underserved Markets. SBA will continue to leverage the SBIC debenture program to support $200 million annually over five years in equity-based impact investments in regions not well served by private financial markets. Two other initiatives—the Small Loan Advantage and Community Advantage programs—will also increase the number of SBA 7(a) loans going to small businesses and entrepreneurs in underserved communities.

Helps Innovative Small Businesses Obtain Early-Stage Financing. SBA will use the Innovation Fund within the SBIC debenture program

to address the capital gap many start-ups face between "angel investor" financing and later-stage venture capital financing. Beginning in 2012 and over five years, up to $200 million in guarantees for matching funds will be available to investors aiming to support innovative companies seeking to ramp up their operations and create new jobs.

Provides Small Businesses with Easy Access to the Full Range of Government Programs and Services Available to Assist Them. The Budget provides $6 million to SBA to implement BusinessUSA, an interagency Administration initiative to streamline and integrate customer service across Federal programs that support small businesses and exporters. This will enable businesses to more quickly identify and connect with the programs they need, and reduce Federal and business costs over the long run. Businesses looking for assistance from the Federal Government will benefit from interacting with one well-coordinated entity, rather than having to search for and solicit a number of separate components.

Expands Entrepreneurship Training Opportunities for Transitioning Veterans. The Budget provides $7 million to SBA to implement the National Veterans Entrepreneurship Training (VET) Program. This new program will provide transitioning veterans with the knowledge and tools to start their own businesses, building on SBA's successful pilot programs for veterans. The VET program will incorporate entrepreneurship training into the Department of Defense's enhanced Transition Assistance Program provided to all departing service members, including an online training curriculum on the fundamentals of small business ownership.

Supports and Reforms Long-Term Disaster Recovery. The Budget will support $1.1 billion in direct loans, the normalized 10-year average, for homeowners and businesses whose property is damaged by natural disasters. The Administration proposes $167 million for disaster loan administrative expenses to operate the program, which will be designated as disaster relief under the cap adjustment under authorized in the Balanced Budget and Emergency Deficit Control Act of 1985, as amended. SBA will streamline staffing and operations to use administrative funds in the most effective and cost-efficient manner.

Makes Tough Cuts

Continues to Support Entrepreneurs While Making Targeted Reductions in Spending. The Budget continues investments in technical assistance programs such as Small Business Development Centers, Microloan Technical Assistance, SCORE, and Veterans Business Development, which provide valuable counseling and training to entrepreneurs. In light of current fiscal constraints, the Budget proposes to terminate the PRIME Technical Assistance program, and includes an overall 8 percent reduction in technical assistance programs.

Improves Cost-Effectiveness

Protects Taxpayer Dollars Through Enhanced Oversight Activities. The Budget provides $19 million for the Office of the Inspector General, a $3 million increase over 2012 enacted funding. This funding will support SBA's efforts to detect and prevent fraud, waste, and abuse in its programs.

Creates Long-Term Savings by Modernizing Information Technology Infrastructure. The Budget supports SBA's efforts to improve the efficiencies of its computing infrastructure, saving an estimated $12 million over five years, by transitioning to a cloud-based model for its network and applications.

Small Business Administration
(In millions of dollars)

	Actual 2011	Estimate	
		2012	2013
Spending			
Discretionary Budget Authority:			
Salaries and Expenses	432	417	424
Business Loans			
Loan Subsidy	83	211	351
Loan Administration	153	148	145
Subtotal, Business Loans	236	359	497
Disaster Loans			
Loan Administration	45	116	0
Subtotal, Disaster Loans	45	116	0
Office of the Inspector General	16	16	19
Office of Advocacy	—	9	9
Total, discretionary budget authority	729	917	949

Small Business Administration—Continued
(In millions of dollars)

	Actual 2011	Estimate	
		2012	2013
Discretionary Cap Adjustment:[1]			
Disaster Relief..	—	—	167
Total, Discretionary outlays...	1,450	1,364	1,388
Mandatory Outlays:			
Business Loan Subsidy Reestimates......................................	4,529	1,643	—
Disaster Loan Subsidy Reestimates......................................	192	156	—
Liquidating Credit Accounts	–8	–7	–7
Surety Bond Guarantees Revolving Fund..............................	—	1	1
Total, Mandatory outlays...	4,713	1,793	–6
Total, Outlays	6,163	3,157	1,382
Credit activity			
Direct Loan Disbursements:			
Direct Disaster Loans...	315	713	1,037
Direct Business Loans	34	27	35
Total, Direct loan disbursements...	349	740	1,072
Guaranteed Loan Disbursements by Private Lenders:			
Guaranteed Business Loans...	19,648	15,867	21,994
Guaranteed Disaster Loans	—	18	57
Total, Guaranteed loan disbursements by private lenders............	19,648	15,885	22,051

[1] The Balanced Budget and Emergency Deficit Control Act of 1985 (BBEDCA), as amended by the Budget Control Act of 2011, limits—or caps—budget authority available for discretionary programs each year through 2021. Section 251(b)(2) of BBEDCA authorizes certain adjustments to the caps after the enactment of appropriations.

SOCIAL SECURITY ADMINISTRATION

Funding Highlights:

- Provides $11.7 billion in discretionary funding, a slight increase over the 2012 level, to maintain core services to workers, retirees, survivors, and people with disabilities.

- Continues investment in program integrity by providing $1 billion to ensure benefits are paid to the right person and in the right amount. In particular, the Budget invests in disability reviews that enhance the long-term integrity of the agency's programs.

- Restores the agency's authority to test disability program changes and funds innovative pilots to help improve educational and employment outcomes for Americans with disabilities.

- Cuts waste by improving efficiency and avoiding unnecessary expenditures.

The Social Security Administration (SSA) administers the Old Age, Survivors, and Disability Insurance program and the Supplemental Security Income (SSI) program. The President believes that Social Security is critical to ensuring that all Americans have the opportunity to retire with dignity and that Americans with disabilities do not have to experience economic hardship. To fund this commitment, the President's 2013 Budget includes $11.7 billion for SSA operations, a slight increase over the 2012 level. It supports disability pilot programs to improve education and employment outcomes for people with disabilities and enhancements to program integrity to cut down on waste, fraud, and abuse.

Protects Social Security for Future Generations

The President recognizes that Social Security is indispensable to workers, retirees, survivors, and people with disabilities and that it is one of the most important and most successful programs ever established in the United States. Although current forecasts maintain the solvency of Social Security paying full benefits until 2036, the President is committed to making sure that Social Security is solvent and viable for the American people, now and in the future. He is strongly opposed to privatizing Social Security and looks forward to working on a bipartisan basis to preserve it for future generations.

Reduces the Disability Appeals Hearing Backlog and Improves Customer Service. The Budget maintains services to the public, which SSA provides through multiple avenues, including the Internet, over the phone, and in-person at hundreds of local offices. A core function for SSA is processing benefit claims from Americans who apply for Disability Insurance or Supplemental Security programs. While the volume of applicants remains high, the Budget provides sufficient resources to prevent large increases in the length of time that people must wait for a decision about whether they qualify for benefits.

The Budget also provides for SSA to continue its progress in lowering the number of people waiting for a disability appeal hearing. In addition, the agency will continue to increase efficiency by holding hearings via video conference for areas of the country with the most cases and increasing the use of online services. By hearing approximately 960,000 cases in 2013, the average processing time will be reduced to SSA's target level of 270 days in September 2013.

Builds the Evidence Base for Disability Program Improvements. The Administration proposes five-year reauthorization of SSA's demonstration authority for the Disability Insurance program. This proposal would allow SSA to test a new round of program innovations. One such innovation would be the Work Incentives Simplification Pilot (WISP), which will test changes in the Disability Insurance return-to-work rules, subject to rigorous evaluation protocols. WISP would eliminate current barriers to employment by simplifying the treatment of beneficiary earnings, potentially increasing the number of beneficiaries that seek and sustain employment.

Improves Services for Children with Disabilities. The Budget supports the continued implementation of the interagency Promoting Readiness of Minors in SSI (PROMISE) pilot, initiated in 2012 to improve outcomes for children in the SSI program. The Department of Education and SSA, in consultation with the Department of Labor and the Department of Health and Human Services, will provide competitive grants to test and evaluate interventions that successfully improve child and family outcomes and reduce the need for children to remain in the SSI program.

Improves Tax Administration by Restructuring the Federal Wage Reporting Process. The Administration proposes to restructure the Federal wage reporting process by reverting to quarterly wage reporting. Currently, wages are reported to the Federal Government once a year. Increasing the timeliness of wage reporting would enhance tax administration and improve program integrity for a range of programs. The Administration will work with the States to ensure that the overall reporting burden on employers is not increased.

Steps up Efforts to Reduce Payment Errors and Boost Program Integrity. The Social Security Administration's program integrity efforts are part of a strong framework for making sure the Government is spending tax dollars efficiently and that SSA pays benefits only to eligible beneficiaries and in the correct amounts.

In 2013, the President's Budget provides $1 billion for SSA program integrity, including completing over 650,000 medical Continuing Disability Reviews that make sure that Disability Insurance and SSI recipients continue to meet the medical criteria for those programs. The Budget includes additional processing capacity within the agency devoted to program integrity, which will lead to over $47.9 billion in further savings. The Budget also requests an additional $140 million in 2012 to fully fund the cap adjustment level of $623 million, as authorized in the Balanced Budget and Emergency Deficit Control Act of 1985, as amended by the Budget Control Act of 2011. This will save an additional $800 million when compared to the current enacted amount for 2012.

Social Security Administration
(In millions of dollars)

	Actual 2011	Estimate	
		2012	2013
Spending			
Discretionary Budget Authority:			
Limitation on Administrative Expenses (LAE) Base[1]	10,550	10,817	10,840
Office of the Inspector General	102	102	108
Research and Development	36	1	41
Total, Discretionary budget authority	10,688	10,920	10,989
Discretionary Cap Adjustment:[2]			
Program Integrity	484	623	751
Total, Discretionary outlays	11,888	11,678	11,723
Mandatory Outlays:			
Old-age, Survivors, and Disability Insurance	725,121	772,812	820,037
Supplemental Security Income [3]	52,681	47,918	54,319
Special Benefits for Certain World War II Veterans	8	6	6
Economic Recovery Payments	17	—	—
Offsetting Collections	−105,338	−80,585	−35,983
All other	101,997	77,322	32,547
Legislative Proposals		—	84
Total, Mandatory outlays	774,486	817,473	871,010
Total, Outlays	786,374	817,473	882,733

[1] The LAE account includes funding, approximately $2 billion each year, from the Hospital Insurance and Supplementary Medical Insurance trust funds for services that support the Medicare program, including implementation of Medicare Reform. The budget authority total for 2011 includes approximately $161 million that is misclassified as discretionary rather than mandatory.

[2] The Balanced Budget and Emergency Deficit Control Act of 1985 (BBEDCA), as amended by the Budget Control Act of 2011, limits—or caps—budget authority available for discretionary programs each year through 2021. Section 251(b)(2) of BBEDCA authorizes certain adjustments to the caps after the enactment of appropriations. Amounts in 2011 are not so designated but are shown for comparability purposes.

[3] This amount does not include the effect of State Supplementation of offsetting collections.

CORPORATION FOR NATIONAL AND COMMUNITY SERVICE

Funding Highlights:

- Provides $1.1 billion, 1 percent above the 2012 funding level, to support the Corporation for National and Community Service's efforts to address national and local challenges through service, while maximizing limited resources.

- Maintains member levels for AmeriCorps at about 82,500, providing Americans with opportunities to serve their communities.

- Eliminates funding for two lower-priority programs in order to preserve key national service priorities.

- Invests in promising new approaches to major community challenges, leverages private and foundation capital to meet these needs, and grows evidence-based programs through a $50 million investment in the Social Innovation Fund.

- Strengthens the Senior Corps and improves the way Federal dollars are spent through competition and a renewed focus on outcomes and impact.

Through volunteering and other forms of public service, millions of Americans each year help address our Nation's greatest challenges and speed our economic recovery. The Corporation for National and Community Service (CNCS) provides an on-ramp for Americans of all ages to serve their community and country in sustained and effective ways throughout their lives, from tutoring at-risk youth to responding to natural disasters and building homes for low-income families. National service expands opportunities and makes positive impacts for both participants and the communities they serve by helping people develop new skills and gain valuable hands-on experience in solving problems in their communities. Some of the most creative solutions to America's challenges have been developed not in Washington, but in communities across the country where citizens work hand in hand to make a difference. The Budget proposes $1.1 billion for CNCS, which reflects the Administration's continuing commitment to providing opportunities for Americans to address local challenges through service, as well as the need to maximize limited resources at a time of fiscal constraint.

Invests in Community Solutions and a Skilled America

Supports National Service. The Budget provides funding for about 82,500 AmeriCorps members, enabling Americans to serve and supporting the efforts of nonprofit organizations to address critical community challenges, from homelessness to hunger to failing schools. The Budget focuses national service resources in those areas where service can achieve the greatest results for communities.

Supports Innovative Non-Profits. Innovative solutions developed in the nonprofit sector for addressing critical national challenges can only be executed if capital is available to develop, evaluate, and replicate successful approaches. The Budget invests $50 million in the Social Innovation Fund to test promising new approaches to major challenges, leverage private and philanthropic capital to meet these needs, and grow evidence-based programs that demonstrate measurable outcomes.

Strengthens Programs that Engage Seniors and Improves the Way Federal Dollars are Spent. Many older Americans are eager to serve our Nation and have a wide range of skills and knowledge to give back to their fellow Americans. For decades, the Senior Corps program has been an important conduit for connecting seniors to local volunteer opportunities. The President's Budget proposes to re-invigorate the program by: using competition to allocate funds to those organizations having the biggest impact in their communities; improving coordination among Senior Corps programs to target resources; focusing the program on outcomes; and evaluating program models to better understand what works.

Eliminates Lower Priority Programs. In this constrained budget environment, the Budget makes difficult choices and reduces lower priority activities in order to preserve investments in other areas. To that end, the Budget eliminates funding for two small, narrowly-focused programs: the Volunteer Generation Fund and the Nonprofit Capacity Building Fund.

Corporation for National and Community Service
(In millions of dollars)

	Actual 2011	Estimate 2012	Estimate 2013
Spending			
Discretionary Budget Authority:			
Operating Expenses	980	962	760
AmeriCorps (non-add)[1]	*676*	*684*	*679*
Senior Corps (non-add)	*208*	*208*	*208*
Social Innovation Fund (non-add)	*50*	*45*	*50*
Payment to the National Service Trust Fund	—	—	209
Salaries and Expenses	88	83	88
Office of the Inspector General	8	4	5
Total, Discretionary budget authority[2]	1,077	1,049	1,062
Total, Discretionary outlays	1,044	759	1,071

Corporation for National and Community Service—Continued

(In millions of dollars)

	Actual 2011	Estimate	
		2012	2013
Mandatory Outlays:			
Interest, National Service Trust[3]	—	7	7
Total, Mandatory outlays	—	7	7
Total, Outlays	1,044	766	1,078

[1] This includes amounts requested for the National Service Trust Fund in 2013.

[2] The 2013 budget authority reflected in this table represents the funds rounded at the account level, while the requested agency level total actually adds to $1,062.6.

[3] This table reflects the correct total mandatory outlay amounts for 2012 and 2013 consistent with the policy in the President's Budget. However, the outlays in the database are erroneously overstated by $61 million in both 2012 and 2013. This error will be corrected in the 2013 Mid-Session Review.

SUMMARY TABLES

Table S–1.   Budget Totals
(In billions of dollars and as a percent of GDP)

	2011	2012	2013	2014	2015	2016	2017	2018	2019	2020	2021	2022	Totals 2013-2017	Totals 2013-2022
Budget Totals in Billions of Dollars:														
Receipts	2,303	2,469	2,902	3,215	3,450	3,680	3,919	4,153	4,379	4,604	4,857	5,115	17,167	40,274
Outlays	3,603	3,796	3,803	3,883	4,060	4,329	4,532	4,728	5,004	5,262	5,537	5,820	20,607	46,959
Deficit	1,300	1,327	901	668	610	649	612	575	626	658	681	704	3,440	6,684
Debt held by the public	10,128	11,578	12,637	13,445	14,198	14,980	15,713	16,404	17,137	17,897	18,678	19,486		
Debt net of financial assets	9,170	10,467	11,358	12,023	12,633	13,281	13,894	14,469	15,095	15,753	16,433	17,137		
Gross domestic product (GDP)	14,959	15,602	16,335	17,156	18,178	19,261	20,369	21,444	22,421	23,409	24,427	25,488		
Budget Totals as a Percent of GDP:														
Receipts	15.4%	15.8%	17.8%	18.7%	19.0%	19.1%	19.2%	19.4%	19.5%	19.7%	19.9%	20.1%	18.8%	19.2%
Outlays	24.1%	24.3%	23.3%	22.6%	22.3%	22.5%	22.2%	22.0%	22.3%	22.5%	22.7%	22.8%	22.6%	22.5%
Deficit	8.7%	8.5%	5.5%	3.9%	3.4%	3.4%	3.0%	2.7%	2.8%	2.8%	2.8%	2.8%	3.8%	3.3%
Debt held by the public	67.7%	74.2%	77.4%	78.4%	78.1%	77.8%	77.1%	76.5%	76.4%	76.5%	76.5%	76.5%		
Debt net of financial assets	61.3%	67.1%	69.5%	70.1%	69.5%	69.0%	68.2%	67.5%	67.3%	67.3%	67.3%	67.2%		

Table S–2. Effect of Budget Proposals on Projected Deficits

(Deficit increases (+) or decreases (−) in billions of dollars)

	2012	2013	2014	2015	2016	2017	2018	2019	2020	2021	2022	Totals 2013–2017	Totals 2013–2022
Projected deficits in the adjusted baseline[1]	1,127	772	662	749	862	815	793	862	944	1,011	1,193	3,860	8,663
Percent of GDP	7.2%	4.7%	3.9%	4.1%	4.5%	4.0%	3.7%	3.8%	4.0%	4.1%	4.7%	4.2%	4.2%
Proposals in the 2013 Budget:[2]													
Short-term measures for jobs growth	178	137	24	10	1	–*	1	1	1	*	*	172	176
Net deficit reduction proposals:													
Health and other mandatory initiatives	11	2	–17	–42	–50	–59	–63	–66	–74	–88	–140	–166	–597
Expiration of high income tax cuts	......	–83	–95	–110	–128	–143	–154	–164	–174	–185	–197	–560	–1,433
Other revenue proposals	*	–20	11	–58	–97	–54	–50	–44	–57	–54	–57	–218	–480
Reductions in Overseas Contingency Operations not reserved for surface transportation	......	......	......	......	–19	–92	–95	–98	–101	–104	–107	–111	–617
Proposed program integrity cap adjustment for IRS and Unemployment Insurance, including mandatory savings	*	*	–*	–1	–2	–3	–4	–4	–5	–5	–5	–6	–28
Proposed Budget Control Act disaster relief cap adjustment	......	5	1	......	......	......	......	......	......	......	......	6	6
Outlay effects of discretionary policy	–*	8	3	–6	–7	–7	–6	–5	–4	–7	–7	–9	–38
Total net deficit reduction proposals	11	–88	–97	–218	–304	–358	–372	–382	–414	–443	–512	–1,064	–3,187
Surface transportation reauthorization:													
Investments in surface transportation	......	*	4	9	13	18	24	22	15	11	8	45	125
Reductions in Overseas Contingency Operations reserved for surface transportation	......	–17	–64	–82	–68	......	......	......	......	......	......	–231	–231
Net cost of surface transportation reauthorization	......	–17	–60	–73	–55	18	24	22	15	11	8	–186	–106
Tax cuts for families, individuals, and businesses[3]	10	25	39	31	32	33	35	36	38	40	43	159	352
Debt service and indirect interest effects	*	1	2	1	–10	–24	–40	–55	–73	–93	–116	–30	–407
Total proposals in the 2013 Budget	200	58	–91	–250	–335	–332	–352	–377	–433	–484	–577	–950	–3,173
Effect of replacing Joint Committee enforcement with 2013 Budget deficit reduction proposals:													
Programmatic effects	......	71	96	105	109	109	109	109	109	109	38	490	966
Debt service	......	*	2	6	13	19	26	32	38	44	50	39	229
Total effect of replacing Joint Committee enforcement	......	71	97	110	122	129	135	141	147	154	88	530	1,195
Resulting deficits in 2013 Budget	1,327	901	668	610	649	612	575	626	658	681	704	3,440	6,684
Percent of GDP	8.5%	5.5%	3.9%	3.4%	3.4%	3.0%	2.7%	2.8%	2.8%	2.8%	2.8%	3.8%	3.3%

* $500 million or less.

[1] See Tables S–4 and S–8 for information on the adjusted baseline.

[2] For total deficit reduction since January 2011, see Table S–3.

[3] Includes the effects of incentives for expanding manufacturing and insourcing jobs and continuing certain provisions through calendar year 2013.

Table S–3. Deficit Reduction Since January 2011

(Deficit reduction (–) or increase (+) in billions of dollars)

	2012–2021	2013–2022
Enactment of 2011 full-year appropriations [1]	-357	-320
Enactment of 2012 full-year appropriations	-565	-598
Budget Control Act discretionary caps for 2013 through 2021 [2]	-681	-791
PAYGO legislation enacted during the 1st Session of the 112th Congress [1]	-7	-11
2013 Budget:		
Short-term measures for job growth	354	176
Tax cuts for families, individuals, and businesses [3]	319	352
Reauthorize surface transportation	117	125
Health and other mandatory initiatives	-446	-597
Expiration of high income tax cuts	-1,236	-1,433
Other revenue proposals	-423	-480
Cap Overseas Contingency Operations (OCO) funding	-741	-848
Proposed program integrity cap adjustment for IRS and Unemployment Insurance, including mandatory savings	-23	-28
Proposed Budget Control Act disaster relief cap adjustment	6	6
Outlay effects of discretionary policy	-31	-38
Debt service	-595	-800
Total deficit reduction since January 2011	-4,309	-5,286
Memorandum, revenue and outlay effects:		
Enacted outlay reductions and 2013 Budget spending proposals	-3,136	-3,777
Enacted receipt increases and 2013 Budget revenue proposals	-1,174	-1,510

[1] Savings totaled through 2021.
[2] Includes program integrity and the cap adjustment for proposed disaster relief.
[3] Includes the effects of continuing certain expiring provisions through calendar year 2013.

Table S–4. Adjusted Baseline by Category¹

(In billions of dollars)

	2011	2012	2013	2014	2015	2016	2017	2018	2019	2020	2021	2022	Totals 2013–2017	Totals 2013–2022
Outlays:														
Appropriated ("discretionary") programs:²														
Defense³	699	709	700	673	678	690	706	722	737	753	769	788	3,446	7,215
Non-defense⁴	600	610	565	546	543	546	553	561	573	585	597	611	2,754	5,682
Subtotal, appropriated programs	1,300	1,319	1,265	1,219	1,222	1,235	1,259	1,283	1,310	1,338	1,367	1,398	6,200	12,896
Mandatory programs:														
Social Security	725	773	820	867	918	970	1,027	1,086	1,149	1,217	1,287	1,361	4,601	10,702
Medicare	480	478	528	564	586	640	660	685	751	811	873	967	2,978	7,065
Medicaid	275	255	283	339	372	402	430	457	486	517	553	589	1,825	4,428
Troubled Asset Relief Program (TARP)⁵	–38	35	12	8	5	2	1	*	*	*	....	....	29	30
Other mandatory programs	631	635	571	595	632	677	680	676	714	745	794	845	3,155	6,930
Subtotal, mandatory programs	2,073	2,175	2,213	2,373	2,513	2,692	2,798	2,904	3,100	3,289	3,508	3,763	12,589	29,154
Net interest	230	223	246	305	384	480	570	645	716	782	846	915	1,985	5,889
Adjustments for disaster costs⁶	*	*	2	5	7	8	9	9	10	10	10	10	31	80
Joint Committee enforcement	....	....	–71	–96	–105	–109	–109	–109	–109	–109	–109	–38	–490	–966
Total outlays	3,603	3,717	3,655	3,807	4,021	4,306	4,526	4,732	5,026	5,310	5,621	6,048	20,315	47,053
Receipts:														
Individual income taxes	1,091	1,179	1,294	1,389	1,506	1,633	1,766	1,894	2,015	2,139	2,267	2,401	7,586	18,303
Corporation income taxes	181	281	365	459	407	381	444	457	472	470	488	501	2,056	4,442
Social insurance and retirement receipts:														
Social Security payroll taxes	566	635	707	742	782	834	883	937	987	1,034	1,093	1,150	3,948	9,150
Medicare payroll taxes	188	203	214	226	239	256	272	289	305	319	337	355	1,206	2,812
Unemployment insurance	56	57	60	62	63	65	62	61	56	57	58	60	313	605
Other retirement	8	9	9	9	9	9	10	10	10	11	12	13	46	103
Excise taxes	72	80	87	97	102	104	110	118	133	140	147	157	500	1,195
Estate and gift taxes	7	11	12	13	14	14	15	16	17	18	19	20	68	159
Customs duties	30	31	34	36	38	39	41	44	46	48	50	52	188	429
Deposits of earnings, Federal Reserve System	83	81	80	61	46	36	36	38	40	42	43	45	259	468
Other miscellaneous receipts	20	24	21	52	67	71	73	77	82	88	94	100	284	724
Total receipts	2,303	2,590	2,882	3,145	3,273	3,444	3,711	3,939	4,164	4,367	4,610	4,855	16,455	38,391
Deficit	**1,300**	**1,127**	**772**	**662**	**749**	**862**	**815**	**793**	**862**	**944**	**1,011**	**1,193**	**3,860**	**8,663**
Net interest	230	223	246	305	384	480	570	645	716	782	846	915	1,985	5,889
Primary deficit	**1,070**	**903**	**527**	**357**	**365**	**382**	**245**	**148**	**146**	**161**	**165**	**278**	**1,875**	**2,773**
On-budget deficit	1,367	1,186	810	689	769	887	839	819	884	954	1,016	1,190	3,994	8,856
Off-budget deficit / surplus (–)	–67	–60	–38	–27	–21	–25	–23	–26	–22	–10	–5	4	–134	–193

Table S–4. Adjusted Baseline by Category [1]—Continued

(In billions of dollars)

	2011	2012	2013	2014	2015	2016	2017	2018	2019	2020	2021	2022	Totals 2013–2017	Totals 2013–2022
Memorandum, budget authority for appropriated programs:														
Defense [3]	711	670	664	676	688	702	717	733	748	765	781	800	3,446	7,273
Non-defense [4]	507	526	509	519	529	539	551	563	576	589	601	616	2,648	5,593
Total, appropriated funding	1,217	1,195	1,173	1,195	1,217	1,241	1,268	1,296	1,324	1,353	1,382	1,417	6,094	12,866

* $500 million or less.

[1] See Table S–8 for information on adjustments to the Budget Enforcement Act (BEA) baseline.

[2] Does not include effects of Joint Committee enforcement.

[3] Reflects revision in security category to consist of accounts in defense function (050).

[4] Reflects revision in nonsecurity category to consist of accounts not in the defense function (050).

[5] Outlays for TARP result from obligations incurred through October 3, 2010 for the Home Affordable Modification Program and other TARP programs.

[6] These amounts represent a placeholder for major disasters requiring Federal assistance for relief and reconstruction. Such assistance might be provided in the form of discretionary or mandatory outlays or tax relief. These amounts are included as outlays for convenience.

Table S-5. Proposed Budget by Category

(In billions of dollars)

	2011	2012	2013	2014	2015	2016	2017	2018	2019	2020	2021	2022	Totals 2013–2017	Totals 2013–2022
Outlays:														
Appropriated ("discretionary") programs:[1]														
Security	838	868	851	768	749	757	771	786	803	820	837	856	3,897	8,001
Nonsecurity	462	450	410	393	385	386	390	397	405	415	420	430	1,964	4,032
Subtotal, appropriated programs	1,300	1,319	1,261	1,160	1,135	1,143	1,162	1,183	1,208	1,236	1,258	1,287	5,861	12,033
Mandatory programs:														
Social Security	725	773	820	867	918	970	1,026	1,085	1,149	1,216	1,287	1,361	4,601	10,699
Medicare	480	478	523	551	569	619	633	654	716	767	822	908	2,895	6,762
Medicaid	275	255	283	338	370	399	423	450	479	510	542	578	1,813	4,372
Troubled Asset Relief Program (TARP)[2]	–38	35	12	8	5	2	1	*	*	*	......	......	29	30
Other mandatory programs	631	711	654	644	665	705	712	716	750	775	821	826	3,381	7,269
Subtotal, mandatory programs	2,073	2,252	2,293	2,409	2,527	2,695	2,796	2,905	3,094	3,269	3,472	3,673	12,719	29,131
Net interest	230	225	248	309	390	483	565	631	692	748	798	850	1,996	5,715
Adjustments for disaster costs[3]	*	*	2	5	7	8	9	9	10	10	10	10	31	80
Total outlays	3,603	3,796	3,803	3,883	4,060	4,329	4,532	4,728	5,004	5,262	5,537	5,820	20,607	46,959
Receipts:														
Individual income taxes	1,091	1,165	1,359	1,476	1,617	1,763	1,912	2,052	2,184	2,319	2,459	2,605	8,128	19,747
Corporation income taxes	181	237	348	430	445	455	473	480	485	494	507	520	2,151	4,637
Social insurance and retirement receipts:														
Social Security payroll taxes	566	572	677	742	781	833	881	936	987	1,034	1,093	1,150	3,915	9,113
Medicare payroll taxes	188	203	214	226	240	257	273	290	306	321	339	357	1,210	2,823
Unemployment insurance	56	57	58	59	75	79	75	73	65	64	66	67	347	681
Other retirement	8	9	10	11	12	12	13	13	14	14	16	17	57	130
Excise taxes	72	79	88	99	104	106	112	120	136	142	150	159	509	1,216
Estate and gift taxes	7	11	13	23	25	27	29	32	34	37	39	42	117	301
Customs duties	30	31	33	36	38	39	41	44	46	48	50	52	188	428
Deposits of earnings, Federal Reserve System	83	81	80	61	46	36	36	38	40	42	43	45	260	468
Other miscellaneous receipts	20	24	21	52	68	71	74	77	83	89	95	101	286	729
Total receipts	2,303	2,469	2,902	3,215	3,450	3,680	3,919	4,153	4,379	4,604	4,857	5,115	17,167	40,274
Deficit	**1,300**	**1,327**	**901**	**668**	**610**	**649**	**612**	**575**	**626**	**658**	**681**	**704**	**3,440**	**6,684**
Net interest	230	225	248	309	390	483	565	631	692	748	798	850	1,996	5,715
Primary deficit / surplus (–)	**1,070**	**1,102**	**654**	**359**	**219**	**166**	**47**	**–56**	**–67**	**–90**	**–117**	**–146**	**1,445**	**969**
On-budget deficit	1,367	1,394	945	695	629	673	634	601	647	667	686	701	3,576	6,877
Off-budget deficit / surplus (–)	–67	–67	–43	–27	–19	–24	–22	–25	–21	–10	–5	4	–136	–193

Table S-5. Proposed Budget by Category—Continued

(In billions of dollars)

	2011	2012	2013	2014	2015	2016	2017	2018	2019	2020	2021	2022	Totals 2013–2017	Totals 2013–2022
Memorandum, budget authority for appropriated programs:[1]														
Security	847	817	788	743	756	769	785	802	819	836	853	874	3,841	8,023
Nonsecurity	370	379	359	366	373	381	389	398	407	416	425	435	1,867	3,947
Total, appropriated funding	1,217	1,195	1,147	1,108	1,129	1,150	1,174	1,199	1,225	1,251	1,277	1,309	5,708	11,970

* $500 million or less.

[1] Discretionary spending levels other than Overseas Contingency Operations reflect the budget authority caps under the Budget Control Act of 2011. The split of discretionary spending between security and nonsecurity after 2013 is based on increasing budget authority in each category by the growth rate in the aggregate discretionary cap.

[2] Outlays for TARP result from obligations incurred through October 3, 2010 for the Home Affordable Modification Program and other TARP programs.

[3] These amounts represent a placeholder for major disasters requiring Federal assistance for relief and reconstruction. Such assistance might be provided in the form of discretionary or mandatory outlays or tax relief. These amounts are included as outlays for convenience.

Table S-6. Proposed Budget by Category as a Percent of GDP

(As a percent of GDP)

	2011	2012	2013	2014	2015	2016	2017	2018	2019	2020	2021	2022	Averages 2013–2017	Averages 2013–2022
Outlays:														
Appropriated ("discretionary") programs:[1]														
Security	5.6	5.6	5.2	4.5	4.1	3.9	3.8	3.7	3.6	3.5	3.4	3.4	4.3	3.9
Nonsecurity	3.1	2.9	2.5	2.3	2.1	2.0	1.9	1.8	1.8	1.8	1.7	1.7	2.2	2.0
Subtotal, appropriated programs	8.7	8.5	7.7	6.8	6.2	5.9	5.7	5.5	5.4	5.3	5.1	5.0	6.5	5.9
Mandatory programs:														
Social Security	4.8	5.0	5.0	5.1	5.0	5.0	5.0	5.1	5.1	5.2	5.3	5.3	5.0	5.1
Medicare	3.2	3.1	3.2	3.2	3.1	3.2	3.1	3.0	3.2	3.3	3.4	3.6	3.2	3.2
Medicaid	1.8	1.6	1.7	2.0	2.0	2.1	2.1	2.1	2.1	2.2	2.2	2.3	2.0	2.1
Troubled Asset Relief Program (TARP)[2]	-0.3	0.2	0.1	*	*	*	*	*	*	*	......	......	*	*
Other mandatory programs	4.2	4.6	4.0	3.8	3.7	3.7	3.5	3.3	3.3	3.3	3.4	3.2	3.7	3.5
Subtotal, mandatory programs	13.9	14.4	14.0	14.0	13.9	14.0	13.7	13.5	13.8	14.0	14.2	14.4	13.9	14.0
Net interest	1.5	1.4	1.5	1.8	2.1	2.5	2.8	2.9	3.1	3.2	3.3	3.3	2.1	2.7
Adjustments for disaster costs[3]	*	*	*	*	*	*	*	*	*	*	*	*	*	*
Total outlays	24.1	24.3	23.3	22.6	22.3	22.5	22.2	22.0	22.3	22.5	22.7	22.8	22.6	22.5
Receipts:														
Individual income taxes	7.3	7.5	8.3	8.6	8.9	9.2	9.4	9.6	9.7	9.9	10.1	10.2	8.9	9.4
Corporation income taxes	1.2	1.5	2.1	2.5	2.4	2.4	2.3	2.2	2.2	2.1	2.1	2.0	2.4	2.2
Social insurance and retirement receipts:														
Social Security payroll taxes	3.8	3.7	4.1	4.3	4.3	4.3	4.3	4.4	4.4	4.4	4.5	4.5	4.3	4.4
Medicare payroll taxes	1.3	1.3	1.3	1.3	1.3	1.3	1.3	1.4	1.4	1.4	1.4	1.4	1.3	1.4
Unemployment insurance	0.4	0.4	0.4	0.3	0.4	0.4	0.4	0.3	0.3	0.3	0.3	0.3	0.4	0.3
Other retirement	0.1	0.1	0.1	0.1	0.1	0.1	0.1	0.1	0.1	0.1	0.1	0.1	0.1	0.1
Excise taxes	0.5	0.5	0.5	0.6	0.6	0.6	0.5	0.6	0.6	0.6	0.6	0.6	0.6	0.6
Estate and gift taxes	*	0.1	0.1	0.1	0.1	0.1	0.1	0.1	0.2	0.2	0.2	0.2	0.1	0.1
Customs duties	0.2	0.2	0.2	0.2	0.2	0.2	0.2	0.2	0.2	0.2	0.2	0.2	0.2	0.2
Deposits of earnings, Federal Reserve System	0.6	0.5	0.5	0.4	0.3	0.2	0.2	0.2	0.2	0.2	0.2	0.2	0.3	0.2
Other miscellaneous receipts	0.1	0.2	0.1	0.3	0.4	0.4	0.4	0.4	0.4	0.4	0.4	0.4	0.3	0.3
Total receipts	15.4	15.8	17.8	18.7	19.0	19.1	19.2	19.4	19.5	19.7	19.9	20.1	18.8	19.2
Deficit	**8.7**	**8.5**	**5.5**	**3.9**	**3.4**	**3.4**	**3.0**	**2.7**	**2.8**	**2.8**	**2.8**	**2.8**	**3.8**	**3.3**
Net interest	1.5	1.4	1.5	1.8	2.1	2.5	2.8	2.9	3.1	3.2	3.3	3.3	2.1	2.7
Primary deficit / surplus (–)	**7.2**	**7.1**	**4.0**	**2.1**	**1.2**	**0.9**	**0.2**	**-0.3**	**-0.3**	**-0.4**	**-0.5**	**-0.6**	**1.7**	**0.6**
On-budget deficit	9.1	8.9	5.8	4.1	3.5	3.5	3.1	2.8	2.9	2.9	2.8	2.7	4.0	3.4
Off-budget deficit / surplus (–)	-0.4	-0.4	-0.3	-0.2	-0.1	-0.1	-0.1	-0.1	-0.1	-*	-*	*	-0.2	-0.1

Table S–6. Proposed Budget by Category as a Percent of GDP—Continued

(As a percent of GDP)

	2011	2012	2013	2014	2015	2016	2017	2018	2019	2020	2021	2022	Averages 2013–2017	Averages 2013–2022
Memorandum, budget authority for appropriated programs:[1]														
Security	5.7	5.2	4.8	4.3	4.2	4.0	3.9	3.7	3.7	3.6	3.5	3.4	4.2	3.9
Nonsecurity	2.5	2.4	2.2	2.1	2.1	2.0	1.9	1.9	1.8	1.8	1.7	1.7	2.1	1.9
Subtotal, appropriated programs	8.1	7.7	7.0	6.5	6.2	6.0	5.8	5.6	5.5	5.3	5.2	5.1	6.3	5.8

*0.05 percent of GDP or less.

[1] Discretionary spending levels other than Overseas Contingency Operations reflect the budget authority caps under the Budget Control Act of 2011. The split of discretionary spending between security and nonsecurity after 2013 is based on increasing budget authority in each category by the growth rate in the aggregate discretionary cap.

[2] Outlays for TARP result from obligations incurred through October 3, 2010 for the Home Affordable Modification Program and other TARP programs.

[3] These amounts represent a placeholder for major disasters requiring Federal assistance for relief and reconstruction. Such assistance might be provided in the form of discretionary or mandatory outlays or tax relief. These amounts are included as outlays for convenience.

Table S–7. Proposed Budget in Population- and Inflation-Adjusted Dollars

(In billions of constant dollars, adjusted for population growth)

	2013	2014	2015	2016	2017	2018	2019	2020	2021	2022
Outlays:										
Appropriated ("discretionary") programs:[1]										
Security	851	746	707	693	685	677	671	665	659	654
Nonsecurity	410	381	363	353	347	342	339	337	331	329
Subtotal, appropriated programs	1,261	1,127	1,070	1,046	1,031	1,019	1,010	1,002	989	982
Mandatory programs:										
Social Security	820	842	865	888	911	935	960	986	1,012	1,039
Medicare	523	535	537	566	562	563	598	622	646	693
Medicaid	283	329	349	365	375	387	401	414	426	441
Troubled Asset Relief Program (TARP)[2]	12	8	5	2	1	*	*	*	......	......
Other mandatory programs	654	626	627	645	632	616	627	628	646	631
Subtotal, mandatory programs	2,293	2,340	2,383	2,467	2,482	2,502	2,585	2,650	2,731	2,803
Net interest	248	300	368	442	502	544	578	606	628	649
Adjustments for disaster costs[3]	2	5	7	8	8	8	8	8	8	8
Total outlays	3,803	3,772	3,828	3,962	4,023	4,073	4,181	4,266	4,356	4,442
Receipts:										
Individual income taxes	1,359	1,434	1,525	1,614	1,697	1,767	1,825	1,880	1,934	1,988
Corporation income taxes	348	417	420	417	420	413	405	400	399	397
Social insurance and retirement receipts										
Social Security payroll taxes	677	721	736	762	782	806	824	838	860	878
Medicare payroll taxes	214	220	226	235	242	250	256	260	267	273
Unemployment insurance	58	58	71	73	67	63	54	52	52	51
Other retirement	10	10	11	11	11	11	11	12	12	13
Excise taxes	88	96	98	97	99	104	113	115	118	121
Estate and gift taxes	13	22	24	25	26	27	29	30	31	32
Customs duties	33	35	36	36	37	38	38	39	39	40
Deposits of earnings, Federal Reserve System	80	60	43	33	32	32	33	34	34	35
Other miscellaneous receipts	21	51	64	65	65	67	69	72	74	77
Total receipts	2,902	3,124	3,253	3,368	3,479	3,577	3,658	3,732	3,820	3,904
Deficit	**901**	**649**	**575**	**594**	**544**	**496**	**523**	**533**	**535**	**538**
Net interest	248	300	368	442	502	544	578	606	628	649
Primary deficit / surplus (–)	**654**	**348**	**207**	**152**	**42**	**–48**	**–56**	**–73**	**–92**	**–111**
On-budget deficit	945	675	593	616	563	517	540	541	539	535
Off-budget deficit / surplus (–)	–43	–26	–18	–22	–19	–22	–18	–8	–4	3

Table S–7. Proposed Budget in Population- and Inflation-Adjusted Dollars—Continued

(In billions of constant dollars, adjusted for population growth)

	2013	2014	2015	2016	2017	2018	2019	2020	2021	2022
Memorandum, budget authority for appropriated programs:[1]										
Security	788	721	713	704	697	690	684	677	671	667
Nonsecurity	359	355	352	348	346	343	340	337	334	332
Subtotal, appropriated programs	1,147	1,077	1,064	1,053	1,042	1,033	1,024	1,014	1,005	999
Memorandum, index of population growth and inflation	1.00	1.03	1.06	1.09	1.13	1.16	1.20	1.23	1.27	1.31

* $500 million or less.

[1] Discretionary spending levels other than Overseas Contingency Operations reflect the budget authority caps under the Budget Control Act of 2011. The split of discretionary spending between security and nonsecurity after 2013 is based on increasing budget authority in each category by the growth rate in the aggregate discretionary cap.

[2] Outlays for TARP result from obligations incurred through October 3, 2010 for the Home Affordable Modification Program and other TARP programs.

[3] These amounts represent a placeholder for major disasters requiring Federal assistance for relief and reconstruction. Such assistance might be provided in the form of discretionary or mandatory outlays or tax relief. These amounts are included as outlays for convenience.

Table S–8. Bridge From Budget Enforcement Act Baseline to Adjusted Baseline

(Deficit increases (+) or decreases (–) in billions of dollars)

	2011	2012	2013	2014	2015	2016	2017	2018	2019	2020	2021	2022	Totals 2013–2017	Totals 2013–2022
BEA baseline deficit	1,300	1,097	598	438	492	556	463	396	411	436	444	483	2,548	4,718
Adjustments for current policy:														
Index to inflation the 2011 parameters of the AMT	....	19	120	115	130	148	169	192	216	242	269	298	682	1,898
Continue the 2001 and 2003 tax cuts	....	....	120	183	198	213	226	233	240	246	253	261	940	2,173
Extend estate, gift, and generation-skipping transfer taxes at current parameters	....	2	5	32	36	40	44	48	51	55	59	62	156	431
Prevent reduction in Medicare physician payments	....	9	26	31	35	41	39	39	46	51	56	65	172	429
Reflect incremental cost of funding existing Pell maximum grant award	....	....	–1	1	7	8	8	6	6	6	6	6	22	50
Subtotal	....	30	270	362	405	450	484	517	558	600	643	692	1,971	4,982
Adjustments for provisions contained in the Budget Control Act:														
Set discretionary budget authority at cap levels	....	....	–27	–49	–62	–71	–76	–82	–87	–92	–99	–103	–284	–746
Reflect Joint Committee enforcement	....	....	–71	–96	–105	–109	–109	–109	–109	–109	–109	–38	–490	–966
Make program integrity adjustments	....	....	–*	–2	–3	–4	–4	–5	–6	–6	–7	–8	–14	–45
Subtotal	....	–*	–98	–146	–169	–184	–190	–196	–202	–208	–215	–149	–788	–1,757
Adjustment for disaster costs[1]	....	*	2	5	7	8	9	9	10	10	10	10	31	80
Reclassify surface transportation outlays:														
Remove outlays from appropriated category	–48	–52	–55	–56	–58	–58	–59	–59	–60	–60	–61	–62	–286	–588
Add outlays to mandatory category	48	52	55	56	58	58	59	59	60	60	61	62	286	588
Subtotal	....	....	....	....	....	....	....	....	....	....	....	....	....	....
Total program adjustments	....	30	174	220	243	274	303	330	366	402	438	553	1,214	3,304
Debt service on adjustments	....	*	1	4	14	31	49	66	85	106	129	157	98	640
Total adjustments	....	30	174	224	257	305	352	397	451	508	567	710	1,313	3,945
Adjusted baseline deficit	1,300	1,127	772	662	749	862	815	793	862	944	1,011	1,193	3,860	8,663

* $500 million or less.

[1] These amounts represent a placeholder for major disasters requiring Federal assistance for relief and reconstruction. Such assistance might be provided in the form of discretionary or mandatory outlays or tax relief. These amounts are included as outlays for convenience.

Table S–9. Mandatory and Receipt Proposals

(Deficit increases (+) or decreases (–) in millions of dollars)

	2012	2013	2014	2015	2016	2017	2018	2019	2020	2021	2022	Totals 2013–2017	Totals 2013–2022
Temporary Tax Relief and Investments to Create Jobs and Jumpstart Growth:													
Tax initiatives:													
Extend temporary reduction in the Social Security payroll tax rate for employees and self-employed individuals	63,153	31,159	......	–72	41	17	8	2	2	1	......	31,145	31,158
Extend 100-percent first-year depreciation deduction for certain property	35,046	14,830	–13,709	–10,284	–7,293	–5,376	–3,503	–2,246	–1,377	–1,029	–935	–21,832	–30,922
Provide a temporary 10-percent tax credit for new jobs and wage increases [1]	14,227	12,601	1,054	1,162	1,048	881	461	458	389	230	164	16,746	18,448
Provide additional tax credits for investment in qualified advanced energy manufacturing project	170	779	1,309	1,215	418	26	–67	–111	–57	–21	–7	3,747	3,484
Provide tax credit for energy-efficient commercial building property expenditures in place of existing tax deduction	......	400	517	367	232	115	32	–2	–2	–2	–2	1,631	1,655
Reform and extend Build America bonds [1]	17	55	95	118	119	118	119	119	119	119	120	505	1,101
Mandatory initiatives:													
Reform and extend unemployment insurance [2,3]	22,620	21,612	......	64	77	116	583	341	40	–37	68	21,869	22,864
Create a Pathways Back to Work fund	3,475	8,400	625	......	......	......	......	......	......	......	......	9,025	9,025
Establish a community college initiative	534	2,134	2,666	2,132	534	......	......	......	......	......	......	7,466	7,466
Provide HomeStar rebates for energy efficient home retrofits	......	300	1,800	2,100	1,020	600	180	......	......	......	......	5,820	6,000
Develop a national network of manufacturing innovation institutes	......	206	131	174	189	139	69	44	28	16	4	839	1,000
Establish advanced vehicles community development challenge	......	150	450	400	......	......	......	......	......	......	......	1,000	1,000
Invest in immediate surface transportation priorities	5,690	18,280	12,090	5,250	3,650	1,480	1,560	960	640	320	80	40,750	44,310
Create infrastructure bank	22	107	478	899	1,186	1,487	1,684	1,411	1,183	859	547	4,157	9,841
Provide for teacher stabilization	15,000	10,000	......	......	......	......	......	......	......	......	......	10,000	10,000
Modernize schools	15,000	6,000	6,000	3,000	......	......	......	......	......	......	......	15,000	15,000
Support first responders	3,000	2,000	......	......	......	......	......	......	......	......	......	2,000	2,000
Support VA conservation jobs	......	50	237	237	238	238	......	......	......	......	......	1,000	1,000
Strengthen the teaching profession	250	2,500	2,250	......	......	......	......	......	......	......	......	4,750	4,750
Continue temporary SNAP assistance	......	369	1,351	23	......	......	......	......	......	......	......	1,743	1,743
Help entrepreneurs and small businesses access capital and grow	1	1	1	......	......	......	......	......	......	......	......	2	2

Table S–9. Mandatory and Receipt Proposals—Continued

(Deficit increases (+) or decreases (−) in millions of dollars)

	2012	2013	2014	2015	2016	2017	2018	2019	2020	2021	2022	Totals 2013–2017	2013–2022
Rehabilitate and repurpose vacant property (neighborhood stabilization)	50	4,650	7,100	3,200	....	....	....	....	....	....	....	14,950	14,950
Total, temporary tax relief and investments to create jobs and jumpstart growth	178,255	136,583	24,445	9,985	1,459	−159	1,126	976	965	456	39	172,313	175,875
Tax Proposals:													
Tax cuts for families and individuals:													
Extend exclusion from income for cancellation of certain home mortgage debt	....	1,153	1,261	292	....	....	....	....	....	....	....	2,706	2,706
Extend American opportunity tax credit (AOTC)[1]	....	672	12,673	12,962	14,066	14,154	15,217	15,610	16,588	17,070	18,358	54,527	137,370
Provide for automatic enrollment in IRAs, including an employer tax credit, and doubling of the tax credit for small employer plan start-up costs[1]	....	....	733	1,203	1,285	1,383	1,555	1,784	2,024	2,333	2,722	4,604	15,022
Expand earned income tax credit (EITC) for larger families[1]	....	73	1,436	1,469	1,487	1,521	1,545	1,575	1,605	1,635	1,663	5,986	14,009
Expand child and dependent care tax credit[1]	....	310	1,088	1,098	1,111	1,114	1,117	1,112	1,099	1,090	1,078	4,721	10,217
Provide exclusion from income for student loan forgiveness for students after 25 years of income-based or income-contingent repayment	....	....	....	....	....	....	....	....	....	....	....	....	....
Provide exclusion from income for student loan forgiveness and for certain scholarship amounts for participants in the IHS Health Professions Programs	....	....	2	2	2	2	2	2	2	3	3	8	20
Total, tax cuts for families and individuals	....	2,208	17,193	17,026	17,951	18,174	19,436	20,083	21,318	22,131	23,824	72,552	179,344
Incentives for expanding manufacturing and insourcing jobs in America:													
Provide tax incentives for locating jobs and business activity in the United States and remove tax deductions for shipping jobs overseas	....	8	8	8	8	8	9	10	10	10	11	40	90
Provide new Manufacturing Communities tax credit	....	19	103	242	394	517	617	702	732	644	456	1,275	4,426
Target the domestic production activities deduction to domestic manufacturing activities and double the deduction for advanced manufacturing activities	....	....	....	....	....	....	....	....	....	....	....	....	....
Enhance and make permanent the research and experimentation tax credit	4,012	7,048	7,834	8,677	9,553	10,441	11,314	12,157	12,991	13,832	14,688	43,553	108,535
Provide a tax credit for the production of advanced technology vehicles	7	53	163	257	413	610	461	434	166	−282	−280	1,496	1,995

Table S–9. Mandatory and Receipt Proposals—Continued

(Deficit increases (+) or decreases (−) in millions of dollars)

	2012	2013	2014	2015	2016	2017	2018	2019	2020	2021	2022	Totals 2013–2017	Totals 2013–2022
Provide a tax credit for medium- and heavy-duty alternative-fuel commercial vehicles	......	44	227	261	310	371	389	177	−42	−25	−15	1,213	1,697
Extend and modify certain energy incentives[1]	460	625	1,781	700	282	109	20	58	86	100	109	3,497	3,870
Total, incentives for expanding manufacturing and insourcing jobs in America	4,479	7,797	10,116	10,145	10,960	12,056	12,810	13,538	13,943	14,279	14,969	51,074	120,613
Tax cuts for small business:													
Eliminate capital gains taxation on investments in small business stock	......	......	......	......	......	214	619	1,018	1,525	2,079	2,536	214	7,991
Double the amount of expensed start-up expenditures	76	322	316	313	311	310	307	302	299	297	296	1,572	3,073
Expand and simplify the tax credit provided to qualified small employers for non-elective contributions to employee health insurance[1]	512	1,077	1,777	2,168	1,987	1,672	1,409	1,215	1,101	981	774	8,681	14,161
Total, tax cuts for small business	588	1,399	2,093	2,481	2,298	2,196	2,335	2,535	2,925	3,357	3,606	10,467	25,225
Incentives to promote regional growth:													
Extend and modify the New Markets tax credit	14	72	184	306	397	465	513	528	466	310	129	1,424	3,370
Designate Growth Zones[1]	......	......	577	1,048	990	934	886	119	−518	−477	−409	3,549	3,150
Modify tax-exempt bonds for Indian tribal governments	......	2	4	8	11	15	19	24	27	31	35	40	176
Allow current refundings of State and local governmental bonds[3]	......	......	......	......	......	......	......	......	......	......	......	......	......
Reform and expand the Low-Income Housing tax credit	1	5	17	35	55	76	98	119	142	165	191	188	903
Total, incentives to promote regional growth	15	79	782	1,397	1,453	1,490	1,516	790	117	29	−54	5,201	7,599
Continue certain expiring provisions through calendar year 2013[1,3]	5,414	13,723	9,295	1,066	541	259	209	238	278	354	394	24,884	26,357
Upper-income tax provisions:													
Sunset the Bush tax cuts for those with income in excess of $250,000 ($200,000 if single):													
Reinstate the limitation on itemized deductions for upper-income taxpayers	......	−4,374	−9,144	−10,038	−11,066	−12,118	−13,149	−14,171	−15,207	−16,285	−17,433	−46,740	−122,985
Reinstate the personal exemption phaseout for upper-income taxpayers	......	−1,510	−3,173	−3,450	−3,745	−4,083	−4,429	−4,793	−5,169	−5,574	−6,016	−15,961	−41,942
Reinstate the 36% and 39.6% rates for upper-income taxpayers	......	−23,101	−32,492	−35,507	−39,133	−42,744	−46,268	−49,839	−53,509	−57,394	−61,567	−172,977	−441,554

Table S–9. Mandatory and Receipt Proposals—Continued

(Deficit increases (+) or decreases (–) in millions of dollars)

	2012	2013	2014	2015	2016	2017	2018	2019	2020	2021	2022	Totals 2013–2017	2013–2022
Tax qualified dividends as ordinary income for upper-income taxpayers ...	....	–21,537	–10,483	–15,624	–20,183	–22,269	–22,529	–22,776	–23,085	–23,615	–24,314	–90,096	–206,415
Tax net long-term capital gains at a 20% rate for upper-income taxpayers	....	–5,811	4,226	1,718	–2,286	–4,681	–5,141	–5,484	–5,822	–6,165	–6,520	–6,834	–35,966
Subtotal, sunset the Bush tax cuts for those with income in excess of $250,000 ($200,000 if single) [4]	....	–56,333	–51,066	–62,901	–76,413	–85,895	–91,516	–97,063	–102,792	–109,033	–115,850	–332,608	–848,862
Reduce the value of certain tax expenditures	....	–27,096	–43,935	–47,457	–51,764	–57,015	–62,263	–66,736	–71,195	–75,899	–80,837	–227,267	–584,197
Total, upper-income tax provisions	....	–83,429	–95,001	–110,358	–128,177	–142,910	–153,779	–163,799	–173,987	–184,932	–196,687	–559,875	–1,433,059
Modify estate and gift tax provisions:													
Restore the estate, gift and generation-skipping transfer (GST) tax parameters in effect in 2009	–103	–150	–8,552	–9,851	–10,791	–11,828	–12,970	–14,191	–15,458	–16,856	–18,150	–41,172	–118,797
Require consistency in value for transfer and income tax purposes	....	–149	–165	–172	–182	–192	–204	–217	–230	–244	–259	–860	–2,014
Modify rules on valuation discounts	....	–766	–1,422	–1,516	–1,626	–1,748	–1,889	–2,038	–2,189	–2,354	–2,531	–7,078	–18,079
Require a minimum term for grantor retained annuity trusts (GRATs)	....	–40	–85	–144	–206	–273	–347	–426	–509	–599	–705	–748	–3,334
Limit duration of GST tax exemption	....	....	....	....	....	....	....	....	....	....	....	....	....
Coordinate certain income and transfer tax rules applicable to grantor trusts	....	–22	–31	–39	–50	–65	–82	–105	–133	–169	–214	–207	–910
Extend the lien on estate tax deferrals provided under section 6166	–2	–5	–9	–13	–16	–17	–18	–19	–20	–21	–22	–60	–160
Total modify estate and gift tax provisions	–105	–1,132	–10,264	–11,735	–12,871	–14,123	–15,510	–16,996	–18,539	–20,243	–21,881	–50,125	–143,294
Reform U.S. international tax system:													
Defer deduction of interest expense related to deferred income of foreign subsidiaries	....	–3,487	–5,926	–6,156	–6,420	–6,693	–3,436	–1,215	–1,258	–1,306	–1,356	–28,682	–37,253
Determine the foreign tax credit on a pooling basis	....	–3,211	–5,457	–5,668	–5,911	–6,163	–6,403	–6,630	–6,865	–7,128	–7,399	–26,410	–60,835
Tax currently excess returns associated with transfers of intangibles offshore	....	–1,498	–2,653	–2,621	–2,550	–2,460	–2,375	–2,290	–2,231	–2,178	–2,117	–11,782	–22,973
Limit shifting of income through intangible property transfers	....	–28	–62	–88	–115	–143	–172	–203	–235	–269	–308	–436	–1,623
Disallow the deduction for excess non-taxed reinsurance premiums paid to affiliates	....	–111	–211	–229	–241	–248	–260	–274	–274	–290	–311	–1,040	–2,449
Limit earnings stripping by expatriated entities	....	–222	–382	–401	–421	–442	–464	–487	–512	–537	–564	–1,868	–4,432
Modify tax rules for dual capacity taxpayers	....	–530	–912	–965	–1,023	–1,081	–1,139	–1,192	–1,245	–1,301	–1,336	–4,511	–10,724
Tax gain from the sale of a partnership interest on look-through basis	....	–158	–218	–229	–240	–252	–265	–278	–292	–307	–322	–1,097	–2,561

Table S–9. Mandatory and Receipt Proposals—Continued

(Deficit increases (+) or decreases (–) in millions of dollars)

	2012	2013	2014	2015	2016	2017	2018	2019	2020	2021	2022	Totals 2013–2017	Totals 2013–2022
Prevent use of leveraged distributions from related foreign corporations to avoid dividend treatment	....	–175	–298	–310	–323	–337	–350	–362	–375	–389	–404	–1,443	–3,323
Extend section 338(h)(16) to certain asset acquisitions	....	–60	–100	–100	–100	–100	–100	–100	–100	–100	–100	–460	–960
Remove foreign taxes from a section 902 corporation's foreign tax pool when earnings are eliminated	....	–10	–20	–27	–36	–46	–50	–50	–50	–50	–50	–139	–389
Total reform U.S. international tax system	....	–9,490	–16,239	–16,794	–17,380	–17,965	–15,014	–13,081	–13,437	–13,855	–14,267	–77,868	–147,522
Reform treatment of financial and insurance industry institutions and products:													
Require accrual of income on forward sale of corporate stock	....	–4	–11	–18	–26	–34	–38	–40	–42	–44	–46	–93	–303
Require ordinary treatment of income from day-to-day dealer activities for certain dealers of equity options and commodities	–37	–152	–240	–254	–270	–286	–303	–321	–341	–361	–383	–1,202	–2,911
Modify the definition of "control" for purposes of section 249	–3	–11	–17	–17	–18	–19	–20	–21	–22	–23	–24	–82	–192
Modify rules that apply to sales of life insurance contracts	....	–14	–38	–46	–58	–70	–84	–99	–115	–133	–154	–226	–811
Modify proration rules for life insurance company general and separate accounts	....	–461	–788	–776	–808	–840	–846	–840	–805	–788	–754	–3,673	–7,706
Expand pro rata interest expense disallowance for corporate-owned life insurance (COLI)	....	–21	–67	–173	–260	–411	–620	–856	–1,216	–1,628	–2,058	–932	–7,310
Total reform treatment of financial and insurance industry institutions and products	–40	–663	–1,161	–1,284	–1,440	–1,660	–1,911	–2,177	–2,541	–2,977	–3,419	–6,208	–19,233
Eliminate fossil fuel tax preferences:													
Eliminate oil and gas preferences:													
Repeal enhanced oil recovery credit [5]	....	....	....	....	....	....	....	....	....	....	....	....	....
Repeal credit for oil and gas produced from marginal wells [5]	....	....	....	....	....	....	....	....	....	....	....	....	....
Repeal expensing of intangible drilling costs	....	–3,490	–2,398	–1,867	–1,760	–1,453	–1,012	–709	–508	–388	–317	–10,968	–13,902
Repeal deduction for tertiary injectants	....	–7	–11	–11	–11	–11	–10	–10	–10	–10	–9	–51	–100
Repeal exception to passive loss limitations for working interests in oil and natural gas properties	....	–9	–11	–10	–9	–8	–8	–7	–7	–7	–6	–47	–82

Table S-9.　Mandatory and Receipt Proposals—Continued

(Deficit increases (+) or decreases (−) in millions of dollars)

	2012	2013	2014	2015	2016	2017	2018	2019	2020	2021	2022	Totals 2013–2017	Totals 2013–2022
Repeal percentage depletion for oil and natural gas wells	......	−612	−1,046	−1,083	−1,122	−1,166	−1,206	−1,242	−1,274	−1,329	−1,385	−5,029	−11,465
Increase geological and geophysical amortization period for independent producers to seven years	......	−61	−225	−339	−310	−226	−146	−68	−15	−3	−7	−1,161	−1,400
Subtotal, eliminate oil and gas preferences	......	−4,179	−3,691	−3,310	−3,212	−2,864	−2,382	−2,036	−1,814	−1,737	−1,724	−17,256	−26,949
Eliminate coal preferences:													
Repeal expensing of exploration and development costs	......	−26	−44	−46	−48	−50	−50	−48	−46	−43	−39	−214	−440
Repeal percentage depletion for hard mineral fuels	......	−185	−177	−172	−168	−168	−170	−174	−175	−176	−179	−870	−1,744
Repeal capital gains treatment for royalties	......	−11	−25	−31	−38	−43	−47	−51	−55	−58	−63	−148	−422
Subtotal, eliminate coal preferences	......	−222	−246	−249	−254	−261	−267	−273	−276	−277	−281	−1,232	−2,606
Total eliminate fossil fuel tax preferences [6]	......	−4,401	−3,937	−3,559	−3,466	−3,125	−2,649	−2,309	−2,090	−2,014	−2,005	−18,488	−29,555
Other revenue changes and loophole closers:													
Increase Oil Spill Liability Trust Fund financing rate by one cent and update the law to include other sources of crudes [3]	......	−55	−72	−72	−72	−73	−75	−74	−75	−75	−74	−344	−717
Reinstate Superfund taxes	......	−1,445	−2,086	−2,036	−1,955	−2,113	−2,193	−2,247	−2,265	−2,281	−2,337	−9,635	−20,958
Make unemployment insurance surtax permanent [3]	......	−974	−1,363	−1,386	−1,410	−1,435	−1,454	−1,466	−1,475	−1,486	−1,487	−6,568	−13,936
Repeal LIFO method of accounting for inventories	......		−5,535	−8,834	−8,399	−8,376	−8,782	−8,738	−8,338	−8,421	−8,359	−31,144	−73,782
Repeal lower-of-cost-or-market inventory accounting method	......		−930	−5,638	−2,315	−1,520	−1,347	−305	−320	−334	−350	−10,403	−13,059
Eliminate special depreciation rules for purchases of general aviation passenger aircraft	......	−54	−174	−268	−304	−357	−376	−278	−162	−119	−114	−1,157	−2,206
Repeal gain limitation for dividends received in reorganization exchanges	......	−48	−81	−84	−86	−89	−92	−94	−97	−100	−103	−388	−874
Tax carried (profits) interests as ordinary income	......	−1,287	−1,935	−1,918	−1,703	−1,426	−1,165	−1,106	−1,171	−1,017	−768	−8,269	−13,496
Expand the definition of built-in loss for purposes of partnership loss transfers	......		−6	−6	−7	−7	−7	−7	−8	−8	−8	−26	−64
Extend partnership basis limitation rules to nondeductible expenditures	......	−6	−67	−74	−83	−89	−94	−97	−100	−105	−111	−319	−826
Limit the importation of losses under section 267(d)	......	−5	−63	−69	−77	−82	−87	−90	−94	−97	−103	−296	−767

Table S–9. Mandatory and Receipt Proposals—Continued

(Deficit increases (+) or decreases (−) in millions of dollars)

	2012	2013	2014	2015	2016	2017	2018	2019	2020	2021	2022	Totals 2013–2017	Totals 2013–2022
Deny deduction for punitive damages	......	......	−24	−35	−35	−36	−36	−37	−37	−39	−40	−130	−319
Eliminate the deduction for contributions of conservation easements on golf courses	−3	−37	−51	−53	−55	−59	−61	−64	−68	−71	−74	−255	−593
Total other revenue changes and loophole closers	−3	−3,911	−12,387	−20,473	−16,501	−15,662	−15,769	−14,603	−14,210	−14,153	−13,928	−68,934	−141,597
Reduce the tax gap and make reforms:													
Expand information reporting:													
Require information reporting for private separate accounts of life insurance companies			−1	−1	−1	−1	−1	−1	−1	−1	−2	−4	−10
Require a certified Taxpayer Identification Number (TIN) from contractors and allow certain withholding		−28	−65	−110	−151	−158	−165	−172	−180	−188	−196	−512	−1,413
Improve compliance by businesses:													
Require greater electronic filing of returns		......	......	......	......	......	......	......	......	......	......	......	......
Authorize the Department of the Treasury to require additional information to be included in electronically filed Form 5500 Annual Reports		......	......	......	......	......	......	......	......	......	......	......	......
Implement standards clarifying when employee leasing companies can be held liable for their clients' Federal employment taxes		−4	−5	−6	−6	−6	−7	−7	−8	−8	−8	−27	−65
Increase certainty with respect to worker classification	−6	−15	−247	−621	−782	−872	−966	−1,062	−1,162	−1,267	−1,378	−2,537	−8,372
Repeal special estimated tax payment provision for certain insurance companies		......	......	......	......	......	......	......	......	......	......	......	......
Eliminate special rules modifying the amount of estimated tax payments by corporations	300	−300	54,700	−5,600	−46,350	−2,750	......	5,600	−5,600	......	......	−300	−300
Strengthen tax administration:													
Streamline audit and adjustment procedures for large partnerships		−50	−221	−105	−128	−161	−192	−210	−214	−216	−217	−665	−1,714
Revise offer-in-compromise application rules		−2	−2	−2	−2	−2	−2	−2	−2	−2	−2	−10	−20

Table S–9. Mandatory and Receipt Proposals—Continued

(Deficit increases (+) or decreases (−) in millions of dollars)

	2012	2013	2014	2015	2016	2017	2018	2019	2020	2021	2022	Totals 2013–2017	Totals 2013–2022
Expand IRS access to information in the National Directory of New Hires for tax administration purposes	......	......	......	......	......	......	......	......	......	......	......	......	......
Make repeated willful failure to file a tax return a felony	......	......	......	......	......	−1	−1	−1	−2	−2	−2	−2	−10
Facilitate tax compliance with local jurisdictions	......	......	......	−1	−1	−1	−1	−1	−1	−1	−1	−3	−8
Extend statute of limitations where State adjustment affects Federal tax liability	......	......	......	......	−1	−4	−4	−4	−4	−4	−4	−5	−25
Improve investigative disclosure statute	......	......	......	......	−1	−1	−1	−1	−2	−2	−2	−2	−10
Require taxpayers who prepare their returns electronically but file their returns on paper to print their returns with a 2-D bar code	......	......	......	......	......	......	......	......	......	......	......	......	......
Allow the IRS to absorb credit and debit card processing fees for certain tax payments	......	−1	−2	−2	−2	−2	−2	−2	−2	−2	−2	−9	−19
Improve and make permanent the provision authorizing the IRS to disclose certain return information to certain prison officials	......	......	......	......	......	......	......	......	......	......	......	......	......
Extend IRS math error authority in certain circumstances [1]	......	−7	−17	−17	−17	−16	−18	−19	−20	−20	−22	−74	−173
Impose a penalty on failure to comply with electronic filing requirements	......	......	......	......	−1	−1	−1	−1	−2	−2	−2	−2	−10
Total reduce the tax gap and make reforms	294	−407	54,140	−6,465	−47,443	−3,977	−1,361	4,117	−7,200	−1,715	−1,838	−4,152	−12,149
Simplify the tax system:													
Simplify the rules for claiming the EITC for workers without qualifying children [1]	......	41	553	563	572	582	589	598	608	619	630	2,311	5,355
Eliminate minimum required distribution (MRD) requirements for IRA/plan balances of $75,000 or less	......	4	8	12	18	25	34	44	56	70	84	67	355
Allow all inherited plan and IRA accounts to be rolled over within 60 days	......	......	......	......	......	......	......	......	......	......	......	......	......
Clarify exception to recapture of unrecognized gain on sale of stock to an ESOP	......	......	......	......	......	......	......	......	......	......	......	......	......
Repeal non-qualified preferred stock designation	......	−30	−49	−49	−48	−45	−42	−37	−33	−29	−26	−221	−388
Repeal preferential dividend rule for publicly offered REITs	......	......	......	......	......	......	......	......	......	......	......	......	......

Table S–9. Mandatory and Receipt Proposals—Continued

(Deficit increases (+) or decreases (−) in millions of dollars)

	2012	2013	2014	2015	2016	2017	2018	2019	2020	2021	2022	Totals 2013–2017	Totals 2013–2022
Reform excise tax based on investment income of private foundations	......	4	4	5	5	5	5	6	6	7	7	23	54
Remove bonding requirements for certain taxpayers subject to Federal excise taxes on distilled spirits, wine, and beer	......	......	......	......	......	......	......	......	......	......	......	......	......
Simplify arbitrage investment restrictions	......	2	10	18	28	38	46	58	68	76	87	96	431
Simplify single-family housing mortgage bond targeting requirements	......	......	......	......	1	1	1	3	3	3	3	2	15
Streamline private business limits on governmental bonds	......	1	4	5	8	9	12	15	16	19	21	27	110
Total, simplify the tax system	......	22	530	554	584	615	645	687	724	765	806	2,305	5,932
Trade initiatives:													
Establish Reconstruction Opportunity Zones:[3]	......	1	5	8	12	19	25	30	33	36	38	45	207
Other initiatives:													
Authorize the limited sharing of business tax return information to improve the accuracy of important measures of our economy	......	......	......	......	......	......	......	......	......	......	......	......	......
Eliminate certain reviews conducted by the U.S. Treasury Inspector General for Tax Administration (TIGTA)	......	......	......	......	......	......	......	......	......	......	......	......	......
Modify indexing to prevent deflationary adjustments	......	......	......	......	......	......	......	......	......	......	......	......	......
Total, other initiatives	......	......	......	......	......	......	......	......	......	......	......	......	......
Total, tax proposals	10,642	−78,204	−44,835	−137,991	−193,479	−164,613	−169,017	−170,947	−192,666	−198,938	−210,442	−619,122	−1,561,132
Mandatory Initiatives and Savings:													
Invest in surface transportation:													
Reauthorize surface transportation (outlays from Transportation Trust Fund)	......	267	3,763	8,646	13,437	18,492	24,063	22,478	15,099	10,645	8,038	44,605	124,928
Invest in immediate surface transportation priorities (non-add; shown above under "Temporary tax relief and investments to create jobs and jumpstart growth")	*5,690*	*18,280*	*12,090*	*5,250*	*3,650*	*1,480*	*1,560*	*960*	*640*	*320*	*80*	*40,750*	*44,310*
Health and other mandatory proposals:													
Agriculture:													
Reduce agriculture subsidies	......	291	−3,560	−2,729	−1,536	−1,788	−3,079	−4,445	−4,607	−4,496	−4,340	−9,322	−30,289
Better target conservation spending	......	−46	−106	−159	−222	−222	−227	−221	−216	−211	−211	−755	−1,841
Permanently reauthorize stewardship contracting	......	−8	−4	2	2	2	2	1	1	1	1	−6	......

Table S–9. Mandatory and Receipt Proposals—Continued

(Deficit increases (+) or decreases (−) in millions of dollars)

	2012	2013	2014	2015	2016	2017	2018	2019	2020	2021	2022	Totals 2013–2017	Totals 2013–2022
Enact Natural Resources Conservation Service (NRCS) fee	....	−22	−22	−22	−22	−22	−22	−22	−22	−22	−22	−110	−220
Enact Animal Plant and Health Inspection Service (APHIS) fee	....	−20	−27	−27	−28	−29	−30	−31	−32	−33	−34	−131	−291
Enact Food Safety and Inspection Service (FSIS) fee	....	−13	−13	−13	−13	−13	−13	−13	−13	−13	−13	−65	−130
Enact Grain Inspection, Packers, and Stockyards Administration (GIPSA) fees	....	−27	−27	−27	−27	−27	−27	−27	−27	−27	−27	−135	−270
Impose biobased labeling fee	....	−1	....	....	....	....	....	....	....	....	....	−1	−1
Extend funding for Secure Rural Schools	54	270	287	198	141	49	10	1	....	....	....	945	956
Outyear mandatory effects of discretionary changes to the Conservation Stewardship Program	....	....	−1	−14	−13	−13	−14	−14	−14	−14	−14	−41	−111
Total, Agriculture	54	424	−3,473	−2,791	−1,718	−2,063	−3,400	−4,771	−4,930	−4,815	−4,660	−9,621	−32,197
Education:													
Provide mandatory appropriation to sustain recent Pell Grant increases	....	....	1,718	5,568	2,693	37	241	892	928	956	984	10,016	14,017
Hold interest rate on subsidized Stafford Loans to 3.4 percent	1,820	1,968	977	371	225	154	78	77	....	....	....	3,695	3,850
Reform and expand Perkins loan program	....	−644	−1,768	−1,395	−1,113	−900	−727	−640	−594	−554	−515	−5,820	−8,850
Adjust guaranty agency loan rehabilitation compensation	....	−3,390	....	....	....	....	....	....	....	....	....	−3,390	−3,390
Overhaul TEACH Grants and replace with Presidential Teaching Fellows	....	....	105	152	156	150	137	−2	−61	−77	−86	563	474
Eliminate in-school interest subsidies for undergraduates after 150 percent of program length	....	−82	−164	−187	−187	−187	−188	−189	−196	−199	−200	−807	−1,779
Establish career academies	....	10	110	270	350	200	60	....	....	126	183	940	1,000
Total, Education	1,820	−2,138	978	4,779	2,124	−546	−399	138	77	126	183	5,197	5,322
Energy:													
Reauthorize special assessment from domestic nuclear utilities [2]	....	−200	−204	−208	−212	−217	−221	−226	−231	−235	−240	−1,041	−2,194
Repeal ultra-deepwater oil and gas research and development program	....	−20	−40	−30	−10	....	....	....	....	....	....	−100	−100
Total, Energy	....	−220	−244	−238	−222	−217	−221	−226	−231	−235	−240	−1,141	−2,294

Table S–9. Mandatory and Receipt Proposals—Continued

(Deficit increases (+) or decreases (−) in millions of dollars)

	2012	2013	2014	2015	2016	2017	2018	2019	2020	2021	2022	Totals 2013–2017	Totals 2013–2022
Health and Human Services (HHS):													
Health proposals:													
Medicare providers:													
Bad debts:													
Reduce Medicare coverage of patients' bad debts	....	−770	−1,900	−2,950	−3,490	−3,730	−4,000	−4,290	−4,590	−4,910	−5,250	−12,840	−35,880
Graduate medical education:													
Align graduate medical education payments with patient care costs	....	....	−830	−940	−970	−1,010	−1,050	−1,110	−1,180	−1,260	−1,340	−3,750	−9,690
Better align payments to rural providers with the cost of care:													
Reduce Critical Access Hospital (CAH) payments from 101% of reasonable costs to 100% of reasonable costs	....	−70	−120	−120	−130	−130	−150	−150	−170	−180	−200	−570	−1,420
Prohibit CAH designation for facilities that are less than 10 miles from the nearest hospital	....	....	−40	−60	−60	−60	−70	−70	−70	−80	−80	−220	−590
Cut waste, fraud, and improper payments in Medicare:													
Reduce fraud, waste, and abuse in Medicare	....	−10	−20	−20	−30	−50	−50	−60	−70	−70	−70	−130	−450
Dedicate penalties for failure to use electronic health records toward deficit reduction	....	....	....	....	....	....	....	....	−180	−200	−210	....	−590
Update Medicare payments to more appropriately account for utilization of advanced imaging	....	−40	−60	−70	−70	−80	−80	−90	−100	−110	−110	−330	−820
Require prior authorization for advanced imaging	....	....	....	....	....	....	....	....	....	....	....	....	....
Drug rebates:													
Align Medicare drug payment policies with Medicaid policies for low-income beneficiaries	....	−3,796	−9,296	−10,438	−11,613	−13,627	−16,080	−18,047	−20,820	−24,068	−27,768	−48,770	−155,553
Encourage efficient post-acute care:													
Adjust payment updates for certain post-acute care providers	....	−30	−840	−1,920	−3,150	−4,420	−5,820	−7,510	−9,300	−11,270	−12,410	−10,360	−56,670

Table S-9. Mandatory and Receipt Proposals—Continued

(Deficit increases (+) or decreases (−) in millions of dollars)

	2012	2013	2014	2015	2016	2017	2018	2019	2020	2021	2022	Totals 2013–2017	Totals 2013–2022
Equalize payments for certain conditions commonly treated in Inpatient Rehabilitation Facilities and Skilled Nursing Facilities (SNFs)	....	−140	−170	−170	−180	−190	−200	−210	−230	−250	−270	−850	−2,010
Encourage appropriate use of inpatient rehabilitation hospitals	....	−180	−210	−210	−220	−230	−230	−240	−250	−260	−270	−1,050	−2,300
Adjust SNF payments to reduce hospital readmissions	....				−210	−250	−260	−280	−300	−320	−330	−460	−1,950
Total, Medicare providers	....	−5,036	−13,486	−16,898	−20,133	−23,777	−27,990	−32,057	−37,260	−42,978	−48,308	−79,330	−267,923
Medicare structural reforms:													
Increase income-related premiums under Medicare Parts B and D	....					−1,430	−2,220	−2,600	−5,137	−7,087	−9,098	−1,430	−27,572
Modify Part B deductible for new enrollees	....						−90	−240	−290	−610	−760	....	−1,990
Introduce home health co-payments for new beneficiaries	....					−10	−30	−50	−70	−80	−110	−10	−350
Introduce a Part B premium surcharge for beneficiaries that purchase near first-dollar medigap coverage	....					−80	−200	−330	−480	−640	−800	−80	−2,530
Strengthen the Independent Payment Advisory Board (IPAB) to reduce long-term drivers of Medicare cost growth	....											....	....
Total, Medicare structural reforms	....					−1,520	−2,540	−3,220	−5,977	−8,417	−10,768	−1,520	−32,442
Interactions	....	−2	68	66	79	56	504	1,485	1,772	2,007	2,076	268	8,112
Medicaid and other:													
Medicaid:													
Phase down Medicaid provider tax threshold beginning in 2015	....			−1,460	−2,050	−2,690	−2,820	−2,970	−3,110	−3,270	−3,430	−6,200	−21,800
Limit Medicaid reimbursement of durable medical equipment (DME) based on Medicare rates	....	−180	−200	−225	−285	−300	−315	−335	−350	−370	−390	−1,190	−2,950
Apply a single blended matching rate to Medicaid and CHIP starting in 2017	....					−3,400	−3,100	−3,100	−2,500	−2,800	−3,000	−3,400	−17,900

Table S–9. Mandatory and Receipt Proposals—Continued

(Deficit increases (+) or decreases (–) in millions of dollars)

	2012	2013	2014	2015	2016	2017	2018	2019	2020	2021	2022	Totals 2013–2017	Totals 2013–2022
Rebase Medicaid Disproportionate Share Hospital (DSH) allotments in FY 2021	......	......	......	......	......	......	......	......	......	–4,080	–4,170	......	–8,250
Expand State flexibility to provide benchmark benefit packages	......	......	......	......	......	......	......	......	......	......	......	......	......
Reduce waste, fraud, and abuse in Medicaid	......	–151	–216	–286	–306	–326	–336	–356	–381	–391	–417	–1,285	–3,166
Extend Transitional Medical Assistance (TMA)	155	640	175	......	......	......	......	......	......	......	......	815	815
Extend Qualified Individuals (QI)	215	695	785	210	......	......	......	......	......	......	......	1,690	1,690
Total, Medicaid	370	1,004	544	–1,761	–2,641	–6,716	–6,571	–6,761	–6,341	–10,911	–11,407	–9,570	–51,561
Pharmaceutical savings: Prohibit brand and generic drug companies from delaying the availability of new generic drugs and biologics	......	–675	–791	–870	–960	–1,037	–1,115	–1,223	–1,325	–1,443	–1,552	–4,333	–10,991
Modify length of exclusivity to facilitate faster development of generic biologics	......	–19	97	8	–327	–426	–505	–603	–654	–683	–713	–667	–3,825
Total, pharmaceutical savings	......	–694	–694	–862	–1,287	–1,463	–1,620	–1,826	–1,979	–2,126	–2,265	–5,000	–14,816
Prioritize Prevention and Public Health Fund investments	......	......	–28	–283	–678	–523	–500	–500	–500	–500	–500	–1,512	–4,012
Accelerate the issuance of State innovation waivers	......	......	......	......	......	......	......	......	......	......	......	......	......
Total, Medicaid and other	370	310	–178	–2,906	–4,606	–8,702	–8,691	–9,087	–8,820	–13,537	–14,172	–16,082	–70,389
Provide administrative expenses for implementation	......	100	250	50	......	......	......	......	......	......	......	400	400
Total, HHS health proposals	370	–4,628	–13,346	–19,688	–24,660	–33,943	–38,717	–42,879	–50,285	–62,925	–71,172	–96,264	–362,242
Extend the child welfare study	1	3	5	6	6	6	6	6	6	6	6	26	56
Strengthen and expand child care access	......	409	634	731	748	750	750	750	750	750	750	3,272	7,022
Improve permanency and safety and child welfare	......	220	243	248	250	250	250	250	250	250	250	1,211	2,461
Modernize child support	......	7	9	182	224	271	283	336	378	380	236	693	2,306
Supplemental Security Income (SSI) effects	......	......	......	–1	–2	–2	–3	–3	–4	–4	–4	–5	–23
SNAP effects	......	......	......	–21	–32	–43	–54	–65	–76	–76	–76	–96	–443
Medicaid effects	......	......	......	10	10	10	10	10	10	10	10	30	80
Foster care effects	......	2	36	36	35	34	34	33	32	31	30	143	303

Table S–9. Mandatory and Receipt Proposals—Continued

(Deficit increases (+) or decreases (–) in millions of dollars)

	2012	2013	2014	2015	2016	2017	2018	2019	2020	2021	2022	Totals 2013–2017	Totals 2013–2022
Make Temporary Assistance for Needy Families (TANF) supplemental grant funding permanent and reduce the annual amount available in the TANF contingency fund	....	....	....	....	....	....	....	....	....	....	....	....	....
Total, HHS	371	–3,987	–12,419	–18,497	–23,421	–32,667	–37,441	–41,562	–48,939	–61,578	–69,970	–90,990	–350,480
Homeland Security:													
Reform the aviation passenger security user fee to more accurately reflect the costs of aviation security	....	–200	–1,139	–1,410	–1,675	–1,950	–2,235	–2,279	–2,324	–2,370	–2,417	–6,374	–17,999
Reform the National Flood Insurance Program by eliminating the premium subsidy for certain properties	....	–45	–119	–225	–335	–483	–649	–704	–778	–834	–909	–1,207	–5,081
Total, Homeland Security	....	–245	–1,258	–1,635	–2,010	–2,433	–2,884	–2,983	–3,102	–3,204	–3,326	–7,581	–23,080
Housing and Urban Development:													
Provide funding for the Affordable Housing Trust Fund	....	10	140	290	230	190	100	20	20	....	....	860	1,000
Interior:													
Extend the Palau Compact of Free Association	29	34	27	24	22	20	14	13	12	11	10	127	187
Reform Abandoned Mine Lands (AML) payments	....	–173	–166	–92	–71	–71	–122	–134	–98	–87	–86	–573	–1,100
Reform hardrock mining on public lands	....	....	–2	–4	–5	–5	–6	–6	–11	–17	–24	–16	–80
Establish an AML hardrock reclamation fund [2]	....	....	–200	–150	–100	–50	....	....	....	....	....	–500	–500
Make permanent net receipts sharing for energy minerals	....	....	–44	–46	–47	–47	–49	–50	–52	–56	–58	–184	–449
Repeal geothermal payment to counties	....	–4	–4	–5	–5	–5	–5	–5	–5	–6	–6	–23	–50
Repeal oil and gas fee prohibition and mandatory permit funds	....	....	–18	–18	....	....	....	....	....	....	....	–36	–36
Impose a fee on nonproducing oil and gas leases	....	–13	–29	–42	–55	–67	–82	–99	–115	–132	–149	–206	–783
Reauthorize the Federal Land Transaction Facilitation Act of 2000 (FLTFA)	....	–3	–3	–8	–9	–3	....	....	....	....	....	–28	–28
Extend funding for Payment in Lieu of Taxes (PILT)	....	398	....	....	....	....	....	....	....	....	....	398	398
Increase duck stamp fees [2]	....	–4	....	....	....	....	....	....	....	....	....	–4	–4
Total, Interior	29	235	–441	–341	–270	–228	–250	–281	–269	–287	–313	–1,045	–2,445

Table S–9. Mandatory and Receipt Proposals—Continued

(Deficit increases (+) or decreases (−) in millions of dollars)

	2012	2013	2014	2015	2016	2017	2018	2019	2020	2021	2022	Totals 2013–2017	Totals 2013–2022
Justice:													
Provide incentives for State medical malpractice reform	......	100	50	50	50	......	......	......	......	......	......	250	250
Labor:													
Establish a universal dislocated workers program [7]	......	......	4,953	4,492	3,802	3,499	3,397	3,499	3,656	3,827	3,995	16,746	35,120
Improve Pension Benefit Guaranty Corporation (PBGC) solvency	......	......	−81	−1,828	−2,275	−2,316	−2,067	−1,713	−1,616	−1,874	−2,210	−6,500	−15,980
Strengthen unemployment insurance system solvency [2,3,8]	1,329	3,958	3,634	−7,856	−9,862	−8,941	−8,752	−5,472	−4,407	−5,043	−4,134	−19,067	−46,875
Reform the Federal Employees' Compensation Act (FECA)	......	−13	−16	−26	−36	−47	−57	−68	−79	−91	−103	−138	−536
Implement unemployment insurance administration cap adjustment [2,3]	......	−22	−53	−75	−93	−107	−107	−108	−107	−91	−98	−350	−861
Enact foreign labor certification fees	......	1	1	1	1	1	1	1	1	1	1	5	10
Total, Labor	1,329	3,924	8,438	−5,292	−8,463	−7,911	−7,585	−3,861	−2,552	−3,271	−2,549	−9,304	−29,122
Transportation:													
Establish a mandatory surcharge for air traffic services [2,3]	......	−647	−668	−692	−719	−744	−767	−783	−798	−813	−829	−3,470	−7,460
Restructure funding for Essential Air Service Program	......	30	50	50	50	50	50	50	50	50	50	230	480
Total, Transportation	......	−617	−618	−642	−669	−694	−717	−733	−748	−763	−779	−3,240	−6,980
Treasury:													
Impose a financial crisis responsibility fee [2]	......	......	−3,252	−6,462	−6,506	−6,784	−7,058	−7,317	−7,652	−7,982	−8,329	−23,004	−61,342
Implement IRS program integrity cap adjustment [2]	......	−421	−1,123	−2,251	−3,455	−4,694	−5,585	−6,200	−6,483	−6,661	−6,779	−11,944	−43,652
Restructure assistance to New York City, provide tax incentives for transportation infrastructure [2]	......	200	200	200	200	200	200	200	200	200	200	1,000	2,000
Authorize the Bureau of Engraving and Printing (BEP) to conduct a coupon program to distribute electronic currency readers [2]	......	−53	−12	−12	−12	−13	−13	−13	−14	−14	−14	−102	−170
Increase levy authority for payments to Medicare providers with delinquent tax debt [2]	−16	−56	−66	−68	−70	−72	−74	−76	−77	−78	−80	−332	−717

Table S–9. Mandatory and Receipt Proposals—Continued

(Deficit increases (+) or decreases (−) in millions of dollars)

	2012	2013	2014	2015	2016	2017	2018	2019	2020	2021	2022	Totals 2013–2017	Totals 2013–2022
Authorize Treasury to locate and recover assets of the United States and to retain a portion of amounts collected to pay for the costs of recovery	......	−2	−2	−2	−2	−2	−2	−2	−2	−2	−2	−10	−20
Provide authority to contact delinquent debtors via their cell phones	......	−12	−12	−12	−12	−12	−12	−12	−12	−12	−12	−60	−120
Allow offset of Federal income tax refunds to collect delinquent State income taxes for out-of-state residents	......												
Total, Treasury	−16	−344	−4,267	−8,607	−9,857	−11,377	−12,544	−13,420	−14,040	−14,549	−15,016	−34,452	−104,021
Veterans Affairs:													
Extend rounding down of cost of living adjustments (compensation)	......	......	−29	−68	−104	−155	−201	−241	−294	−329	−374	−356	−1,795
Extend rounding down of cost of living adjustments (education)	......	......	−4	−4	−4	−4	−4					−16	−20
Allow occupancy by a dependent child to satisfy VA home loans occupancy requirement	......	1	1	1	1	1	1	1	1	1	1	5	10
Allow for Government furnished headstones [9]	......	......										......	......
Expand work study activities [10]	......	......										......	......
Increase cap on vocational rehabilitation contract counseling	......	1	1	1	1	1	1	1	1	1	1	5	10
Exclude temporary residence adaptation grants from Specially Adapted Housing (SAH) grants [11]	......												
Replace the SAH program's grant limit [12]	......	......						1	1	1	1	......	4
Amend visual impairment standard for SAH grant	......	3	3	3	1	1	1	1	1	1	1	11	16
Restore eligibility for housing adaptation	......	6	6	6	6	7	7	7	8	8	9	31	70
Provide SAH grants to veterans living with family	......	6	6	6	7	7	7	8	8	9	9	32	73
Extend supplemental service disabled veterans insurance coverage [13]	......												
Expand eligibility for veterans medallion for headstones [14]	......											......	......
Total, Veterans Affairs	......	17	−16	−55	−92	−142	−188	−222	−274	−308	−352	−288	−1,632

Table S–9. Mandatory and Receipt Proposals—Continued

(Deficit increases (+) or decreases (−) in millions of dollars)

	2012	2013	2014	2015	2016	2017	2018	2019	2020	2021	2022	Totals 2013–2017	Totals 2013–2022
Corps of Engineers:													
Reform inland waterways funding [2,3]	......	−82	−113	−113	−113	−113	−113	−113	−113	−113	−114	−534	−1,100
Other Defense -- Civil Programs:													
Increase TRICARE pharmacy benefit copayments	......	−256	−335	−542	−678	−936	−1,131	−1,335	−1,575	−1,865	−1,993	−2,747	−10,646
Increase TRICARE pharmacy benefit copayments (accrual effect)	......	979	1,012	1,069	1,130	1,195	1,264	1,336	1,413	1,495	1,581	5,385	12,474
Increase annual premiums for TRICARE-For-Life (TFL) enrollment	......	−141	−287	−436	−586	−627	−672	−716	−764	−816	−872	−2,077	−5,917
Increase annual premiums for TFL (accrual effect)	......	404	416	439	463	490	518	548	579	613	648	2,212	5,118
Provide additional accrual payments to the Medicare-Eligible Retiree Health Care Fund	......	−271	......	......	......	......	......	......	......	......	......	−271	−271
Total, Other Defense -- Civil Programs	......	715	806	530	329	122	−21	−167	−347	−573	−636	2,502	758
Environmental Protection Agency:													
Enact Pesticide Registration and Premanufacture Notice Fees	......	−77	−88	−95	−97	−101	−104	−107	−110	−114	−116	−458	−1,009
Establish Hazardous Waste Electronic Manifest System [2]	......	......	......	−6	−4	−3	−3	−3	−3	−3	−3	−13	−28
Total, Environmental Protection Agency	......	−77	−88	−101	−101	−104	−107	−110	−113	−117	−119	−471	−1,037
Office of Personnel Management:													
Increase employee contributions to the Civil Service Retirement System (CSRS) and the Federal Employees Retirement System (FERS) [2]	......	−898	−1,803	−2,749	−2,835	−2,932	−3,036	−3,137	−3,240	−3,345	−3,452	−11,217	−27,427
Offer a phased retirement option for FERS and CSRS employees [2]	......	−12	−36	−60	−85	−113	−93	−88	−83	−78	−72	−306	−720
Accrual effects of phased retirement and elimination of the FERS Supplement for new employees	......	5	17	28	40	51	67	83	100	116	134	141	641
Streamline Federal Employees Health Benefits Program pharmacy benefit contracting (health proposal)	......	......	−72	−154	−165	−176	−189	−204	−219	−236	−259	−567	−1,674
Total, Office of Personnel Management	......	−905	−1,894	−2,935	−3,045	−3,170	−3,251	−3,346	−3,442	−3,543	−3,649	−11,949	−29,180
Social Security Administration (SSA):													
Improve collection of pension information from States and localities	......	13	20	17	−211	−456	−593	−626	−566	−529	−481	−617	−3,412

Table S-9. Mandatory and Receipt Proposals—Continued

(Deficit increases (+) or decreases (−) in millions of dollars)

	2012	2013	2014	2015	2016	2017	2018	2019	2020	2021	2022	Totals 2013–2017	Totals 2013–2022
Enact Disability Insurance Work Incentives Simplification Pilot	......	5	10	15	22	25	13	......	......	......	......	77	90
Establish Workers Compensation Information Reporting	......	5	5	......	......	......	......	......	......	......	......	10	10
Enact SSA quarterly wage reporting	......	20	30	90	......	......	......	......	......	......	......	140	140
Extend SSI time limits for qualified refugees	......	41	43	......	......	......	......	......	......	......	......	84	84
Medicaid effects	......	11	11	......	......	......	......	......	......	......	......	22	22
SNAP effects	......	−7	−7	......	......	......	......	......	......	......	......	−14	−14
Lower electronic wage reporting threshold to 100 employees [15]	......	......	......	......	......	......	......	......	......	......	......	......	......
Conform treatment of state and local government EITC and CTC for SSI [14]	......	......	......	......	......	......	......	......	......	......	......	......	......
Terminate stepchild benefits in the same month as step-parent [16]	......	......	......	......	......	......	......	......	......	......	......	......	......
Total, SSA	......	88	112	122	−189	−431	−580	−626	−566	−529	−481	−298	−3,080
Other Independent Agencies:													
Civilian Property Realignment Board:													
Dispose of unneeded real property	......	−140	−260	−380	−990	−130	−100	−120	−120	−120	−120	−1,900	−2,480
Postal Service:													
Enact Postal Service financial relief and reform:													
PAYGO impact	7,106	3,119	−3,005	−4,005	−4,005	−4,005	−4,005	−4,005	−4,005	−4,005	−4,005	−11,902	−31,927
Non-scorable impact	500	1,750	3,000	4,000	4,000	4,000	4,000	4,000	4,000	4,000	4,000	16,750	36,750
Railroad Retirement Board (RRB):													
Allow the electronic certification of certain RRB benefits	......	......	......	......	......	......	......	......	......	......	......	......	......
Telecommunications Development Fund:													
Provide no new funding for the Telecommunications Development Fund	−3	−7	−7	−7	−7	−7	−7	−7	−7	−7	−7	−35	−70
Total, other independent agencies	7,603	4,722	−272	−392	−1,002	−142	−112	−132	−132	−132	−132	2,914	2,274
Multi-Agency:													
Enact National Wireless Initiative	−50	229	−3,870	−8,144	−5,595	−1,479	582	−388	−969	−546	−774	−18,859	−20,954
Adjust payment timing	......	......	......	......	......	......	......	......	......	......	−44,000	......	−44,000
Establish hold harmless for Federal poverty guidelines	......	......	......	......	......	......	......	......	......	......	......	......	......
Total, multi-agency	−50	229	−3,870	−8,144	−5,595	−1,479	582	−388	−969	−546	−44,774	−18,859	−64,954
Total, health and other mandatory proposals	11,140	1,849	−18,449	−44,012	−54,034	−63,405	−69,131	−72,783	−80,670	−94,437	−146,927	−178,050	−641,998

Table S–9. Mandatory and Receipt Proposals—Continued

(Deficit increases (+) or decreases (−) in millions of dollars)

	2012	2013	2014	2015	2016	2017	2018	2019	2020	2021	2022	Totals 2013–2017	Totals 2013–2022
Total, mandatory initiatives and savings	11,140	2,116	−14,686	−35,366	−40,597	−44,913	−45,068	−50,305	−65,571	−83,792	−138,889	−133,445	−517,070
Total, mandatory and receipt proposals, including measures for jobs growth	200,037	60,495	−35,076	−163,372	−232,617	−209,685	−212,959	−220,276	−257,272	−282,274	−349,292	−580,254	−1,902,327

Note: For receipt effects, positive figures indicate lower receipts. For outlay effects, positive figures indicate higher outlays. For net costs, positive figures indicate higher deficits.

¹The estimates for this proposal include effects on outlays. The outlay effects included in the totals above are as follows:

	2012	2013	2014	2015	2016	2017	2018	2019	2020	2021	2022	2013–2017	2013–2022
Provide a temporary 10-percent tax credit for new jobs and wage increases		615										615	615
Reform and extend Build America Bonds	105	607	1,610	2,854	4,185	5,614	7,127	8,703	10,331	12,019	13,973	14,870	67,023
Extend AOTC			5,940	6,018	6,477	6,494	6,950	7,041	7,538	7,649	8,210	24,929	62,317
Provide for automatic enrollment in IRAs, including an employer tax credit, and doubling of the tax credit for small employer plan start-up costs			140	218	220	225	231	234	238	244	247	803	1,997
Expand EITC for larger families		71	1,429	1,462	1,481	1,515	1,539	1,569	1,599	1,629	1,657	5,958	13,951
Expand child and dependent care tax credit			314	324	337	346	359	369	375	384	391	1,321	3,199
Extend and modify certain energy incentives	1,147	178	706	209	95	65						1,253	1,253
Expand and simplify the tax credit provided to qualified small employers for non-elective contributions to employee health insurance	34	73	120	147	134	113	95	82	74	67	53	587	958
Designate Growth Zones			23	24	27	27	29					101	130
Continue certain expiring provisions through calendar year 2013	97	455	595									1,050	1,050
Extend IRS math error authority in certain circumstances		−4	−9	−9	−9	−9	−10	−10	−11	−11	−12	−40	−94
Simplify the rules for claiming the EITC for workers without qualifying children		24	486	495	503	512	518	526	535	545	554	2,020	4,698
Total, outlay effects of receipt proposals	1,383	2,019	11,354	11,742	13,450	14,902	16,838	18,514	20,679	22,526	25,073	53,467	157,097

²The estimates for this proposal include effects on governmental receipts. The receipt effects included in the totals above are as follows:

	2012	2013	2014	2015	2016	2017	2018	2019	2020	2021	2022	2013–2017	2013–2022
Reform and extend unemployment insurance	2	−40	−37	44	62	104	572	330	29	−48	57		
Reauthorize special assessment from domestic nuclear utilities		−200	−204	−208	−212	−217	−221	−226	−231	−235	−240	−1,041	−2,194
Establish an AML hardrock reclamation fund			−200	−200	−200	−200	−200	−200	−200	−200	−200	−800	−1,800
Increase duck stamp fees		−14	−14	−14	−14	−14	−14	−14	−14	−14	−14	−70	−140

Table S–9. Mandatory and Receipt Proposals—Continued

(Deficit increases (+) or decreases (−) in millions of dollars)

	2012	2013	2014	2015	2016	2017	2018	2019	2020	2021	2022	Totals 2013–2017	2013–2022
Strengthen unemployment insurance system solvency	....	2,990	3,634	−7,856	−9,862	−8,941	−8,752	−5,472	−4,407	−5,043	−4,134	−20,035	−47,843
Implement unemployment insurance administration cap adjustment	....	....	1	2	6	14	28	33	40	62	61	23	247
Establish a mandatory surcharge for air traffic services	....	−647	−668	−692	−719	−744	−767	−783	−798	−813	−829	−3,470	−7,460
Impose a financial crisis responsibility fee	....	....	−3,252	−6,462	−6,506	−6,784	−7,058	−7,317	−7,652	−7,982	−8,329	−23,004	−61,342
Implement IRS program integrity cap adjustment	....	−421	−1,123	−2,251	−3,455	−4,694	−5,585	−6,200	−6,483	−6,661	−6,779	−11,944	−43,652
Restructure assistance to New York City, provide tax incentives for transportation infrastructure	....	200	200	200	200	200	200	200	200	200	200	1,000	2,000
Authorize the BEP to conduct a coupon program to distribute electronic currency readers	....	−53	−12	−12	−12	−13	−13	−13	−14	−14	−14	−102	−170
Increase levy authority for payments to Medicare providers with delinquent tax debt	−16	−56	−66	−68	−70	−72	−74	−76	−77	−78	−80	−332	−717
Reform inland waterways funding	....	−82	−113	−113	−113	−113	−113	−113	−113	−113	−114	−534	−1,100
Increase employee contributions to CSRS and FERS	....	−898	−1,803	−2,749	−2,835	−2,932	−3,036	−3,137	−3,240	−3,345	−3,452	−11,217	−27,427
Implement a phased retirement option for Federal employees	....	−1	−2	−3	−4	−6	−5	−4	−3	−2	−1	−16	−31
Total receipt effects of mandatory proposals	−14	778	−3,659	−20,382	−23,734	−24,412	−25,038	−22,992	−22,963	−24,286	−23,868	−71,409	−190,556

[3] Net of income offsets.

[4] The Administration also proposes to restore the estate, gift and GST tax parameters in effect in 2009. The total effect on receipts of allowing the Bush tax cuts to expire for high-income taxpayers is shown below:

	2012	2013	2014	2015	2016	2017	2018	2019	2020	2021	2022	Totals 2013–2017	2013–2022
Sunset the Bush tax cuts for those with income in excess of $250,000 ($200,000 if single)	....	−56,333	−51,066	−62,901	−76,413	−85,895	−91,516	−97,063	−102,792	−109,033	−115,850	−332,608	−848,862
Restore the estate, gift and GST tax parameters in effect in 2009	−103	−150	−8,552	−9,851	−10,791	−11,828	−12,970	−14,191	−15,458	−16,856	−18,150	−41,172	−118,797
Total, effect on receipts of allowing the Bush tax cuts to expire for high-income taxpayers	−103	−56,483	−59,618	−72,752	−87,204	−97,723	−104,486	−111,254	−118,250	−125,889	−134,000	−373,780	−967,659

[5] The proposal is estimated to have zero receipt effect under the Administration's current economic projections.
[6] The Administration also proposes to repeal the domestic manufacturing deduction for oil and gas and other fossil fuel production. The effects of repeal on receipts, which are included in the estimates of the Administration's proposal to target the domestic production activities deduction, are shown below:

	2012	2013	2014	2015	2016	2017	2018	2019	2020	2021	2022	Totals 2013–2017	2013–2022
Repeal domestic manufacturing tax deduction for oil and gas production	....	−574	−986	−1,043	−1,105	−1,169	−1,231	−1,289	−1,346	−1,404	−1,465	−4,877	−11,612

Table S–9. Mandatory and Receipt Proposals—Continued

(Deficit increases (+) or decreases (−) in millions of dollars)

	2012	2013	2014	2015	2016	2017	2018	2019	2020	2021	2022	Totals 2013–2017	Totals 2013–2022
Repeal domestic manufacturing tax deduction for coal and other hard mineral fossil fuels	....	....	−13	−23	−24	−26	−28	−29	−30	−31	−33	−34	−114	−271
Total, effect on receipts of repealing the domestic manufacturing tax deduction for oil and gas and other fossil fuels	....	−587	−1,009	−1,067	−1,131	−1,197	−1,260	−1,319	−1,377	−1,437	−1,499	−4,991	−11,883

[7] This proposal would also result in discretionary savings of $7.7 billion over 10 years.
[8] Totals include the effects of interest on unemployment insurance loans to States.
[9] This proposal has outlays of less than $500,000 per year. The total cost over 2013–2022 is $1 million.
[10] This proposal has outlays of less than $500,000 per year. The total cost is $1 million from 2013–2017 and $2 million from 2013–2022.
[11] This proposal has outlays of less than $500,000 per year. The total cost is $1 million from 2013–2017 and $3 million from 2013–2022.
[12] This proposal has outlays less than $500,000 per year in years 2013–2018. The total cost is $2 million from 2013–2017.
[13] This proposal has outlays of less than $500,000 per year. The total cost is $1 million over 2013–2017 and $3 million over 2013–2022.
[14] This proposal has outlays of less than $500,000 per year. The total cost over 2013–2022 is also less than $500,000.
[15] This proposal has no estimated costs.
[16] This proposal has outlays of less than $500,000 per year. The total savings are $1 million over 2013–2017 and $4 million over 2013–2022.

Table S–10.   Bridge Between Total Mandatory and Receipt Proposals and PAYGO Scorekeeping

(In billions of dollars)

	2012–2017	2012–2022
Grand total, mandatory and receipt proposals from Table S–9	–380	–1,702
Adjustments for net savings and costs from Table S–9 not counted for PAYGO purposes:		
Surface transportation reauthorization costs offset with Overseas Contingency Operations savings	45	125
Program integrity savings generated by increased discretionary funding, and other non-PAYGO effects	15	–34
Total adjustments	59	91
Total savings from mandatory and receipt proposals under PAYGO scorekeeping	**–439**	**–1,793**
Memorandum, PAYGO costs included in the adjusted baseline:		
Extend AMT relief and index to inflation the 2011 parameters	701	1,917
Extend estate, gift, and generation-skipping transfer taxes at current parameters	157	433
Continue the 2001 and 2003 tax cuts	940	2,173
Prevent reduction in Medicare physician payments	181	438

Table S–11. Funding Levels for Appropriated ("Discretionary") Programs by Category

(Budget authority in billions of dollars)

	2010 Actual	2011 Actual	2012 Enacted	2013 Request	2014	2015	2016	2017	2018	2019	2020	2021	2022	2013–2017	2013–2022
								Outyears						Totals	
Discretionary Policy by Category:[1]															
Security agencies	684.4	687.8	684.0	686.0	698.4	711.6	725.3	741.0	757.4	774.5	791.5	808.5	829.5	3,562.3	7,523.7
Nonsecurity agencies	400.4	371.0	373.6	356.8	363.3	370.1	377.3	385.5	394.0	402.9	411.8	420.6	430.9	1,853.1	3,913.3
Total, Base Discretionary Funding	**1,084.8**	**1,058.8**	**1,057.6**	**1,042.8**	**1,061.8**	**1,081.7**	**1,102.6**	**1,126.5**	**1,151.4**	**1,177.4**	**1,203.3**	**1,229.2**	**1,260.4**	**5,415.4**	**11,437.0**
Discretionary Cap Adjustments and Other Funding (not included above):[2]															
Overseas Contingency Operations[3]	162.6	159.4	126.5	96.7	44.2	44.2	44.2	44.2	44.2	44.2	44.2	44.2	44.2	273.4	494.2
Disaster relief	....	....	10.5	5.6	....	....	....	....	....	....	....	....	....	5.6	5.6
Program integrity[4]	0.5	0.5	0.9	1.8	2.3	2.8	3.2	3.7	3.7	3.8	3.9	4.0	4.1	13.9	33.4
Other emergency/supplemental Funding[5]	9.6	–1.3	....	–*	....	....	....	....	....	....	....	....	....	....	....
Grand Total, Discretionary Budget Authority	**1,257.6**	**1,217.5**	**1,195.5**	**1,147.0**	**1,108.2**	**1,128.7**	**1,150.0**	**1,174.4**	**1,199.3**	**1,225.3**	**1,251.3**	**1,277.3**	**1,308.6**	**5,708.3**	**11,970.2**
Memorandum, Grand Total Discretionary Budget Authority Adjusted for Inflation and Population:															
Security	947.2	905.3	840.7	788.2	721.4	712.6	704.3	697.0	690.4	684.0	677.4	670.7	666.8	3,623.4	7,012.7
Nonsecurity	443.2	395.7	389.6	358.8	355.2	351.7	348.3	345.5	342.6	339.8	337.0	334.0	332.0	1,759.4	3,444.8
Grand total	1,390.4	1,301.1	1,230.3	1,147.0	1,076.6	1,064.2	1,052.6	1,042.5	1,033.0	1,023.8	1,014.4	1,004.7	998.8	5,382.8	10,457.6

* $50 million or less.

[1] The 2013 Budget proposes discretionary funding levels at the caps included in Title I of the Budget Control Act of 2011 with separate categories for "security" and "nonsecurity" programs for 2013 and a single discretionary category for 2014–2021. These caps have been adjusted downward to reflect the Administration's proposal to reclassify certain Surface Transportation programs as mandatory, as shown in the Preview Report in the Budget Process chapter of the *Analytical Perspectives* volume. For purposes of this presentation, the security and nonsecurity categories are increased from 2013 based on growth in the overall discretionary category but do not reflect specific policy decisions. For 2022, programs are assumed to grow at current services.

[2] Where applicable, amounts in 2012 through 2021 are cap adjustment amounts designated pursuant to Section 251(b)(2) of the Balanced Budget and Emergency Deficit Control Act of 1985 (BBEDCA), as amended. Amounts in 2010 and 2011 are not so designated but are shown for comparability purposes.

[3] The Budget includes placeholder amounts of $44.2 billion per year for Overseas Contingency Operations (OCO) in 2014 and beyond. These amounts reflect the Administration's proposal to cap total OCO budget authority from 2013 to 2021 at $450 billion but do not reflect any specific decisions or assumptions about OCO spending in any particular year.

[4] Amounts in 2012 include requested increased funding for BBEDCA program integrity adjustments.

[5] Amounts are not designated as emergency funding pursuant to Section 251(b)(2)(A) of the BBEDCA, as amended. These amounts include congressionally-designated emergencies, rescissions of funding provided in the American Recovery and Reinvestment Act of 2009 (P.L. 111–5), and other supplemental funding.

Table S–12. Funding Levels for Appropriated ("Discretionary") Programs by Agency

(Budget authority in billions of dollars)

	2010 Actual	2011 Actual	2012 Enacted	2013 Request	2014	2015	2016	2017	Outyears 2018	2019	2020	2021	2022	Totals 2013–2017	2013–2022
Base Discretionary Funding by Agency:[1]															
Security Agencies:															
Defense[2]	530.1	528.3	530.5	525.4	533.6	545.9	555.9	567.3	579.3	592.4	605.4	617.9	634.2	2,728.2	5,757.4
Energy - National Nuclear Security Administration[2]	9.9	10.5	11.0	11.5	10.8	11.0	11.2	11.4	11.7	11.9	12.2	12.4	12.8	55.9	116.8
Homeland Security	39.8	41.9	39.7	39.5	39.8	40.5	41.2	41.9	42.8	43.7	44.7	45.7	46.8	202.8	426.5
Veterans Affairs[3]	53.1	56.4	58.5	61.0	63.1	64.2	65.5	66.9	68.3	69.8	71.3	72.8	74.8	320.6	677.7
State and other international programs[4,5]	50.8	50.1	43.7	48.0	48.9	49.8	50.8	51.9	53.0	54.2	55.3	56.5	58.0	249.3	526.3
Intelligence Community Management Account	0.7	0.7	0.5	0.5	0.6	0.6	0.6	0.6	0.6	0.6	0.6	0.7	0.7	2.9	6.1
Allowance for security agencies[6]	....	....	....	....	1.8	-0.4	0.3	1.0	1.8	1.8	1.9	2.5	2.2	2.6	12.8
Subtotal, Security Agencies[7]	684.4	687.8	684.0	686.0	698.4	711.6	725.3	741.0	757.4	774.5	791.5	808.5	829.5	3,562.3	7,523.7
Nonsecurity Agencies:															
Agriculture[4]	25.1	21.5	22.0	21.4	22.6	23.1	23.5	24.0	24.6	25.1	25.7	26.2	26.9	114.6	243.0
Commerce	13.9	5.6	7.7	8.0	8.3	8.6	8.9	9.4	10.4	11.5	17.7	9.8	9.7	43.3	102.3
Census Bureau	7.2	-0.7	0.9	1.0	1.2	1.3	1.5	1.8	2.6	3.6	9.6	1.6	1.2	5.9	25.0
Education	64.3	68.3	67.4	69.8	70.3	71.2	72.2	73.3	74.4	75.5	76.7	77.9	79.2	356.9	740.6
Energy (excluding National Nuclear Security Administration)	16.6	15.2	15.3	15.6	16.3	16.6	16.9	17.3	17.6	18.0	18.4	18.8	19.3	82.6	174.8
Health and Human Services[8]	84.4	78.5	78.3	71.7	79.8	81.3	82.9	84.7	86.5	88.5	90.4	92.4	94.6	400.3	852.6
Housing and Urban Development	42.8	37.1	38.2	35.3	39.2	40.0	40.8	41.7	42.6	43.6	44.6	45.5	46.7	197.0	420.0
Interior	12.1	11.7	11.3	11.4	11.8	12.1	12.3	12.6	12.8	13.2	13.4	13.7	14.1	60.2	127.4
Justice	27.6	26.9	26.8	17.9	27.7	28.3	28.8	29.5	30.1	30.8	31.5	32.2	33.0	132.2	289.8
Labor	13.5	12.5	13.2	12.0	12.0	11.3	11.5	11.8	12.0	12.3	12.5	12.8	13.0	58.6	121.2
State and other international programs[4]	0.1	0.1	0.1	0.1	0.1	0.1	0.1	0.1	0.1	0.1	0.1	0.1	0.1	0.6	1.3
Transportation	14.7	13.7	13.7	13.8	14.1	14.4	14.7	15.0	15.3	15.7	16.0	16.4	16.8	72.0	152.2
Treasury	13.4	13.4	13.2	12.6	13.7	14.1	14.5	14.9	15.4	15.9	16.4	16.9	17.3	69.8	151.6
Corps of Engineers	5.5	4.9	5.0	4.7	4.8	4.9	5.0	5.1	5.2	5.3	5.5	5.6	5.7	24.6	51.9
Environmental Protection Agency	10.3	8.7	8.5	8.3	8.5	8.7	8.9	9.1	9.3	9.5	9.7	9.9	10.1	43.5	91.9
General Services Administration	0.4	-1.0	-1.0	-0.8	-1.2	-1.3	-1.3	-1.4	-1.4	-1.4	-1.4	-1.5	-1.5	-5.9	-13.2
National Aeronautics and Space Administration	18.7	18.4	17.8	17.7	18.0	18.4	18.7	19.1	19.6	20.0	20.4	20.9	21.4	92.0	194.2
National Science Foundation	6.9	6.8	7.0	7.4	7.5	7.6	7.8	8.0	8.1	8.3	8.5	8.7	8.9	38.3	80.8
Small Business Administration	0.8	0.7	0.9	0.9	1.0	1.0	1.0	1.0	1.0	1.1	1.1	1.1	1.1	4.9	10.4
Social Security Administration[8]	8.9	8.6	8.8	9.0	9.2	9.4	9.5	9.7	9.9	10.1	10.4	10.6	10.8	46.8	98.6
Corporation for National and Community Service	1.2	1.1	1.0	1.1	1.1	1.1	1.1	1.1	1.2	1.2	1.2	1.3	1.3	5.5	11.6
Other agencies	19.1	18.1	18.2	18.9	19.3	19.6	20.0	20.4	20.8	21.3	21.8	22.2	22.7	98.1	207.0

Table S–12. Funding Levels for Appropriated ("Discretionary") Programs by Agency—Continued

(Budget authority in billions of dollars)

	2010 Actual	2011 Actual	2012 Enacted	2013 Request	Outyears 2014	2015	2016	2017	2018	2019	2020	2021	2022	Totals 2013–2017	2013–2022
Allowance for nonsecurity agencies[6]	......	......	......	......	–21.1	–20.3	–20.5	–20.8	–21.7	–22.7	–28.7	–20.7	–20.3	–82.8	–196.9
Subtotal, Nonsecurity Discretionary Budget Authority[7]	**400.4**	**371.0**	**373.6**	**356.8**	**363.3**	**370.1**	**377.3**	**385.5**	**394.0**	**402.9**	**411.8**	**420.6**	**430.9**	**1,853.1**	**3,913.3**
Discretionary Cap Adjustments and Other Funding (not included above):[9]															
Overseas Contingency Operations[10]	162.6	159.4	126.5	96.7	44.2	44.2	44.2	44.2	44.2	44.2	44.2	44.2	44.2	273.4	494.2
Defense	162.3	158.8	115.1	88.5	88.5	......	......	......	......	......	......	......	......	88.5	88.5
Homeland Security	0.2	0.3	0.3	......	......	......	......	......	......	......	......	......	......	......	......
Justice	0.1	0.1	......	......	......	......	......	......	......	......	......	......	......	......	......
State and other international programs	......	0.3	11.2	8.2	......	......	......	......	......	......	......	......	......	8.2	8.2
Overseas Contingency Operations outyears	......	......	......	......	44.2	44.2	44.2	44.2	44.2	44.2	44.2	44.2	44.2	176.6	397.4
Disaster Relief	......	......	10.5	5.6	......	......	......	......	......	......	......	......	......	5.6	5.6
Agriculture	......	......	0.4	......	......	......	......	......	......	......	......	......	......	......	......
Commerce	......	......	0.2	......	......	......	......	......	......	......	......	......	......	......	......
Homeland Security	......	......	6.4	5.5	5.5	......	......	......	......	......	......	......	......	5.5	5.5
Housing and Urban Development	......	......	0.1	......	......	......	......	......	......	......	......	......	......	......	......
Transportation	......	......	1.7	......	......	......	......	......	......	......	......	......	......	......	......
Corps of Engineers	......	......	1.7	......	......	......	......	......	......	......	......	......	......	......	......
Small Business Administration	......	......	......	0.2	0.2	......	......	......	......	......	......	......	......	0.2	0.2
Program Integrity[11]	0.5	0.5	0.9	1.8	2.3	2.8	3.2	3.7	3.7	3.8	3.9	4.0	4.1	13.9	33.4
Health and Human Services	......	......	0.3	0.3	0.3	0.4	0.4	0.4	0.4	0.5	0.5	0.5	0.5	1.8	4.2
Labor	......	......	......	*	*	*	*	*	*	*	*	*	*	0.1	0.3
Treasury	......	......	......	0.7	1.0	1.3	1.6	2.0	2.0	2.0	2.1	2.1	2.2	6.7	17.1
Social Security Administration	0.5	0.5	0.6	0.8	0.9	1.1	1.2	1.3	1.3	1.3	1.3	1.3	1.3	5.3	11.8
Other Emergency/Supplemental Funding[12]	9.6	–1.3	–*	......	......	......	......	......	......	......	......	......	......	......	......
Defense	–1.9	......	......	......	......	......	......	......	......	......	......	......	......	......	......
Energy	–1.5	–1.3	......	......	......	......	......	......	......	......	......	......	......	......	......
Health and Human Services	0.2	......	......	......	......	......	......	......	......	......	......	......	......	......	......
Homeland Security	5.5	......	–*	......	......	......	......	......	......	......	......	......	......	......	......
State and other international programs	6.1	......	......	......	......	......	......	......	......	......	......	......	......	......	......
Small Business Administration	1.0	......	......	......	......	......	......	......	......	......	......	......	......	......	......
Other emergency/supplemental funding	0.4	......	......	......	......	......	......	......	......	......	......	......	......	......	......
Grand Total, Discretionary Budget Authority	**1,257.6**	**1,217.5**	**1,195.5**	**1,147.0**	**1,108.2**	**1,128.7**	**1,150.0**	**1,174.4**	**1,199.3**	**1,225.3**	**1,251.3**	**1,277.3**	**1,308.6**	**5,708.3**	**11,970.2**

Table S–12. Funding Levels for Appropriated ("Discretionary") Programs by Agency—Continued

(Budget authority in billions of dollars)

	2010 Actual	2011 Actual	2012 Enacted	2013 Request	Outyears									Totals	
					2014	2015	2016	2017	2018	2019	2020	2021	2022	2012–2016	2012–2021
Memorandum: 2013 Budget Defense Request versus 2012 Budget Defense Request [13]															
2012 Budget for Defense	n/a	n/a	553.0	570.7	586.4	598.2	610.6	621.6	632.8	644.1	655.7	667.5	n/a	3,540.4	6,140.6
Savings resulting from 2013 Budget policy	n/a	n/a	–22.5	–45.3	–52.8	–52.2	–54.7	–54.2	–53.5	–51.8	–50.3	–49.6	n/a	–227.5	–486.9

* $50 million or less.

[1] The 2013 Budget proposes discretionary funding levels at the caps included in Title I of the Budget Control Act of 2011 with separate categories for "security" and "nonsecurity" programs for 2013 and a single discretionary category for 2014–2021. These caps have been adjusted downward to reflect the Administration's proposal to reclassify certain surface transportation programs as mandatory, as shown in the Preview Report in the Budget Process chapter of the *Analytical Perspectives* volume.

[2] The Department of Defense (DOD) levels in 2014–2022 include funding that will be allocated, in annual increments, to the National Nuclear Security Administration (NNSA). Current estimates by which DOD's budget authority will decrease and NNSA's will increase are, in millions of dollars: 2014: 677; 2015: 712; 2016: 767; 2017: 781; 2018: 798; 2013–2022: 7,109. The DOD and NNSA are reviewing NNSA's outyear requirements and these will be included in future reports to the Congress.

[3] The Veterans Affairs total is net of medical care collections.

[4] The Security category for State and other international programs is comprised entirely of international affairs (function 150). This includes funding for international food aid programs in the Department of Agriculture.

[5] The variances in the Security category for State and other international programs base funding are due in part to definitional differences in Overseas Contingency Operations (OCO). A comparison of total international affairs funding, including both base and OCO funds, can be found in the State and other international programs chapter of this volume.

[6] The 2013 Budget includes allowances, similar to the Function 920 allowances used in Budget Resolutions, to represent amounts to be allocated among the respective agencies to reach the notional security and nonsecurity levels for 2014 and beyond. These notional levels are determined for illustrative purposes based on the overall growth of the discretionary category being applied on a proportional basis to the 2013 security/nonsecurity caps but do not reflect specific policy decisions.

[7] Amounts in 2011–2012 exclude changes in mandatory programs enacted in appropriations bills since those amounts have been rebased as mandatory, whereas amounts in 2013 are net of these proposals. The individual agency chapters in this volume provide a comparative look at the gross funding levels from year to year.

[8] Funding from the Hospital Insurance and Supplementary Medical Insurance trust funds for administrative expenses incurred by the Social Security Administration that support the Medicare program is included in the Health and Human Service total.

[9] Where applicable, amounts in 2012 through 2021 are cap adjustment amounts designated pursuant to Section 251(b)(2) of the Balanced Budget and Emergency Deficit Control Act of 1985 (BBEDCA), as amended. Amounts in 2010 and 2011 are not so designated but are shown for comparability purposes.

[10] The Budget includes placeholder amounts of $44.2 billion per year for OCO in 2014 and beyond. These amounts reflect the Administration's proposal to cap total OCO budget authority from 2013 to 2021 at $450 billion but do not reflect any specific decisions or assumptions about OCO spending in any particular year.

[11] Amounts in 2012 include requested increased funding for BBEDCA program integrity adjustments for the Department of Health and Human Services (+$270 million) and the Social Security Administration.

[12] Amounts are not designated as emergency funding pursuant to Section 251(b)(2)(A) of the BBEDCA, as amended. These amounts include congressionally-designated emergencies, rescissions of funding provided in the American Recovery and Reinvestment Act of 2009 (P.L. 111–5), and other supplemental funding.

[13] These amounts exclude funding designated as OCO.

Table S–13. Surface Transportation Proposal [1]

(In billions of dollars)

	Six-Year Total (2013–18)	Ten-Year Total (2013–22)
Budget authority: [2]		
Transportation Trust Fund (TTF):		
Baseline funding, current law Highway Trust Fund-financed activities (HTF)	315	544
Baseline funding, BA-funded accounts shifted to the TTF	26	45
Proposed funding increases, surface transportation (PAYGO)[3]	135	135
Subtotal, Transportation Trust Fund	476	724
General Fund:		
Immediate transportation investment (2012)	50	50
Total budget authority, surface transportation	526	774
TTF Financing: [4]		
Baseline outlays, current law HTF-financed activities	324	
Baseline outlays, BA-funded accounts shifted to the TTF	19	
Baseline HTF revenue	–250	
Subtotal, six-year baseline revenue gap	94	
Proposed funding increases, surface transportation (PAYGO)[3]	135	
Offset from Overseas Contingency Operations (OCO)	231	

[1] The proposal is described in greater detail in the Budget Process chapter of the *Analytical Perspectives* volume.

[2] All amounts are mandatory budget authority.

[3] Proposed budget authority would produce $125 billion in outlays, subject to PAYGO, over 2013–2022. However, to ensure the proposal is fully paid for, the Budget finances the full $135 billion of budget authority.

[4] Proposed funding increases are the same for the six- and ten-year horizons because outyear funding levels return to baseline. Similarly, OCO financing only covers the six-year baseline funding gap and all new outlays associated with the proposal. All outlays are reclassified as mandatory, derived from either contract authority or budget authority.

Table S–14. Economic Assumptions[1]

(Calendar years)

	2010 Actual	Projections											
		2011	2012	2013	2014	2015	2016	2017	2018	2019	2020	2021	2022
Gross Domestic Product (GDP):													
Nominal level, billions of dollars	14,527	15,106	15,779	16,522	17,397	18,448	19,533	20,651	21,689	22,666	23,659	24,688	25,760
Percent change, nominal GDP, year/year	4.2	4.0	4.5	4.7	5.3	6.0	5.9	5.7	5.0	4.5	4.4	4.3	4.3
Real GDP, percent change, year/year	3.0	1.8	2.7	3.0	3.6	4.1	4.0	3.9	3.2	2.7	2.5	2.5	2.5
Real GDP, percent change, Q4/Q4	3.1	1.7	3.0	3.0	4.0	4.2	3.9	3.8	2.8	2.6	2.5	2.5	2.5
GDP chained price index, percent change, year/year	1.2	2.1	1.7	1.7	1.6	1.8	1.8	1.8	1.8	1.8	1.8	1.8	1.8
Consumer Price Index[2], percent change, year/year	1.6	3.2	2.2	1.9	2.0	2.0	2.1	2.1	2.1	2.1	2.1	2.1	2.1
Interest rates, percent:													
91-day Treasury bills[3]	0.1	0.1	0.1	0.2	1.4	2.7	3.8	4.1	4.1	4.1	4.1	4.1	4.1
10-year Treasury notes	3.2	2.8	2.8	3.5	3.9	4.4	4.7	5.0	5.1	5.1	5.1	5.3	5.3
Unemployment rate, civilian, percent[4]	9.6	9.0	8.9	8.6	8.1	7.3	6.5	5.8	5.5	5.4	5.4	5.4	5.4
Memorandum, January unemployment rate forecasts:[4,5]													
Blue Chip Low Ten	9.6	9.0	8.3	7.6									
Blue Chip High Ten	9.6	9.0	9.0	8.9									
FOMC Central Tendency[6]	9.6	8.7	8.2–8.5	7.4–8.1	6.7–7.6								
CBO[7]	9.6	9.0	8.8	9.1	8.7	7.4	6.3	5.7	5.5	5.5	5.4	5.4	5.3

Note: A more detailed table of economic assumptions is in Chapter 2, "Economic Assumptions," in the *Analytical Perspectives* volume of the Budget, Table 2–1.

Sources: CBO, The Economic Outlook: January 2012; January 2012 Blue Chip Economic Indicators, Aspen Publishers, Inc.; Federal Reserve Open Market Committee Projection Materials, January 25, 2012.

[1] Based on information available as of mid-November 2011.
[2] Seasonally adjusted CPI for all urban consumers.
[3] Average rate, secondary market (bank discount basis).
[4] Annual average.
[5] After the economic assumptions for the Budget were finalized, the unemployment rate declined notably. Alternative forecasts are presented to reflect a range of current projections based on more recent data.
[6] Fourth quarter values.
[7] Projection based on current law.

Table S–15. Federal Government Financing and Debt

(Dollars amounts in billions)

	Actual 2011	Estimate										
		2012	2013	2014	2015	2016	2017	2018	2019	2020	2021	2022
Financing:												
Unified budget deficit:												
Primary deficit (+)/surplus (–)	1,070	1,102	654	359	219	166	47	–56	–67	–90	–117	–146
Net interest	230	225	248	309	390	483	565	631	692	748	798	850
Unified budget deficit	1,300	1,327	901	668	610	649	612	575	626	658	681	704
As a percent of GDP	8.7%	8.5%	5.5%	3.9%	3.4%	3.4%	3.0%	2.7%	2.8%	2.8%	2.8%	2.8%
Other transactions affecting borrowing from the public:												
Changes in financial assets and liabilities:[1]												
Change in Treasury operating cash balance	–252	2	....	....	....	....	....	....	....	....	....	....
Net disbursements of credit financing accounts:												
Direct loan accounts	50	138	162	157	149	135	126	117	110	108	106	111
Guaranteed loan accounts	10	10	11	1	–*	1	–*	1	1	–2	–5	–5
Troubled Asset Relief Program (TARP) equity purchase accounts	–2	–27	–15	–15	–5	–1	–4	–2	–1	–3	–*	–*
Net purchases of non-Federal securities by the National Railroad Retirement Investment Trust (NRRIT)	–1	–*	–1	–1	–1	–2	–1	–1	–1	–1	–1	–1
Net change in other financial assets and liabilities[2]	5	....	....	....	....	....	....	....	....	....	....	....
Subtotal, changes in financial assets and liabilities	–190	123	157	141	143	134	121	115	108	102	100	104
Seigniorage on coins	....	–*	–*	–*	–*	–*	–*	–*	–*	–*	–*	–*
Total, other transactions affecting borrowing from the public	–190	123	157	141	143	134	121	115	108	102	100	104
Total, requirement to borrow from the public (equals change in debt held by the public)	1,109	1,450	1,059	809	752	783	733	690	733	760	781	808
Changes in Debt Subject to Statutory Limitation:												
Change in debt held by the public	1,109	1,450	1,059	809	752	783	733	690	733	760	781	808
Change in debt held by Government accounts	126	137	138	143	174	182	201	228	173	165	151	124
Change in other factors	*	1	1	1	1	2	1	1	1	1	2	2
Total, change in debt subject to statutory limitation	1,236	1,587	1,198	953	928	967	936	920	908	926	933	934
Debt Subject to Statutory Limitation, End of Year:												
Debt issued by Treasury	14,737	16,323	17,520	18,471	19,398	20,363	21,298	22,218	23,125	24,051	24,984	25,918
Adjustment for discount, premium, and coverage[3]	9	11	12	13	14	16	16	17	18	18	18	18
Total, debt subject to statutory limitation[4]	14,747	16,334	17,532	18,485	19,412	20,379	21,315	22,235	23,143	24,069	25,002	25,936

Table S–15. Federal Government Financing and Debt—Continued

(Dollars amounts in billions)

	Actual 2011	Estimate										
		2012	2013	2014	2015	2016	2017	2018	2019	2020	2021	2022
Debt Outstanding, End of Year:												
Gross Federal debt:[5]												
Debt issued by Treasury	14,737	16,323	17,520	18,471	19,398	20,363	21,298	22,218	23,125	24,051	24,984	25,918
Debt issued by other agencies	27	28	28	29	29	28	28	27	27	26	24	22
Total, gross Federal debt	14,764	16,351	17,548	18,500	19,427	20,392	21,326	22,245	23,152	24,077	25,008	25,940
Held by:												
Debt held by Government accounts	4,636	4,773	4,911	5,055	5,229	5,411	5,613	5,841	6,015	6,180	6,330	6,454
Debt held by the public[6]	10,128	11,578	12,637	13,445	14,198	14,980	15,713	16,404	17,137	17,897	18,678	19,486
As a percent of GDP	67.7%	74.2%	77.4%	78.4%	78.1%	77.8%	77.1%	76.5%	76.4%	76.5%	76.5%	76.5%
Debt Held by the Public Net of Financial Assets:												
Debt held by the public	10,128	11,578	12,637	13,445	14,198	14,980	15,713	16,404	17,137	17,897	18,678	19,486
Less financial assets net of liabilities:												
Treasury operating cash balance	58	60	60	60	60	60	60	60	60	60	60	60
Credit financing account balances:												
Direct loan accounts	718	856	1,018	1,175	1,323	1,459	1,585	1,701	1,811	1,919	2,025	2,136
Guaranteed loan accounts	–22	–12	–1	–*	–1	1	1	2	3	1	–4	–10
TARP equity purchase accounts	75	48	33	18	14	12	9	7	6	2	2	2
Government-sponsored enterprise preferred stock	133	164	173	177	177	177	177	177	177	177	177	177
Non-Federal securities held by NRRIT	21	21	20	18	17	16	14	13	12	11	9	8
Other assets net of liabilities	–25	–25	–25	–25	–25	–25	–25	–25	–25	–25	–25	–25
Total, financial assets net of liabilities	958	1,111	1,278	1,422	1,565	1,699	1,820	1,935	2,043	2,145	2,244	2,349
Debt held by the public net of financial assets	9,170	10,467	11,358	12,023	12,633	13,281	13,894	14,469	15,095	15,753	16,433	17,137
As a percent of GDP	61.3%	67.1%	69.5%	70.1%	69.5%	69.0%	68.2%	67.5%	67.3%	67.3%	67.3%	67.2%

* $500 million or less.

[1] A decrease in the Treasury operating cash balance (which is an asset) is a means of financing a deficit and therefore has a negative sign. An increase in checks outstanding (which is a liability) is also a means of financing a deficit and therefore also has a negative sign.

[2] Includes checks outstanding, accrued interest payable on Treasury debt, uninvested deposit fund balances, allocations of special drawing rights, and other liability accounts; and, as an offset, cash and monetary assets (other than the Treasury operating cash balance), other asset accounts, and profit on sale of gold.

[3] Consists mainly of debt issued by the Federal Financing Bank (which is not subject to limit), debt held by the Federal Financing Bank, the unamortized discount (less premium) on public issues of Treasury notes and bonds (other than zero-coupon bonds), and the unrealized discount on Government account series securities.

[4] The statutory debt limit is $16,394 billion, as increased after January 27, 2012.

[5] Treasury securities held by the public and zero-coupon bonds held by Government accounts are almost all measured at sales price plus amortized discount or less amortized premium. Agency debt securities are almost all measured at face value. Treasury securities in the Government account series are otherwise measured at face value less unrealized discount (if any).

[6] At the end of 2011, the Federal Reserve Banks held $1,664.7 billion of Federal securities and the rest of the public held $8,463.5 billion. Debt held by the Federal Reserve Banks is not estimated for future years.

OMB CONTRIBUTORS TO THE 2013 BUDGET

The following personnel contributed to the preparation of this publication. Hundreds, perhaps thousands, of others throughout the Government also deserve credit for their valuable contributions.

A

Kate D. Aaby
Andrew Abrams
Chandana Achanta
Brenda Aguilar
Shagufta I. Ahmed
Steven D. Aitken
Jameela R. Akbari
David Alekson
Julie Allen
Victoria L. Allred
Lois E. Altoft
Aaron Ampaw
Robert B. Anderson
Kevin Archer
Anna R. Arroyo
Emily E. Askew
Ari Isaacman Astles
Lisa L. August
Renee Austin

B

Peter M. Babb
Susan Badgett
Kenneth Baer
Jessie W. Bailey
Paul W. Baker
Carol Bales
Catherine A. Ballinger
Kifle Bantayehu
John W. Barkhamer
Bethanne Barnes
Patti Barnett
Jody Barringer
Avital Bar-Shalom
Mary C. Barth

Sarah Bashadi
Nancy B. Beck
Jennifer Wagner Bell
Steven Bennett
Sam K. Berger
Lindsey R. Berman
Scott A. Bernard
Elizabeth Bernhard
Boris Bershteyn
Tricia Bixby
Mathew C. Blum
James Boden
Melissa B. Bomberger
Debra Bond
Dan Bonesteel
Cole Borders
David S. Bortnick
Constance J. Bowers
Bill Boyd
Chantel M. Boyens
Betty I. Bradshaw
Nicole A. Bradstreet
Amanda Branting
Joshua J. Brammer
Michael Branson
Shannon Bregman
Andrea Brian
Candice M. Bronack
Jonathan M. Brooks
Calla R. Brown
Dustin S. Brown
Elizabeth M. Brown
Jamal T. O. Brown
James A. Brown
Kelly D. Brown
Michael Brunetto
Paul Bugg
Tom D. Bullers

Robert Bullock
Erin Boeke Burke
Benjamin Burnett
Ryan M. Burnette
John D. Burnim
John C. Burton
Mark Bussow

C

Jill F. Cahill
Kathleen Cahill
Steven Cahill
Patrick Campbell
William H. Campbell
Mark F. Cancian
Eric D. Cardoza
J. Kevin Carroll
William S. Carroll
Scott Carson
Adam Case
Mary I. Cassell
David Cassidy
Benjamin Chan
Daniel E. Chandler
James Chase
Anita Chellaraj
Michael C. Clark
Rosye B. Cloud
Daniel Cohen
Allison L. Cole
John J. Colleran
Victoria Collin
Debra M. Collins
Kelly T. Colyar
Nicole E. Comisky
David C. Connolly
Martha B. Coven

Joshua Cover
Catherine Crato
Victoria P. Criado
Joseph Crilley
Ann M. Crocker
Rosemarie C. Crow
Michael F. Crowley
Craig Crutchfield
C. Tyler Curtis
William P. Curtis

D

Neil B. Danberg
J. Michael Daniel
Kristy L. Daphnis
Michael P. Darling
Alexander J. Daumit
Joanne Davenport
John Davis
Ken Davis
Margaret B. Davis-Christian
Anne M. Decesaro
Joshua DeLong
Brian Dewhurst
John H. Dick, Jr.
Frank DiGiammarino
Jason Dixson
Angela M. Donatelli
Paul Donohue
Bridget C. E. Dooling
Shamera Dorsey
Lisa Driskill
Laura Duke

E

Jacqueline A. Easley
Mabel E. Echols
Jeanette Edwards
Emily M. Eelman
Lisa Ellman
Noah Engelberg
Michelle A. Enger
Sarah J. Engle
Sally Ericsson
Victoria Espinel
Edward V. Etzkorn
Rowe Ewell

F

Emmy Fa
Chris Fairhall
Robert S. Fairweather
Edna T. Falk Curtin
Michael C. Falkenheim
Kara Farley-Cahill
Christine Farquharson
Kira R. Fatherree
Dick Feezle
Nicole A. Fernandes
Patricia A. Ferrell
Lesley A. Field
Craig Fischer
Mary Fischietto
E. Holly Fitter
Mary E. Fitzpatrick
Michael A. Fitzpatrick
Darlene B. Fleming
Tera Fong
Keith Fontenot
James Ford-Fleming
Nicholas A. Fraser
Marc Freiman
Farrah B. Freis
Virginia French
Nathan J. Frey
Rob Friedlander
Patrick J. Fuchs

G

Arti Garg
Marc Garufi
Thomas Gates
Jeremy J. Gelb
Jennifer Gera
Melissa Geraghty
Brian Gillis
Dori Glanz
David Glaudemans
Joshua Glazer
Kimberly G. Glenn
Gary Glickman
Ja'Cia D. Goins
Jeffrey Goldstein
Oscar Gonzalez
Dan Gordon
Robert M. Gordon
Zachary Graber
Tom Grannemann
Kathleen Gravelle
Richard E. Green
Aron Greenberg
Fumie Y. Griego
Hester Grippando
Rebecca Grusky

H

Michael B. Hagan
Christopher C. Hall
Erika S. Hamalainen
Kathleen D. Hamm
Christina Hansen
Eric V. Hansen
Linda W. Hardin
Dionne M. Hardy
Tom Harker
David Harmon
Patsy W. Harris
Brian Harris-Kojetin
Nicholas R. Hart
David S. Hartman
Paul Harvey
Tomer Hasson
David J. Haun
Laurel Havas

Mark H. Hazelgren
John Henson
Kevin W. Herms
Alex Hettinger
Gretchen T. Hickey
Michael Hickey
Beth N. Higa
Heather A.
    Higginbottom
Cortney J. Higgins
Mary Lou Hildreth
Andrew Hire
Thomas E. Hitter
Jennifer Hoef
Joanne Cianci Hoff
Adam Hoffberg
Stuart Hoffman
Troy Holland
Jim Holm
Peter M. Holm
Grace Hu
Kathy M. Hudgins
Jeremy D. Hulick
James Hundt
Alexander T. Hunt
Lorraine D. Hunt
James C. Hurban
Jaki Mayer Hurwitz
Kristen D. Hyatt
Dana J. Hyde

I

Tae H. Im
Janet Irwin
Paul Iwugo

J

Laurence R. Jacobson
Carol D. Jenkins
Aaron Joachim
Barbara A. Johnson
Carol Johnson
Kim I. Johnson
Michael D. Johnson
Bryant A. Jones
Danielle Y. Jones

Denise Bray Jones
Lisa M. Jones
Scott W. Jones
Hee K. Jun

K

Julie A. Kalishman
Richard Kane
Jacob H. Kaplan
Irene B. Kariampuzha
Jenifer Karwoski
Nathaniel Kayhoe
Regina Kearney
Dan Keenaghan
Matthew J. Keeneth
Hunter Kellett
John W. Kelly
Ann H. Kendrall
Nancy Kenly
Amanda R. Kepko
Paul E. Kilbride
Cristina Killingsworth
Barry D. King
Kelly Kinneen
Carole E. Kitti
Ben Klay
Sarah Klein
Irene Konow
David Koppel
Emily Kornegay
Steven M. Kosiak
John Kraemer
Lori A. Krauss
Alison C. Kukla
Joydip Kundu
Christine J. Kymn

L

Katherine T. LaBeau
Leonard L. Lainhart
Chris LaBaw
James A. Laity
Chad A. Lallemand
Lawrence L. Lambert
Emily R. Langner
Daniel LaPlaca

Eric P. Lauer
Jessie LaVine
Michael A. Lazzeri
Amanda I. Lee
David Lee
Jessica Lee
Karen Lee
Nicholas C. Lee
Sarah S. Lee
Gerard F. Leen
Susan Leetmaa
Bryan León
Jeremy León
Andrea Leung
Stuart Levenbach
Ariel D. Levin
Jacob J. Lew
Anthony Lewandowsky
George Lewis
Sheila D. Lewis
Wendy Liberante
Richard A.
   Lichtenberger
Kristina E. Lilac
Lin C. Liu
Patrick G. Locke
Brandi M. Lofton
Aaron M. Lopata
Alexander W. Louie
Adrienne C. Erbach
   Lucas
Kimberley Luczynski
Thomas S. Lue
Gideon F. Lukens
Sarah Lyberg
Autumn Lynch
Randolph M. Lyon

M

Chi T. Mac
Debbie Macaulay
Ryan J. MacMaster
John S. MacNeil
Natalia Mahmud
Claire A. Mahoney
Mikko Makarainen
Kathryn (Katie)
   Malague

Margaret A. Malanoski
Thomas J. Mancinelli
Dominic J. Mancini
Sharon Mar
Celinda A. Marsh
Brendan A. Martin
Kathryn Martin
Mitchel Martin
Rochelle Wilkie
   Martinez
Meg Massey
Surujpat J. Adrian
   Mathura
Shelly McAllister
George McArdle
Karen R. McBride
Alexander J.
   McClelland
Jeremy McCrary
Anthony W. McDonald
Christine McDonald
Katrina A. McDonald
Renford McDonald
Luther McGinty
Christopher McLaren
Robin J. McLaughry
Andrew McMahon
William J. McQuaid
William J. Mea
Heta K. Mehta
Inna L. Melamed
Flavio Menasce
Jessica Nielsen Menter
Gordon B. Mermin
Richard A. Mertens
Justin R. Meservie
P. Thaddeus
   Messenger
Michael Messinger
Shelley Metzenbaum
William L. Metzger
Laurie A. Mignone
Joanna M. Mikulski
Julie L. Miller
Kimberly Miller
Asma Mirza
Joe Montoni
Cindy Moon
Jamesa C. Moone

Marcus Childs Moore,
   Jr.
Odette N. Mucha
Meagan Muldoon
Moira Mack Muntz
Jennifer Winkler
   Murray
Chris Music

N

Jennifer Nading
Jeptha E. Nafziger
Larry Nagl
Janice Nall
Barry Napear
Allie Neill
Adam Neufeld
Melissa K. Neuman
Betsy Newcomer
Joan F. Newhart
John Newman
Kimberly A. Newman
Kevin F. Neyland
Teresa Nguyen
Abigail P. Norris
Douglas A. Norwood
Jennifer Nou
Tim H. Nusraty

O

Erin L. O'Brien
Devin O'Connor
Matthew J. O'Kane
Matthew Olsen
Steve Onley
Farouk Ophaso
Rebecca Ore
Jared Ostermiller
Tyler J. Overstreet
Brooke Owens

P

Ben Page
Jennifer E. Park
Sangkyun Park
Joel R. Parriott

John Pasquantino
Terri B. Payne
Jacqueline M. Peay
Mike Perz
Falisa L. Peoples-Tittle
Kathleen Peroff
Andrew B. Perraut
Larry Pertosa
Andrea M. Petro
John R. Pfeiffer
Stacey Que-Chi Pham
Carolyn R. Phelps
Karen A. Pica
Joseph T. Pika
Joseph G. Pipan
Alisa M. Ple-Plakon
Rachel C. Pollock
Ruxandra I. Pond
Celestine M. Pressley
Jamie Price Pressly
Larrimer Prestosa
Marguerite Pridgen
Robert B. Purdy

Q

John P. Quinlan

R

Jonathan E. Rackoff
Lucas R. Radzinschi
Latonda Glass Raft
Jose Angelo Ramilo
Jamil Ramsey
Maria Raphael
Jeffrey Reczek
McGavock D. Reed
Tiffany Reeser
Rudy Regner
Paul B. Rehmus
Jake Reilly
Meg Reilly
Sean Reilly
Thomas M. Reilly
Scott Renda
Richard J. Renomeron
Kent Reynolds
Keri A. Rice

M. David Rice
Gavette A. Richardson
Shannon Richter
Emma K. Roach
Benjamin Roberts
Donovan O. Robinson
Marshall Rodgers
Alexandra Rogers
Meredith B. Romley
Adam J. Ross
David Rowe
Mario D. Roy
Chris Rupar
Latisha Russell
Ross A. Rutledge

S

Fouad P. Saad
John Asa Saldivar
Dominic K. Sale
Azita Saleh
Mark S. Sandy
Kristen J. Sarri
Ryan J. Schaefer
Erik K. Scheirer
Lisa A. Schlosser
Andrew M. Schoenbach
James Schuelke
Margo Schwab
Nancy Schwartz
Jasmeet K. Seehra
Will Sellheim
Nirav Shah
Pinal R. Shah
Shahid N. Shah
Emily L. Sharp
Dianne Shaughnessy
Paul Shawcross
Rachel C. Pollock
Gary Shortencarrier
Mary Jo Siclari
Matthew J. Siegel
Sara R. Sills

Angela M. Simms
Rhonda M. Sinkfield
Lauren Sinsheimer
Jack A. Smalligan
Curtina O. Smith
Jan Smith
Jeannemarie Smith
Nikolis R. Smith
Joanne E. Snow
Sarah Snyder
Silvana Solano
Timothy C. Sommella
Kathryn B. Stack
Scott Stambaugh
Melanie A. Stansbury
Andrea M. Staron
Nora Stein
Gary Stofko
Carla B. Stone
Shayna Strom
Shannon Stuart
Tom Suarez
Stephen Suh
Brett J. Sullivan
Kevin J. Sullivan
Jessica Sun
Cass R. Sunstein
Indraneel Sur
Daniel S. Sutton
Daniel R. Suvor
Jennifer Swartz
Benjamin R. Sweezy

T

Teresa A. Tancre
Naomi Stern Taransky
Benjamin K. Taylor
Myra Taylor
Richard P. Theroux
Raina Thiele
Judith F. Thomas
LaTina Thomas
Will Thomas

Courtney B.
  Timberlake
Thomas Tobasko
Toinita Tolson
Richard Toner
Taryn H. Toyama
Gilbert Tran
Minh-Hai Tran-Lam
Susan M. Truslow
Donald L. Tuck
Benjamin J. Turpen
Grant K. Turner

U

Nick Uchalik
Darrell J. Upshaw

V

Matthew J. Vaeth
Kathleen M. Valentine
Ofelia M. Valeriano
Amanda L. Valerio
Cynthia A. Vallina
Sarita Vanka
Steven L. VanRoekel
David W. Varvel
Areletha L. Venson
Alexandra Ventura
Patricia A. Vinkenes
Dean Vonk
Kathy Voorhees
David Vorhaus
Ann M. Vrabel

W

James A. Wade
James "Rusty" Walker
Martha A. Wallace
Katherine K. Wallman
Heather V. Walsh
Sharon A. Warner

Gary Waxman
Mark A. Weatherly
Bessie M. Weaver
Jeffrey A. Weinberg
Maggie Weiss
Philip R. Wenger
Daniel Werfel
Mike Wetklow
Arnette C. White
Kamela G. White
Kim S. White
Sherron R. White
Chad S. Whiteman
Sarah Widor
Mary Ellen Wiggins
Shimika Wilder
Debra L. (Debbie)
  Williams
Monique C. Williams
Ross D. Williams
Julia B. Wise
Julie A. Wise
Sarah Wolek
Daryl Womack
Drew T. Wonacott
Gary Wong
Raymond Wong
Lauren Wright
Sophia Wright

Y

Abra Yeh
Melany N. Yeung
Theany Yin

Z

Jeff Zients
Gail S. Zimmerman
Rachel Zinn
Rita Zota

www.ingramcontent.com/pod-product-compliance
Lightning Source LLC
Chambersburg PA
CBHW081437170526
45166CB00008B/2232